Principal Succession

SUNY Series, Educational Leadership

Daniel L. Duke, Editor

Principal Succession

Establishing Leadership in Schools

Ann Weaver Hart

Foreword by William Greenfield

State University of New York Press

Published by
State University of New York Press, Albany

© 1993 State University of New York

Printed in the United States of America

For information, address State University of New York Press,
State University Plaza, Albany, N.Y. 12246

Production by M. R. Mulholland
Marketing by Fran Keneston

Library of Congress Cataloging-in-Publication Data

Hart, Ann Weaver, 1948–
    Principal succession : establishing leadership in schools / Ann
Weaver Hart.
        p.   cm. — (SUNY series, educational leadership)
    Includes bibliographical references (p.   ) and index.
    ISBN 0-7914-1291-1 (cloth : alk. paper). — ISBN 0-7914-1292-X
(pbk. : alk. paper)
    1. School principals — United States. 2. Leadership. I. Title.
II. Series. III. Series: SUNY series in educational leadership.
LB2831.92.H37 1993
371.2'012—dc20   91-45300
                                                                             CIP

BK
18 50

10 9 8 7 6 5 4 3 2 1

To Randy Bret Hart

Contents

Tables   ix

Foreword   xi

I   Foundations of Leader Succession in
Theory and Research   1

1. Changing Principals   5
Principal Succession   6
Principal Socialization   10
Principal Professional Socialization Research   17
Summarizing Organizational Socialization
    for Succession Research   21
2. Leader Succession Research   43
Succession Effects   45
Succession as a Boundary Delineating
    Leadership Effect   52
Succession Context in Organizations   55
Stages of Managerial Succession   57
Leadership and Leader Succession   62
Combining and Expanding Views of Succession   87
3. The Conceptual Roots of Organizational Socialization   89
Interaction: The Fundamental Unit of Analysis   91
Multiple Process Theories of Interaction   97
Self-concept   119
Outcomes   132

II   Principals in Succession: A Potpourri of Experiences   139

4. A Faculty's Perspective of a Succession   143
The Setting   143
How the Faculty Experienced the Succession   145
The Teachers' View of Organizational Socialization   158
Contributions from Organizational Socialization   158

5. An Outsider Successor's Personal View   165
   The Succession Setting   165
   The New Principal   168
   The Social Dynamic of a Succession   168
   The Insider's View of Organizational Socialization   184
6. The Professional and Organizational Socialization
   of Principals: Analysis of Additional Research   197
   Studies of Newly Appointed Principals   199
   The Organizational Socialization of New Principals   230

III   Leader Succession and Socialization:
       The Future in Research and Practice   243

7. Implications for Research on Leader Succession
   in Schools   247
   Issues in the Organizational Socialization of Principals   252
   Implications for Research Methodologies   256
   Research Propositions   258
8. Improving Leader Succession in Schools   265
   Socialization Stages   273
   Groups Empower Principals through Social Validation   274
   School Leaders Should Demonstrate Valued
     Knowledge and Skills   277
   The Socialization of Principals Can Be
     Deliberately Influenced by Superiors   279
   Current Practice Promotes a Custodial Response   290
   Socialization Occurs With or Without Planning   290
   People Expect Change During Succession   292
   The Need for Stability and the Need for
     Creativity Will Conflict   294
   School Leaders Can Affect the Processing
     of Information that Shapes Interpretations
     and Actions During Succession   295
   Socially Incongruent Leaders Can Succeed
     and Contribute   297

Notes   303

References   305

Index   339

Tables

1.1	Organizational Socialization Tactics	28
1.2	Socialidation Outcomes	39
7.1	A Research Synthesis	250

Foreword

The attention by educational scholars and policymakers to succession reflects their interest in the quality of a school's formal leadership and, ultimately, its educational effectiveness. Professor Hart's work contributes substantially to our understanding of succession by offering the field a fresh perspective on these concerns, and by providing administrators, scholars, and policymakers with a more complete view of leader succession, and its challenges and opportunities.

Her important and timely contribution invites us to think about succession not as an "event," but rather as a complex social process characterized by interactions among a school's faculty and their new principal, and among the principal and others. In weaving a new and more complete portrait of this phenomenon, Ann Hart's work advances the field considerably by introducing this new and more powerful vantage point for the study and the design of administrator succession.

Succession is conceptualized as an interactive process through which one is integrated into membership in the organization. As this process unfolds in school settings, an administrator undergoes a group membership boundary passage resulting in varying degrees of acceptance and legitimacy by the school's faculty (and others). As the data reported here so clearly illustrate, the manner in which this transition is negotiated has many ramifications for the successor as well as for teachers and others.

The results portrayed offer a vivid picture of the variables associated with the social dynamics of succession. Integrating concepts from the literatures of professional and organizational socialization, administrator succession, and leadership, this work considerably extends traditional approaches to describing and explaining a common but not well understood fact of administrative life. Four central concepts guide her exploration: socialization tactics; socialization stages; personal and social contexts shaping socialization; and socialization outcomes.

After introducing key studies from the professional and organizational socialization literature, and reflecting upon the intellectual heritage of the concept of organizational socialization, the author describes two cases of succession (one offering a faculty's perspective on succession, and the other providing a successor's view of the experience). The two cases then are complemented by an integrated review of the results of recent principal succession and organizational socialization studies.

These glimpses into the realities of succession provide a heightened awareness of the complexities and possibilities attending the process, and underscore its significance as an organizational phenomenon presaging the capacity of a principal to successfully and effectively influence and lead a school faculty. The illustrations provided by Professor Hart effectively bring to life the complex ideas grounded in theories of organizational socialization, and the stories embedded in these illustrations are examplars of the complexities of administrators' lives in schools. Everyone involved in or otherwise acquainted with the process of succession will find many familiar landmarks in these pages!

These data provide us with good illustrations of a school's social and cultural dynamics, of the opportunities available to a newly-arrived administrator to build legitimacy with teachers and students (that are seized by some and frequently missed by others), of the consequences for new-comers of mistaken assumptions, of the inevitability of the unanticipated, and of the myriad other realities of school life. The effect is a new awareness of the subtleties and complexities of succession, and a more complete view of the challenges and opportunities this process represents for school districts, teachers, successors themselves, and for scholars interested in understanding career and organizational dynamics in education.

For scholars, the integration of the organizational socialization ideas with the traditional concerns of succession researchers yields a multitude of fresh questions and avenues for inquiry. Differences in succession contexts, in organizational socialization tactics and assumptions, in gender, ethnicity, and race, in the "stock of knowledge, attitudes, values, and skills" of successors, and many other potential variables are waiting to be studied. What are the recurring dilemmas of succession across contexts? For adminis-trators...and for teachers? What happens when a new principal is appointed, and what are the short and long-term consequences of responses by faculty and by the successor to this event and associated social processes? These and other important and provocative questions stimulated by the perspective offered in these pages promise a rich and varied landscape for those interested in the study of succession and the development of theory about career and organizational dynamics in educational administration.

Similarly, for school district administrators and other educational policymakers, the framework portrayed in these pages offers a new basis for systematically designing and shaping succession processes and outcomes. For administrators themselves, much is offered regarding potential strategies for enhancing the process—both in terms of increasing one's capacity to effectively negotiate the process, and to use the process itself as a professional growth opportunity. As these pages illustrate, the process of succession brings with it great potential for individual and organizational development. For school districts, the potential to "design" succession represents a recurring opportunity to deliberately influence leadership development and school change. In a very real way, this conception offers school districts a promising but largely untapped avenue by which to shape the development of schools and school leaders.

Professor Hart's scholarship yields a rich panoply of powerful new concepts and emergent issues to consider as administrator succession and its correlates are explored. Whatever the reader's perspective, be it that of school researcher, graduate student, or school administrator, each will be stimulated by this book. The ideas crafted here represent an important shift in our thinking about succession, and the result is a more powerful and dynamic framework for inquiry, action, and policy development than has heretofore been available. In summary, this work adds substantially to our view of administrator succession, and I'm confident readers will find these pages engaging as well as intellectually stimulating!

William Greenfield
Portland State University

I

Foundations of Leader Succession in Theory and Research

This section provides an overview of the major issues in theory and research related to leader succession. While principals and those who work with them find the experiences that come with a succession event salient and disruptive (whether positive or negative), inquiry related to succession and to the interaction of individuals with important groups to which they belong remains diffuse and poorly synthesized. Section I attempts a synthesis of sorts, addressing a "persistent problem confronting the social sciences...the interrelationship of the individual and group" (Monane, 1967, p. 1). More importantly, this relationship poses a persistent problem for people assigned to lead established social and professional groups like those found in schools. Principals are given the specific charge to lead, to exert formal authority over the school. Voluntary action by teachers and others directed toward the important goals new leaders hope to pursue, however, depends on new leaders' abilities to secure the validation, support, and affirmation of the group as a whole. This affirmation emerges from group processes that are complex, inter-active, and diffuse. At the same time, principals must adhere to district norms and policies, pursuing goals and objectives set out by their superiors. Because of this complexity, those who undergo a principal succession find the experience important but difficult to analyze and even more difficult to influence. Conflicting advice abounds: bide your time; seize the day; don't make waves; capitalize on your window of opportunity; be creative; follow the superin-tendent's lead. . . .

Chapter 1 begins the discussion by examining major issues that arise when a change in school principals occurs. It provides an overview of the debate about leader succession that has occurred during the past several decades and a conceptual framework based on organizational socialization that alters the focus of this inquiry from the principal to the interaction between the new principal and the organization—the school and district.

Chapter 2 is a review of the research commonly labeled leader succession. It presents the major themes that have dominated this tradition and examines the shortcomings that have led some writers to declare the approach moribund, at least in education (Ogawa, in press).

Chapter 3 presents an overview of long-standing traditions in the social and behavioral sciences from which the organizational socialization literature springs. This chapter relies heavily on theories developed in sociology, psychology, and social psychology. While a mastery of the material in this chapter is not necessary to understand organizational socialization, it places the perspective within the intellectual traditions on which it draws. It addresses the persistent problem of individual creativity versus group power that all who seek to be 'leaders' in schools will be led to feel. Those who seek a deeper understanding of the intellectual roots of a school's influence on those who work there and vice versa will find the chapter a helpful introduction to some important ideas. Those who hope to use this book to improve their own or others' leader succession experiences in schools will not suffer a substantial loss of understanding if they omit Chapter 3 from their reading.

1

Changing Principals

When a person holding an influential office in a formal organization (such as a manager or chief executive) is replaced, the effects reverberate throughout the organization. The magnitude of this experience and its impacts on relationships, expectations, and outcomes may vary, but all feel its effects. Succession brings the issue of leadership close to the surface of organizational consciousness at all levels. Those who appoint new leaders, those who work with them, and those whose lives may be affected by them watch for signs that the change will make a positive difference in their work lives and outcomes. The effects are felt by the new manager as well. Before and after succession, newly appointed administrators strive for success under the pressure of personal and professional transition.

Leader succession is a frequent and widespread occurrence in all kinds of organizations. In one study, managers reported averaging between five and six new management assignments in their careers (Gabarro, 1987). The attention given by governing bodies, superiors, and subordinates alike to the selection and integration of new formal leaders and the resources organizations allocate to assure the best possible outcomes illustrate the importance placed on this event. Scholars, too, examine succession. Referring to the long tradition of this work in educational administration, Miklos (1988, p. 63) said: "An assumption underlying the research on administrative succession is that a change of administrators is a significant event in the history of an organization." The interest of scholars springs both from the importance attached to leader succession by participants and from its potential for revealing the role of leaders in organizational outcomes.

From anthropology to political science, writers have chronicled the people, events, processes, and principles associated with succession to leadership roles. Their focus differs, but the core interest remains in the values and processes shaping transition to formal authority.

In anthropology, scholars study the rules of property transfer and ascension to high office. They often focus on hereditary succession and the rules governing interpersonal relationships in small groups that succession reveals in different cultures (Goody, 1966). In political science, scholars examine the methods by which government officials gain high office. Sociologists take advantage of succession to study social groups when relationships are in transition and close to the surface. These transitions reveal important aspects of the stable interaction patterns and underlying structures characterizing the social group.

Succession to high office in organizations has been studied under a number of rubrics: executive succession (Brady & Helmich, 1985; Carlson, 1962); administrative succession (Grusky, 1960, 1964, 1969); managerial succession (Gouldner, 1952); and bureaucratic succession (Grusky, 1964). Each group of studies concerns itself with the replacement of formal leaders at different levels. Each has yielded results that provide important pieces of the succession puzzle. The primary focus of this book, because it concerns itself with the impact of new formal leaders on schools and vice versa, is managerial or administrative succession, but the general term leader succession provides a useful name for the replacement of key officials in formal organizations. Throughout the text, unless studies cited refer to a specific level of succession (such as chief executive officer), leader succession, managerial succession, and principal succession will be used interchangeably, as will formal leader and leader. This decision was made in spite of the realization that "leadership" may be a much more rarified form of social influence than "management" and is not necessarily exerted by all who fill formal leadership roles (Pfeffer, 1978, 1981b).

This chapter is an overview of the literature related to leader succession with a focus on principals. It includes studies primarily concerned with principal succession, leader socialization, principal professional socialization, and organizational socialization. The chapter introduces major issues related to the organizational socialization of new leaders that shape the discussion in subsequent chapters.

Principal Succession

A principal's succession affects all who work in and with a school. It creates a period of "apprehension and fear of the unknown with high expectations being held" by principals, teachers, and district superiors alike (Weindling & Earley, 1987, p. 67). In addition to the traditional concern over the appointment of principals new to the profession, which is happening at a high rate (Baltzell & Dentler, 1983), researchers find that school leaders are often transferred from one assignment to another. In Great Britain, turnover rates stand at 7 percent per year (Weindling & Earley, 1987). Since the Education Reform Act [1988] passed in that country, bringing with it sweeping changes in the role of the head, a number of heads have expressed the desire to retire (possible at age fifty-five) or leave the profession. Weindling speculates that these turnover rates may consequently increase substantially (Weindling, 1991).

While those responsible for appointing and studying new leaders ponder the important questions that shape the process and its outcomes, scholars interested in effective schools identify the principal as a key figure in school effectiveness—its orchestrator and shepherd— drawing additional attention to the importance of principal succession. Edmonds argued that "one of the most tangible and indispensable characteristics of effective schools is strong administrative leadership, without which the disparate elements of good schooling can neither be brought together nor kept together" (Edmonds, 1979, p. 32). In a comprehensive review of the literature on effective schools, Bossert, Dwyer, Rowan, and Lee (1982) concurred, concluding that effective principals create conditions for success by providing coherence to instructional programs, conceptualizing instructional goals, setting high and attainable academic standards, staying informed of policies and teachers' problems, making frequent classroom visits, creating incentives for learning, and maintaining student discipline. Other scholars also name the principal as a factor in school goal achievement (Brookover, et al, 1979; Corcoran, 1985; Purkey & Smith, 1983). More recently, Leithwood, Begley, and Cousins (in press) found over fifty empirical articles published since the middle 1970s that assert that principals have a substantial impact on schools.

Major reforms designed to use knowledge about formal leaders' effects on schools to improve the preparation, induction, and professional development of school principals have coincided with the development of succession and effective schools research (Leithwood, Steinbach & Begley, in press; Murphy, 1990). Those committed to the improvement of educational administration as a profession seek new ways to enhance the success of talented aspiring school leaders and improve the means through which they are prepared, inducted, and supported in their professional work (Duke, 1987; Hart, Sorensen & Naylor, 1992; National Policy Board, 1989).

But the dynamics and critical features of an effective principal/school relationship, although tantalizingly close to view and frequently included in testimonials and ideological statements, remain somewhat ephemeral. Students and instructors alike recognize a gap between formal instruction in the practice of administration and the demands of practice. These demands often pressure new school leaders to abandon skills and knowledge acquired in preservice education and conform to existing patterns of practice. Principals taking on their first professional assignments must find ways to connect and integrate their professional knowledge and experience. Principals moving to new assignments must carefully assess what attitudes and behaviors to take with them and what dynamics and unique challenges face them at the new school (Porter, Lawler & Hackman, 1975). For principals new to administration or new to a particular school, critical relationships and interaction patterns among themselves, their superiors, and the school social system are inchoate at the time of their appointment. They form during the uncertainty preceding succession, throughout selection, and into the succession, when the new administrator is deeply embroiled in a complex social process and when time to reflect on their experiences may be difficult to find. As a principal seeks to become a functioning leader and understand her relationships with others in the group, she ultimately is concerned with seeing her own fit—experience rendered meaningful through insight (McNeil, 1969). For those who appoint new leaders, uncertainty remains long after critical succession events occur. Were their decisions appropriate?

The mix of person and group is unique for each succession. This uniqueness poses dilemmas for those who study succession. If we examine it only from the perspective of the principal, we fail to explain the history of the event or the school and are unable to account for the conduct of people involved. But if we go too far in focusing on outcomes and ignore the dynamic mix of people, processes, and contexts that shape succession (the classic "black box" studies) and the schools and districts in which succession occurs, we lose track of the qualities and power of the individual. We fail to tap the uniqueness and creativity of the single person that stimulates much of our interest in leadership in the first place.

A quick reading of the literature on leader succession reveals that the individual perspective has dominated. Only those who challenge the basic assumption that leaders have any substantive effect (Pfeffer, 1981a, 1981b) have raised alternative voices. One might even argue after reviewing this literature that taking charge of a school, district, or other formal organization is a lonely, individual experience, and that the new leader should always be the focus of attention (Miskel & Cosgrove, 1985). While this view acknowledges the importance placed on leadership roles in our culture, it leaves much about managerial succession unexamined, unexplained, and superficially understood. It does this by focusing in isolation on only one, albeit important, element in a highly social event. Many who study leader succession focus on the effects of the lone heroic leader who operates as a free agent acting to affect others. Even those who apply contingency perspectives, which attend to environmental favorableness, focus on the leader's actions. This view is flawed, misrepresenting the social nature of the organizations in which formal leaders work. In reality, the social relationships between formal leaders and their hierarchical subordinates and superordinates play an important part in their influence on the school.

> We cannot force others to give us their approval, regardless of how much power we have over them, because coercing them to express their admiration or praise would make these expressions worthless. . . . There are fundamental differences between the dynamics of power in a collective situation and the power of one individual over another. The weakness of the isolated subordinate limits the significance of his approval or disapproval of the superior. The agreement that emerges in a collectivity of subordinates concerning their judgment of the superior, on the other hand, has far-reaching implications for developments in the social structure. (Blau, 1964, p. 17, 23)

Research affirms the need for a multidirectional view of leadership.

> The findings of . . . researchers . . . provide firm evidence for the view that influence-processes between superiors and subordinates are two-way rather than one-way. It might still prove to be the case that leaders influence their subordinates more than subordinates influence their leaders. But the studies make clear the manner in which subordinate actions can cause leaders to perceive subordinates in certain ways and consequently to employ certain behaviors towards them rather than others. (Smith & Peterson, 1988, p. 40)

Firestone (1989) described this organizational reality aptly in a study of the "cultural politics of executive succession" by superintendents.

He found that current enthusiasm for dramatic leadership achieved by manipulating organizational culture was not supported by his case studies of superintendent succession. Instead, he questioned the assumption that the superintendent is a free actor when choosing the direction of cultural change in school districts. Roberts (1989a, 1989b) echoed these conclusions in a series of case studies of new high school principals. Adding to the criticisms of leader succession research in education, Ogawa (in press) argued that traditional succession frameworks have failed to add significant insights for almost a decade.

By overemphasizing the study of formal leaders as single, self-conscious, and self-actualized people, one runs the risk of missing major components of the succession process. The new principal misses the mechanisms by which she is shaped by the social forces around her and through which her self-awareness emerges. The group misses opportunities for cooperative action and improved succession outcomes. Research and practice justify a broader view including the complex social context in which succession takes place. "The meaning that organizational members attach to succession merits future study conducted within a broader conceptual framework than that of previous research" (Miklos, 1988, p. 65).

Principal Socialization

Another rich body of theory and research provides a view somewhat different from traditional leader succession perspectives—drawing attention to the leader and the context simultaneously. This view is based in socialization theory and research. Socialization is simply the "learning of social roles" (Merton, Reader & Kendall, 1957). It involves individuals' adjustments and adaptations to the expectations of a group. These adjustments make cooperative effort possible and represent an orientation toward the common needs of the group. Through this process, people come to internalize the values, norms, and beliefs of the groups to which they belong and to accept the meanings these groups ascribe to events, other people, and ideas. In the process, principals come to behave in ways consonant with the expectations of the school but not enslaved by it. Referring to principals, Leithwood, Begley, and Cousins (in press, p. 10) said, "The ideal socialization process positions one at the point of sharpest focus: not so close as to render the corporate image a fuzzy blur; nor so far away as to make the detailed features of the image unrecognizable."

As adults, we experience socialization each time we join an existing group. Research on the socialization of first-time principals investigates the major variables molding the process of becoming a principal (Duke et al., 1984; Greenfield, 1985a, 1985b; MacPherson, 1984; Miklos, 1988; Parkay, et al., 1989; Roberts, 1989b; Wright, in press). This tradition emphasizes the impacts of the existing core of administrators, training, university preparation, and professional associations on the new principal. As Leithwood, Steinbach, and Begley (in press) explain, socialization is "those processes by which an individual selectively acquires the knowledge, skills and dispositions needed to adequately perform a social role, in this case the school principalship."

The socialization of principals to the profession or occupation of school administration begins in training or preparation programs. While some writers believe that teacher socialization begins this process, others provide persuasive arguments that educational administration is a distinct profession with its own norms and values in which "aspiring professionals learn the importance of specialized knowledge (expertise), as well as the values and ethics that guide the use of this knowledge" (Duke, 1987, p. 262). As principals secure administrative jobs and interact with other administrators they internalize the norms, values, and behaviors generally accepted as part of their professional role. This process is known as professional socialization, a unique aspect of socialization that will be described in greater detail later in the chapter. Studies explore the professional socialization of principals—in their preservice, during anticipatory socialization as teachers, in their formal training, and as new principals in their first years as administrators (Duke et al., 1984; Greenfield, 1985a; Weindling & Earley, 1987). Writers describe the means by which new principals come to adapt to the expectations attendant to their role, thrive, and prosper.

When principals enter a district and/or school as new members of the social group, they experience another form of socialization— organizational socialization. Organizational socialization differs from professional socialization (Schein, 1986). It teaches a person the knowledge, values, and behaviors required in a particular role within a particular organization. These values and norms may be very different from those the person learned as part of his professional socialization.

Organizational socialization—immediate, salient, and persuasive—often overpowers the effects of carefully structured professional socialization (Bucher & Stelling, 1977; Duke, 1987). Guy (1985) asserted that the need to fit into the immediate work environment makes organizational socialization more salient and immediate than experiences that precede it. The organization controls a person's evaluation and reward structures and provides social and personal reinforcement for compliance to immediate social norms and expectations. Organizational norms consequently tend to displace those learned during professional socialization.

First-time principals experience a double socialization experience—professional socialization to school administration and organizational socialization to their immediate work setting. They must break into a new social group and a new profession simultaneously (Van Maanen, 1976, 1977a, 1977b). In all kinds of professions including teaching, carefully planned formal study and internship experiences often yield to the immediate press of the organizational context in which work occurs (Blase, 1985; Bullough, 1990). Because of the power of this force, Duke (1987) suggested that principals' superiors can develop specific leadership orientations in new administrators (such as instructional leadership) through organizational socialization. They can do this by fostering changes in orientations and training, evaluation systems, incentives, and sanctions provided by the district.

Van Maanen and Schein (1979, p. 211) provided a vivid description of what happens during organizational socialization:

> [Experienced members] must...find ways to insure that the newcomer does not disrupt the ongoing activity on the scene, embarrass or cast disparaging light on others, or question too many of the established cultural solutions worked out previously....The manner in which this teaching/learning occurs is...the *organizational socialization process* [emphasis in the original].

Peter Blau (1964, pp. 275–276) also described the function of this process:

> [T]he process of socialization results in many of the legitimating values of organized community life being passed on to future generations, and these are the institutionalized values that sustain and invigorate the external forms of institutions, which without them would be dead skeletons.

Organizational socialization binds the members of work organizations into communities with far deeper ties than those forged through previous experiences or formal structure.

Although organizational socialization has received limited attention in education literature, important research has been done on the professional socialization of teachers and principals. An established body of research traces the processes through which teachers come to accept expectations for equality, privacy, and cordiality, often overcoming the effects of preservice socialization in norms of collegiality, experimentation, and interaction (Bullough, in press; Little, 1982; Lortie, 1975; Hoy & Rees, 1977; Hoy & Woolfolk, 1990).

The Social Context as a Source of Leader Power

The influence of organizational socialization consequently extends to all members of a group, including formal leaders such as principals. By examining the socialization of leaders, one acknowledges that leaders are part of a social context that wields a combined source of power over their beliefs and actions greater than the power of either previous professional socialization or their own formal authority:

> If the . . . qualities of the individual are said to be derived from experience in society, there is no logical sense in beginning serious scientific inquiry into the effect (the role-related, social self), while ignoring the cause (society, and ipso facto, socialization). . . . The nature of the "society" presented in socialization must be described. (Wentworth, 1980, p. 8)

Organizational socialization, then, examines the effects of leaders and organizations from many directions, recognizing that leader successors are newcomers who must be integrated into existing groups, validated by social processes, and granted legitimacy by subordinates and superiors before they can have significant impacts on actions taken by others. Authority granted by the members of the group in this way differs from other forms of influence to which people voluntarily submit. Blau (1964, p. 200) distinguished this socially validated authority as leadership:

> It may be suggested that the distinctive feature of authority is that social norms accepted and enforced by the collectivity of subordinates constrain its individual members to comply with directives of a superior. Compliance is voluntary for the collectivity, but social constraints make it compelling for the individual. In contrast to other forms of influence and power, the

pressure to follow suggestions and orders does not come from the superior who gives them but from the collectivity of subordinates. These normative constraints may be institution-alized and pervade the entire society, or they may emerge in a group in social interaction. The latter emergent norms define leadership. . . .

Scott (1987) calls this endorsed leadership. In contrast to the authority and power granted by the collective, the authority rooted in formal position is limited in scope to the performance of duties that meet a minimum standard. Only actions required by policy and directive can be controlled by principals relying on formal authority. Effective management, Blau asserted, is impossible on the basis of formal authority alone. Duke and his colleagues (1984) found this to be true for new principals. They found that faculties were the most important source of influence, satisfaction, *and* dissatisfaction new principals experienced during their first year.

In addition to revealing individual power, succession is a good time to study group effects on leaders in schools, for "the influence of the organization upon the individual peaks during passage" (Van Maanen & Schein, 1979, p. 224). The behavior of newly assigned principals (not just first-time principals) changes as a result of their interactions with people in the school and district (Hartup & Coates, 1972). The authority these principals eventually exert beyond the limited power of office emanates from the people within the social system in which they work.

Group effects on new managers deserve increased attention for a number of reasons. First, interaction on the job may be the most important factor in helping newcomers become effective members of work organizations (Louis, Posner & Powell, 1983). Second, new leaders learn new roles. Providing additional support for the belief that socialization plays a critical part in creating effective leaders in schools, Greenfield (1985b) asserted that the role-learning outcomes of socialization serve as primary criteria for later success. Further-more, the learning of needed attitudes, values, and beliefs in the school context are central to gaining the acceptance of others in similar and superordinate leadership roles and of the school. He argued that the social structure of the school organization is a powerful mediating force affecting work activities and outcomes. Moral socialization, as well as technical socialization, exerts critical force over the eventual professional identity of principals. Third, socialization's influences on leaders are well documented (White, 1978). Managers' attitudes, self-concept, and professional identity resulting from socialization experiences have long been a focus of study (Berlew & Hall, 1966–67).

Organizational Socialization: Tapping the Power of the Context

The traditional succession literature relies on methods and assumptions that address the outcomes of succession in general and the traits of the leader and structure that predict these outcomes. This approach is accused of reflecting an exaggerated concern with organizational control, image management, and status quo pattern maintenance (Nicholson, 1984). In contrast, succession studies that add organizational socialization factors advance understanding and practice in three ways: (1) to identify organizational circumstances when the decision to change leaders might be advantageous; (2) to understand the social dynamics of succession across time; and (3) to examine the interaction effects of groups and individuals on succession outcomes.

Case studies go farther toward advancing these purposes than do other forms of succession inquiry that have dominated the last two decades. In fact, complex interactions within the organization were the focus of the earliest succession studies (Gouldner, 1954; Guest, 1962). Occasionally, cases revealing the dynamics of leader succession processes within organizations continue to offer intriguing new insights (Gephart, 1978; Oskarsson & Klein, 1982; Salaman, 1977). In schools, too, studies of principal succession provide a look at dynamics that may trigger or suppress major shifts in ideology and practice (Hart, 1988; Ogawa, 1991; Starbuck, Hedboerg & Greve, 1977).

A principal may adapt and prosper personally, however, without contributing to school improvement. Schools need their new principals to become integrated into the group, but they also need creativity and new ideas. These two needs make the effects of socialization during leader succession critical factors shaping future events in the school. These needs seem contradictory. They do work at cross-purposes if successors fail to find a productive balance between them in each situation. One must not assume that all social learning is positive. The new principal's acceptance of established solutions that have not been productive or are blatantly unproductive is a negative outcome of succession. Although thorough learning and acceptance of the existing culture through socialization may always be immediately *adjustive* for an individual in that such learning will reduce the tension associated with entering an unfamiliar situation, such learning, in the long run, may not always be adaptive, since certain cultural forms may persist long after they have ceased to be of individual value. (Van Maanen & Schein, 1979, pp. 212–213)

This book aims to use the conceptual insights provided by organizational socialization to expand research on leader succession. It pursues a fourfold purpose: (1) to lay out a conceptual foundation from organizational socialization that can be applied to leader succession; (2) to show how new research on the succession of school leaders can be better understood through the use of this framework; (3) to develop the research implications of this expanded view; and (4) to illustrate how organizational socialization and leader succession research in concert can be used by school districts and by new principals to improve the outcomes of succession. The advantages of this approach are several. First, principals are appointed with the expectation that they will take charge of a specific school. By studying the principal isolated from the school and from her superiors, researchers risk applying a level of analysis that may limit generalizability while misrepresenting the fundamental nature of the experience. Second, socialization, although continuous throughout a career, is most intense and problematic for a person just before and just after a particular boundary passage. Succession may be among the most important professional transitions principals ever make. Third, leader succession affects many people in a school, stimulating interactions and breaking up routines that require people to reestablish shared expectations, work patterns, and relationships. Succession may be one of the most common forms of organizational change accessible to researchers for study. It also may be a unique opportunity to implement important changes in schools.

Research and practice give reasons to believe, therefore, that an understanding of organizational socialization can help shape our understanding of succession and its outcomes. It can do this by helping new principals better understand and respond to the factors shaping their responses to work and the immediate social context, thus cushioning the effects of oversocialization so persuasively criticized by Pfeffer (1978). Taking charge is a powerful experience for which few principals are adequately prepared (Weindling & Earley, 1987). Pfeffer and others contended that the socialization of managers assures a uniformity that suppresses creativity and the diverse options that might be necessary to address the complex dilemmas and needs of schools—in effect, that managers of all kinds are "oversocialized." Socialization also has been named as an important factor in the seeming intransigence of educational administration to the changes attempted in preservice graduate school education programs (Hart, Sorensen & Naylor, 1992).

This intransigence is a real but not insurmountable challenge. "It is the social context of leadership actions which gives them their meaning and consequently their effect" (Smith & Peterson, 1988, p. 61). Organizational socialization reveals the interactive and group character of leadership. As Schein (1985, p. 197) argued, in a mature group "leadership comes to be seen as a shared set of activities rather than a single person's trait, and a sense of ownership of group outcomes arises." Others assert the social nature of new principals' part in schools more radically: leadership is an attribute not of individuals but of social systems (Dachler, 1984). The knowledge that social groups possess a singular power related to leadership but distinct from individual influence can expand understanding and increase educational leadership. This is the major contribution an organizational socialization perspective can make to leader succession.

Principal Professional Socialization Research

I noted earlier that principal professional socialization research is well developed when compared with organizational socialization. An understanding of professional socialization, which builds on research on the professions (Schein, 1971a), helps set the stage for its expansion to include organizational socialization.

The principal professional socialization literature yields a number of important insights into the development of school management professionals (Duke et al., 1984; Greenfield, 1985a, 1985b; MacPherson, 1984; Miklos, 1988). Among the most noted studies are those completed by Duke and Greenfield.

Duke and his colleagues (1984) identified in the literature four features of professional socialization to the principalship role that they applied to a reflective study of successful veteran principals' first years. These features were (1) duration of the socialization period; (2) mechanisms of socialization; (3) relationships between expectations and the realities of the job; and (4) formal and informal preparation for school administration. They found that the principals in their sample generally marked the end of their professional socialization period around the completion of their *first year* as principals. Principals viewed all their professional experiences, including those as teachers, as part of their overall socialization. Thus, Duke, et al. began with anticipatory socialization, moving through entry into the principalship, and concluding with a period of development or "metamorphosis" (Van Maanen, 1976). The researchers concluded that the induction period can be of varying length, but the vast majority of their subjects no longer felt like rookies at the end of the first year.

Socialization mechanisms identified by principals in the Duke study were both formal and informal. Only two of thirty-two veterans participating and two of fourteen novices described receiving any formal orientation to the principalship by their employing districts. The researchers labeled this practice "sink or swim" socialization. While half were given written job descriptions, many were vague and offered little guidance about the districts' expectations. Principals argued that informal processes dominated their experience. They learned about the norms and expectations of the principalship and of their district (sometimes solicited, sometimes by chance) from a variety of sources: former principals under whom they had worked; predecessors, secretaries, and teachers in the school; central office administrators. The dominant source of information was other principals in the district.

The critical factor shaping the all-important informal socialization process for these principals was other people. "Consistent with the general literature on socialization, first year principals seem to be very concerned about their acceptance by others and gratified when it occurs" (Duke et al., 1984, p. 23). The faculty, in fact, was the most important source of influence on new principals, followed by assistant principals and students.

> Clearly the people within the school building where one is principal serve as the most important influences on one's performance as principal. For second year principals there are additional important influences: other principals in the district, central office personnel and the principal with whom one had worked as a teacher or intern. (Duke et al., 1984, p. 19)

However, major sources of *support* and major sources of *influence* were not necessarily the same. Teachers constituted the primary source of both satisfaction and dissatisfaction for new principals.

Differences between principals' expectations and the job they experienced—surprises (Louis, 1980b)—elicited strong emotional responses from the principals in the Duke study. "Subjects conveyed considerable emotion as they described the unexpected loneliness of the principalship, the unanticipated time pressure, and the disconcerting feelings of unpreparedness. . . ." The researchers concluded that the principals apparently had lacked "an appreciation of the complexity of the principalship" (p. 26).

Finally, formal and informal preparation for administrative work during the anticipatory (training and aspiration) stage of professional socialization shaped principals' experiences. However, the principals placed far less emphasis on the importance of their formal course work in universities than on informal factors in shaping even this phase.

Greenfield (1985a, 1985b, 1977a, 1977b) also inquired into the professional socialization of principals. In his early studies (1977a & b), Greenfield examined the phases of candidacy to administrative positions and argued that interpersonal, social process, and organizational context variables led to an administrative perspective. Greenfield (1985a) found that socialization to administration is informal and largely random, It occurs over a variable time frame, requires candidates to gradually divest themselves of their identities as teachers, and depends to a large measure on the context, which shapes both role-learning and role-enactment for candidates and novices.

In later studies, Greenfield (1985b) revealed dynamics influencing the transition to administrative work in schools, asserting that professional socialization has two primary objectives: moral socialization and technical socialization. Moral socialization is concerned with values, norms, and attitudes attendant to the career group. Technical socialization focuses on knowledge, skills, and techniques needed to perform adequately as a school administrator. He pointed out that "different socialization responses are a function of differences in organizational socialization tactics, contexts, and conditions" (Greenfield, 1985a, p. 3).

Recent research in Canada adds to the work of Duke and Greenfield. Leithwood, Steinbach, and Begley (in press) studied a group of new Canadian school administrators, attending primarily to less formal socialization in search of evidence linking socialization (both prior to and after appointment to a principalship) with instructional leadership. The researchers applied a stage framework that conceptualized professional socialization as initiation, transition, and incorporation in four major areas—relationships; experience with the formal organization; formal training; and outcomes (image of the principal's role; skills and knowledge; and norms and values). They found that both preservice and serving principals valued most those experiences that related directly to their work and occurred *in schools*. They also found that socialization experiences thought to promote and develop instructional leadership had no impact on the value and importance principals placed on instructional leadership tasks in their work. These findings raise questions about the causal relationship among professional socialization experiences, psychological development, and actual work behaviors and values (Frese, 1982, 1984).

A number of other studies contributed to professional socialization knowledge in educational administration. MacPherson (1984) criticized this work, asserting that studies of anticipatory, preservice socialization yield scant knowledge of the early years of an administrative career when organizational socialization and professional socialization occur simultaneously. Others added to the criticism. They pointed out that site level factors shape professional socialization; task specific learning; the mastery of practical, routine tasks (DuBose, 1986); feelings of isolation; the need for technical assistance from the district (Alvey, 1983; Marrion, 1983); and the influence of assistant principals and office staff. These factors mold the way principals "learn the ropes."

These studies of entry into the profession of school administration reveal means through which newcomers become functioning school administrators. A major gap in knowledge remains, however. We know very little about the relative advantages of thorough socialization, which can suppress personal qualities, creativity, and originality. This dampening effect can result in failure. The two extremes along the continuum from total internalization to alienation highlight the need to understand the relationship between uniqueness and continuity in leader succession experiences. The optimum socialization level along this continuum may depend on the needs of the school in each succession. Organizational socialization literature, with its emphasis on the interaction between the new member and the group, provides an apt framework for exploring this continuum. An overview of major issues stimulating thought and research in organizational socialization provides important clues to factors deserving renewed attention from researchers and practitioners in schools.

Summarizing Organizational Socialization for Succession Research

Four key themes dominate the discourse on organizational socialization applicable to school leader succession inquiry: (1) tactics used in the socialization process; (2) socialization stages through which new members pass; (3) the personal and social contexts that shape the entire process; and (4) the outcomes or effects of socialization practices likely to result from these factors.

Organizational Socialization Tactics

People in transition from one role to another in organizations experience organizational socialization (Van Maanen, 1978). Both deliberately and unconsciously, organizations apply a number of tactics to integrate new members. The decision to leave the socialization of newcomers to chance, dependent on the mix of people, issues, power, and events that happen to coincide, is of itself a tactic. Writers describe a number of categories of socialization tactics likely to affect new members. This list of tactics is by no means exhaustive, and districts may change their tactics continually, depending on developing circumstances.

Van Maanen and Schein (1979) provided one of the most quoted and tested set of categories for analyzing socialization tactics. Using paired comparisons, they suggested that tactics are collective or individual; formal or informal; sequential or random; fixed in time or variable; serial or disjunctive; and demanding investiture or divestiture. Definitions of these categories follow.

Jones (1986) modified the classification of these characteristics. He argued that socialization occurs in three areas: context, content, and sociality. By context, Jones meant that socialization is either collective or individual and formal or informal. The content (what a new member learns) is either sequential or random and fixed or variable. And the sociality of socialization is either serial (with role models) or disjunctive and involves investiture or divestiture.

Although their labels seem overly technical at first glance, these categories are useful when looking at the tactics organizations use to socialize new members. The *context* a person encounters can involve him alone or in a group of other new members (collective or individual). It also may be carefully planned and formalized by the organization. The *content*—what is learned—may be set up in sequence, much like a set of courses in mathematics that build one upon another and must be taken in order. It also may constitute a body of knowledge requiring no particular sequence, and this can be acquired in random order, depending on chance or convenience. Additionally, a new member may be given a fixed amount of time to master the content or allowed to set her own time frame. Finally, the context can be used as a socialization tactic. *Socialization* can occur under the strong influence of role models (serial) or free of role models (disjunctive). The whole experience can also be designed to require that the new member divest himself of old identities and concepts of self (divestiture) or that she reaffirm and reinforce her existing professional self-concept (investiture).

Interest in socialization includes the interaction of all these tactics and their effect on the new member and the group. Scholars also examine substantive changes in new members (Wentworth, 1980). What core social beliefs and values might have to be adopted before new members can function as an accepted part of the group? How completely must these core values or behaviors be adopted? How dependent or independent is the new member?

> The novice can be relatively powerless in an ultimate way, yet actively influence the face-to-face process of socialization. The novice then may also inject control and power into the socialization relationship. This is to say, the members' culture is not presented in a vacuum. It is presented *to* someone so that its precise quality is historically and concurrently modified in the interaction between member and novice. The content of socializing activity is thus modified by the very structure of the interaction situation. Socialization is then related to the context of its presentation. (Wentworth, 1980, p. 69)

When the new member is also the functional leader of the group, this influence clearly is enhanced. As a new leader enters the group, "socialization not only presents a world, it constructs one" (Wentworth, 1980, p. 134).

Context. Collective socialization tactics require specific choices; *individual* socialization can be structured deliberately or result from benign neglect. During collective socialization, new principals go through a series of activities together (perhaps training in instructional supervision). Individual processing takes new principals through their experiences alone. While those socialized independently tend to be less homogeneous than members of a cohort, the newcomer is more likely to feel lonely, and the quality of the experience can be highly varied. The continuity of experience a collective process promotes is no guarantee of predictable outcomes, however. Even though newcomers may be "processed" in the same way, they will experience that process differently. Past experiences and personal characteristics exert tremendous influence.

Each context tactic has advantages and disadvantages. Individual socialization leads to relatively high levels of role conflict and ambiguity, but it also enhances innovation. Collective and highly structured activities promote commitment and job satisfaction (Jones, 1986), but they suppress creativity and change. None of the studies in education surveyed for this review applied institutionalized, planned processes to any great extent. For principals and other managers, "individual socialization" (Van Maanen, 1978) is most likely. This seems also to be the case for teacher mentors and leaders (Little, 1990). It is

> most likely to be associated with hierarchical boundaries where preparation for promotion requires the complex learning of skills, attitudes, and values, and where specific judgments of a given individual must be made by certain others in the organization as to the person's "fitness" for promotion (or demotion). (Van Maanen & Schein, 1979, p. 235)

The context in which principals undergo socialization may also be more or less *formal*. Formal socialization, designed to incubate specific norms and expectations, can be used by schools, although it rarely is. Others depend on informal arrangements. Mentors play a large part in formal and informal socialization tactics. Sometimes a new principal works almost exclusively with an assigned mentor (Dansereau, Graen & Haga, 1975; Dienesch & Liden, 1986; Hunt & Michael, 1983). These arrangements receive considerable praise (Daresh & Playko, 1989). Other times, mentor relationships develop informally. Reliance on mentors leaves the quality of the working relationship between mentors and newcomers to chance. Outcomes are highly vulnerable to quality control problems, particularly when mentors receive little or no guidance about their role or the goals the district wants them to pursue. These problems appear repeatedly in studies of teacher mentor programs, for example (Little, 1990).

Mentors also constrain innovation. By turning the socialization of newcomers over to long-time members of the group, organizations virtually guarantee the reproduction of existing roles (Van Maanen, 1978). Even when mentors and new principals have a good working relationship, the results may be undesirable.

A study in the insurance industry illustrates this vulnerability to personal relationships (Blau, 1988). The quality of the relationship between mentors and management interns had direct and moderating effects on outcomes for the interns. It affected feelings that interns met expectations, the clarity of roles, commitment to the organization, and performance. Relationships also affected the interaction of role clarity and intern performance, despite the managers' abilities. These findings raise important questions about the wholesale, unstructured use of mentors in education to socialize new principals, teachers, and teacher leaders.

Formalization has its advantages and disadvantages. Some researchers find that a highly formalized socialization process produces a custodial orientation (recreation of the existing order). Newcomers try to play the established part exactly as it was designed and filled by others. Informal socialization may stimulate more creativity and innovation, but it also produces "more extreme responses in either the custodial or innovative directions than formal socialization" (Van Maanen & Schein, 1979, p. 240).

Earlier in this review, I reported the conclusions of Duke et al. (1984) and Greenfield (1985a, 1985b) that formal socialization is rarely employed by school districts to develop new principals. Weindling and Earley (1987) confirmed this conclusion, finding a paucity of formal socialization procedures in their British sample. Only 26 percent of their sample of secondary heads experienced any formal induction lasting more than one day. Most induction occurred during the first part of the year, and even introductions at the school were cursory and superficial. They took place so soon after the formal appointment that heads had forgotten the people to whom they were introduced by the time they actually took over their positions. Weindling and Earley found one major exception, a district with plans for a seminar for new heads, senior advisers, and experienced heads. Time and resource constraints limited this program. One of the major findings of their five-year study was that districts should "have a planned program of induction for new heads" including a number of features: (1) more time for newly appointed managers to visit their new schools; (2) arrangements for outgoing heads to produce full written reports for their successors; (3) carefully planned introductory visits to the new assignment; (4) an induction course; (5) a handbook for new heads; and (6) the assignment of experienced mentors (Weindling & Earley, 1987, p. 190).

Content. When a succession occurs, the new principal must master a specific knowledge content. When the tactic requires that content exposure must follow an established and ordered set of steps, it is sequential. In order to achieve full membership in the role, the new members or new role incumbents must pass through these steps without deviation. During random socialization, the steps required to master the content are flexible, ambiguous, or continually changing. Some writers contend that, by sequencing the content, an organization builds high commitment among new members (Nota, 1988). In educational administration, the content of new learning is seldom ordered beyond simple orientation meetings at the beginning of a school year. Like the formal context or structure, this tactic receives little attention.

The timetable in which a newly assigned principal must master content can be fixed or variable. A fixed time requirement under which steps must be taken—such as five-year doctoral studies or a twelve-week instructional leadership course—tightens the control of the organization. It also limits the duration of newcomer status. After formal training is complete, teachers and administrators report almost totally random and variable socialization. Clearly, little attention is paid to this influential tactic in educational organizations.

Sociality. When principals follow in someone's footsteps and strong role models exist, they experience serial socialization. During disjunctive socialization, the newcomer has no significant role models and *may* build a whole new role. An absence of role models leaves new principals more free to innovate and more ambiguous about what is expected of them in the new role. Consequently, it is a two-edged sword. Teacher leaders, for example, often must create their own roles as they go along, leaving them both more unsettled and more free to be creative than are new teachers who model their actions after the existing corps (Hart, 1987; Little, 1990). Successor principals can experience disjunctive socialization if they differ significantly in personal characteristics from those who commonly are principals. Women and ethnic minority members, for example, report significant stress (disjunction) in their pursuit of success. They often feel that they must negotiate their way through more ambiguity with less support than their more conventional peers because few people like them have preceded them in the role (Ortiz & Marshall, 1988; Valverde, 1980).

But a lack of role models also has its benefits. Researchers find strong evidence that, when innovation is needed, "the socialization process should minimize the possibility of allowing incumbents to form relationships with their likely successors" (Van Maanen & Schein, 1979, p. 250). Just as mentors can suppress innovation, role models can limit thinking and constrain options. While principals without role models need social support, they can tap individual creativity and spark new ideas.

A second aspect of sociality tactics employed during organizational socialization requires that the principal either strengthen or abandon an existing self-image. Duke (1987) referred to the potential this tactic holds when he recommended that teachers be encouraged to demand instructional leadership from principals and that instructionally oriented teachers be recruited into administration. The first recommendation requires that traditional candidates divest themselves of conventional roles (manager, bookkeeper). The second requires that administrative recruitment programs seek out and promote those who possess desired skills and values. When a new work assignment reinforces the professional identity of a person, the existing sense of self at work is invested—affirmed and supported. When the new work assignment challenges a person's professional identity and causes a substantial adjustment in the self-concept, divestiture occurs. The existing sense of self-concept is disaffirmed and subverted (Van Maanen & Schein, 1979).

This tactic possesses power that springs from the group. When a principal abandons her status as a teacher, for example, she also abandons central operating assumptions and devalues old skills. Divestiture might force a successor to acquire new skills or apply existing skills to the new situation; investiture might encourage him to press for innovation in his new role in the school. Superiors should be aware of the potential impacts of these effects.

Investiture and divestiture remain difficult concepts to differentiate during socialization, however, partly because they depend on self-concept as much as on organizational processes. The nebulous features of investiture and divestiture as socialization tactics deserve elaboration. Because every principal enters a new assignment with an established professional identity, some pressure on this self-concept will occur. We know little about the levels of pressure that may be most productive under what conditions.

The investiture/divestiture tactic can best be illustrated with an extreme example—military succession. Frequently, the military employs processes that assault previous status, degrade the sense of self, and require a new definition of the person dependent upon and completely loyal to the organization. The goals of the military match these processes well. But in education, the needs of a district and a particular school may be less clear. When principals who already have desired skills feel affirmed, they will be more likely to strike out, to modify the practices of the predecessor, to innovate. When they feel disaffirmed, they recreate structures and patterns that already have secured the affirmation and support of the group, avoiding the personal assault and social alienation that innovation invites.

This conflict and ambiguity between affirmation and disaffirmation appears in studies of work redesign for teachers, too (Hart, 1990a, 1990b; Smylie & Denny, 1990). Scholars find that teacher leaders deliberately minimize their own contributions and the substantial innovation they accomplish. They fear ostracism and criticism from other faculty members (Hart & Murphy, 1990). Teachers report that the emotional and personal costs of divestiture accompanying some leadership roles are too high. Some resign their positions as a result of this social pressure (Hart, 1990a).

When the paired categories of organizational socialization tactics just discussed are translated into general terms, they fall into five major factors at two levels. The factors of socialization features include the nature of events; the time frame in which events occur; the formality of structure; the social context shaped by superiors and predecessors; and the content. These factors occur at the individual or organizational/collective level. Table 1.1 illustrates how these tactics can be conceptualized as structural features and levels. Note that the events, time, structure, context, and content are depicted in the dichotomous pairs suggested by Van Maanen and Schein. Each of these tactics is susceptible to deliberate intervention and planning. Each is likely to result in different effects.

The outcomes of each of these tactics at individual or group levels can be predicted by research. The challenge facing scholars and practitioners, however, is to give insight to professionals who must use this knowledge in unique and complex settings under constraints researchers seek to control.

Managerial transition research offers a conceptually consistent look at the outcomes of leader succession. Citing Fromm (1941), Nicholson and West (1988, p. 1) suggest that "one might even argue . . . that one of the main functions of culture is to cushion and protect us from our fundamental insecurities about change." They go on to assert that

> the most anxiety-inducing questions about the meaning of our existence, the uncertainty of the future, and the nature of identity, are solved for us, partially at least, by the mechanisms of cultural transmission—the socialization of values, beliefs and behaviours and the institutionalization of social relationships.

TABLE 1.1

Organizational Socialization Tactics

LEVEL

		Individual	Collective
	Events: random sequential		
	Time: fixed variable		
ASPECTS	Structure: formal informal		
	Role Models: without with		
	Content: Role Disaffirming Role Affirming		

Stages of Socialization

In addition to deliberate tactics, scholars use stage frameworks to illuminate steps through which all newcomers pass during organizational socialization. In many ways, the stages are similar to the succession stage frameworks reviewed later in Chapter 2, but they emphasize interaction, not the passage of time and critical events. Linear models see stages moving through steps along a continuum until they reach equilibrium and integration in the new setting. Iterative and cyclical perspectives see the process continuing perpetually (as do Miskel & Cosgrove, 1985). Whatever their labels, three stages reappear in the literature. They identify periods of learning and uncertainty, gradual adjustment during which outcomes (custodial or organizational change) begin to emerge, and stabilization. Three major categorizations are presented in the following discussion.

Encounter, Adjustment, Stabilization. Nicholson and West (1988) are among those who find that managers view their successions as cycles of recurring, interdependent, and continuous phases. Because managers experience multiple successions that each include organizational socialization, they move continually through anticipation and preparation, through encounter and adjustment, and then to stabilization. They then prepare for and anticipate the next transition. Anticipation is akin to the preparation stage Merton, Reader, and Kendall (1957) called anticipatory socialization. The other three stages require elaboration.

Encounter (arrival) requires much learning. It can be cognitive and affective. Cognitive learning during entry into a new setting sometimes is called sense making (Louis, 1980b). The demands of sense making on the new principal during encounter appear to depend on three factors: (1) the amount of change—differences in the status, role requirements, and work environment between the new and old positions; (2) contrast—the carry-over involving people; and (3) surprise—unmet positive and negative expectations. Stress-coping during encounter focuses on feelings. Writers like Hopson and Adams (1976) examine the ways in which people cope with feelings of change during job change, applying the stages of grief to this research. Others, while acknowledging that job change is stressful, see it as less dramatic (Feldman, 1976).

The adjustment phase involves the task of fitting in. The new principal must reach accommodation with the work role, the people with whom she interacts and the culture of the new school. Nicholson and West contend that the adjustment phase technically is organizational socialization at the work site.

Some adjustment factors include mentors and supervisors (Weiss, 1978), group dynamics (Moreland & Levine, 1983), job characteristics (Dawis & Lofquist, 1984), evaluation, and influence (Feldman, 1976). The personal outcomes of socialization emerge during this stage. Some scholars seek changes in individual identity, even personality (Mortimer & Lorence, 1979; Brousseau, 1983; Kohn & Schooler, 1983), as a result of adjustment.

Nicholson and West treat stabilization and preparation stages (for the next change) together, since "it may not be uncommon to find that stabilization never occurs" (1988, p. 14). These writers find that the vast majority of interest in leadership, work outcomes, assessment, management control, job satisfaction, and job design focuses on stabilized work structures and relationships, treating people as if they have "no past and no future."

For new school leaders, this stage requires that they negotiate two new sets of relationships simultaneously—one with superiors and one with faculty, staff, and students (Duke et al., 1984). And it may involve a continuing informal negotiation among all these people akin to the "social contracting" relationship of leadership (Fulk & Cummings, 1984). The cyclical nature of the stages also requires that people continually project into the future, combining their appraisal and assessment of current work performance with preparation for future transitions.

Anticipation, Accommodation, Role Management. Feldman's (1976) three-stage entry model relies on many of the same concepts as Nicholson and West's. Feldman described differences in content and kind during anticipatory socialization, accommodation, and role management. Anticipatory socialization, he argued, encompasses the complete process of "getting in" to the new group, from preparation through selection and early entry. Its success depends on two measures: the extent to which the expectations of the new member and the organization are realistic, and the degree to which the newcomer is well matched with his or her new role (Watts, Short & Well, 1987). In Feldman's model, the accommodation stage involves four events. First, the newcomer is initiated to the new job. Second, the newcomer is initiated into a group of fellows and interpersonal relationships. Third, through the interaction processes, the group and the newcomer come to see how this person fits into this organization, uses time, and works toward common goals. Finally, the newcomer and the group come to an agreement about this person's fit in the group and evaluate his performance. The final stage in Feldman's model is role management—settling in. During this final stage, the newcomer resolves conflicts about how his work fits into the organization (and into life outside of work) and resolves the conflicts that arise within the work itself.

Confrontation, Clarity, Location. Other writers also apply stage frameworks to the study of organizational socialization. Wanous (1980) categorized stage frameworks as primarily based on the passage of time or on the occurrence of crucial events. Stage frameworks, he contended, must answer two basic questions: how are the stages related to each other? and how does one move from one stage to another? He offered a model that he believes answers these questions.

During the first stage, confrontation, the newcomer must confront and accept the reality of the new social setting. Expectations are confirmed or disconfirmed, conflicts between personal values and needs and the climate of the organization are confronted, and the aspects of self that the new setting will reinforce or suppress are discovered. Wanous's second stage involves the newcomer's achievement of *role clarity*. The tasks of the new job are assessed. Interpersonal relationships with subordinates, peers, and superiors emerge. The newcomer learns to cope with resistance to change on the part of established members of the group. The differences between the group's evaluation of the newcomer's performance and her own evaluation are confronted. And the newcomer learns to cope with ambiguity. During the third stage of socialization, the newcomer locates herself in the context by learning which behaviors are congruent with expected behaviors. Increased commitment to the organization, an altered or reaffirmed self-image and values, and new interpersonal relationships develop. Feelings of mutual acceptance should result.

Other stage frameworks contribute insight into the dynamics of organizational socialization. Buchanan's staged model is similar to Feldman's but uses the passage of time to delineate the three stages—basic training and initiation (year one), performance (years two, three, and four), and organizational dependability (year five and beyond). Also like Feldman's, Porter, Lawler, and Hackman's stages depend on the accomplishment of steps. They examine prearrival (anticipatory), encounter (accommodation), and change and acquisition (settling in). However, they evaluate the outcomes of the final stage in four areas—self-image, formation of new relationships, adoption of new values, and acquisition of new behaviors—all related to personal, not organizational, outcomes.

Each stage presents different challenges for new principals and may be susceptible to influence from different tactics. First, anticipation provides a period of varying length in which the new leader can gather information about the job and make preparations (e.g., principals and lead teachers can acquire skills in the observation of instruction and mentor relationships). The level of anxiety people feel during this stage appears to depend on such factors as the previous experiences they have to draw on, the amount of forewarning they have, and the relationship with the new superior.

During encounter, managers (Nicholson & West, 1988) report that their major source of anxiety is performance, whether their contributions will be valued, and whether they will like their work. Women feel significantly higher levels of presuccession or pretransition anxiety about performance and the value of their contributions than do men. The encounter stage also presents a reality shock in which surprise is the primary feature (Louis, 1980b). Reality usually differs markedly from expectations (Richards, 1984), but this period can be one of "excitement, optimism, and discovery" (Nicholson & West, 1988, p. 98). Major sources of discovery are work context (atmosphere, training or learning opportunities, and communications and decision making), job content (the nature of the work, the people, and the supervision), and personal responses or effects (performance, reactions and feelings, impacts on life-style). Surprises occur in transitions to new organizations *and* in transitions within organizations. Negative surprises tend to outweigh positive, particularly those related to people and the environment. Outcomes emerge during stabilization when the personal and organization ramifications of a change in principals becomes apparent.

Personal and Social Context

Tactics and stages occur in a context that sets the stage for the succession experience. New leaders enter an existing social world. Even if this existing world prescribes behavior so tightly that creativity is seen as a "breach of the rules" (Wentworth, 1980, p. 58), it "does not exert an irresistible hold" over the newcomer. Each new leader brings a personal perspective, outside influences, and "creative skepticism" to the experience. When a new principal is appointed, a work group and corps of superiors with a preexisting culture precedes her. The leader's entry requires that she learn the nature of this culture while striving to effect some changes within it (Crouch & Yetton, 1988). Neither the prior qualities of a leader nor the prior qualities of the existing group adequately explain the outcomes of successions (Smith & Peterson, 1988). Taken together, they constitute the third major theme of organizational socialization.

Personal Context. New members—their talents, preferences, characteristics, thinking, and experiences—form the personal context in which successions occur. Writers interested in understanding the impact of a career on personal development are strongly embedded in this tradition and adopt a number of different perspectives. Some are centered in a view of the career as an unfolding evolutionary process; some rely on psychological theories of adult development; and some synthesize the adult and career perspectives (Manning, 1977).

Those who take a career approach often adopt a lifelong evolutionary view of career as an accumulation of role-related experiences over time (Hall, 1987; Louis, 1980a). The life cycle tradition in adult psychology provides a similar view, pointing to common phases of development. This perspective has received much popular attention (Erikson, 1950). Another group of sociologists and psychologists takes a more flexible position, seeking patterns of change in individuals' life spans but avoiding hard and fast rules about the particular kind of changes that will or will not take place. Researchers in this tradition examine situational/professional self-concept and its interaction with core self-concept as values, intellectual functioning, and sense of self-direction change with experience (Brousseau, 1983; Kohn & Schooler, 1983).

Social Context. The social structure at the time of a succession constitutes the primary context for socialization. It is the human system into which integration is sought. Some assert that culture is so fundamental to organizations that organizations are cultures (Pondy et al., 1983; Smircich, 1983). To tap the power of this context, a new principal or teacher leader (Hart, 1990a) must come to understand and be able to use the fundamental values, beliefs, and assumptions about worth that drive and energize the group. Schein's (1985) cultural analysis questions provide excellent guidance for such an analysis.

Human systems theory provides another useful framework for understanding the social context of succession. The organizational level of the new member and dynamics of interaction shape the effects of the socialization system from a human systems view. The level of organization at which the newcomer or new ideas enter the system influences judgments and reactions by members of the group. Someone entering as a new principal or lead teacher, for example, receives very different responses than a new teacher. Three central features of human systems strongly affect interactions during organizational socialization. They are similarity of group members; frequency of interaction or contact among group members; and the tendency of people to interact with people like themselves and limit the frequency and intensity of their contact with people who are different (Gecas, 1981).

The first and second of these features—the impact of contact on positive feelings and similarity of members—affect the selection and entry stages of leader socialization. People generally accept the notion that the similarity of group members and frequency of contact among members positively affect feelings, increasing liking among the members and creating positive responses. This belief leads many to recommend more communication in schools as an intervention strategy when problems arise. Monane (1967) points out that this belief is unfounded. Positive affect outcomes depend on the legitimacy of interaction. Neither increased similarity nor increased contact appear "independently or jointly productive of positive affect in systems where hostility is the legitimate expected" outcome of contact (Monane, 1967, pp. 28–29).

Monane uses the example of the Apache to illustrate this phenomenon. Among the Apache, son-in-law/mother-in-law contact is frowned on and produces negative feelings when it occurs. Much energy is devoted to preventing contact. The salutary impacts of communication also depend on the makeup of the social system. Monane (1967, p. 59) explains:

> The amount of communication among components, however, appears to have little impact in either setting or changing a system's emotional tone. Increases in association do not in themselves yield bounties of affection; decreases do not necessarily deepen hostility. . . . What appears essential is not the amount of communication and interaction but the total system in which they operate: the components (including affect) of that system and the environment impinging upon it.

We find these effects in research on school reform. Many policy makers call for more communication between principals and faculties, more teamwork, and more teacher peer supervision. There are many recommendations to increase the number and length of principal classroom visits to improve schools and positive feelings. In the absence of support from the social system, affirmation by professional beliefs and norms, and support from the environment, these reforms can cause problems. When they are not seen as legitimate, they can cause resentment and restrict productive work (Firestone & Bader, 1991).

Another example of the importance of contact, communication, and similarity can be drawn directly from the traditional succession research. Opportunity and diversity in school leadership are important values. Consequently, the social incongruence of new principals receives attention from writers interested in succession effects (Hart, 1988; Pounder, 1988, 1989; Valverde, 1980). The perception of social incongruence presents a challenge, because it leads to limited contact, communication blocks, and low perceived legitimacy. Surface characteristics of these principals present initial barriers during succession. In the social context they must emphasize and highlight their similarities, thus improving their acceptance by the group.

Finally, people tend to increase their interactions with those similar to themselves and limit their interactions with those with whom they feel dissimilar. This tendency poses problems for newcomers, their superiors, and their new colleagues. First, school and community members' perceptions that new principals don't fit may lead to their isolation. They may seek to protect the system from their influence and "shortcomings." Second, newcomers might intentionally or unintentionally intensify perceptions of incongruence by drawing attention to differences by their behavior, because they do not realize how they are perceived. On the other hand, new principals might highlight similar experiences, characteristics, and beliefs and deemphasize dissimilar ones to help create a social environment in which they are seen as legitimate.

Human systems theory also provides insight into interaction dynamics between new leaders and the existing group. Weick (1976) argued that many of the organizational outcomes we observe in schools can be explained as a result of the nature of schools as "loosely coupled systems." This loose coupling makes early contacts slow to develop. Healthy reactions need to spread through the school for relationships to develop. "In systems of high organization, the action of one member toward a particular entrant (a person or an idea, for example) is likely to trigger similar action by other members as well" (Monane, 1967, p. 24). If schools are loosely coupled, having low organizational linkages, the interaction process new principals experience could have two features. First, it could take more effort for principals to establish socially validated authority relationships (Blau, 1964; Dornbusch & Scott, 1975) with teachers, parents, and supervisors and, eventually, with the school as a whole than if linkages were more tightly coupled. On the other hand, early, strong responses by superiors or influential teachers and parents to the new principal and her ideas could trigger similar responses from others. This effect would be particularly strong for those with whom principals have close contact. It could create a chain reaction of responses—positive or negative.

Outcomes or Effects

While succession research looks for organizational effects, socialization reveals both personal and organizational effects. The addition of the personal perspective—with personal and organizational outcomes then becoming features of the setting (Miskel & Cosgrove, 1985)—is one important contribution of organizational socialization to succession. Outcomes occur in personal, structural, and cultural dimensions. These outcomes immediately become part of the developing context, a much less static view of succession than the traditional succession literature (see Chapter 2).

Scholars predict a number of outcomes from combinations of these features and the level of tactics available. Predicted outcomes also take place at the personal or organizational level and involve several aspects of the role. A custodial response from the new leader would be the most static outcome of a succession. This means that the inherited past dominates, at both the individual and organizational levels. All aspects of the role remain virtually unchanged, and the new leader is much like the predecessor. The successor literally becomes the custodian of an unchanged social niche in the organization. Van Maanen and Schein (1979) predicted a custodial response when the process is sequential, and variable, includes role models, and shapes a new professional identity. New leaders essentially imitate their predecessors, learn the requirements of the job, and use customary strategies and actions to meet these requirements.

Content innovation occurs with changes in the way the new principal performs his role. This second outcome is most likely when socialization is collective (new ideas and innovation are stressed), formal, random, fixed, and without role models. The new principal accepts traditional norms and goals but changes tactical alternatives, tasks, and the knowledge base on which he draws to get his work done.

Last, role innovation is the most innovative outcome. Role innovation refines the mission and goals of the role as well as its content. It is predicted when socialization is individual, informal, random, and disjunctive and affirms a strong professional identity. When role innovation occurs during socialization, the new principal rejects most of the norms governing conduct and performance. She makes a genuine attempt to redefine the ends as well as the means (Schein, 1971b).

These predictions cover only a small proportion of the possible combinations of features and levels of organizational socialization outcomes. Empirical research leaves much territory unexplored. Jones

(1986), for example, examined the outcomes of planned organizational socialization in 102 new MBA graduates. He found that collective organizational level socialization generally encourages a custodial response while individual processes are more likely to result in innovation. He also found that a custodial response is very common and, unlike Van Maanen and Schein, observed this replication under processes that affirmed identity and were fixed in time. He also emphasized that individual differences in self-efficacy moderate these outcomes. But restrictive *content* likely follows formality.

Other views of socialization outcomes provide further insight. Nicholson (1984) focused directly on personal and role development—change in person or change in the role (content and basic function). He theorized that personal development is most likely when socialization is sequential (involving cumulative learning), occurs with role models, and requires that one abandon or redefine professional identity. Change, then, is a major theme. On the other hand, role development is more likely when socialization is random, occurs without role models, and affirms professional identity.

Nicholson's (1984) outcome categories also differ somewhat, emphasizing affective states and coping responses; identity changes in which new values, skills, and dispositions emerge; and behavior. He reminds us that affect has a powerful impact and should not be discounted. Successful socialization is facilitated by friendship and strong affective bonds (Sherman et al., 1986). Organizations pay a high price for disaffection. Wanous (1980) estimated that socialization operates as one of the five most important factors creating feelings of alienation and resignations. Nicholson (1984) further developed his work by exploring four adjustments—replication, absorption, determination, and exploration—depending on the personal disposition of the new manager, the new role requirements, and organizational socialization. When neither the new principal nor the role change, replication is the result. This is a custodial response. When little about the role changes but considerable personal development takes place in response to the role requirements, absorption occurs. While this response is also custodial, the new principal experiences personal growth and development. It can be a form of human resource development. When little personal change occurs, but significant content or role innovation takes place, determination is the outcome. And when both the role and the person change, exploration occurs. Depending on the needs of the organization, any of these outcomes can be functional or dysfunctional.

Two dimensions of managers' jobs—novelty and discretion—exert further influence over outcomes. The greater the novelty, the greater the likelihood that a principal will develop new skills and perspectives. The greater the discretion, the more likelihood that a principal will attempt role innovation. Older, higher status, generalist managers are more likely to say they are role innovators (Nicholson & West, 1988). Since both principal growth and school improvement are desired outcomes of most successions, Nicholson and West (1988, p. 110) report a research finding of great interest:

> High role innovators are more likely than low innovators to report having experienced personal change as a result of their last job change. This indicates, in the terminology of the theory of work role transitions, that "exploration" is more common as an adjustment mode than pure "determination."

The creative and innovative work that can result when principals receive new assignments deserves as much attention as does the effect of macro-level education reform (West, Farr & King, 1986).

A major question remains unanswered: What is the cumulative effect of socialization experiences in adult work and professional settings over time? The effect is individual, not organizational, because each principal's experiences are unique. Over time, in homogenous work groups in which people have similar, frequent, salient, and valued experiences, socialization may result in similar personal outcomes often because it represents a shared ordeal among newcomers (Becker et al., 1961; Lortie, 1968). Yet so little is known about how people process information and experience over time (Weick, 1977) that the relative accumulated effect of a series of socialization experiences in various groups is unknown (Thomas & Griffin, 1983). "The meanings of job change are highly personal. We would need to take an individualized biographical perspective to fully appreciate how they fit into the lives and careers of managers" (Nicholson & West, 1988, p. 211). This approach has been termed a "worthwhile endeavor" for future research.

> If job change has the power to effect changes in identity as well as in organizational performance then how the transition process is managed has a vital bearing on the well-being and effectiveness of organizations. It would appear that few organizations recognize this. (Nicholson & West, 1988, p. 212)

Nonetheless, socialization also creates an "organizational mind" of sorts that shapes actions and policy for everyone involved (Mitroff, 1983). One final factor affecting the quality of succession/transitions is the quality of feedback and recognition given to new leaders—an area in which Nicholson and West found most organizations to be deficient. Principal socialization research paints a similar picture—some new principals report going months on end with no contact with their superiors and absolutely no feedback about how they are perceived (Duke et al., 1984; Greenfield, 1985a, 1985b).

The possible outcomes of organizational socialization tactics that various writers predict can occur at the personal and organizational level. Different kinds of change may occur, including personal growth and development or content and role innovation. Combinations of change and status quo outcomes at personal and organizational levels may be more or less desirable. Table 1.2 provides a summary of possible outcomes.

TABLE 1.2

Socialization Outcomes

Features		*Outcomes*
Custodial:		
absorption	→	personal development
replication	→	no personal or role development
Organizational Change:		
determination	→	content/role innovation
exploration	→	content/role innovation *and* personal development

A custodial response preserves the status quo; it can also result in the personal development of the new principal. Organizational change requires more complex outcomes and can result in changes in the content of the role or in the fundamental assumptions and functions of the role. Research on the most successful managerial successions suggests that the ideal outcome is a combination of personal growth and organizational change (exploration).

The impacts of the social and personal context on outcomes receive more attention in empirical literature than the impacts of tactics. Contexts are far more difficult for the organization to control with policies and procedures. It is in context that the new principal exerts her greatest impact. Tactics employed by the organization

affect her personal development and orientation toward organizational change, but interactions with superiors and with the school
shape the social validation emphasized at the beginning of this
chapter. This is where the new principal can exert the greatest
influence over her own succession, recognizing the impact of the group
on her as she works to affect the achievement of the group while also
working to develop a foundation of social power (French & Raven,
1959).

Summary

    While succession researchers and those who appoint new
principals customarily acknowledge the critical part new appointees
to leadership positions play in schools, they generally accept the
assumption that the primary influence flow is downward from the
principal to the school. But organizations protect against the intrusion
of new members by routinization and a number of additional formal
and informal social system mechanisms, one of which is socialization
(Gouldner, 1954). Most people who work in schools assume that
succession will occur and that the effects of a new principal on the
school will be felt in its structure, social interactions, and performance. Yet others show how organizations "minimize the succession
crisis" (Gross & Etzioni, 1985) by socializing newcomers and laying
obstacles in their paths.
    Principal succession is of interest to people concerned with many
aspects of schools. Those who study leadership; those who appoint and
transfer principals; those who work in schools; principals' superiors;
and school board members have different but complementary interests
in principal succession and its outcomes. In this chapter, I have argued
that isolating the study of principal succession from the study of
organizational socialization creates artificial and unnecessary
barriers to understanding this important organizational event as an
interaction process and to interventions by superiors and principals.
Succession and socialization research present two views of the same
event involving the same people—the one view focused on the school
and district effects on the newcomer, the other concentrated on the
newcomer's effect on the group. The tension between a school's need
for creativity and the need for principal integration into the group
remains a factor in shaping succession outcomes. Principal
professional socialization research to date lays a strong foundation
for the expansion of inquiry to include new and experienced successors
and group and individual creativity. By expanding analyses to include

organizational socialization, the dynamics and variables leading to a healthy balance between the power of the group and the creativity of the individual can be promoted (Emerson, 1962; Frese, 1982).

Chapters 2 and 3 review two bodies of literature on which this discussion of leader succession is based. Chapter 2 presents traditional organizing frameworks for studying leader succession in schools. Chapter 3 provides an overview of thought contributing to the organizational socialization framework on which this book is based.

Since no body of knowledge exists in isolation, Chapter 3 presents an overview of the conceptual roots of the organizational socialization literature in the social sciences. It explores the theoretical traditions of organizational socialization in social and behavioral science. This chapter can be viewed as background material, a glimpse at the debt organizational socialization and leader succession scholars owe to the intellectual traditions on which their work is based. As background material, it is not necessary to understand and benefit from the underlying principles on which the book is based and may be overlooked by those interested primarily in applying organizational socialization to the improvement of leader succession experiences in schools. For those interested in a foray into theories that undergird this analysis, Chapter 3 provides a beginning.

2

Leader Succession Research

For three decades social scientists have examined leadership by those holding formal organizational roles through the lens of change. Managerial succession research originally was founded on the belief that leaders make a difference in organizations and that managers can exercise leadership. Research projects were designed in part to discover whether succession per se affected organizations in predictable ways and in part to determine how this important event could be made more successful for the organization and the successor. To their dismay, scholars found as many different outcomes of succession as there were cases and data bases accumulating in the literature. These diverse findings reflected the ambiguity and complexity of research findings in the general leadership literature (Stogdill, 1974). The research on administrative succession in schools proved no exception. Ogawa (in press) reviewed the succession research applying traditional frameworks. He declared the usefulness of recent findings from this approach seriously limited.

Leadership succession research developed into four branches: (1) the search for succession effects, isolated from general leadership effects, and for the individual, social, and environmental factors that affect it; (2) the use of succession to define the tenure of different managers in order to isolate the impact of their leadership on organizational performance; (3) the study of personal, social, and organizational variables interacting during succession and their relevance in revealing a general leadership factor in formal organizational roles; and (4) the delineation of the stages through which the process of succession takes place across time. The first of these approaches, the search for succession effects, was a response to the widespread practice, common in all kinds of organizations, of changing formal leaders when performance falters. Change for its own sake also is valued by some as a management policy. In education, many superintendents believe that principals should remain in one school for a limited number of years and act on that belief, regularly transferring school administrators. Researchers questioned the assumption inherent in this behavior—that managerial succession improved performance—and set out to test it.

The second approach used changes in managers to distinguish the tenure of one formal leader from that of another to study general leadership effects. It often relied on the quantitative analysis of large data bases on organizational performance coupled with data on managerial change in the search for the leader effect. In a very broad way, scholars reasoned, variance in performance should be associated with the tenure of different managers if they affect organizational outcomes. Each of these two approaches contributed to the development of succession research. A broad range of analytical techniques applied to succession and the events preceding and following it consequently has been pursued.

Although less common, a third approach was also taken. Some researchers studied the interactions among social and personal factors in the organization during managerial succession. Like those who study organizational socialization, they capitalized on times of change to study the general leadership factor as it finds expression in interactions within the group. The rationale on which these writers based their work springs from the theory of Weber and Bierstedt that "power appears when relationships are not quite routine" (Wentworth, 1980, p. 118). They also accept the assumption that power and influence are vital resources in organizational management (Kotter, 1979, 1982, 1985).

The fourth approach to leadership succession research joined the study of general succession effects with context and content factors in a stage framework. Because succession events appear to be time bound, scholars in this tradition reasoned that more complete understanding of the stages characterizing effective successions would expand knowledge about ascension to leadership and help people improve the quality of succession experiences. It addressed these questions: How does succession occur? Through what stages does succession pass? How do we know when succession is successfully completed? What thought patterns affect positive outcomes? (Manz et al., 1988).

Each of these four branches of leadership succession research contributed to the development of the field. They are discussed in further detail below.

Succession Effects

The question whether succession per se is a salutary or disruptive event in organizations remains unanswered. More specifically, the answer seems to be, it depends. In a review of succession literature, Brown (1982) found studies supporting the full spectrum of possible outcomes; succession improved, disrupted, and had no effect on organizational performance. Carroll (1984) argued that, rather than try to sort out whether or not succession has positive effects, researchers should look at conditions under which succession will have different effects, such as changes in supervisory leadership patterns (Koch, 1978). As Pfeffer and Davis-Blake (1986, p. 81) pointed out, "the consequences of successions are likely to vary dramatically depending on the conditions surrounding them." These findings emerged from all types of organizations and research designs, a disparity leading some researchers to abandon the question of succession effects per se.

Positive Effects

The judgment that managerial succession has positive effects springs primarily from case studies applying qualitative methods to the question. Two very different cases illustrate the observations leading to this conclusion. While the setting, environment, and circumstances differed widely in the two cases, making comparisons difficult, they provided important impetus to further exploration of the succession effect. The lack of comparability and failure to find common factors contributing to positive or negative outcomes in succession case studies shook scholars' confidence in the applicability of the case study method to advance this research, however.

One of the first cases with a positive outcome that attracted attention was prepared by Guest (1962), who observed a new manager who was successful in taking charge. He was able, through careful use of informal contacts, to improve interactions and communication in the auto plant in which he succeeded to top management. He carefully accumulated personal relationships—through the formal structure and informal floor contacts with the workers—that made it possible for him to accomplish substantive and structural changes. Through this process, he gathered vital technical knowledge, learned about subordinate needs, and created a power base in the organization. The observed outcomes of this study led Guest to argue that succession can be a positive organizational event.

A second case with a positive outcome often cited by succession writers was prepared by Salaman (1977), who studied a succession in a small manufacturing plant. In this case, the retired manager posed a threat to the successor by continuing to exercise considerable influence. Salaman's case raised important questions about the power of the predecessor to influence the process and outcomes of managerial succession. He observed members of the group praising and idealizing the predecessor. The "Rebecca Myth," first described and named by Gouldner (1954) in his landmark study of succession, appeared in this succession. Named after Daphne du Maurier's famous novel *Rebecca*, the Rebecca Myth is an emerging process through which predecessors are idealized by members of the group, regardless of their objective qualities or the group's assessment of them during their tenure. In Salaman's case, this dynamic exerted a strong influence, but the new manager, a highly charismatic authoritarian leader, was able to overcome its negative effects and complete a successful succession.

Negative Effects

Unlike the research resulting in positive assessments of succession, conclusions that succession disrupts and is, therefore, a dysfunctional event arose from studies taking a number of conceptual perspectives and applying a variety of methods. Often factors leading to positive outcomes in early case studies resulted in negative outcomes in other cases, and correlation analyses yielded bleak predictions about the usefulness of succession as a management strategy.

Gouldner's (1954) judgment of succession was negative. He argued that many factors combine to make succession a disruptive experience in an organization. Observing a succession in the management of a gypsum mine, he watched the new leader violate highly entrenched social norms. Subordinates reacted negatively; the new leader fell back on hierarchical authority, increasing tension and stress. Organizational members responded by spreading the Rebecca Myth mentioned above, an idealization of the performance of the predecessor. Unlike the event Salaman described, the myth persisted despite its lack of veracity. His conclusion: disruption results when an important member of the group leaves and is replaced.

Other, more recent, studies in very different settings support Gouldner's conclusion. In a case study of a psychiatric unit, Oskarsson and Klein (1982) highlighted a variety of dangers attendant to managerial change. Both before and after succession, they found feelings of apprehension and strong differences of philosophy between the work group and the new leader. These feelings resulted in conflict, withdrawal, and regression to unproductive behaviors. Once a group begins to view itself as beleaguered, they found, a new manager has a particularly difficult task. Work may need to cease while members focus on relationships and attempt to reestablish productive patterns. Whether this beleaguered state occurs or not, the succession itself is disruptive; the new leader may be perceived as an intruder, performance may fall, the organization may regress.

Context-free succession studies also resulted in negative conclusions about impacts. The win/loss records of athletic teams provided one of the earliest uses of quantitative data in succession studies. When a team loses consistently, the coach often is fired. Scholars asked whether this convention serves any purpose aside from catharsis for owner and fans. The results of athletic team analyses provided little support for the belief that changing leaders improves performance. Grusky (1963), finding that baseball teams with the poorest performance records had the highest succession rates, argued that succession is a vicious circle. Poor performance causes succession, which is disruptive and leads to further poor performance. Gamson and Scotch (1964) explained the continued faith in the practice of firing losing coaches and managers as "ritual scapegoating," a way of making sense of nonsense. Other studies reporting negative outcomes were conducted on the financial health of business firms. Beatty and Zajac (1987) studied the impact of announced succession in the chief executive officers on overall worth of firms and found both insider and outsider successions to cause a statistically significant drop in the overall value of the firms.

No Effect

Perhaps more disturbing to those who appoint or study leaders in organizations than disagreement over the positive or negative effects of succession was the contention that it does not matter. According to the results of some studies, outcomes fail to validate the belief that a change in managers could improve or degrade performance; it serves no substantive purpose.

Like the studies supporting the disruptive effect of succession, research on the win/loss records of athletic teams provided much of the evidence leading to this dismal assessment of succession effects. Perhaps the judgment that succession is a nonevent is best represented by the arguments of Gamson and Scotch (1964) mentioned in the preceding section. They interpreted succession in baseball is a "ritual scapegoating" process having little impact on performance.

The manager is offered up as a sacrifice for an unsuccessful team performance. Expanding on this argument, Eitzen and Yetman (1972) observed that the predominant variable influencing the performance of athletic teams is an artifact of probability, not team leadership—the regression effect. The performance of strong teams tends to regress downward toward the mean performance level, and weak teams' performance tends to regress upward.

This ritualistic explanation, decoupled from substantive performance differences, also was the foundation of Gephart's (1978) explanation for the processes leading to a forced succession in the leadership of a university student organization. Once the impetus to remove a leader grows to a consensus, he explained, group members begin a process of status degradation to justify and rationalize the decision. Not until the incumbent is clearly and systematically portrayed as unsuitable does succession take place. The scapegoat can be marked and purged through status degradation.

In another study of athletic teams, Allen, Panian, and Lotz (1979) concurred with those disassociating succession from organizational outcomes. They maintained that the succession factor makes far too small a contribution to organizational performance to be important. In a time series study of major league baseball teams between 1920 and 1973, they set out to assess the relative adequacy of succession theories as explanations for organizational performance. While they confirmed previous conclusions that frequency of succession is negatively related to team performance, they pointed out that only a very small proportion of the variance in performance can be explained by succession. A far more potent predictor, past performance (also the most powerful predictor of student performance), led them to call for succession research focused on structures, policies, and environments rather than outcomes. Implicit in their conclusion is the belief that something important in the social structure of organizations is affected by the process of succession and is worthy of investigation.

Quantitative data from schools contributed to the pool of evidence leading to the rejection of succession's effect on organizational performance. With a study of principal succession, Miskel and Owens (1983) supported the thesis that administrative succession has no effect in schools. They examined effects on a variety of outcomes—structural linkages, perceived organizational effectiveness, job satisfaction of teachers, and student attitudes. No impact of principal succession on these measures of school performance was discernible in their data.

In a recent revival of the search for positive effects that sought to capitalize on the advantages of large data pools, Rowan and Denk (1984) examined actuarial performance data from schools. They sought to isolate the principal succession effect and the circumstances under which leader succession is likely to be most advantageous. Their analysis revealed that succession is disruptive in schools where students are primarily of high socioeconomic status (SES) and helpful in schools of low SES, supporting arguments that succession itself can be either positive or negative depending on a variety of organizational and environmental factors. Their results affirmed that investigations of succession outputs may be less promising than examinations of contextual factors.

A number of explanations have been offered for these outcomes of research. Writers who subscribe to the argument that the succession of an individual leader makes little or no difference in organizational performance often explain outcomes by pointing to the enormous constraints on leaders. Lieberson and O'Connor's (1972) often-cited study of major industrial organizations falls in this category. It provided evidence of the triviality of succession effects and the constraining power of context. This evidence is commonly used to support the argument that large organizations are inertia bound and slow to respond to any change, even the succession of a powerful and prominent formal leader (Hambrick & Mason, 1984; Hannan & Freeman, 1984; Samuelson, Galbraith & McGuire, 1985). Writers place heavy emphasis on the total variance in performance that different leaders appear to affect when they offer up skeptical assessments of the overall impact of leaders.

The question of positive, disruptive, or absent effects of succession provides a clue to why interaction dynamics in contexts accompanying succession might be worthy of more attention: "The inherent social disruption caused by successions may be one reason why a new manager's ability to develop effective working relationships discriminates so strongly between the failed and successful successions" (Gabarro, 1987, p. 166).

Contextual Constraints

Context, then, becomes the alternative focus of interest (Thomas, 1988). Pfeffer (1978, 1981b) offered a number of explanations for the failure of those filling formal leadership positions to affect organizational performance—all contextually based. He attributed the absence of evidence that administrators influence organizational performance to three sets of constraints: the similarity of people working in administrative positions; the nature of administrative work; and the organizational and external environments in which administrators operate.

Administrators' Similarity. The first constraint on the influence of administrators identified by Pfeffer and discussed in the preceding chapter on administrator socialization is the similarity of people in the administrative pool. These similarities result, he argued, from administrator selection, socialization, and training. Selection processes contribute to the homogeneity of administrators, because superiors tend to select candidates with whom they share social characteristics. Kanter (1977) referred to this as "homosocial reproduction." Homosocial reproduction operates in all types of organizations, including public schools. Baltzell and Dentler (1983) noted that educational administrators,particularly superintendents, tend to favor individuals who mirror their own social and personal characteristics when selecting administrators. This is one explanation for the relative exclusion of women and members of minority groups from educational administration, because the field has been dominated by white, Protestant, males (Valverde, 1980; National Commission on Excellence in Educational Administration, 1987; Pellicer, Anderson, Keefe, Kelly & McCleary, 1988a, 1988b; Tyack & Hansot, 1982). In short, school administrators tend to look alike.

Another reason for the similarity of administrators is formal education and training. Pfeffer observed that most administrators undergo similar formal training and informal socialization experiences. In preparation for public school careers, the vast majority of administrators have completed university based, graduate training programs. These programs generally vary little (Duke et al., 1984). Training usually provides exposure to such topics as school law, school finance, school politics, administrative and organizational theory, instructional supervision, the principalship, and personnel administration. This uniformity results in administrators who act on the basis of similar knowledge and assumptions.

Informal socialization extends the homogenizing effect of formal education. For example, almost all school administrators were once classroom teachers and identify their teaching as part of their professional socialization experience (Duke et al., 1984). After leaving the classroom, they typically follow a common career route from assistant principal to principal and, in some cases, to the superintendency. Studies of administrator socialization discussed in Chapter 1 (Pitner & Ogawa, 1981; Greenfield, 1985a, 1985b) generally conclude that administrators develop common orientations as a result of their shared professional socialization experiences. Thus, they tend to operate from a common set of assumptions and beliefs (Tyack & Hansot, 1982).

The Social Nature of Administrative Work. A second contextual constraint on the impact of managerial succession lies in the social nature of administrative work. Pfeffer (1978) suggested that many organizational elements (such as formal job descriptions and informal role expectations) limit managerial discretion. In addition, administrators typically avoid making important unilateral decisions such as resource allocation or personnel selection.

In public schools, examples of these constraints abound. Teachers expect principals to buffer them from parents. Most principals have very limited control over resource allocations and personnel decisions. And union agreements and board policies prevent principals from making unilateral decisions about instructional programs and materials.

Organizational Settings. Pfeffer identified a third source of constraint on administrator influence: the settings in which they work. Circumstances over which administrators have little or no control exist both within organizations and in their external environments. These circumstances influence operations and, thus, performance. Technology, social norms, and standard operating procedures typically are deeply embedded in organizations. Therefore, they are not easily changed by administrators.

In public schools, examples of these organizational factors abound. A principal new to a school inherits a faculty that is likely to have well-developed norms that guide social interactions as well as the day-to-day operation of the school. She will also find that instructional programs have been implemented and textbooks have been adopted, purchased, and used. Even the physical layout of the building can limit the types of instructional programs that can be implemented.

External environmental factors, such as contracts with suppliers, market conditions, and government regulations, also influence the structure and operation of organizations. Because these constraints persist over time, they greatly reduce the discretion and, therefore, the influence of administrators. Many environmental constraints impinge on public schools. They include the norms of local communities, the policies of state and federal agencies, court rulings, and innovations in instructional technology. Not only must educational administrators respond to forces in the environment, they also find that the alternatives available to them in making decisions are defined by the interests of powerful constituencies in their environments. For example, when an administrator hires teachers, only those candidates who have met state standards for a teaching credential and, often, only those who have passed muster for the personnel director can be considered.

Succession as a Boundary Delineating Leadership Effects

A second tradition of succession research uses the event to delineate the boundary between the tenures of different managers. A body of quantitative work that sought to control contaminating variables and establish general leadership effects developed within this tradition. It addresses two distinct questions:

> One concerns the extent to which leader differences account for performance variations within each [organization] over time. This is indicated by the proportion of variance unexplained by contextual variables that is accounted for by leader differences. The second question concerns the extent to which leader differences account for the total variation displayed by the whole set of organizations, which includes both within- and between [organization] variance. . . . Since the two bases for assessment are different, it is not surprising that the conclusions in each case are different. They only appear contradictory if it is assumed that they are different answers to the same question rather than answers to two different questions. (Thomas, 1988, p. 398)

One should keep this distinction in mind when reviewing the actuarial studies of succession effects, for it is within each organization that differences can be found.

Lieberson and O'Connor (1972) were among the pioneers of the actuarial approach to the study of succession, which used the event to distinguish among managers and depended on large existing data banks. They examined succession to chief executive officer (CEO) positions in business and industry by isolating leadership, corporate, and environmental factors that might influence performance. Using sales, earnings, and profit margins as output measures in manufacturing, they first controlled for trends in the economy and in each industry and for past corporate performance. They then adjusted their data for a time lag between succession and the appearance of effects. Lieberson and O'Connor found that the effect of change at the helm varied: 6.5 percent of the difference in sales; 4.5 percent of the difference in income; and 14.5 percent of the difference in profit was attributable to the people holding leadership positions. These findings attributed variance to top managers but did not draw conclusions about the positive or negative direction of effects. They described these influences as small but interesting, justifying further examination. In an attempt to explain the modest magnitude of their findings, they augmented their analysis with a discussion of constraints on leadership. Those who argue that succession makes no difference in organizational performance cite this small effect on total performance variance as evidence, but Lieberson and O'Connor said that the significance of their findings rests in the contribution of leadership to the unexplained variance (1972, p. 123).

Weiner and Mahoney (1981) attempted to decompose the factors contributing to performance in business, arguing that a relatively large number of small influences may be important. Their results were not encouraging, explaining only 54.4 percent of the variance in profitability in their 1981 study and convincing them that many factors contributing to performance on the outcomes they measured are simply not included in the current actuarial models. In a further explanation for their disappointing findings, they argued that the role of the leader may be most important during growth, change, and crisis and, thus, not apparent in longitudinal data. This argument brings the logic of succession research full circle, for managerial succession is a common period of change and sometimes of crisis in organizations.

The method used by Lieberson and O'Connor was also applied to governments, schools, and school districts. Salancik and Pfeffer (1977), using the intermediate variable of budget allocations as their measure of mayoral influence on city governments, obtained results similar to those of Lieberson and O'Connor. They interpreted these results as evidence that leadership in organizations is not only constrained but may serve no real role in performance. As Pfeffer later argued more completely (1978, 1981b), the role of leadership may be better explained as attribution, a process by which group members make sense of observed outcomes for which they have no logical explanation by attributing them to the leader.

Ogawa and Hart (1985) and Hart and Ogawa (1987) replicated the business and government actuarial studies in schools and school districts. Arguing that small (as much as 9.4 percent of variance) but identifiable differences in school and district performance on mathematics and reading tests attributable to the tenure of principals and superintendents are important, they used results similar to those obtained by Lieberson and O'Connor, Salancik and Pfeffer, and Weiner and Mahoney to defend and advocate a search for the nature of the effects, both positive and negative. Because only about 15 percent of the variance in student achievement is attributable to between-school differences (Jencks et al., 1972) and as much as 32 percent of the remaining between-school variance can be attributable to stable school-level properties (Rowan, Bossert & Dwyer, 1983), they judged the discovery of some variance attributable to leaders worthy of further investigation. In organizations as complex and multifaceted as schools with ambiguous goals and unclear technologies (March, 1976), these percentages did not appear to them to be trivial. Rowan and Denk (1984) added power to the actuarial research in schools, finding that school socioeconomic status moderated the leader succession effect.

Several contradictions in obtained results and their interpretation by researchers arose in the actuarial research tradition. First, most of these studies provided evidence of some, if small, effects of individuals in formal leadership roles on outcomes when other factors were controlled. But researchers judged the relative importance or triviality of observed impacts differently. Salancik and Pfeffer argued that these performance differences were meaningless. Lieberson and O'Connor found them worthy of further exploration, because, as mentioned earlier, the impact on total variance unexplained by multiple and complex contextual factors was important. Ogawa and Hart concurred, arguing that they provide evidence of an individual leadership effect, diluted by the constraints of the organization and of the methodology.

Second, formal leaders may influence some aspects of organizational performance more than others. This possibility led to conflicts over which outcome measures to choose when pursuing research into succession effects. Findings may be artifacts of the performance measures chosen rather than a limitation of individual or organizational effect. Thomas (1988, p. 397) found in his study of firms in the United Kingdom, for example, that "paradoxically, the data show that leadership doesn't make a difference and that it does." He explained this finding by pointing to differences in organizations' levels of performance over time and the varying constraints over leadership's impact on different performance outcomes. And other researchers (Day & Lord, 1988) continue to present a compelling case that individual leaders make a difference.

Finally, the methodology itself has been attacked. Critics contend that findings are an artifact of the method rather than the organizational variables of interest. Recent evidence, however, suggests that the actuarial approach can continue to offer insight into the large-scale study of leader/outcome relationships and provides "definite support for the individualist view of leadership" effects on organizational performance (Thomas, 1988, p. 388).

Regardless of the explanations offered for diverse findings, expectations for the magnitude of significant effects, lack of appropriate outcome measures, and methodological limitations, researchers continue the search for leadership effects through the vehicle of managerial succession research. Many writers continue to believe in the power of individual leaders to influence organizational outcomes (Smith, Carson & Alexander, 1984). As much of the research suggests, the effect of change in leadership on organizations is not uniformly predictable and depends in large measure on context variables (Rowan & Denk, 1984). The exact nature of these contingencies remains largely unexplored, however.

Succession Context in Organizations

A third use to which scholars put managerial succession events in the study of leadership and organizations springs from a recognition that context affects succession and from traditions of theory and research in sociology and social psychology. As Miklos (1988) pointed out, participants see succession as an important organizational event. Based on assumptions that social and personal factors may be more explicit and therefore more apparent during periods of change, this research examines the effects of succession on newly appointed formal leaders, the context in which succession takes place, and the features of the organizations that successors are expected to lead. A variety of social and psychological factors, examined in interaction, play parts in this dynamic view of managerial succession.

Gephart (1978) influenced the contextual research with his carefully constructed examination of the processes through which a social group comes to the conclusion that a formal leader must go. His description of status degradation emphasized the importance of group social psychological processes during a change in formal leaders—ways in which people come to share a common explanation and make sense of social events. Gephart insisted that before a group will accept the forced succession of its leader, the status of this person who formerly played an important and respected part in the group must be degraded through a series of social processes. His status degradation effect fills a role similar to that played by ritual scape-goating (Gamson & Scotch, 1964) and attribution (Pfeffer, 1981b)—a way of making sense of otherwise nonsensical organizational events.

Although sense making was used as evidence that succession has no substantive effect on organizations, people's explanations should not be discounted. Scholars from many fields find that explanations and attributions contribute understanding to difficult circumstances and affect behavior. Attribution functions in many ways: "The conditions and consequences of the perception of self-as-cause have become a major focus of contemporary attribution theory. Especially relevant. . . are the self-attributions individuals make with regard to personal control over events that affect them" (Turner, 1988, p. 19). People thus attribute cause to themselves and to powerful people in their social groups—the principal, the general manager, the valued teacher, the parent. They then may act on these attributions, creating effects (Hart, 1988).

This social psychological approach to studying succession has been applied to principal succession research. Ogawa and his colleagues (Fauske & Ogawa, 1987; Ogawa & Smith, 1985; Ogawa, 1991) used a sense-making framework to examine a voluntary retire-ment and subsequent succession of the principal in an elementary school. Taking up where Gephart's focus on the predecessor left off, their extended case study asked how the members of a school faculty make sense of the retirement of their principal and the subsequent succession of another principal appointed to the school. They found that the existing social organization and expectations of the group played a significant part in shaping the positive and negative judgments of faculty and staff, drawing attention to the important interplay between a new formal leader and existing social structures.

Crow (1990) and Lamoreaux (1990) applied very different methodologies to the study of principals' successions and came to similar conclusions—that interpersonal aspects most often are identi-fied by new principals and aspiring principals as the critical factors shaping their work. Crow's survey subjects focused on the importance of interpersonal and school climate issues. Lamoreaux's educational criticism portrayed a successful new principal for whom vision became the most important factor in succession. He said her "vision. . . is a vision of caring, of sharing, and of relationships. It is a vision that she models when working with students and staff" (Lamoreaux, 1990, p. 18).

Similarly, Hart (1987, 1988) turned her attention to the interpretations of the new principal, asking how the newly appointed formal leader makes sense of the dynamic interplay of self with the established social group. Providing one person's "native view" (Gregory, 1983), she too found that the social structure of the existing organization, its needs as perceived by current members, and its sacred and tacit practices (Corbett, Firestone & Rossman, 1987) exert tremendous influence over perceived outcomes. She concluded along with Blau (1964) and Dornbusch and Scott (1975) that the group's social validation of the legitimate authority of a new leader was a critical part of a succession experience and provided the underpinnings of the right to act in behalf of the group.

Scholars interested in the socialization of newly appointed leaders (their work was reviewed in Chapter 1) fit well within this third tradition of succession research. Duke et al. (1984), Greenfield (1985a, 1985b), and MacPherson (1984) emphasized how much of an impact the early professional socialization of principals plays in their subsequent professional identities and in their functioning as formal school leaders. Acknowledging the impact social factors have on the new member, regardless of the formal authority associated with the new role, these writers turned the attention of practitioners and scholars interested in the impacts of new principals on schools away from an exclusive examination of the personae, talents, and actions of the new principal and toward the social power of the existing group and the dynamic interactions among members of the whole.

Stages of Managerial Succession

Acknowledging the interaction dynamics in succession events, recent models provide a fourth approach to understanding succession. These models attempt to synthesize the impacts of leadership, change, and culture on the organization across time. They examine the processes and stages of interaction among people and context variables. These studies point to factors like the breadth and rigor of the search for a successor, the presence of insider favorites with power in the organization, crises brought on by performance failure, the power and expertise of selection agents or sponsors, and successor contacts.

Gordon and Rosen (1981) reviewed the inconclusive succession literature and recommended two process models to unify disparate results. The first called for the explication of factors relevant to succession stages—presuccession, succession, and postsuccession.

Presuccession in this model begins with the events leading to a change in managers and postsuccession ends when the new manager's presence is no longer novel. The second model depends on the tradition of situation-shaped leader outcomes focused on situational variables important to organizational succession, including group history, successor origin, selection process, mandates for change, and response to succession. Miskel and Cosgrove (1985, p. 89) modified Gordon and Rosen's two models to frame a review of succession research for application to education—capitalizing on process, context, and outputs resulting during prearrival, arrival, and succession effects stages. The important prearrival factors they identified were reasons for the succession, selection processes, reputations of leaders, and orientations of leaders. During arrival, they identified demography, organizational structure, school culture, educational programs, successor actions, community, and school effectiveness as important. And succession effects included changes in reputations, orientations, and arrival factors (which set the stage for the next succession). In all these attempts at a unification theory for managerial succession, traits, behaviors context, and interactions play important parts.

Stages of organizational entry intrigue writers interested in a wide range of questions related to leadership succession (Jentz et al., 1982). Friedman (1986, p. 192) focused his attention on the processes characterizing the actual replacement of the incumbent, dividing the prearrival stage into four parts: (1) establishing the need for a succession event, (2) determining selection criteria, (3) selecting candidates, and (4) choosing among the candidates. While he acknowledged that these categories artificially rationalize the process (and the steps may be reversed on some occasions), Friedman contended that an understanding of succession requires detailed analysis of each of these four stages, including who is involved, the reasons they give for their decisions, procedures followed, the time span over which events take place, and the amount of organizational effort expended—time, energy, and financial resources.

Redlich (1977), too, argued that stages characterize the process of leadership succession: anticipatory; appointment; inauguration; honeymoon; assertion of personality, style, and programs; working through differences; and establishment of equilibrium. Wanous, on the other hand, saw the process as less fragmented. He argued that people in the recruitment stage (presuccession in the Gordon and Rosen model) know very little about the organizations they may hope to join and may have very unrealistic expectations about what they hope to gain and contribute to the new organization. The impact of unrealistic expectations in the presuccession stage remains generally unaddressed by research, although findings suggest they may significantly affect subsequent disillusionment and turnover among new managers (Wanous, 1980).

Gabarro (1987) relied on another stage framework, describing his observations from studies of seventeen general and functional new managers. His goal was to delineate criteria on which one can judge whether or not a succession is complete. He concluded that leader succession involves five major stages: (1) taking hold, (2) immersion, (3) reshaping, (4) consolidation, and (5) refinement.

In the taking hold stage, managers are so pressed by the exigencies of grasping the new situation that they engage in little sense making and the attendant "double-loop learning" that reflection makes possible (Argyris & Schon, 1974). This is a time of concrete experience and active experimentation. The immersion stage involves more reflection (Schon, 1983). Reflection leads to more abstract conceptualization of the nature of the organization, because this period provides the opportunity to learn from the actions of the previous stage and examine underlying social assumptions governing behavior. The reshaping stage is heavily action oriented—a period of active experimentation and concrete observation exploiting the more reflective learning that took place during the immersion stage. Consolidation corresponds in Gabarro's estimation to the entire range of learning during succession, from the concrete experience to the active experimentation by the new manager. The final stage, refinement, represents a period of fine-tuning and relatively little major additional learning (p. 173).

When the succession is successful, Gabarro argued, the new manager has taken charge. Taking charge, he said, is "the process by which a manager establishes mastery and understanding of the organization, its tasks, people, environment and structure, practices, and performance." The process is completed only when "he or she has mastered it in sufficient depth to be managing the organization as efficiently as the resources, constraints, and the manager's own ability allow" (Gabarro, 1987, p. 6). When the succession stabilizes, the new manager and the members of the group work out mutually acceptable expectations and begin to trust each other as they work together toward common goals (Gabarro, 1979).

Success most frequently occurred in Gabarro's studies in conjunction with three effective behaviors on the part of successors. Successful new managers were effective at (1) assessing the organization and diagnosing its problems, (2) building a management team focused on a set of shared expectations, and (3) bringing about timely changes that addressed organizational problems. These studies failed to support the conventional wisdom that new administrators should wait and see before making changes, revealing instead a three pronged wave of changes within the first six months of a new manager's tenure and a strong and healthy pattern of working relationships with others in the organization (Gabarro, 1987, p. 57). In order for these two conditions to occur, "deep diagnostic" work requiring skilled reflection on the part of the new manager was needed to reconceptualize the work group. Gabarro suggested that the success of this condition may depend on a new manager's ability to learn and desire to accept and master a new situation.

As with other views of succession, stage frameworks acknowledge the interaction of factors. Among these interactions, selectivity during the selection stage plays a major part. Researchers find that moderate and low selectivity increases the need for intense formal and informal socialization as a means of quality control (Argyris, 1954; Alderfer, 1971). Yet this same characteristic, a too close matching between individuals and organizations such as that criticized by Pfeffer (1978), often leads to low levels of innovation and concomitant constraints on performance (Wanous, 1980).

The arrival stage specifically receives attention as a time of adjustment for new managers (Greenblatt, 1983). Studies of this phase look remarkably like those labeled organizational socialization by other writers. Black (1988) studied the degree, mode, and facet of adjustment by American expatriate managers in Japan in search of clues about the nature of major transitions to new settings. Basing his study on the work of Pinder and Schroeder (1987), Black found that role novelty, ambiguity, conflict, discretion, and overload increased problems with adjustment. He observed three degrees of adjustment: (1) honeymoon; (2) hostility; and (3) complete. During the honeymoon period, new managers feel enthralled with their new environments, finding everything about them stimulating and exciting. Members of the organization respond in kind. During hostility, the new managers find that some important old behaviors that have served them well in the past are inappropriate, but they have nothing with which to replace them. They acquire new skills and the ability to negotiate the expectations of those in the new setting. Complete adjustment, Black contended, occurs only when the new manager knows the expectations of those in the new setting and can properly behave without undue anxiety.

The modes of adjustment observed by Black parallel those in work transition theory reviewed in Chapter 1 (Nicholson, 1984). Managers adjust to new settings by replicating the behavior of others and making minor adjustments in their own identity or behavior to fit new roles; by absorption into the new role, changing their own behavior and attitudes to fit the new setting; by determination, changing little in themselves but altering their new role; and by exploration, adjusting themselves and the role in a relationship of mutual growth. In the process, a person's work history, career, and the transition experience shape personal and organizational outcomes (Nicholson, 1987; Nicholson & West, 1987, 1989).

Arrival similarly captures the attention of much recent research on new principals. In a body of work known as the "Beginning Principals Study" (Parkay & Hall, in press), a number of scholars focused their attention on this difficult and important time in managerial succession. Based on many case studies, they argue that new principals suffer performance anxiety and difficulty controlling the nature of their professional work during the difficult first year as a principal.

In managerial succession research, a potent image for the arrival stage can be found in its characterization as the "process of taking charge." Gabarro (1987) provided a powerful description of this process at multiple levels of management, describing the "stages of learning and action that characterize the taking-charge process; the situational and personal background factors that bear on the process; and the patterns of behavior that distinguish successful transitions from those that fail" (1987, p. vii). Common and salient (occurring three to nine times in the average manager's career), succession shapes the experiences of every person who works in organizations (Kotter cited in Gabarro, 1987). Quoting from an interview, Gabarro provided a vivid account:

> You go through an early period of first trying like hell to learn about the organization. You're faced with a set of problems that are foreign to you. You have to learn about the people and their capabilities awfully fast, and that's the trickiest thing to do. At first you're afraid to do anything for fear of upsetting the apple cart. The problem is you have to keep the business *running* while you *learn* about it. (Gabarro, 1987, p. 1)

During arrival a number of unique problems can arise. Some new principals report unrealistic expectations from the faculty. In

Weindling and Earley's (1987, p. 67) study of new heads in Great Britain, all sixteen of their case study subjects described an "air of expectancy," saying that "many staff were excited and optimistic, looking to the head for a fresh start and knowing that the new head would want to introduce changes." Some saw this "sincere welcome" as undue pressure to work miracles, pressure to achieve as the "new champion or savior." One new head said, "I think the staff here had unrealistic expectations of me and wanted someone who could 'walk on water.'"

Leadership and Leader Succession

The preceding discussion briefly reviews the major traditions of the succession literature. The remainder of this chapter highlights the commonalities of succession and leadership literature by expanding this review and drawing comparisons with well-known research traditions. This comparison makes it possible to look at succession itself as an organizational variable and upon the succession to formal leader roles as a dynamic personal and organizational event involving all the members of a school or other formal organization.

Leaders hold an important place in Western culture. Myth and history recount their exploits. Political leaders who have forged the destinies of nations (Morgenthau, 1972) and transformed political history (Burns, 1978) fascinate and inspire us. Social commentators document the effort to understand leadership in thousands of published studies that treat leaders as central agents in the function of social systems ranging in size and complexity from small groups of elementary school students to professional baseball teams to multinational corporations (Bass, 1981). Belief in the individual importance of leaders remains strong (Thomas, 1988).

Education is not immune to the belief in leaders. For a long time, educational administration has emphasized the impact of leadership on schools. Recently, increased concern over the performance of American public schools has led to heightened interest in leadership among a broader range of educators. While those in educational administration now emphasize the role of the principal as "instructional leader" (Bossert et al., 1982; Duke, 1987), scholars in other areas speak and write of leadership provided by newly empowered teachers (Carnegie, 1986; Holmes Group, 1986). In Great Britain, a Department of Education and Science (DES) Green Paper entitled "Education in Schools" stated, "The character and quality of the head teacher are by far the main influence in determining what a school sets out to do and the extent to which it achieves those aims." Heads must function as "both a 'leading professional' and a 'chief executive'" (quoted in Weindling & Earley, 1987, p. 1).

In spite of this widespread conviction about the power of leadership, some scholars question the belief that people filling formal leader roles exert meaningful influence on organizational outcomes. These critics point to the failure of research reviewed in the first sections of this chapter to uncover clear and consistent relationships between leadership variables and organizational performance. They argue that leaders' discretion to make changes in and influence organizations is limited by complex and pervasive constraints.

The ambiguity found in succession studies thus reflects the wide variety of outcomes found in studies of leadership in general. Stogdill (1974, p. 7), after reviewing research and theory generated over a twenty-year period, concluded: "There are almost as many different definitions of leadership as there are persons who have attempted to define the concept." This conclusion exemplifies what Bennis (1990) termed the slipperiness and complexity of leadership.

Three sets of factors commonly reappear in the study of leadership, regardless of the definition applied, however: the traits and attributes of leaders, leaders' behaviors, and the settings in which leadership is exerted. Research has moved from (a) the identification of the traits of individual leaders to (b) the identification of the situational determinants of leadership to (c) the description and examination of the behavior of leaders and finally to (d) the explication of the interplay of these three factors, the contingency approach (Hoy & Miskel, 1991). With the exception of contingency theorists, scholars customarily have treated each dimension of leadership in isolation. But contingency theories of leadership, too, focus on only a few variables at a time (Immegart, 1988). Similarly, research tends to examine the influence of leadership on a variety of outcomes. Studies in educational settings examine the relationships between leadership and teachers' satisfaction, motivation, and morale and the climate and academic achievement of schools (Hoy & Miskel, 1991).

Leaders' Traits

The personal traits of leaders receive much attention (Yukl, 1989). For example, leaders are described as the members of groups who possess the greatest number of desirable personality traits. Etzioni (1964) defined leadership as "power based predominantly on personal characteristics. . . ."

Early studies consequently sought traits of leaders that distinguished them from those who were not leaders. These studies identified intelligence, alertness, verbal facility, originality, judgment, scholarship, knowledge, athletic accomplishments, dependability, initiative, persistence, aggressiveness, self-confidence, desire to excel, activity, sociability, cooperation, adaptability, humor, socioeconomic position, and popularity (among others) as traits of leaders (Bass, 1981). Stogdill divided the many desirable leadership traits appearing in the proliferation of lists into five categories: capacity, achievement, responsibility, participation, and status. He concluded that traits failed to identify leaders. Results of trait studies also were contradictory, with traits identified as advantageous in one study showing up as dysfunctional in others. Leaders were sometimes assertive and aggressive, sometimes mild-mannered and restrained. Some were quick and decisive; others were reflective and diplomatic (Hoy & Miskel, 1991).

Although the trait approach yielded inconsistent findings, it later reemerged in various guises. For instance, the National Association of Secondary School Principals recently developed the Assessment Center to assess the extent to which candidates for administrative positions possess requisite skills. The Assessment Center is being widely adopted by school systems. Such approaches to administrator screening are based on the assumption that the skills needed to lead are known, carrying on the traditional search for leaders with necessary traits (McCleary & Ogawa, 1989). Critics are quick to point out, however, that not only do traits predict performance poorly, but the systems through which scholars rate leadership are suspect (Phillips, 1984).

The Situation

Abandoning the frustrating search for leaders' traits, scholars turned to circumstances, or situations, to explain leadership in a search for situational factors that influence the behavior and success of leaders (Campbell et al., 1970; Campbell, 1977). They postulated that contextual variables such as organizational size, structure, and climate, role characteristics, and subordinate characteristics influenced leadership (Hoy &, Miskel, 1991).

Situation research investigated a number of variables that seemed to be associated with leadership. First, it looked at structural properties of the organization such as size, hierarchy, and formalization. Second, it asked about the influence of organizational climate (openness, participativeness, group atmosphere) on leaders. Next, it turned to the characteristics of roles. These included things like position power, type and difficulty of the assigned tasks, strategy, and procedural rules (Smith & White, 1987). Finally, it examined subordinate characteristics. Studies questioned the influence of knowledge and experience, tolerance for ambiguity, responsibility, and power on leadership. Some scholars argue that organizational characteristics can be designed to create relationships and behaviors that substitute for leaders—permitting and enhancing healthy information exchange, promoting productive decision-making processes, and providing for the exercise of authority without a designated leader (Fiedler & Garcia, 1987). Most scholars reject the assertion that the situation makes the leader, calling it "unduly restrictive and counterproductive" (Hoy & Miskel, 1991, p. 256).

Leaders' Behavior

Research and thinking on leadership took a major step when scholars began to focus their attention on leaders' behavior. Definitions of leadership reflecting this focus have a distinctly action-based flavor. For example, Hemphill (1964) wrote: "To lead is to engage in an act that initiates the process of solving a mutual problem." Similarly, many authors, including Stogdill (1974, 1980) and Lipham (1964), defined leadership as behaviors that facilitate the attainment of organizational goals. Like the trait-centered definitions that preceded them, behavioral definitions also resulted in some contradictory assertions. Fiedler (1957) described leadership as a function assigned to certain organizational members—directing and coordinating group activities; Katz and Kahn (1978) defined leadership as the influence exerted on the behavior of organizational members that exceeds compliance to "routine directives." The former assumes that leadership is bound to certain roles, while the latter suggests that leadership exceeds formal roles.

Beginning with the work of a group of Ohio State University researchers (Fleishman, 1953, 1957; Halpin & Winer, 1957; Hemphill & Coons, 1950), leader behaviors were observed and catalogued into two main categories: consideration for people and initiating structure that fosters task accomplishment. A number of other studies (Blake & Mouton, 1964; Bowers & Seashore, 1966; Cartwright & Zander, 1968; Getzels & Guba, 1957) identified similar couplets of leader behaviors (Hoy & Miskel, 1991). More effective leaders were found to be high on both dimensions: attending to organizations' tasks while taking care of members' feelings. Despite the developing consensus that leaders manifest two types of behavior that can be classified as either task completion or human relationships (or some combination), the search for behavioral effects on measurable outcomes remains incomplete.

Contingency: Traits and Behaviors in Context

Writers disappointed with the ability of traits, behavior, or situations to explain leadership effects in isolation brought these approaches together to form the contingency approach. Theorists posited that the effectiveness of task or relations-oriented behaviors was contingent on situational conditions such as task structure, the leader's position power, leader-member relations, and subordinates' characteristics (Fiedler, 1957; Vroom, 1976).

Yukl (1989), upon reviewing this array of definitions and conflicting research findings, suggested that researchers should design studies that would illuminate the ramifications of a total range of definitions. Hoy and Miskel (1991) and Immegart (1988), writing in the educational administration literature, drew similar conclusions. Hoy and Miskel closed their chapter on leadership by proposing a "schema of variables for the study of leadership." Their schema included leadership traits, situational characteristics, leader behavior, and leader effectiveness. Immegart offered a broad model of leadership that included nine variables, arguing that "the number of aspects, dynamics, and variables that are examined in leadership research must be increased" (Immegart, 1988, p. 274).

More recently, interest in the complex interplay among organizational and personal factors has turned writers' attention toward less concrete and more symbolic conceptualizations of the contingencies shaping leaders' influence. Firestone (1989) found evidence that the "chief executive may be a . . . link between national and organizational cultures" in schools. This link may, he argued, be the reason there is so much evidence that superintendents are hired by school boards with specific agendas (Carlson, 1962). Pfeffer (1981b) characterized organizations as essentially two dimensional—symbolic and substantive—and argued that managers exert little influence on the substantive dimension of organizations but manipulate symbols to maintain both the compliance of organizational members and the legitimacy of the organization among stakeholders in the external environment.

But other writers see the distinction between substantive and symbolic and the search for interest from the manager to the group as not only overly restrictive but inaccurate. First, they look at the impact of leaders on culture, tending to ignore the impacts of organizational culture on new leaders. This focus is criticized and examined further in subsequent chapters of this book. Second, culture is cast in the organizations literature as either something that organizations have—a variable—or as something that organizations are—a root metaphor (Smircich, 1983). If one adopts the latter position, then, "organizations are understood and analyzed not mainly in economic or material terms, but in terms of their expressive, ideational, and symbolic aspects" (Smircich, 1983, pp. 347–348). From this perspective, the distinction that Pfeffer drew between the substantive and symbolic dimensions of organizations is artificial. If culture is the organization, then culture is necessarily inseparable from any part of the organization. The allocation of resources and production processes— the substantive dimension—reflects organizations' cultures. The contribution of administrators is real, and the ultimate success or longevity of the organization may hinge on their effectiveness in the symbolic, cultural dimension. Presenting a compelling case for the importance of this ineffable yet observable impact, Schein (1985) said that it could be the most important function of leadership.

Smircich (1983) would concur with Schein. She described one treatment of organizational cultures as systems of shared thought or systems of knowledge and belief. The patterned behaviors that characterize an organization result from people acting and knowing within an organization's system of knowledge and belief. It follows from this view of organizations that leaders might exert influence by affecting how others make sense of organizational reality. Leaders' influence in the cultural dimension exceeds attribution; leaders affect performance by affecting culture. They shape defined reality, meanings, beliefs, and expectations on which people act.

Despite Pfeffer's (1978, 1981b) separation of the symbolic and substantive dimensions, scholarship sustains belief in symbols and meanings as substantive factors affecting organizational life. Effects appear to be multidirectional, not always flowing from leader to group. These effects are affirmed, for example, by cognitive perspectives on organizational culture. Moreover, accumulating evidence indicates that interpretations influence substance.

The results of some experimental research support this view. For example, Green and Novak (1982) manipulated feedback from supervisors and leader-member exchange. They found that information about work from superiors accounted for significant variance in subordinates' performance and attitudes about work design. These results are confirmed in other studies (Griffin, 1983; O'Connor & Barrett, 1981).

This attention to organizational culture is reflected in a body of work on the induction and professional socialization of new principals undertaken by the scholars associated with the "Beginning Principals Study" referred to briefly in the preceding discussion (Curcio & Greene, 1989; Daresh, 1986; Hall & Hord, 1987; Parkay et al., 1989; Playko & Daresh, 1989; Roberts, 1989a, 1989b; Roberts & Wright, 1989; Wright, in press). It fails to support the predictions of Schein and Smircich, however. The researchers hoped to find social, personal, and cultural linkages recognized, exhibited, and manipulated by beginning principals as part of their ascension to leadership in high schools (Roberts, 1989a). Focusing on the new principal's impact on school culture, not on the culture's impact on the new principal, these researchers were disappointed in their findings. While theory (and the work of other writers) suggests that school culture should exert important influence on principal succession as well as other organizational factors (Blanch, 1989), new high school principals' concerns, they found, centered on "being the boss, being in control, and being responsible" (Roberts, 1989a, p. 19). Culture is a complex phenomenon, deeply imbedded in a social whole (Smircich, 1983). One year may have been much too soon to observe any effect of principals on culture. Yet Roberts and her colleagues found principals not only lacking influence on but paying little heed to school culture.

Succession research can also be seen as the traits, situation, and behavior of new managers entangled within a social context. Because succession research themes parallel those of the mainstream literature in leadership, contingencies often are conceptualized as moderators of the advantageous and disadvantageous traits, behaviors, and situations accompanying managerial succession. In the discussion that follows, which draws parallels between succession and leadership research, contingency issues appear within each section. The chapter then turns to the newer streams of research focused on the symbolic dimension of leadership during succession so well portrayed by Schein (1985). As Brown concluded in his review:

> If the relationship between succession and effectiveness does vary with the unpredictability of the environment . . ., then the long search for a uniform succession effect (across organizational context and over time) has clearly been fruitless. If however, there is a conditional relationship it may be possible to begin to assess realistically the circumstances in which administrative change is likely to produce improved performance. (Brown, 1982, p. 15)

With this move toward the symbolic and cultural dimensions of leadership and groups, writers turn toward long-established traditions of social interaction theory and sociology examined in greater detail in Chapter 3.

Succession and Traits

Ironically, renewed focus on circumstances moderating the usefulness of managerial succession resurrected interest in leader traits. A variety of traits were reexamined in succession contexts. Traits of interest included the full gamut identified in the mainstream of leadership research, including administrator experience (Pfeffer & Davis-Blake, 1986). It also added several new traits of more recent social interest, including race, sex, religion, origin (geographic and cultural), and social class. The insider/outsider status of the successor and his or her family relationships in the organization have also been added.

Sex. The sex of a successor to formal leadership changes the responses of organizational members and the outcomes they attribute to the new leader. Several research projects support the accusation that people are more likely to attribute a group's performance to a leader's behavior when the leader is male. This outcome holds true even if those involved are unaware of any bias. Rice, Bender, and Vitters (1980) attributed this factor to an "unconscious ideology." Other researchers also argue that the sex of newly assigned leaders influences the interaction of group members and group performance (Garland & Price, 1977; Hollander, 1978; Terborg, 1977).

Another feature of sex related to succession is its impact on expectations for preparation. Superiors seem more likely to insist that women (as opposed to men) fulfill assistant or apprenticeship roles. In Great Britain, for example, Weindling and Earley (1987) found that 25 percent of men worked as acting head teachers before being appointed to their first headship while 40 percent of women were assigned acting roles first. In their sample, women spent significantly more time in teaching and as deputy heads and were older at their first appointment. Additionally, they found that some evidence exists that sex is a factor in employment discrimination. They said, "[W]omen with children were three times as likely as men to have been demoted en route to a headship. Men rarely experienced demotion after absence from teaching, even when they had worked outside the education system" (1987, p. 25).

Because of an interest in equal opportunity unanticipated in the 1950s when trait research was first abandoned by scholars of leadership, the problems of social incongruity remained largely unexplored. Succession research joined a growing body of literature on the impact of social biases for and against certain physical and social traits. Once affirmative action resulted in the appointment of new leaders from previously underrepresented groups, the factors moderating their success became of interest.

Insider/Outsider. Another trait factor, the status of successors as insiders or outsiders, is the subject of extensive succession research. Studies examine the likelihood of outsider or insider appointment contingent on many factors. These include the status of the predecessor as a person of long tenure, organizational performance, successor's leadership style (applying contingency theories), growth in the organization's major field, and organizational size. They find also that outcomes of insider or outsider appointments differ.

One influential body of work on insiders and outsiders was done in education. Carlson (1962, 1972) examined the appointment of superintendents. He found that insiders and outsiders have an equal likelihood of appointment when a board of education is satisfied with the district. However, insiders tend to be adapters rather than innovators and may lack a clear mandate from their superiors. Their leeway is often hampered by the previous administration. Outsider appointments are more likely when a board is dissatisfied with the direction of the district. Outsiders are innovators, feel the board expects change, and benefit from strong board commitment. While these findings are supported by data from other kinds of organizations, the variables affecting the success of insiders and outsiders are complex. They may spring from social interactions that facilitate certain behaviors; they may arise from differences in the norms of the organization where either insider or outsider appointments prevail; or they may be a function of the cosmopolitan or local orientation of the majority within the organization, people who tend to move or remain loyal to a given organization during their careers (Carlson's place-bound and career-bound administrators).

Helmich (1974, 1977) and Helmich and Brown (1972) sought a greater understanding of the correlations and causes of observed differences between insiders and outsiders. In a series of studies including pre- and postsuccession factors and using several data sets, they concluded that the outsider/insider context in management succession has distinct features that hold across organizations. Like Carlson, they concluded that insiders tend to stay in office longer (Helmich, 1977). To further test these findings in business and industry, these researchers examined organizational change independent of other influences. After controlling for organizational performance, leadership styles, intensity, size, and industry growth, Helmich and Brown (1972) found that outsider succession does indeed result in more organizational change than does insider succession. Other research confirms these outcomes. Fewer subordinates are replaced when insiders succeed to leadership roles, and fewer changes are made in executive role constellations (Gabarro, 1987). Insider succession can also result in problems when one or more existing assistant or aspiring principals unsuccessfully applied for the position (Weindling & Earley, 1987). In times of poor performance or when the environment is uncertain and problematic, scholars find that outside successors are more likely to make strategic internal changes and to be more effective in implementing successful turnarounds in performance than are successors appointed from inside the organization (Helmich, 1974; Helmich & Brown, 1972; Reinganum, 1985; Samuelson, Galbraith & McGuire, 1985).

Insiders also have problems and advantages. Daum (1975) found that promotion from within can be dysfunctional. He argued that the composition and characteristics of the work group strongly influence the positive or negative potential of insider appointments. High internal rivalry raises particular obstacles against the success of an insider. These findings are strongly supported by Birnbaum's (1971) discovery that colleges use outsider succession patterns in the presidency to limit internal rivalries.

Outsiders have a number of advantages, as long as they can avoid being labeled as "deviant" by the group (Becker, 1963). They have been found to effectively suspend the social system of interest groups and cliques, giving greater flexibility and latitude in ameliorating internal conflict to everyone involved. By doing so, they may make it possible to redirect the course of the organization (Gabarro, 1987). Outsiders make more personnel changes (Grusky, 1963; Helmich, 1975; Helmich & Brown, 1972), which may or may not be advantageous.

School principals are the subject of another group of studies probing the insider/outsider question. Ganz and Hoy (1977) attempted to expose a relationship between the principal as change agent and his or her work history. Reinforcing other studies, they found that outsiders are more inclined to view change in their schools as necessary for job advancement, are more career committed, and describe themselves as facile at persuading their superiors of the need for change. They are also described more frequently by their faculties as change agents in the school. These data are confirmed in more recent research. Cosgrove (1986) found that none of her subjects, all insider (in the district) successors to the principalship, felt they had a mandate for change from district executives or the school board.

As would be expected, the relative advantage of insider or outsider succession is strongly contextual. Several generalizations, springing from a variety of settings, are warranted. Outsiders tend to make more changes—in rules, structures, personnel, and procedures. They see change as important for their success, and feel that they have a mandate and that change is expected. Outsiders are less constrained by previous contacts, internal rivalries, and social patterns and owe no organizational debts. They also lack important informal information about the organization and an understanding of its history. During high intraorganizational conflict or when socialization needs are strong, this lack of knowledge may critically hamper their ability to form coalitions or to act decisively or quickly on accurate information.

Factors affecting responses to outsiders and insiders have yet to be thoroughly explored. The presence of a favorite son or daughter who is passed over for an outsider may restrict a new manager. Other traits of the successor may meld or clash with norms in the new organization. Surface qualities of insiders (or the absence of knowledge about personal traits of an outsider) may shape early expectations and perceptions, limiting or facilitating early success, if opportunities to demonstrate critical skills valued by the group are scarce. The length of time a predecessor holds office may or may not influence the likelihood of an outsider appointment. And some studies suggest that, unlike the unknown outsider, an insider never really gets a honeymoon period, because the "new" leader is seen as a continuation (more or less) of the status quo (Weindling & Earley, 1987).

The insider/outsider trait and the selection or prearrival stage also have been found in some studies to interact. For school leaders, Weindling and Earley (1987, p. 71) found that some heads felt that a "shortlist" of internal candidates who clearly had no chance at a position is created by superiors to create the appearance that insiders are given serious consideration. This "perceived 'poor' treatment of internal candidates had a deleterious effect not only on the individuals concerned, but also on the staff as a whole." As one head put it long after her own appointment, "It might make them feel better if they were all shortlisted." She saw the shortlist of insiders as a management strategy designed to control the behavior of those who are passed over.

Many questions about insider/outsider succession remain unresolved. While some studies suggest that infrequent succession favors outsiders (Carlson, 1962; Helmich, 1977), other data (Helmich's 1974 study of 140 manufacturing firms) fail to support this hypothesis. The definition of insiders is also nebulous, depending on the perceptions of those involved. For example, a new principal may be considered an insider or an outsider if he originates from another school in the district; this distinction may arise out of tradition, personal beliefs, group norms, or the mix of events. Weindling and Earley (1987) found in Great Britain that the majority of new heads are appointed from outside their local education authority *and* their school. In the national cohort of 188 new secondary heads they surveyed, only 10 percent were appointed from within the same school and 40 percent from within the local education authority (LEA) or district. Because insider successions are rare, they were forced to deliberately select schools for their case study sample that included some internal appointments (one fourth). These researchers raised the question, Is the local appointing authority or the school the appropriate level of analysis when studying insider/outsider effects? While "the advantages to be gained from appointing an internal candidate [seem] to be quite small and [are] probably outweighed by the disadvantages," superiors must still contend with the strongly held belief that appointment to leadership roles is an important reward for long and loyal service (Weindling & Earley, 1987, p. 179). Gabarro's (1987, p. 161) conclusions summarizing findings in private industry concur: "Industry insiders initiate more change than industry outsiders" and "an explicit decision to search outside the firm is very likely a reflection of an explicit desire by a board to bring about change."

Relationships: Kinship and Personal Ties. Relationship traits among people affect succession. These relationships can be personally established or based on kinship ties. Nepotism has plagued many school districts, particularly in small communities in the United States where mobility in the education profession is not the norm. In one small community in a western state, for example, it is not uncommon for the high school principal to be the nephew of the superintendent and for the elementary school secretary to be his wife. It is not rare to find kinship affecting generations of appointments to school leadership positions in a community or state, even when overt nepotism is not apparent (Buchanan, F., forthcoming).

The subtle effects of kinship on leader succession particularly interest some writers outside education. Boldt (1978) examined succession to leadership positions among Hutterites. In an environment of limited opportunities or oversized or slow fissioning colonies, he found that kinship exerted strong influence on leader succession. When opportunities are less restricted, these connections play a less important role. These findings may explain some of the outcomes of leader appointments in schools in small communities. The scarcity of school leadership positions is obvious in a community where there may be one elementary school and one 7–12 high school whose principal is also the district superintendent (a common situation in states such as Iowa, which had 140 school districts in 1990).

Family and personal relationships also affect managerial succession in businesses. If the chief executive officer is a partial owner of the corporation, the factors affecting succession are substantially altered (Salancik & Pfeffer, 1980). When boards of directors include family members, managers are far less likely to suffer involuntary succession during periods of poor performance (Allen, Panian & Lotz, 1979). The relationships between management and boards continue to intrigue scholars (Mizruchi, 1983).

Personal linkages reveal relationship traits akin to family. Because formal leaders "do differentiate between subordinates" and "group averages of subordinate perceptions do not show the same relations with measures of leader style as do individual subordinate perceptions" (Smith & Peterson, 1988, pp. 36–37), the exchanges between a newly appointed leader and each person in the established group will be important to the outcome of succession. Some writers find these differences compelling. They justify an approach that differentiates between subordinates and interventions related to the successor-member relationship (Smith & Peterson, 1988). Differentiations among new principals and their superiors may be similarly in order.

Succession and Behavior

As in the general leadership literature, the behavior of a successor is identified as an important factor in succession. For example, Yukl and Nemeroff (1979) offered a nine-category dissection of traditional task and consideration (human relations) behaviors, arguing that behavior manifested in leader-follower interaction is the critical dimension in succession. Schreisheim & Kerr (1979) contended that research should concentrate on the behavior of people in groups leading to productivity, drive, and cohesiveness. A number of behavioral categories have received attention from scholars and practitioners—behavior designed to accomplish tasks, support personal needs, and initiate change.

Task-centered and Person-centered Behaviors. The task/person duality of leader behaviors so important to the progress of the general leadership literature resurfaced in succession studies. These behaviors aimed at task accomplishment and human relations became important for succession researchers as they searched for succession's impacts. The person or human relations dimension appears in research demonstrating that, when a successor is perceived as unfeeling, critical, or different in vital ways from the group, anxiety and productive collapse may result (Oskarsson & Klein, 1982).

The task dimension of behavior also affects judgments of new leaders. When a successor is seen as competent in crucial tasks, her acceptance by the group is facilitated (Hollander & Julian, 1978). New subordinates tend to be more receptive to successors with clear task expertise, those who have proven themselves on required tasks (Goldman & Fraas, 1965). Beliefs about task competence are not solely dependent on observed behavior, however. The ability of sponsors and the expectations of superiors, subordinates, and peers exert influence over judgments of task abilities (Lieberman, 1956). Additionally, some group dynamics seem to create task-oriented leaders, with those who emerge naturally from groups tending to be more active in defining tasks and task-related problems, proposing solutions and procedures, and soliciting solutions from others.

Writers emphasize the importance of interpersonal dynamics, citing Mintzberg's (1973) classic. He showed that executives spend 78 percent of their working time interacting with others and as much as 50 percent interacting with subordinates. Quality working relationships are associated with positive performance and personnel evaluations (Liden & Graen, 1980). Positive working relationships are associated with three salient outcomes. First, the successor and others develop mutual expectations. Second, they come to trust each other in the general effort they all expend in behalf of the work. And third, they develop a bond of mutual influence "beyond that which is accorded the new manager and the subordinate by virtue of their roles" (Gabarro, 1987, p. 101).

In spite of the importance of both task and interpersonal behaviors during succession, the clarity of the distinction made here is somewhat artificial. New managers find that, even when they identify problems that require their attention, it is not always clear whether these problems are a result of the person or persons involved or the way their work is structured. The importance of diagnosis and reflection early on during a new manager's tenure cannot, consequently, be understated (Gabarro, 1987).

In schools, both task and person behaviors receive attention. Each is given credit for affecting outcomes. Comer (1980) argued that interpersonal relationships moderate student achievement in schools, and many scholars and practitioners call on principals to create the personal environment necessary for effective schools (Corcoran, 1985; Purkey & Smith, 1983). Darling-Hammond, Wise, and Pease (1983) contended that the value stance of school leaders shapes the values of others that yield these outcomes. Principals can improve the likelihood of student achievement through the emphasis on achievement as a core value. Yet Kunz and Hoy (1976) found that task behaviors are more influential in gaining acceptance for new principals than human relations behaviors, evidence underscoring the enhanced receptivity of groups to competent and knowledgeable successors revealed by experimental research (Hollander & Julian, 1978).

Changes in human relations and task are also used to assess the relative value of succession. Child and Kieser (1981) believed that succession is a positive event, because it provides an opportunity for new personal and leadership styles to develop, work and social patterns to emerge, and networks of communication in the organization and with the environment to grow. From this perspective, succession is good because it opens minds to new possibilities.

A large body of scholarship related to task and person behaviors by managers during succession has accumulated. In spite of these efforts, it provides little in the way of guidance for any successor to act in a given context. Although researchers attempt to identify critical dimensions of task and personal behaviors by new leaders, they criticize the lack of cues for action provided by all this research (Argyris, 1979, pp. 54–55).

Change-centered Behavior. In addition to supportive or task-directed behaviors, those designed to initiate change have received attention in succession research. In all kinds of organizations, succession elicits expectations for change. Many successions occur as a result of belief in a need for change, and studies affirm that people expect a new manager to make changes.

Change associated with managerial succession takes a number of forms. In one group of studies, change occurred in patterns related to stages. Observing that change takes place in a sequence of stages alternating between learning and action, Gabarro (1987) described three periods of change common during succession: (1) early on during the taking-hold stage, (2) during a reshaping period following immersion in the organization's social and structural nature and intense learning, and (3) as the new manager consolidates his or her position. In Gabarro's seventeen cases, the greatest period of change followed deep immersion in the organization.

Along with its association with various stages in a succession, change is associated with successor background and situation factors. Successors come to an organization with a set of skills, beliefs, and expectations learned in other settings. The extent and nature of this experience seem to have a major effect on the way in which change is approached. Prior experience "profoundly influences the manager's actions and what he tends to focus on, as well as the kinds of problems he is likely to face" (Gabarro, 1987, p. 7). Another important situational factor successors use to shape change, experience within the enterprise at hand, influences the pace and scope of change. Industry insiders make more and faster changes than industry outsiders. "[I]n this respect they took hold more quickly" (Gabarro, 1987, p. 48).

This interaction of change with the insider/outsider factor affects many variables. Discretion to act may, for example, be an important factor moderating the impacts of succession. Hambrick and Finkelstein (1987) asserted that low managerial discretion is associated with older chief executives, internal promotions, low pay, and low involuntary turnover among top managers. In contrast, high discretion is most common when top management is young, is promoted from outside, exhibits a tendency toward risk-taking, is highly paid, and experiences high involuntary turnover.

In schools, the expectation for change is no less pronounced. In the sense that almost all educational administrators are industry insiders, the relative rate of change might be predicted to be fairly rapid. Studies of school administration successions affirm that change plays a part in expectations and actions. Only 10 percent of new managers and 9 percent of more experienced heads in one study said no major changes had been introduced in their schools during the first year of their tenure (Weindling & Earley, 1987). The majority of these changes originated with the successor, and they often related to the image of the school, especially when the community had a low opinion of its school. Moreover, new heads said that the pacing and timing of change played critical parts in their success. Planning for change began immediately upon succession, and many new managers who thought they would wait for the year to end found they could not delay. New school heads recognized "the importance of being seen by staff as someone who could get things done" (p. 103). Faculties, too, expected change. Weindling and Earley found that virtually everyone expected that change would accompany succession. The only exception they found was in a school where a former deputy head (insider) was appointed.

Assessments of the benefits of change reveal less consensus. In the British study, reactions to change were "largely favourable in six schools, largely negative in four schools and mixed in the remaining six schools" (1987, p. 106). Five years later, however, the researchers discovered that criticism often accompanied the "go slow" decision:

> Before they take up their post, new heads are often given one of two pieces of conflicting advice: "Go in and make an impact," or "Do nothing for a year." The current research suggests that both are misguided. New heads need to make some early changes which are not controversial and are, in fact, welcomed by the majority of staff. At the same time they should carefully assess the situation and plant the seeds for future innovation. (Earley, Baker & Weindling, 1990, p. 25)

By way of advice for new heads, one of Earley, Baker, and Weindling's respondents said, "Timing is important. You have got to be an opportunist, rather than simply assuming you can introduce any change just when you want to. Seize the opportunity when you see an interest. You have got to have the support of people who are going to make the change" (1990, p. 24).

Some major dilemmas related to change behavior remain for new managers. Although studies reveal the salutary effects of timely and appropriate change following succession, judgments of timeliness and appropriateness remain a matter of care, reflection, and judgment. Tension remains between the need to move quickly and in a timely fashion in order to avoid the loss of opportunity and the need to respond to and thoroughly understand organizational problems and needs. Gabarro (1987, p. 91) concluded that decisive change may be the more important behavior, as the new manager "may lose credibility because he appears indecisive."

Succession and Situation

The final dimension prominent in leadership research, situation, also appears in succession literature. If anything, situation has received greater attention with more productive results than in mainstream leadership research. Studies focus on many different situational variables moderating the positive or negative impact of traits and behaviors on succession outcomes, including such things as power, the existence of succession systems in the organization, organizational size, the stability of the organization, its environment, and its performance, precipitating events, and implicit theories held in common by members of the organization. In general, organizational demography remains of interest to succession researchers (Wagner, Pfeffer & O'Reilly, 1984).

Power. Power, for example, is a situational variable related to (but more general than) the kinship trait. In addition to its relational power inherent in kinship, reward power, coercive power, legitimate power, expert power, and referent power moderate overall effects of succession (Smith & Peterson, 1988). Salancik and Pfeffer(1980), Allen and Panian (1982), and James and Soref (1981) studied the relationship between corporate ownership, controlling interests, connections, organizational performance, and succession. These studies and others reveal that the greater the external control of an organization's management the greater the frequency of executive succession (Allen, 1981; Allen & Panian, 1982; McEachern, 1975).

Although involuntary succession is inversely related to corporate (as well as athletic team) performance (Friedman, 1985; James & Soref, 1981), power moderates this relationship (Salancik & Pfeffer, 1980). Partial ownership in a corporation by the chief executive officer affects length of tenure. Additionally, control and performance interact to protect managers from forced succession. Not surprisingly, the relationships of managers, including family representation on boards of directors or controlling interest in significant blocks of voting stock, are also directly related to their longevity. Particularly during periods of poor performance, managerial power is inversely related to the probability of succession (Allen & Panian, 1982; Gordon & Rosen, 1981).

Power receives less attention in educational succession research than in private industry. Recently, however, power in school board–administration relationships reemerged as a topic of study. Researchers tie political power and elections at the state level to outcomes of school board elections and the careers of superintendents (Firestone, 1989, 1990).

Succession Systems. Many types of organizations, including school districts, established systems for identifying and developing future leaders. The presence and features of these systems are the subject of study by a number of writers (Carroll, 1984; Friedman,

1986; Hall, 1986). Hall (1987) found that a major interest in the development of succession systems springs from perceived needs to identify and develop future leaders within organizations and help them develop into viable candidates for available positions. According to Hall (1987, p. 236), a number of organizations fail to develop succession systems, relying instead on the "one-position staffing" system: "How can we find the best qualified individual for this particular job?" When organizations rely on this method, they must find people already prepared to meet the demands of the new position. A more appropriate system would be replacement planning (if emphasis is placed on future positions and needs rather than on specific jobs) and succession planning (emphasizing a future orientation and focuses on candidates' learning needs).

Friedman (1986) contended that the succession event provides insufficient information about the potential impact of leadership succession on outcomes, even when moderated by the effects of context. There, too, an organization's implicit and explicit succession systems exert influence. He defined succession systems as "the rules and procedures that form the context for a typical succession event (i.e., a change in job incumbency) including executive development and placement practices" (Friedman, 1986, p. 192). Because "all organizations face the challenges and opportunities inherent in the need to replace current leaders," all organizations have systems, however implicit or explicit, for managing this critical event.

Testing this belief in the power of succession systems and the hypothesis that quality succession systems will lead to superior reputations and performance, Friedman (1986) examined the correlations of seven characteristics of succession systems with reputation and financial performance in 235 private firms: (1) level of formalization, (2) presence of checks and balances, (3) sufficient resources allocated to the system, (4) availability of information on people and positions, (5) use of technical competence criteria, (6) use of political criteria, and (7) formal staff role. He found that the level of formalization per se played no role in either reputation or organizational performance. When top management was involved in nominations, other managers were rewarded for developing subordinates, and other checks and balances came into play in succession processes, positive relationships were found. Additionally, sufficient resources, information systems, access to information, and influence on selection by a professional staff were positively associated with performance. Political criteria and insider appointments were also positively associated with outcomes.

Friedman also uncovered a common flaw in planning for succession: "The monitoring and remunerating of executives on the basis of their performance as developers of people, a powerful means by which to ensure adequate attention to succession and development issues, is a relatively uncommon practice" (1986, p. 201). He found that firms more often apply cultural criteria (taking part in the ongoing social system, fitting in) than political criteria (loyalty, network ties) during the decision making. And fitting in becomes more important as one ascends the hierarchy. Fitting in is a commonly used criterion for identifying and grooming future school administrators. Principals report that they chose an administrative career only after a principal or other school leader encouraged them (Campbell et al., 1987).

Another characteristic of the succession system receiving some attention—matching managers to the strategies they are expected to implement—gets mixed reviews. This matching strategy is observed in school districts when principals are labeled "change agents" or are matched by ethnicity or background to a school. Gupta (1986) pointed out that, while deliberate attempts to match managers to strategy does result in more effective strategy implementation, it may not always be feasible, necessary, or desirable to do so. Because some need for strategic flexibility and management development always exists, superiors risk creating motivational problems when people are labeled "turnaround" managers or "risk-averse harvesters." Because managers are constrained in their latitude to take action, the time and effort taken to match managers to strategic assignment may not be justified.

Size. Organizational size is a situational factor of succession examined at some length with ambiguous results. Studies have attempted to determine whether the size of the organization is linked to the frequency, form, or outcome of succession. While Grusky's (1960) and Kriesburg's (1962) data suggest that size and succession rates are highly correlated, Gordon and Becker (1964) disagreed. Holding age of executive, compensation rates, and other related factors constant, they found no clear relationship between the size of organizations and succession. Because size and succession rates are confounded by other situational variables—organizational history, technological differences, industry differences, retirement policies, and executive benefits—they rejected the direct relationship that might be suggested by simple correlations (Sonnenfeld, 1986).

Other attempts to isolate the effects of size on succession link size with situational variables such as inside/outside succession or profitability (Kriesburg, 1962). Worrell and Davidson (1987), contrary to Reinganum (1985), found that large firms, like smaller firms, are susceptible to the succession effect. They also tied size to insider/outsider succession and the death of the predecessor, finding a low reported incidence of outsider succession consistent with those reported by Dalton and Kesner (1983). In education, size functions as a variable in succession at the district level. Operating to restrict opportunity in small districts, size may also contribute to the perception that insider successions are more fair (Hart, 1987; Oskarsson & Klein, 1982).

Stable Performance. While size received much attention as a situational variable in the context of succession, Brown (1982) argued that the stability of the organization's performance environment is far more critical. In school districts, for example, infrequent superintendent succession is more common in rural, close knit, stable communities where districts also tend to be small. Their urban counterparts—larger, more diverse, and more subject to conflict—have higher succession rates. In these complex environments, ritual scapegoating is blamed by some urban superintendents for high turnover (Scott, 1982).

As was pointed out early in this chapter, involuntary succession rates tend to be inversely related to organizational performance (Dalton & Kesner, 1985; James & Soref, 1981; Schwartz & Menon, 1985). The more dismal the performance, the more frequent succession will be. However, succession rates are also tied to personal choice— in this case the desire of leaders to disassociate themselves from unsuccessful organizations. And poor organizational performance is just one precipitating factor in succession. Better understanding of the subtle impacts of resignations, dismissals, and incentive-based retirements on remaining organizational members is suggested. Forced successions may inspire resentment in remaining organizational members while legitimate factors—death, promotion, voluntary retirement—may provide a positive environment for a new manager (Grusky, 1963). While the likelihood that succession might lead to increased organizational performance is examined carefully by many researchers, the organizational factors leading to the firing of top managers is of equal interest.

Scholars thus work to tie the rate and nature of succession to performance. Following an extensive review of the literature, House (1988) concluded that involuntary succession at top levels of management (except in cases of illness or death) occurs predominantly in response to problematic organization and *perceptions* of declining performance. These findings concur with those of Grusky (1961) and Gamson and Scotch (1964), who argued that the functional role of succession was explainable as scapegoating or sense making.

Poor performance is often blamed as the precipitating factor in involuntary succession (Fredrickson, Hambrick & Baumrin, 1988; Friedman, 1986), yet studies of the dismissal of chief executive officers find that organizational performance explains less than one-half the variance in CEO dismissal and turnover rates (James & Soref, 1981; McEachern, 1975; Salancik & Pfeffer, 1980). More complete models of dismissal include the governance, organizational, industry, and individual (incumbent manager and predecessor) factors that come into play and emphasize the organizational nature of succession. Multiple factor models acknowledge that the personal characteristics and perceived self-interests of governing boards (concern for friendships, image, wealth, reputation, and so on) and the sociopolitical features of the organization moderate outcomes. In public institutions such as schools, these public governance and political factors exert tremendous influence. Sociopolitical features include such things as the board's expectations and attributions, board members' allegiances and values, the availability of alternative administrators and the incumbent administrator's power (i.e., control over community interest groups and key contacts). These more complete models also include traits and ongoing involvement by the predecessor (as a stockholder or member of the board) in the organization (Fredrickson, Hambrick & Baumrin, 1988; Meyer, 1979; Pfeffer, 1981b; Salancik & Pfeffer, 1980).

Some situational factors moderating succession remain completely outside the control of an organization. One of these is the death of a top manager. Worrell and Davidson (1987) found in a study of the stock market covering seventeen years, for example, that the price of common stock in large, publicly held corporations rose following the death of a chief executive officer and the appointment of an internal successor when the effects of moderating factors were controlled. Another situational factor outside the control of management is the age of the organization. Organizational age interacts with other factors to affect the outcomes and processes of managerial appointments. Even when controlled for executive style, form, performance, size, growth, and base technology, older firms promote more insiders than outsiders and long-lasting organizational forms yield to the pressure exerted by inertia (Helmich, 1975, 1978). At the same time, rapid rates of turnover at the top management echelons tend to slow the pace of organizational growth (Helmich, 1977). Inertia exercises major influence in long-lived institutions such as school systems.

Implicit Theories of the Organization. Any impact a newly appointed manager might have on the established group is constrained by yet another situational factor—implicit theories or beliefs about what the organization is or ought to be (Brief & Downey, 1983). These operational norms constrain potentially powerful changes a new manager might make and may exist at the societal, career, organizational, or work site levels. Schools clearly are subject to inertia (Hannan & Freeman, 1984).

When writers use inertia or context (Thomas, 1988) to explain the muted effects of succession, the social psychological features of organizations come into play. Only a few studies have, however, applied the context of these models to the study of succession. These studies rely heavily on sense making and cognition theories to help frame group beliefs as a situational variable moderating succession effects (Gephart, 1978; Hart, 1988; Ogawa, 1991).

Another implicit theory imbedded in organizations and affecting leadership succession relates to beliefs about the nature of an organizational career (Hall, 1987). In some models (Milkovich, Anderson & Greenhalgh, 1976), the career is represented as a structural feature of the organization, a series of hierarchical positions. Executive succession under these models presents a pressing organizational concern, because the individual people involved sometimes see the process as a tournament in which they joust with other candidates and win promotion. Hall (1986) contended that hierarchical models prevent organizational learning and actively inhibit the growth in executives necessary for successful integration and learning, yet schools clearly conceive of principal succession in exactly these terms.

Peer Support. A number of succession studies emphasize the role of peer support in creating a favorable situation for succession. If new CEOs can bring along with them a number of important subordinates, for example, their own success appears to be enhanced (Grusky, 1969). Weindling and Earley (1987) found that many faculty members expect new heads to bring in their own people. Those who accompany a new leader may have a decided advantage. Three decades ago, Grusky (1969) addressed the question of subordinate and successor relationships and found that an assistant who comes with a successor will eventually dominate an inherited assistant, even though people value integration.

Peer support plays a critical part in the success of newly appointed managers, however. Weindling and Earley's (1987) interview subjects identified supportive assistants as a primary source of support for new heads. Duke et al. (1984), too, contended that an assistant principal and helpful colleagues in similar positions in the district provide important peer support during the transition following succession. In private industry, in public administration, and in school administration the presence or absence of peer support is an important situational factor facilitating and hindering managerial succession.

In yet another sense, peers provide support that enables new managers to bridge the organizational transition between themselves and their predecessor (Brady & Helmich, 1985). Scholars find that allies within the existing social group can be invaluable to a new manager as they assist in this difficult process. Predecessors sometimes attempt to impede the changes attempted by a successor (Hart, 1988; McGivern, 1978), and peer support can be critical in identifying and shaping outcomes.

Predecessor Status and Assessment. As the above examples illustrate, the predecessor exerts powerful influence over the succession experience. Other direct examples abound. Gordon and Rosen (1981) argued that a popular predecessor is not an easy act to follow; members of the group will constantly compare the newly appointed leader unfavorably with their valued predecessor. The idealization of the predecessor becomes a difficult obstacle for successors. Weindling and Earley (1987) found that school leaders experience their successions in part as a function of their predecessors' style and behavior. Heads most frequently rated serious difficulties associated with consultation and communication with faculty members, for example, as a result of the practices and style of previous heads. Their subjects argued that the most important factor in adjustments to predecessor/successor differences was a function of their ability to learn as much as possible about the style of their predecessors and then deliberately set up transition changes that capitalized on qualities and failings alike.

The Symbolic Dimension in Succession. While succession literature has not traditionally addressed issues relevant to the symbolic context of organizations that Pfeffer, Schein, and others emphasize in organizational leadership, case studies provide tantalizing stories of the impact of symbols and organizational culture on leader succession. Writers use the words and concepts of symbol, meaning, and understanding but seldom emphasize this aspect of the succession process. A brief perusal of succession scholars' work, however, provides insight into the factors they observed that point to the importance of meaning and belief.

The harmony of succession research with cultural views of organizations appears strikingly in the use of words. Writers describe feelings, perceptions, expectations, and beliefs. They assess the importance of legitimacy, authority, and reputation and use the language of ritual, myth, and status to explain observed outcomes. These concepts are central to a view of organizational lives fraught with meaning, of actions based on belief in whole or in part divorced from "objective" reality. A few examples illustrate the prominence of these themes in the succession research tradition.

One example appearing frequently, the effect of a crisis mentality on people's attitudes and behavior during succession, is tightly coupled with belief. Hamblin (1958) found that a group believing it faces an imminent crisis will tend to move to replace a leader who appears to lack a specific solution to the problem. The quality of the solution is less important than its specificity. Once the decision to purge a leader is reached, people use a variety of methods that feature meaning and belief as tools to an end to bring about succession. Status degradation (Gephart, 1978) is among these symbolic processes, as is ritual scapegoating (Gamson & Scotch, 1964), and these processes may have no concrete benefit.

A second example of the function of meaning relates to the impact of selection agents. New leaders often receive reputational credit (as competent and desirable leaders) when their selection agents or perceived selection agents are seen as valued experts at critical tasks (Knight & Weiss, 1980). New group leaders chosen by people perceived to have great task expertise are themselves seen as more skillful and able to exert greater influence over valued tasks than those whose selection agents are not well respected on critical dimensions (Hollander, Fallon & Edward, 1977; Hollander & Julian, 1978). Not only do group members assess a new leader more favorably if the selection agent is seen as competent, but groups often project the actual characteristics of the sponsor onto the successor. Additionally, other selection factors influence group beliefs, including the perception that the selection process was rigorous, wide ranging, and competitive (Hollander, Fallon & Edwards, 1977). Superintendents' talents or agendas thus can transfer to principals whose appointment they control or substantially affect (Hart, 1987).

The reasons and motives driving a succession and affecting attitudes, beliefs, and expectations about a new manager provide a third function of meaning and symbol during successions. When people perceive the reasons for change as legitimate (death, voluntary retirement, or promotion of the predecessor), researchers find them less likely to hold negative attitudes toward the successor than if a succession is believed to have been forced or the result of unfair organizational processes (Grusky, 1963). This salutary effect of legitimacy also improves a groups' attitudes toward changes that might ensue. Ogawa and Smith (1985) observed a school faculty that assumed that change would come with a new principal who followed a voluntary retirement. However, the legitimacy of precipitating causes for succession is also complicated by the availability of promotional opportunities. Gordon and Rosen (1981) maintained that frequency of opportunity is a critical variable shaping subordinates' reactions to successors, symbolizing their own promotion opportunities and, subsequently, their responses to a new manager. If opportunities are infrequent, new managers face more resistance and resentment than when other opportunities may come along at any time. Hart (1987) found this to be the case in a principal succession.

In summary, symbol and meaning appear frequently in research, suggesting they function ubiquitously in leader-member relationships interpreting succession. If human actions and interpretations are the "stuff from which organizations are made" (Greenfield, 1975), then a potentially powerful route toward understanding leadership during succession emerges from intensified study of the meaning that goes into realities created by those who experience them (Gregory, 1983). As Miskel and Cosgrove (1985) conclude, influencing the perceptions of subordinates may be the most critical function of school leaders.

Combining and Expanding Views of Succession

In this chapter, a review of managerial succession research organized around prevailing themes in leadership inquiry reveals a quickening interest among writers and practitioners in the interplay among substantive and symbolic dimensions of organizations during leader succession. These dimensions include personal characteristics, beliefs, and actions and organizational/social characteristics, cultures, and interactions as well as environment and context. With increasing frequency, those interested in the impact of formal leaders on organizations point to participants' interpretations of each of these important dimensions and the impacts of these interpretations on subsequent actions.

Some of the research reviewed here points toward the growing application and potential usefulness of more comprehensive interaction perspectives on succession. The dynamics of leader succession as a complex social event involving important individuals, social groups, and their interactions suggest that much can be learned from social and interactive rather than individually based points of view. The socialization theory and research outlined in Chapter 1 offer one such perspective applied profitably to principal professional socialization research in the past. When combined with the insights on individual creativity and initiative brought by leader succession views, this perspective widens the vistas of school leader literature and practice. The following chapter presents an overview of the foundations of socialization. These traditions undergird organizational socialization research.

3

The Conceptual Roots of Organizational Socialization

Socialization has been studied from many points of view. Psychologists seek to understand each person's experiences. Cultural anthropologists are concerned with the development of the typical adult in a particular culture. Social psychologists assess the influence of a group on each person within it. Sociological studies seek insight into the impacts of socialization on people within the institutions and groups that make up society (McNeil, 1969; Merton, 1949). In a professional field such as education, each of these perspectives offers information that can help the people who work in schools understand their experiences from different points of view. This chapter presents an overview of some theories and research in the social and behavioral sciences that provide a foundation for organizational socialization theories.[1]

In Chapter 1, four themes dominating the literature on organizational socialization were introduced: socialization tactics; stages of socialization; personal and group context; and outcomes. In this chapter, the roots of these themes in psychology, sociology, and social psychology are explored. The forces motivating people to interact, the social processes of interaction, and the social structure environments and outcomes of interaction are related to the four central themes of organizational socialization. This chapter develops no new theory but rather illustrates the application of traditional analytical frameworks to the analysis of leader succession. Many of the theories presented in the discussion that follows informed the study of leadership in the past, although from slightly different perspectives. Dyadic relationships, for example, are fundamental to exchange views of leadership (as described by Blau and others).

The ideas on which this chapter draws provide a glimpse at the development of thought in socialization. Research results illuminate the processes by which people acquire their individual traits and idiosyncracies, their motives, values, opinions, and beliefs. They probe the impacts of schools on new principals and of principals on the shared values, opinions, standards, and beliefs of people in a school. Social learning theory, for example, shows how a principal and school can depend on each other and change together, and how people must continually deal with the "paradox of mutual indeterminism" (Bandura, 1978). From sociology we gather additional clues to the effects of a school on a newly appointed principal. From psychology, in addition to insight into the effects of individual teachers on a new principal, we secure help avoiding "one of the greatest errors of omission in the field of leadership by giving little attention to the processes whereby leaders rely upon themselves as sources of strength or support" (Smith & Peterson, 1988, p. 160). We probe the power of individual will and agency (James, 1979, 1984). From social systems theory we gather intriguing insights into the mechanisms through which powerful and established system determinants often block the attempts of new principals to affect change, altering the principal instead, making him or her more like the existing members of the system. In systems theory, this process is known as "component convergence" (Monane, 1967, p. 32). A new principal thus may experience a form of "conversion" to existing behavioral norms and attitudes rather than affect change in a new school. And once strong reactions toward a new principal begin to develop, they are "likely to trigger similar action by other members" (Monane, 1967, p. 24).

The chapter is organized around central issues of social interaction: (a) unit of analysis; (b) processes; (c) self, other, and role; and (d) social structure. First, the usefulness of interaction as a unit of analysis in research involving social groups (such as schools) is examined and two approaches to interaction analysis in organizations are introduced. The second section builds on the illustrations provided in section one and attends specifically and in detail to interaction processes on which organizational socialization draws to construct its models of characteristics and stages. Some multiple process theories of interaction (e.g. exchange, ethnomethodology, symbolic interactionism, dramaturgy, interaction rituals) are reviewed. The third section of the chapter explores multiple concepts of self, others, and roles that create the personal and social context of organizational socialization. It shows how ideas introduced by theories such as symbolic interactionism provide a conceptual foundation for the interpretive frameworks so often used to explain the symbolic and cultural aspects of school leadership. Concepts of social structure like those that characterize each school are presented in the final section. This section emphasizes the role of social patterns necessary for a school culture to develop, evolve, and be passed on to others.

Interaction: The Fundamental Unit of Analysis

When a new principal is appointed to a school, those who appoint her and those who will work with her care most about the impact of the succession on themselves and the school. A newly appointed principal, too, experiences succession both alone and as a new member of a social group—the school. If a new principal is also new to the district, he must learn to function within the school and district social groups at many levels. He must interact with individuals, subgroups, and coalitions that develop over issues arising as a natural course of work in the school, and established groups in his new role.

Interaction can be broadly defined as the overt actions (including language), covert deliberations and plans, and physical presence and gestures of one person that influence others in a continuing cycle of exchange and communication. Interaction occurs along a number of fronts in schools: among individuals; among individuals and subgroups; and among subgroups. It stands midway between psychological, individual views of leadership that examine a principal's thoughts, talents, and actions and macro organizational views of social structure that pay little or no attention to the idiosyncratic dynamics that are the rich and messy stuff of each leader succession. An interaction perspective views the individual and his psychology as critical to the process of organizational socialization (Jones, 1983).

The distinction between action and interaction is less troublesome than it might first seem. Weber, for example, argued that action is social (becoming interaction) when it is meaningfully oriented to the actions of others, a condition aptly met by principal succession events. Interaction can be rational (calculated and deliberate), affectual (determined by feelings and emotions), or traditional (dictated by customs and habit) (Turner, 1988, p. 6). For example, the succession studies reviewed in Chapter 2 often examined the rules and formal processes through which new leaders are selected. The interactions involve rational and clearly observable steps that are followed. These studies also reveal approaches to selection that have become established by tradition. An example of this form of interaction can be found in the experiences reported by many principals: their principal or another school administrator approaches them, tells them they would make fine school leaders, and suggests they ought to get an administrative certificate. To no one's surprise, they receive the next administrative position that becomes available. When others are involved, people choose to interact or not, depending on the level of motivation. Turner (1988, p. 7) contends that to understand the processes through which people are motivated to interact, form value orientations, develop a line of action, interact, and structure social relations (i.e., while accomplishing organizational socialization), one must focus on the interaction as the basic unit.

Models of interaction serve to frame and clarify the important factors common to different principal succession events. Case studies tell vivid stories that often resonate with the experiences of others, such as the experience of being singled out and annointed (so to speak) for an administrative position. People usually excluded from these traditional forms of succession interactions find that they sometimes place almost insurmountable barriers in their way. The search for patterns (in theory and practice) adds to these rich details by providing models that can be repeated or modified and transferred from one person and school to another. When descriptive studies are combined with the patterns developed from more generalizable forms of analysis, a richer view of leader succession emerges. Turner (1988) and Schein (1985) provided two useful models of interaction that can be aptly applied to principal succession processes.

Schein's View of Culture Structuring Interaction

Schein contended that organizational culture provides one framework for the structuring effects of interaction in organizations. In fact, he defined organizational culture as an outcome of interaction among group members and between the group and elements in its environment. Schein asserted that culture is

> the deeper level of *basic assumptions* and *beliefs* that are shared by members of an organization, that operate unconsciously, and that define in a basic "taken-for-granted" fashion an organization's view of itself and its environment. These assumptions and beliefs are *learned* responses to a group's problems of *survival* in its external environment and its problems of *internal integration*. They come to be taken for granted because they solve those problems repeatedly and reliably. This deeper level of assumptions . . . culture . . . is a *learned product of group experience* and is, therefore, to be found only where there is a definable group with a significant history [emphasis in the original]. (Schein, 1985, pp. 6–7)

Schein conceded that people share other, less generalized and abstract meanings for organizational culture as well. For example:

1. *Observed behavioral regularities* when people interact, such as the language used and the rituals around deference and demeanor. This could include such things as the use of first names among teachers who address their principal as "Doctor" or the expectation that a teacher can always walk through the principal's open door and receive an immediate hearing for a professional concern.
2. The *norms* that evolve in working groups, such as the particular norm of "a fair day's work for a fair day's pay . . ." Teachers who arrive too early or leave to late too often suffer sanctions from other teachers if they violate this norm.
3. The *dominant values espoused* by a school, such as "high academic standards" or "individualized instruction."
4. The *philosophy* that guides a district's policy toward employees and/or students, such as "every student matters" or "teachers are professionals."
5. The *rules* of the game for getting along in the school or district, "the ropes" that a newcomer must learn in order to become an accepted member.
6. The *feeling* or *climate* that is conveyed in an organization by the physical layout and the way in which members of the organization interact with customers or other outsiders.

In addition to these commonly shared meanings, a new principal must come to know about interaction patterns that are so established as a part of the school itself that they are passed on to new members as if they are objective reality and a preferred part of life (Louis, 1980b). Football players never take exams during fall term, or teachers take professional leave days for the elk hunt. The interactions among teachers, administrators, parents, students, and staff must themselves be the focus of study in order to get at the patterning that culture represents and that shapes all understanding and actions.

Schein (1985, p. 314) also applied this model of culture as patterned group interaction to his analysis of leadership. He viewed leadership as managed cultural change, but he warned, "Do not assume that culture can be manipulated like other matters under the control of managers. Culture controls the manager more than the manager controls culture, through the automatic filters that bias the manager's perceptions, thoughts, and feelings."

Turner's View of Motivation, Interaction, and Structure

Turner provided a unified theory of interaction that differs from Schein's patterned view of culture, because it attempts to unify motivation, interaction, and social structure. Motivational processes energize and mobilize people to interact; interactional processes highlight how people use symbols and gestures (including language), plans, and physical presence to send signals to others and to interpret received signals; and structural processes are the patterns that result and become established in a school. These patterns allow people to repeat and organize their interactions (akin to Schein's view of culture). Because interaction in each situation is viewed as indeterminate and spontaneous, a model like Turner's helps focus attention on the dynamics and elements of the interactions that occur during each principal succession. The three elements of Turner's model deserve some further elaboration.

Motivational Processes. The first processes in Turner's interaction model are motivational. Motivation plays a part because people are more or less willing to mobilize themselves and expend effort to interact with others in their work in schools. Because of surface differences of race, ethnicity, or sex, for example, teachers may avoid interacting with a new principal, thus limiting his influence. Motivation theory has a long history of interest in education related to both students and teachers, but it generally focuses on the motivation of individuals to perform their work or to improve their performance. Many theories of interaction in sociology and social psychology focus on motivational processes, among them exchange (Homans, 1961; Blau, 1964), ethnomethodology (Garfinkel, 1967), symbolic interactionism (Blumer, 1969; Mead, 1934), dramaturgy (Goffman, 1959), and ritual interaction (Collins, 1987). Some of these same theories offer insight into interaction process and resulting social structures, as well. For example, Turner (1988) contended that exchange theory, often applied to leadership studies (Yukl, 1989; Blau, 1964) as well as other social interactions, is a theory of motivation. Exchange theory attempts to explain why teachers choose to interact (with a new principal, for example, to get something from him or her in return for loyalty or desired behaviors) not what they do when they interact.

Motivation to interact springs from a number of different sources. People can be motivated to obtain some profit or achieve some self-interest such as influence over a new principal's beliefs and actions (exchange, utilitarianism). Other motivations also drive people to interact in schools, such as the need to affirm one's identity as a valuable teacher (Mead, 1934; Turner, 1988), participate in a ritual or tradition such as graduation (Durkheim, 1915), gain group acceptance (as a "leader"), or help form a common version of reality (a definition of what is really happening) on which others will act. In the last instance, for example, a superintendent might be motivated to take an active part in principal appointments to shape others' view of her as an instructional leader with high standards, thus leading to the perception that she is improving instruction in a school district.

Interactional Processes. Interaction processes make up the second element of Turner's model. They follow upon the motivation to interact by including what people "actually do when they influence each other's behavior" (Turner, 1988, p. 16). In the interaction process, people signal a course of behavior, interpret their own signals, and interpret the signals of others. They then act in response to their interpretations, and the cycle repeats itself. Symbolic interactionism (Blumer, 1969; Mead, 1934), discussed below, provides a noteworthy example of theories explaining how this occurs.

Interaction process theories often focus on descriptions of the dynamics of interaction, an essential ingredient of any organizational socialization theory. Mead (1934), for example, acknowledged that many animals, even plants, send out signals to other organisms in the environment—color, scent, sound, markings. These signals can be received, and the receipt of the signal can alter the behavior of another organism. (A fly may land on a plant, enticed by color or odor; a teacher who aspires to administration may alter his patterns of dress to conform more closely to those of administrators.) The original sender then might alter its behavior in turn. (The Venus flytrap may close on the fly when touched, digesting its meal gradually over the ensuing days; the principal may ask the teacher to represent her at a meeting.) Human interaction is qualitatively different from simple forms of interaction. Humans use word symbols that mean the same or essentially the same things to other humans. People can take on the roles and interpret the gestures of others and deliberately play a part or take a different perspective. They possess a capacity for using themselves as the guidelines from which they organize responses. They have the capacity to think, imagine, rehearse alternatives, foresee outcomes, avoid inappropriate responses, and select a course of action. And finally, humans can understand and assume the perspective of groups or communities of attitudes, like professions—teachers—or established organizations ("in this district we always have prayer at graduation").

To this insight of Mead, Schutz (1932) added the idea of selective perception with which people frame their beliefs about self, how they think and act, and how they interpret situations and save that information as stocks of knowledge. This contribution of "stocks of knowledge" as a precise view of ordered past experiences is an important one. It may shape a teacher's beliefs about a new principal's supervision methods (as interference versus caring attention), delegation of authority, or decision-making style. Schutz suggested that interactional processes can then be used by individuals to construct a myth of the self—through presentation and interpretation skills, what Goffman (1959) called the presentation of self (one of the multiple process models of interaction discussed later in this chapter). It is important to remember that the presentation of self depends on no factual reality. It has been described as "a model of the self as a modern-day myth that people are forced to enact rather than a subjective entity that people privately possess" (Collins, 1985, p. 215). In succeeding chapters, examples of new principals who present themselves as a "teachers' principal," the "professional woman," or the "leader of the band" illustrate how this can happen.

Leader succession studies have capitalized on the insight offered by interaction process theories. Gabarro (1987) contended that, while the conditions leading to succession are important, the dynamics of taking charge are the most influential factors shaping outcomes. The organizational and interpersonal dynamics he found to affect these outcomes include "the stages of learning and action that characterize the taking-charge process; the situational and personal background factors that bear on the process; and the patterns of behavior that distinguish successful transitions from those that fail" (Gabarro, 1987, p. vii). Gabarro asserted that postarrival factors studied in traditional succession research emphasize the dynamics of interaction (see Chapter 1). To illustrate this point, he cited Gordon and Rosen (1981), who emphasized the importance of mutual observation between the new manager and group members, judgments about the accuracy of the perceived or expected characteristics of the new manager, the new manager's actions and reactions (including the gathering and processing of information), and the manager's development of power and influence. Chapters 4 and 5 illustrate how these perceptions, judgments, and actions can shape leader succession in schools.

Structuring Processes. Structuring, the third element of Turner's unified theory of interaction, explains how and why social interactions become structured—repeated across time and space (Parsons, 1937;

Parsons, 1978). Schein (1985) would see this as the creation of culture as structure. Repetition is a necessary condition for an organizational culture or structure to form and persist and is often the criteria applied by scholars to judge a leader's impact on a group (Schein, 1985; Smith & Peterson, 1988). Some scholars go beyond viewing process and structure as interchangeable (Bosworth & Kreps, 1986). Culture, repeated patterns of social interaction and expectations, is a powerful mechanism through which principals influence their schools (Deal & Peterson, 1990; Pettigrew, 1979). Consequently, the structuring processes of interaction during principal succession create a foundation for long-term positive or negative effects on the school that go beyond actual events. When structuring occurs as a result of succession, outcomes begin to emerge. As succession effects become entrenched, these structures make alternative assumptions and patterns "virtually undiscussible" (Schein, 1985, p. 33). Inequalities become deeply locked within the system (Blau, 1977).

Structuring processes that occur during major changes sometimes clash with traditional social structures—those that members of the group have internalized and bring with them from other, similar experiences. In some cases, these fixed "sets of symbols" (Wentworth, 1980) are so firmly ingrained and shared that a "new" culture forming in a newly established work organization is merely a recreated culture transplanted through the members of the group to the new setting. This appears to happen when new schools are built and principals and faculty members are transferred from existing schools in a district. Under these circumstances, researchers find a "new school" that looks almost exactly like all other nearby schools. Professional training, conventions of behavior, even routines are transferred, and the culture is simply recreated (Blanch, 1989).

Schein and Turner provided two views that illustrate the usefulness of interaction as a unit for analyzing leader succession. A number of theories that explore interaction processes also increase our understanding of leader succession.

Multiple Process Theories of Interaction

Process theories of interaction often are applied as research frameworks to leadership studies—to explain followers' and leaders' behavior or the nature of their social contract. These theories include concepts such as utility, behavior, exchange, ritual, talk, and sense making (interpretation).

Many process theories explaining motivation to interact depend on a very rational view of choice and behavior. They assume that people weigh the relative costs and benefits of a choice and the utility or appeal of outcomes or payoffs they expect. They also assume that values are clear, and that people will remember their losses and gains in past exchanges and use that memory when making future choices. Rational theories assume that people have access to the relevant information necessary to weigh the various advantages or disadvantages of interaction and the conscious ability to assess the relative utility or value of projected outcomes. Were this true, educators involved in a succession would choose to interact in the process on the basis of unambiguous notions about the purpose of schools and the effects on outcomes candidates for a position might have. They would know what they want, remember what principals had succeeded or failed to give them in the past, and know what each candidate was likely to be able to give. They then would choose to interact after weighing all these data. Other process theories of interaction apply much less rational assumptions to the analysis of exchange. Ethnomethods, for example, relies on the understanding of "folk practices" by those who participate in them, concepts of belonging, and the definition of facts. Symbolic interactionism explores concepts of self and other, trust, signals, gestures, and information processing within attributed meaning. Dramaturgy reveals the self as constructed myth. Interaction ritual traces chains and profits of exchange. Each of these views provides insight into the processes being experienced by teachers and principals during succession.

Exchange

"The basic principles underlying the conception of exchange may be briefly summarized. An individual who supplies rewarding services to another obligates him. To discharge this obligation, the second must furnish benefits to the first in turn" (Blau, 1964, p. 89). In exchange theories, the relationships between a principal and a teacher (or teacher leader and teacher) are personal and dependent on the relative profit each can derive from the relationship. Profit can take many forms—power, influence, money, advantageous work assignments. For exchanges to work, the people involved need not maximize their rewards (win), they need only make some profit in the exchange, and that profit may reflect progress toward goals accepted by others in the school (Blau, 1964), such as a favorable schedule or room assignment.

Exchange theory does not depend totally on the assumptions of rationality discussed above. Processes can be nonrational, nonlogical, nonmaximizing, and unconscious. They do, however, depend on calculations and negotiations over what valued resources a new principal must be willing to give up (control over a decision) in order to receive valued resources from teachers (support for a new discipline program). Resources have broad social as well as economic meanings. Social obligations become a web of loyalties that may be called in on any number of issues. Teachers who have benefited from a union's assistance during salary negotiations may feel obligated to oppose a site-based management or mentor teacher plan that the union opposes, for example. The most "crucial distinction is that social exchange entails *unspecified* obligations.... [It engenders] feelings of personal obligation, gratitude, and trust" (Blau, 1964, p. 93). From this perspective, interactions among teachers and a new principal may emerge from the flow of exchanges and resulting obligations involving valued resources, emotions, and social obligations. Formal authority plays a minor part.

An understanding of the nonrational aspects of exchange is essential to apply it to an expanded view of principal succession. Expectations, for example, play a critical part in the value people assign to the resources being exchanged. If teachers value time for professional preparation, then time is a valued "currency." "The satisfactions human beings experience in their social associations depend on the expectations they bring to them as well as on the actual benefits they receive in them" (Blau, 1964, p. 143). People also tend to develop values based on past experiences. Teaching provides an apt example, for it is a profession in which intrinsic, service rewards have been abundant and monetary rewards sparse. The majority of teachers say that intrinsic rewards are more important to them than salary, yet the reasons for this expressed value may lie as much in the scarcity of monetary rewards as it does in the thrill of working with children. Researchers find that people tend to describe the rewards they value in their work to match the rewards available from their work, and it is not possible to determine which comes first (Salancik & Pfeffer, 1977).

Consequently, the study of exchange in social relationships "must take into account the ways in which the values of the rewards being exchanged are modified by the expectations of the participants and, ultimately, by the previous distribution of rewards that govern these expectations" (Blau, 1964, p. 144). Teachers' and principals' expectations can take a number of forms: (1) general expectations of the total benefits that can be accrued in all the aspects of work and relationships in the school; (2) expectations about a particular person—ways in which he or she can give rewards for the interaction and ways in which the rewards conform to accepted standards; and (3) expectations that, when the costs of working together are deducted (time, loss of autonomy, and so on), the comparative rewards of the interaction warrant the effort (Blau, 1964). In the first case, a person may be unwilling to engage in site-based decision making at the urging of a new principal because she lacks the belief that she will benefit or her working life be improved by her investment of time and effort. In the second case, the teacher may simply disbelieve a principal's assertion that he can provide the promised rewards (money for summer time, for example). In the last case, a teacher may look at the balance sheet between costs and rewards and conclude that the costs outweigh the promised benefits. In all three cases, expectations would suppress teacher participation.

At the most personal level, exchange is sometimes conceived as a series of favors that make people grateful, lead to expressions of that gratitude, and make doing favors enjoyable. "One good deed deserves another." Many principals and teachers never move past this level in their exchange relationships, and such relationships sometimes lead to accusations that a teacher is "kissing up" or that a principal is "buying" favors. On a more positive note, exchange can provide a means through which a new principal gradually becomes an integrated member of the school, a process through which the necessary ties binding her or him to people in the school can be established.

Exchange processes are not limited to the individual level. Group obligations, too, can develop. Exchange theories view this group effect as an outcome of personal (dyadic) exchanges. As a new principal gradually provides valued outcomes for the school as a whole, for example, shared values are marshalled to become currency in a social contract of sorts. Exchange theory postulates that this process creates legitimate power for a new leader and transforms obligations into authority. As was pointed out earlier, "managerial practices that advance the *collective* interest of subordinates create *joint* obligations" (Blau, 1964, p. 207). Loyalty and compliance with the new principal's leadership thus become social obligations enforced by the majority of teachers in the school (Festinger, 1957). If this occurs, a principal will no longer need to rely solely on the personal obligation of a few loyal teachers, nor on the formal authority of his position as a source of power.

Exchange theory has also been applied directly to leadership research. Hollander (1979), for example, equated leadership with exchange. He argued that leadership can be reduced to exchanges for rewards between a leader and the group or individuals within the group. As a form of contingency theory, Hollander said that a combination of a new leader's and group members' traits, the group's tasks, and norms governing their behavior will determine the skills and values that define the rewards sought through the exchange process. Hollander argued that loyalty and the acceptance of a leader develop over time as exchanges take place. As leaders demonstrate their competence at tasks valued by the group and conform to group norms, they provide benefits to individuals and to the group. In turn, they accumulate credit for future exchanges. Validation also results, securing for the principal the right to be different, to make changes. By exhibiting an ability and willingness to contribute to the organization and demonstrating commitment to the organization, administrators accumulate what Hollander (1958, 1960, 1979) called "idiosyncrasy credits." These credits purchase for the holder the right to deviate from rigid expectations and group norms without penalty, showing that the organization's impact on the new leader, building her commitment, has been successful (Buchanan, 1974).

Hollander believed that the rights secured through the accumulation of idiosyncrasy credits can carry principals through major changes in a school (i.e., in goals, structure, and operations) and the conflicts that may result, as long as the validation of the group remains in force. Teachers, students, and parents may be willing to suspend judgment and participate in innovations about which they have doubts. Administrators who hold no credits, whose authority remains unvalidated, possess no such mandate and are unable to function as leaders, especially during difficult times. They then must rely only on positional and legal forms of authority (Blau & Scott, 1962). Social exchange theory also suggests that teachers not only accept the innovative ideas of administrators who have sufficient credit but expect them to initiate changes in response to problems. Leaders thus secure the right to alter both goals and processes (Lipham, 1964; Selznick, 1957). In his examination of great leaders in history, Burns (1978) asserted that leaders provide the means for followers to attain something of value to them, while followers give compliance and willingness to be led and are transformed and enhanced in the process. Some leader-follower exchanges are transactions—bargains or trades. Followers benefit personally, growing and developing in the process, when leadership reaches its highest potential; however, this transformation of followers is the essence of leadership. Sergiovanni (1991) conceptualized this contribution as "value added leadership." These concepts provide illustrations of the concrete ways people can exert "heroic" or "cultural" leadership in education.

This social exchange perspective would support an argument that new principals gain influence through the social interactions that occur as part of the succession process. When they first join a school, new principals' bases of influence have not yet been formed. They exchange benefits and favors with teachers, superiors, parents. Exchanges involve material or psychological benefits (e.g. respect, esteem, and approval) or both.

Exchanges limit future choices as well. As relationships (and obligations) develop, a form of mutual determinism (Bandura, 1978) structures future options in a gradually narrowing spiral.

When we talk of leadership, we often lapse into heroic language and expect dramatic outcomes, but exchanges need not be of heroic proportions to function. They can be and often are very utilitarian. In one study, a superintendent exchanged votes in the appointment of a junior high school principal for support for a new name for a school (Firestone, 1990). In other research, exchanges of simple favors, supplies, or support appear to build relationships between new leaders and the groups (Gabarro, 1979). Seemingly ordinary and simple processes in daily life can build into communities and societies (Blau, 1964).

> To be sure, each individual's behavior is reinforced by the rewards it brings, but the psychological process of reinforcement does not suffice to explain the exchange relation that develops. This social relation is the joint product of the actions of both individuals, with the actions of each being dependent on those of the other. The emergent properties of social exchange consequent to this interdependence cannot be accounted for by the psychological processes that motivate the behavior of the partners. (Blau, 1964, p.4)

A number of criticisms have been lodged against this very rational view of motivation to interact. First, it isolates incidences, deemphasizing chains of responses and individual preferences. The assessment of value or benefit and the cost of the exchange is internal for each individual. It may be hard to tell what a teacher wants as opposed to what "teachers" want. Second, it depends on the assumption that people have unambiguous and well-ordered hierarchies of value. Teachers, parents, and others know what they want and in what order. Third, it relies on people's ability to calculate their choices on the basis of clear values, complete information, experience with profits and losses, and maximized benefit. Particularly in a profession characterized by unclear goals and ambiguous outcomes, this may be unreasonable.

Ethnomethods

Another approach to understanding interaction processes, ethno-methods, relies on detailed analyses of interaction processes among people, especially the analysis of talk (Gronn, 1982; Heritage, 1984). This seems a uniquely suitable method of understanding principals' leadership, because the vast majority of their interactions are verbal (Martin & Willower, 1981; Kmetz & Willower, 1982). By understanding how patterns among new principals, teachers, and others develop, scholars hope to uncover the processes through which succession effects emerge. By better understanding the patterns in which they are becoming embroiled, new principals can hope to affect them.

Ethnomethods can be defined as implicit practices in a group that create a presumption that all in the group share a common world (Cicourel et al., 1974; Garfinkel, 1967; Heritage, 1984). These implicit practices often are called folk practices (Turner, 1988). By concentrating on subtle conversational patterns, scholars seek to learn about processes of interaction and implicit assumptions and beliefs about reality held in common by members of a group.

The most extreme applications of ethnomethodology as a theory of social interaction assert that folk practices and the common perceptions they create are the *only* social reality. Social reality in this view of interaction creates an underlying sense of "facticity" that may be divorced from all outside assessments of objective reality. This decoupling of experience of outsiders' "objectivity" does not matter, however, because facticity lies outside the limited concept of fact. At the same time, it serves the same purpose for the members of the group. Garfinkel (1967) goes so far as to assert that the social realities scholars study are not real in any objective sense, that by telling a story or an account and labeling objects with talk, groups document what is real through the grammar of language, pauses, assertions, patterns of turn taking, insertions of verbal fillers in interactions. Thus, a study of interaction from this point of view requires one to acknowledge that reality is contextually constructed through mutual account making and account taking by the people in each setting. Accounts are the only realities; reality is illusionary (Turner, 1988).

This rather esoteric discussion about what is real and what is illusion actually serves a concrete purpose in understanding interactions among the people who work in schools. If people act on their realities, illusionary or not, the question of their substantive reality seems moot. Consequently, pure ethnomethodologists refuse to engage in debates about what is real; they attend only to the realities upon which people act. If, for example, teachers view a new principal as a "hatchet man," hired by the school board to "clean house," their interactions with that principal, the language they use to explain their responses, and the outcomes will reflect that reality. Distrust and caution will affect actions and degrade relationships.

A number of scholars interested in culture and leaders draw on these traditions. Schein (1985) acknowledged the importance of understanding a group construction of reality when he cautioned researchers trying to study organizational cultures that they cannot rely on insiders for complete descriptions. Insiders cannot tell an outsider about basic assumptions in the group and how they are patterned without assistance, because these patterns have "dropped out of awareness and are taken for granted" (Schein, 1985, p. 113). Patterns develop to the point that they are past being assumptions and are part of the facticity accepted by the group. Van Maanen and Barley (1984) provided additional insight into the power these realities can exert as forms of social control. They described social worlds as forms of communal control (and this includes control over a new principal or other school leader). They pointed out that an understanding of these social worlds provides important additional insight to rational studies of interaction.

In ethnomethods, talk among members of the group serves as the primary means through which facticity is established. People must talk together about a succession event, interpret the meanings others are beginning to develop, and share their interpretations with each other to establish a group version of what is happening. While we often view communication as interaction involving the symbols, grammar, and syntax of talk, the traditions of ethnomethods help us see how it also involves validity claims (Habermas, 1984). People communicate and assert claims about the legitimacy of their beliefs and assertions. They may meet the norms and cultural standards of the group and establish the sincerity of their intentions and actions. A series of these exchanges and feedback loops then creates the group version of the facts. During succession or any important organizational process, this perspective hypothesizes that the real experience is forged through the communication process.

If a common version fails to emerge, however, the group's strong need for a commonly held view forces people to talk more and more intently to repair the damage or to cover up discord. If a succession is turbulent, for example, talk among school members will increase as people seek to come to a common view of what is happening. Discordance becomes so painful when it remains unresolved that interactions absorb group members' attention and energy. People have less energy to meet other needs, including work, until the discord is resolved. As the research on principal succession affirms, leader succession is disruptive and will necessitate the use of some work energy to create a new, commonly held view of the school that includes the new member.

Conversation becomes an important focus, because conversations, particularly the use of jargon accepted and understood by members of the group, can give people a feeling "that they are part of a larger solidarity." Solidarity in the form of jargon then frames the real world, the interpretations and claims of all the members of the group about what actually is happening and what it means. Teachers, for example, can talk about needing "support" from a principal without having to explain what they mean by support. Special education teachers can talk about IEPs and LEAs with assurance that everyone who is in the group knows what they mean. Were this not the case, teachers and principals could not feel (even if it is something of an illusion) that they share a dependable, factual, and fixed world in which to work.

Another contribution of ethnomethods emerges from its view of the content of talk and ways in which it can be manipulated by existing members of a group (teachers) when interacting with new members (the new principal). Jones (1986), for instance, asserted that newcomers respond to a group in unique ways, because they receive different kinds of information than established members. By giving or withholding information or providing information in particular ways, those already at a school can shape the interpretations and responses of a new principal until he or she gradually comes to accept the existing, shared reality. Some established members of a school community may be very assertive, moving to present their view of the school to a new principal in an attempt to affect the thinking of this influential new member. Deliberate stories or myths frequently told to newcomers to teach them a cultural content may provide only part of the story and may or may not match with actual assumptions that operate (Smith & Simmons, 1983), so a new principal is well advised to withhold early judgments about the nature of the actual shared reality operating to shape teachers' work, parents' attitudes, and interactions with superiors.[2]

Symbolic Interactionism

In the preceding section, the means through which ethnomethods exert a shared reality in a group were presented as an exchange of symbols and gestures. This symbolic interactionism is offered as one explanation for the effects of communication that sustains a shared view of experiences. In addition to exploring the enduring means through which people communicate and interact through symbols, symbolic interactionist theory examines ways in which people develop self-concepts and assess themselves based on their beliefs about how others see and evaluate them (Edwards & Klackars, 1981). As such, it provides a foundation for exploring how a new principal might come to view herself and how others in the school can shape that view. More generally, the theory provides one model for the ways in which the social role of principal might develop as a result of these processes. Unlike ethnomethods, which relies on talk as the primary method for establishing beliefs about social experiences, symbolic interaction examines symbols in many forms such as talk, physical gestures, intonation of voice, and facial expression.

The roots of symbolic interactionism lie in the collected lectures and writings of George Herbert Mead (1934). Its promise lies in its power to reveal and explain human experiences centered in the family, social groups, and work groups from which all people draw support and purpose. Its challenge lies in the abstract nature of symbol and gesture interpretation. Its basic assumption is that individuals, not groups or organizations, create and sustain group beliefs through interactions with others (Van Maanen & Schein, 1979).

Awareness and the acquisition of knowledge form the foundation of symbolic interaction. Each person must be aware, learn, and signal other people in order for the processes to work. The theory relies a great deal on the psychological notions of cogition to explain this process. Cognition involves perception, recognition, conceptualization, judgment, and reasoning on the part of each person (Rosenthal & Zimmerman, 1978). It also requires that knowledge is absorbed in some abstract form to be generalized and transferred to other, similar situations. The construct of cognition is complex and is often explained and best understood in the context of social learning through interaction:

Cognition is a *method of processing information*. It refers to all of the processes that enable an individual to represent and deal with the external environment symbolically or imaginally. The individual does not react to stimulation from the distal environment in raw physical form, but first interprets and represents these stimuli. These representations then instigate and guide most subsequent behavior. [It is] both a repository of past experiences and a complex information processing device. (Rosenthal & Zimmerman, 1978, pp. 1, 2)

Thus each person involved in a succession will bring to the experience an existing abstract framework that explains similar processes they have experienced. As events unfold and gestures and signals are sent and interpreted, this abstract model of leader succession may be confirmed or modified, and the interpretations of others—teachers, parents, superiors—will help to shape its modification. This information processing is not just thinking but reaction and response to other people, events, and things. Pondy (1978) goes so far as to label leadership itself a "language game."

No single person can be the focus of inquiry into symbolic interaction (which fits the study of leader succession aptly), because symbolic interaction requires a number of specific conditions. First, symbols must be exchanged—words, gestures, facial expressions. This exchange requires that someone send a message for which he or she intends meaning and that someone receive the message. Second, a receiver must interpret the message. Third, those involved must share, at minimum, some common meaning for the gesture or symbol. Fourth, a return message is usually sent. This requires that someone receive the message, examine and interpret his or her internal response, and then, in some state of self-knowledge more or less well developed, send a message in return. The return message can even be a deliberate disregard for the message received. Fifth, the meanings and interpretations of symbols are learned through social experience, through ongoing interactions with others (much like the talk in ethnomethods). Social learning forms the foundation on which all subsequent interactions are based. While meanings that were not intended by a new principal may be attributed to him by teachers, for example, simply asking the principal what he intended will provide only incomplete insight into subsequent events, because no message exists apart from its receivers. Finally, concepts of self and group, needs for inclusion in the group, and the need to understand what is real shape ongoing group interpretations of information and symbol exchange. In this way information is processed and a shared meaning of events and experiences is created by people in a school (Blumer, 1969). This phenomenon of symbol exchange and interpretation is often referred to as social information processing, and it can result in very different meanings being assigned to the same set of events by different social groups. For example, Blau asserted that authority, which requires voluntary compliance, develops out of the social norms of groups and is "exactly as voluntary as conformity with social norms generally" (1964, p. 209). Blumer (1969) went further, arguing that the environment includes only those things that people know about and recognize. Consequently, humans confront a world that they "must interpret in order to act rather than an environment to which [they] respond...." (p. 15).

The critical part symbolic interactionism plays in groups sheds light on the part played by new principals as they interact with others in a school. The principal must send messages, signaling her plans and vision, even her self-concept. These signals play a critical role in the social information processing associated with succession. They create a place for the new principal, as well as change the dynamics of the social group. Collins (1987) described this need to create a sense of membership and inclusion in social relations that drives the dynamics of groups. Consequently, one can assert that a new principal needs to belong as well as lead; teachers need to feel their principal is one of them. Giddens (1984) agreed, asserting that a need for trust in others—that other people are reliable and that their responses are predictable—drives much of the interaction behavior observed in groups and related to the interactions in which people are willing to engage. This need for inclusion may be especially high when one is a newcomer to an established social group:

> When we experience a new cultural situation, we feel a need to respond, react, "do the right thing," fit into the situation, remove the tension of uncertainty, gain acceptance, establish communication, or the like. We find it difficult just to observe the situation and tolerate the feelings of alienation and tension that it may arouse. (Schein, 1985, p. 28)

A new principal also risks assault on her core self-concept during transition periods such as succession. A person may "perceive himself, have perceptions of himself, communicate with himself, and act toward himself" (Blumer, 1969, p. 62). Self-concept within the formal role of principal may conflict with individual needs. During succession, group members may withhold information from the new leader. Ashford (1989) asserted that people often have difficulty assessing themselves because they have difficulty obtaining the necessary information, must balance the desire to understand what they should be doing and how well they have done with the costs to the ego they suffer when hearing negative feedback, and the negative implications of seeking information about themselves in the group when it may be perceived as a sign of weakness or insecurity. This may be a particularly difficult task for a newly appointed principal who is supposed to be strong and lead.

People's need to be included in groups serves an important function in organizational socialization. This (Van Maanen & Schein, 1979) means that newcomers to hierarchical levels (like principals) remain on the edge of organization affairs for some time while members of the group assess their trustworthiness. "When the socialization process does not work optimally, when the new member does not learn the culture of the host group, there are usually severe consequences" (Schein, 1985, p. 42). The interplay between group cultures and individual careers creates a complex environment far less dependable than many would hope (Schein, 1971a, 1971b, 1978, 1984, 1986). Greenfield, while not applying a symbolic interactionist framework per se to his studies of principal professional socialization, nevertheless asserted that researchers have much to learn from studies that depend on the same traditions. These studies illuminate "the interplay between social processes, social contexts, and social-ization outcomes as these are reflected in the behaviors of individuals and in the understandings that are developed as incumbents come to terms with their work, their careers, and themselves" (1985a, pp. 6–7).

Coming to terms and achieving inclusion are critical outcomes of symbolic interaction within groups. They mean that people develop an implicit account of reality or a shared factual world (called facticity by the ethnomethodologists) that functions in several ways. First, it adds the power of responsiveness. People can understand and respond with decreasing expenditure of energy and decreasing uncertainty. Second, it contributes trust to the principal-school interaction. With trust, members come to know that others in the group are reliable and that their responses are predictable. Third, it provides for the whole group—new principal and all others—the confidence that reality has a meaning that they hold in common (Giddens, 1984).

The first contribution of a shared factual world that develops between a new principal and other members of the group, power of responsiveness, is a natural outgrowth of the frequency and perceived success of interactions. It springs from integration and inclusion, from skill among those in a school in accurately interpreting the meanings others intend in their symbolic gestures. It allows people to respond in an understandable way. You need only join a close knit family for an evening of conversation and jokes or a faculty meeting in a tight-knit school to see immediately that many of the subtleties of communication and interaction are lost on you. The power of inclusion cannot be underestimated. For example, a lack of shared under-standing can cause "diffuse anxiety" (Turner, 1988, p. 59) and may be difficult for a person experiencing it to identify. Yet, people "seem to know implicitly the criteria for assessing whether or not they are excluded from a group" (Turner, 1988, p. 60). Inclusion can have an anxiety-reducing function making it possible for a new principal to function effectively:

> [H]umans would experience high levels of anxiety if they could not sort out from the mass of stimuli those that are important and those that are not. Once we learn how to think about our primary task; have goals, means, and information systems; and agree on how to communicate, relate to each other, and conduct our daily affairs, we also have a system for sorting out from the mass of input the things that must be attended to, and a set of criteria for reacting to them. (Schein, 1985, pp. 82–83)

The need for inclusion may be acute for newly appointed principals, for they need to be able to respond and seek responses quickly in order to do their work. In a study of a national cohort of 188 new secondary heads in Great Britain (Weindling & Earley, 1987), 59 percent of the respondents reported feelings of isolation.

The second contribution to the group made by a strong shared reality—trust—emanates from a belief that people can predict others' responses to common events. If a student disrupts an assembly, teachers can count on the nearest faculty members to take action to end the disruption. If a fight breaks out on the playground, the closest adult will stop the fight. Within a profession, trust provides an implicit sense of predictable behavior from others (Turner, 1988; Gabarro, 1987). Common knowledge leads to common actions springing from trust that others in the group are reliable and that their responses are predictable (Giddens, 1984). Thus, when a new principal establishes that he possesses the common experiences, critical and valued skills, and values and beliefs that drive the actions of others in the school, that principal contributes to the trust necessary for healthy interaction.

Ontological security, the sense that things are as they appear (Turner, 1988), provides the final contribution of a strong sense of shared reality to a school or other group. It affirms that what is, what exists in a social experience, is visible and understood. For a person to feel ontological security in a social situation, she must believe that no critical dimensions of the situation remain hidden.

The common world constructed through interaction also includes role structures within the group, although it accepts that role structures are fluid, constantly created and recreated rather than fixed and rigid. This fluidity may actually contribute to new principals' ability to affect critical roles that influence the success of schools. Some scholars, in fact, assert that leaders play a potent role in creating this reality (Smith & Peterson, 1988). External sources of meaning in a school—experiences with other principals, work structures, teaching and learning strategies, customary ways of doing things—affect interpretations of events surrounding the succession of a principal and focus and interrupt the attention of everyone involved. An additional effect arises from individual sources of meaning—experiences and interpretations (Markus & Zajonc, 1985). Smith and Peterson (1988, p. 89) argued that to understand leadership one must accept and address the real psychosocial world in which "different sources of meaning could even affect very basic aspects of event perception." Over two decades ago, Blau (1964, p. 67) described the effect of interpretations from high and low status members of organizations on social events:

> Since the judgments of a person who commands respect are more likely to be accepted as correct than those of one who does not, superiors have a better chance to earn gratitude with either their supportive approval or their critical suggestions for improvement, whereas inferiors take a greater risk of incurring contempt by their approving agreement or of provoking annoyance by their critical disagreement.

This influence should not be underestimated. It has been found to have greater power to affect behavior than rewards for exemplary behavior or the threat of punishment (Markus & Zajonc, 1985).

Smircich and Morgan (1983) viewed the influence of leaders on group interpretations or sense making as a series of stages. First, leaders draw attention to certain elements in the overall flow of organizational experience. A principal might take every opportunity to emphasize the potential of new technologies as instructional tools, for example. This attention-drawing process frames elements for interpretation: technology is important to my teaching. Second, elements are interpreted by organizational members within the wider context of the organization. While leaders may have specific interpretations in mind, other participants derive their own interpretations: I need to use more advanced technology in my teaching. Third, people act on the meanings they construct and associate with other elements: I attend workshops, write grant applications, and apply for time in the school computer lab with my students. Pfeffer (1981b), who discounts the effects of leadership on organizations as symbolic rather than substantive, suggested that the interpretation of social information may be a major function of management:

> Organizing involves not only the structuring of behaviors, a process that must be continually reaccomplished, but also the structuring of information and meaning, a process that must also be continually reaccomplished. Indeed, what the social psychological experimenter does in the laboratory may be one of the more important tasks of management making certain information salient and pointing out connections between behaviors and subsequent attitudes. . . . creating meaning systems and consensually shared interpretations of events for participants. (Pfeffer & Lawler, 1980, p. 54)

New principals' ability to exert influence over social interpretations serves a functional purpose in schools during succession. Gabarro, for example, described how shared expectations during the process of taking charge exert influence. In order to work through shared expectations, the new principal should invest time and effort to influence priorities and settle differences arising in the organization. The first three to six months are a critical time during which a new principal's expectations can be communicated by action and by the use of symbolic communication—"rallying cries and themes" (1987, p. 86) that communicate beliefs about what is important. In this way, successful new principals actively work to affect the information processing associated with their successions to leadership and the development of three qualities in their working relationships that are particularly salient to success: mutual expectations, trust, and influence. Social information processing can go the other way, too, as Gabarro and Kotter (1980) asserted in their discussion of "managing your boss."

Other research in work settings provides examples of the power of social information processing to shape people's judgments of the value and appropriateness of their experiences. Podsakoff, Todor, and Skov (1982) found that people react better to incentive rewards they believe are contingent on performance than when they believe the rewards are based on other factors. They concluded that one cannot assume that a specified reward offered by a superior will always have a predictable impact. And Peterson (1985) showed that teachers respond very differently to direct instructions from a principal. Their responses depend in large part on whether they believe they already know what needs to be done. These examples of the power of belief and meaning to shape events in schools is further supported by Bass's (1985) finding that people who rate their leaders high on their ability to transform their interpretations, aspirations, and expectations (Burns's transformational leadership) also rate them high on effectiveness. In this research, leaders who relied on exchange for influence were seen as less effective. Control over information and its meaning, contacts among group members and with the environment, and communication with others serve as major sources of power (House, 1988). At the same time, "the individual is not a neutral observer but an active constructor of social reality" (Turner, 1978, p.7).

The formal and informal power of people involved in exchanges also moderates the outcomes of symbolic interaction and should not be overlooked in analyses of information processing (although more emphasis has been given to power in exchange theory). Experimental studies of small groups reveal that high-ranking members dominate the communication and tend to control the sending and receiving of information. Their interpretations have more impact on actions, as well (Monane, 1967).

Studies of school leadership give additional credence to these analyses. In the most extensive longitudinal study to date on leader succession in schools, Weindling and Earley (1987, p. 55) found the access to insider information provided by informants to be highly valued by new heads in secondary schools in England. During succession, new heads "particularly valued senior staff who had an 'ear to the ground' ". The information they chose to share often played a significant part in new heads' ability to successfully block attempts to deny them critical information and seek out additional sources of information. Additionally, the researchers found that heads who consulted teachers and communicated with them regularly, sharing and using information to avoid the impression of "fait accompli pronouncements" met with more approval from the faculty. They also found that information processing can take other political forms. The negotiated interpretations of events and the meanings of experiences that result form an important base on which formal leaders then act and on which they hope to influence the actions of others: "On the one hand, formal leaders negotiate an interpretation of events upon which their *own* actions can be based. On the other hand, they then engage in processes of negotiating meanings with *others* and attempting to influence their actions" (Smith & Peterson, 1988, p. 131).

Negative examples of this process in schools can also be found. In five of the sixteen in-depth case studies of headship succession conducted by Weindling and Earley, they found that

> adverse reactions had been generated by the new heads' constant reference to their "old" school and the implied criticism of the "new" school and its staff. Frequent reference to the need for change, accompanied by comments as to how well arrangements worked at the head's last school, upset many teachers. (1987, p. 74)

Information processing aimed at judgments about the school by those in the environment was interpreted by faculties as a critical responsibility of school leadership. In fact, new heads identified the creation of a better public image of the school as one of only two external problems they felt they faced that were either serious or very serious (p. 154). Most problems for new heads came from within the school and these, too, involved interpretations.

While social information processing is seen as a critical responsibility of school leaders, a too-optimistic view of a formal leader's ability to control social information processing in the social context can misrepresent its complexity. It is important to reemphasize that information processing emerges from fluid and dynamic processes, dominant meanings require shared understanding but not consensus, and the final meaning is never set (Hosking & Morley, 1988). Additionally, newly appointed principals may have difficulty deliberately affecting the beliefs and interpretations of the faculties in their schools through the use of communication. Roberts, in a study of first-time high school principals, found that

> stories circulating among faculty members were not principal-initiated, positive, culture-building tales but rather complaints in which the new principal was often the target. Making changes

without sufficient communication, being critical of all instead of a guilty few, being negative about faculty . . . , constantly pointing out errors, and even being inappropriately silent [were common mistakes]. (1989a, pp. 16–17)

Roberts's study illustrates the difficulties a newly appointed principal faces when trying to shape shared beliefs and meaning and the ways in which teachers and others communicate and interpret information in schools. Other studies reveal similar problems (Alvey, 1983). Rather than a stimulus for cultural change, many new leaders find the organizational culture shapes the environment of their careers (Schein, 1984).

One approach to social interaction that takes an individual view offers a final look at social information processing that deserves note. This view is best represented by social learning theory. Social learning has been described as those processes concerned with the behaviors and attitudes people acquire by observing and interacting with others and modeling what they have observed in their own behavior (Hartup & Coates, 1972). Social modeling and learning can shape teachers' behaviors during a principal succession. As the teachers observe others' actions and reactions to events associated with the succession, these responses convey information about appropriate responses. Teachers then distill the common attributes of the observed and modeled behavior and abstract a general principle or conclusion about the event. If similar events occur, this learning transfers to times when and where similar behavior might be appropriate. When social learning has occurred, those who observe and learn can behave in ways the model might behave in similar circumstances, "even though subjects had never witnessed the model's behavior in these new situations" (Bandura, 1972, p. 37). Although social learning theory relates directly to the feedback and consequences arising from the social environment, it emphasizes vicarious reinforcement and self-reinforcement (Blumer, 1969). By taking a psychological view of the social learning process, it focuses on the behavior that results from modeling rather than on emerging social realities. By doing so, it adds a critical individual component to the total picture of people's interpretations of principal succession.

Dramaturgy and Interaction Rituals

While their impact on studies of administration has been less pronounced than exchange theory and symbolic interactionism, two additional theories from social psychology add to an interaction analysis of leader succession. These frameworks are dramaturgy and interaction ritual. They explore the dramatic, ritualistic aspects of interaction—dramaturgy from the perspective of the individual actor presenting herself to a school during succession and interaction rituals from the perspective of the group or school acting out its meaningful rituals during succession.

Dramaturgy. Dramaturgy emphasizes the importance of the self-concept in shaping interactions. While a number of scholars expanded the study of interaction to present a coherent view of the self (Blumer, 1969; Stryker, 1980; Rosenberg, 1979), Goffman's (1959) theory of dramaturgy unquestionably has had the most profound impact on interpretations.

The impact of Goffman's theories springs from the lure of "the presentation of self." Goffman posited that people interact with others as actors on a stage, presenting themselves in ways they view as most advantageous in a given situation. Furthermore, these presentations change from stage to stage, depending on a person's reading of each social context. And some people are better at the presentation of self than are others.

The presentation of self during principal succession could involve two important factors identified by Goffman. First, principals skillful at the presentation of self will be apt and astute self-monitors; they will observe and attend to the social demands of the new school. They will watch themselves and others in the new context and monitor their own behavior for its appropriateness and for the responses it receives. They will be able to behave in different ways in different situations, depending on the behavior expected by the group (or subgroup, such as parents, student assemblies, school board meetings; not surprisingly, Goffman found that actors and politicians tend to be good self-monitors). New principals who are skilled self-monitors "prove themselves" to the group, a major problem for newcomers or for people transferred to a new role within an organization (Schein, 1971b). Second, self-monitors always will be aware of a front stage and a back stage to their behavior. Frontstage behavior requires the most careful adjustment for a particular audience and strict adherence to accepted and expected actions. Backstage behavior is reserved for insiders to a tight social group and may allow (or encourage) letting down, dropping some of the monitoring and careful control otherwise expected. Astute actors understand both self-monitoring and front- and backstage settings. They assess the stage, frame their behavior, and act out rituals.

Goffman's research provided a significant framework for understanding the actions of people in groups. He recognized that

> macrostructures and collective orientations circumscribe what actors do in concrete interaction. This willingness to recognize the significance of Durkheim's insights into the importance of shared collective orientations and ritual has placed him at odds with most microtheorists, who reject structural and functional modes of theory. (Turner, 1988, p. 92)

Turner (1988, p. 95) praised Goffman's contribution to interaction theory along three important dimensions: (1) He recognized that everyday life is punctuated with rituals marking group membership and structuring interactions. (2) He advanced theory by providing a conceptualization of the "ecology" and "geography" of interaction as crucial aspects of the process through which people communicate. (3) He transformed the definition of the setting or situation from a static, status quo structure to a dynamic and active process of framing and reframing.

Theories of dramaturgy raise questions about the core and situational concepts of self that affect succession and about self-conscious interpretations and adjustments principals make to a new school. If self-monitoring is all-encompassing, prevalent, and influential in every interaction, the existence of a stable, situation-free definition of self may be in question. Self-presentation is not only a functional mechanism for promoting harmony and success in social interactions, it may also be a defense mechanism. Overused, it may suppress information and overwhelm a stable psyche. When this suppression is internal, a new principal may repress important aspects of herself or allow only information that confirms a preconceived self-conceptualization to be acknowledged and dealt with. Contradictory and critically important information from the school could be ignored—what Schon (1983) calls selective inattending—or the source of the information impugned to avoid dealing with it. A new principal may, in this kind of situation, be in danger of losing the best she has to offer the school in the search for acceptable behavior. He also may be committing a common problem-solving error (Barrows, 1988). Additionally, when presentations of self fail to yield either overt confirmation and affirmation of the core or accepted situational selves, presentation activities may increase. People may work harder to present appropriate images, seeking the desired response from the group. If these responses are not forthcoming, anxiety can increase, setting off escalated efforts to sustain the self-concept (Turner, 1988). Another criticism: the presentation may be artificial, not just adaptive. Critics accuse self-presentation of being "a model of the self as a modern-day myth that people are forced to enact rather than a subjective entity that people privately possess" (Collins, 1985, p. 215).

The presentation of self can thus be a curse or a blessing for a new school leader. Overused, it can bury potential contributions as the individual continually plays to the school audience. A principal might be accepted yet fail to have any substantial impact. Ignored, the need for self-monitoring can lead to fatal social errors that prevent a new leader from ever being given the chance to have an impact.

While the presentation of self is the core concept in dramaturgy, Goffman did not confine himself to this perspective. He also asked important questions about the social effects of staged behavior. He emphasized that, as people act out their presentations and repeat them over time, they frame group rituals that become established forms of interaction—the function of ritual making (Goffman, 1974). These group rituals then form an independent feature of interaction.

Interaction Rituals. Goffman defined ritual making as a primary function of dramaturgy (Goffman, 1967). By doing so, he turned the focus from the individual to the group. Collins (1987) synthesized a number of constructs from traditional interaction theory to include concepts of talk and conversation, rituals and solidarity, exchange and inequality, power and conflict. He analyzed conflict as a series of ritual chains in which people use their resources to extract profit from others within the core group.

Some of the concepts central to dramaturgy for individuals emerge in Collins's group rituals and concept of cultural capital. He argued that people assess the basic nature of situations—as work or as practical, ceremonial, or social interactions. They then direct their energy toward different goals. Teachers, principals, and others might draw these assessments during a succession, then direct their efforts on the basis of these judgments. Goals would depend on three types of interactions into which people decided a situation falls. First, work situations like schools require that people interact to establish their place in the group authority structure, division of labor, and ranking system. Second, ceremonial situations like a commencement revolve around a different form of conversation aimed at establishing a place in the rituals of the group and increasing the sense of belonging and membership. Finally, social situations like faculty relationships require people to use their resources to enhance their standing in groups. They then promote prestige, authority, and secure relationships that further establish their favorable place in the group. When conversations directed toward each of these situations are successful, Collins posits that people enhance their "cultural capital" and desire to keep conversations going or to repeat successful encounters. These repeated interactions or chains of conversation over time create social structures that can be produced and reproduced.

Cultural capital might be a critical resource of a new principal. When the effort to increase cultural capital is unsuccessful, people will increase their level of effort to try to recoup their losses. When they fail, they begin to withdraw. People may seek to avoid situations that cause them to lose cultural capital, and their conversation will become perfunctory and highly ritualized and will involve little expenditure of energy. New principals who see themselves failing to achieve integration may take this outcome as a danger signal that they are slipping away from the centers of influence. In one study, a new principal literally barricaded herself in her office when her attempts to forge a new organizational structure in a school resulted in conflict and rejection (Hart & Murphy, in press).

The function of ritual making as a social activity, too, has been used by scholars to assess leader succession. Firestone (1989) observed dynamics he called "competitive dramaturgy." These dynamics emerged as part of the "cultural politics" within a school district and were associated with the succession of a superintendent. They centered in two policy areas: desegregation and personnel policies. The new superintendent and powerful interest groups within the district eventually squared off in a series of ritual actions whose function appeared to be the dramatization of the values of fairness and equality.

Self-concept

Another major construct in the social sciences, self-concept, can extensively influence the outcomes of leader succession by affecting the responses of every participant. Scholars have found that individual interpretations of the self in isolation, in specific roles, and in relation to others deserve attention in their own right.

Concepts of Self

Several views of the self provide frameworks from which to explore the relationships among members of a group and of the group with one member (such as a new principal). These views raise questions about the concept of self that adults hold. Does it vary substantially or only very gradually over time? Does it depend on particular situations (e.g., as parent, son or daughter, professional)? Related to these two stationary features of the self-concept, researchers study transition in self-concept, attribution of characteristics to the self in different settings and groups, and the part the social and psychological concept of "self" plays during interactions (Swann, 1983).

Stable Self-concept. Definitions of self-concept vary, but they generally center around the characteristics people attribute to themselves. Scholars see this view grounded in either an internal, primarily psychological source, or an external, sociological, source relying on the appraisals of others. Self-concept is "a vague but vitally felt idea of what I am like in my best moments, of what I am striving toward and have some encouragement to believe I can achieve, or of what I can do when the situation supplies incentives for unqualified effort" (Turner, 1968, p. 98). Thus, self-concept can be viewed as a theory that a person holds about himself in interaction with the rest of the world (Epstein, 1973).

When infants interact with their families and, subsequently, with others in their culture, their personalities and self-concepts gradually are formed (Costa & McCrae, 1980). While they bring a set of talents and characteristics to these interactions, their interpretations of their qualities and of their value in a social context are constructed through this series of interactions. This process is sometimes conceptualized as the internalization of the social expectations and values surrounding each person, although researchers do not agree about the relative power of others' views to change a self-concept. Shrauger and Schoeneman (1979) concluded, following a review of fifty studies of self-concept, that the power of others' opinions to affect the adult self-concept is in doubt. They asserted that people's self-perceptions and their beliefs about ways in which others perceive them agree substantially. But self-perceptions and others' actual views are poorly related.

A substantial majority of sociologists see socialization as the primary process through which infants and children develop a self-concept. These scholars see the internalization of social assessments of the self as the outcome—a passive individual process of receiving social conditioning. In part, this view derives from the work of Margaret Mead and others who sought the "cultural antecedents of the personality" (Wentworth, 1980, p. 24). Early in life, children's interactions are most frequently with people important to them, and the credibility and value of other's evaluations have been found to significantly affect children's self-concept (Webster & Sobieszek, 1974). In adults, as well, many conceive of self-concept as a form of negotiated identity, "inseparable cause and consequence in social interaction" (Gecas, 1982, p. 11) or an outcome of the internal dialogue with self (Blumer, 1969). Whatever the balance of socially constructed or innate self-concepts (the nature-nurture debate), the socialization experiences of children that result in a fairly stable self-concept by the time they are young adults are often called primary socialization. Mead (1934) described this stable image of the self as a structured set of meanings that people have about themselves in all situations.

The relative stability of the core self-concept affects the process and outcomes of social interaction, especially during critical events such as leader succession. A number of interaction theories acknowledge that self-esteem and consistency are important factors shaping interaction (i.e., dramaturgical analyses and role theory). Some scholars, pointing to highly successful self-monitors (to use Goffman's term), suggest that no stable self-concept exists, that all is situational. Giddens's (1984) inquiry convinced him that this was not the case, that concepts of self become ingrained so that people can draw on them in a self-monitored dialogue or "discursive consciousness" that allows them to talk about and explain their actions to themselves. Concepts of self provide an unconscious "practical consciousness" on which they can draw while, at the same time, adding new information from their interactions with others to their stocks of practical knowledge. Whatever the case, a new leader immediately finds the self in question and under scrutiny by the group.

Situational Self-concept. The focus of this book is change—a change among formal leaders in schools. Change exerts pressure derived from the situation. A substantial body of research provides evidence that cumulative adult experiences shape situational self-concepts that may differ from their beliefs about the stable, best self. Ongoing interactions affect people's concepts of themselves, their abilities, skills, and interests in particular groups—in higher education, at work, and in the community. These experiences are classified as secondary socialization (Wentworth, 1980).

> Secondary socialization is...specific (adult) role-oriented learning of functional utility for the system. Whereas the "actor" is the significant unit for the personality system, the "role" is the basic unit of the social system; during secondary socialization they meet and become one. (Wentworth, 1980, p. 36)

Symbolic interactionism theory provides one explanation for the processes through which gradual changes in core and situational self-concepts occur (Blumer, 1969). During the course of an important event such as succession, people's actions become stimuli for the actions of others, which are received, interpreted, and given a response in turn. The response action becomes both a response and a new stimulus, and the interpretations a person gives to this feedback process become a reflective form of self-conditioning (Mead, 1934). Using the metaphor of a scientific experiment involving the conditioning of a rat, Morris (in Mead, 1934, p. xviii) explained that symbolic interactionism

> is able to give a penetrating analysis of such reflection in terms of the self-conditioning of the organism to future stimuli in virtue of being able to indicate to itself through symbols the consequences of certain types of response to such stimuli. This account is able to explain the behavior of [the scientist] in conditioning the rat, and not merely the resulting behavior of the conditioned rat.

It also provides the scientist with a way to examine her own responses.

Investiture and divestiture (reviewed in Chapter 1) are two situational factors in succession that affect the situational self-concept. Van Maanen and Schein (1979) theorized that these processes function in all organizational socialization experiences. Investiture ratifies and confirms the viability and usefulness of the personal characteristics of new group members. It tends to be smooth and trouble free. Divestiture serves a different purpose, stripping away the value of new members' existing characteristics and rebuilding the self-image based on assumptions in the new setting.

Attempts to apply the notion of self-concept to theories about people's behavior and growth in work situations illustrate the importance of the self-concept in understanding how people choose to act during a leader succession event. A central feature of self-concept in interaction theory holds that, in various situations (like those in which a formal leader works to affect the attitudes and actions of the group), people conceive of themselves in ways uniquely suited to the particular situation. A principal might have one concept of herself in association with leadership in a school, another formed as a result of volunteer work in the community, another centered in experiences as a teacher. These self-concepts and the roles people play in organizations can sometime come into conflict (Bacharach,

Bamberger & Conley, 1990). Situational self-concept thus plays an important part in understanding social interactions among adults developing in part as a result of secondary socialization experiences—"the learning of social roles" (Merton, Reader & Kendall, 1957). The experienced world creates transitory images of the self in a particular interaction setting (Mead, 1934). "Short-term events do not easily change a person's values, but they can change the subset of values that guide action at a particular time" (Smith & Peterson, 1988, p. 52).

Adults typically move in and out of many important groups during their lifetimes, some of them related to work. When moving into their field of work, people experience some of the most intense secondary socialization experiences they will have. Consequently, the initial induction into a profession (the professional socialization reviewed in Chapter 1) is often the focus of scholars' attention when studying situational self-concept. "Professional socialization is. . . multidimensional in that students simultaneously acquire new views of self along with role behaviors" (Olesen & Whittaker, 1977, p. 160).

Jarring transitions to new settings (those that a person feels are unsuccessful) challenge the situational self-concept. People often mobilize to do something about these assaults (Swann, 1983). They also act to affect the dynamics they are experiencing. These actions then reestablish a "predictable and patterned rhythm to interactions" (Turner, 1988, p. 60). Understanding this normal course of events in which anxiety results from nonroutine and unintegrated social relations, new managers can make efforts to set up routines and social integration (Giddens, 1984). Anxiety experienced when tension between the dispositional and situational self or the core self and the peripheral self occurs in a new situation can be the target of deliberate action by the person involved who is "mobilized to do something about it" (Turner, 1988). Many of the dynamics observed in leader succession research may be an outgrowth of this process—the movement to rectify incongruencies between succession feedback and situational self-concept. The stress and conflict associated with transition and change in work arrangements in schools is well documented (Bacharach, Bamberger & Mitchell, 1990).

Scholars examining instructional leadership among principals provide vivid examples of the potential impacts of stable versus variable professional self-concepts (Leithwood, Steinbach & Begley, in press). In one study, the resilience of firm professional identities was aptly demonstrated by principals who were given many experiences designed to socialize them as instructional leaders yet continued to choose action priorities focused on legal and managerial issues.

Others see the constant adjustment in situational self-concept as less disturbing, more a part of the normal course of life events. When people detect discrepancies between a contextual standard and their own behavior, they simply seek to reduce the discrepancy (Carver & Scheier, 1981). When this system breaks down, self-assessment dysfunctions lead to inappropriate or unproductive behavior (Ashford, 1989).

Concepts of Others

Just as scholars recognize core and situational self-concepts, they divide views of others in social settings into two groups (Mead, 1934): generalized others or all others; and communities of others from which to evaluate oneself and orient responses. These communities not only have certain characteristics in common, they also possess "stocks of knowledge" (Schutz, 1932). From this last concept of others, a new principal might choose to act on the basis of his beliefs about what teachers know and believe, generalizing to all teachers or all teachers in similar schools.

Beliefs held about others thus play an important part in the interaction processes between new principals and schools. As the discussion about symbolic interactionism above illustrates, people take on the roles or interpret the gestures of others and mentally assume a perspective they believe is congruent with the attitudes of the group with which they are communicating—they assume a perspective of the generalized other or communities of attitudes to frame their self-evaluation and shape their conduct. New principals' beliefs about the others in the school coupled with their concepts of self as principals would be primary variables determining how they think, communicate, and interpret the responses of others. When the new principal is well integrated, he learns the social norms of the group and comes to see himself as part of the school.

Schein described how this abstract notion of self and others plays itself out when formally appointed leaders interact with the collective others in their groups:

> [W]hen we observe that the behavior of a number of people is coordinated into a larger pattern, that there is a consistency among a number of separate elements, we are led to generalizations about how formal or informal a given organization is, how autocratic, bureaucratic, or participative it is, or how open or closed it seems to be. (Schein, 1985, p. 26)

New group members then look for patterns because they cannot productively deal with randomness or meaninglessness. He also argued that this construct of "stocks of knowledge" or generalized other constituting patterns of behavior affects the success of attempts to merge two or more existing groups. Using the analogy of corporate mergers, he pointed out that "the philosophy or style of the company; its technological origins, which might provide clues as to its basic assumptions; and its beliefs about its mission and its future" often explain the failures of such mergers (Schein, 1985, p. 34). Schein appealed in part to sociodynamics theory (Alderfer & Cooper, 1980; Schein & Bennis, 1965) to help explain how and why people share a common view in integrated groups. Revealing interpersonal and emotional processes related to inclusion and identity and to control, power, influence, acceptance, and intimacy, he asserted that no attempt to understand leadership can ignore these social variables (Schein, 1985, p. 150).

These factors in sociodynamics make it difficult for anyone to exercise leadership in mature organizations where cultures are firmly established over time. They make the outcomes of school culture and principal succession studies focused on culture much less puzzling, however. These organizational cultures form the social structure in which the interactions of organizational socialization during leader succession take place.

Establishing Structures of Interaction

In the introduction to this chapter, structuring processes were defined as those interactional processes that allow people to organize and repeat interactions in a stable pattern over time. When combined with accepted and ongoing roles, the imbedded social structure of the group is created.

A major portion of this imbedded structure is embodied in organizational culture. Schein (1985) emphasized that the culture of an organization is more than behavioral regularities, norms, values, philosophy, rules, or climate. It is

the deeper level of *basic assumptions* and *beliefs* that are shared by members of an organization, that operate unconsciously, and that define in a basic "taken-for-granted" fashion an organization's view of itself and its environment. These assumptions and beliefs are *learned* responses to a group's problems of *survival* in its external environment and its problems of *internal integration*. They come to be taken for granted because they solve those problems repeatedly and reliably. This deeper level of assumptions is to be distinguished from the "artifacts" and "values" that are manifestations or surface levels of culture but not the essence of culture. (pp. 6–7)

The patterned and accepted nature of culture in this definition is critical to understanding its fundamental part in group interactions during socialization as it is "taught to new members as the correct way to perceive, think, and feel in relation" to the problems the group faces (Schein, 1985, p. 9). Into this established structure of behaviors and roles—characteristic, systematic patterns of interactions among elements of a social group—newly appointed formal leaders must move, seeking to affect and shape productive behaviors as an outsider and new member also subject to the socialization interactions experienced by all new members (Biddle & Thomas, 1966; Sergiovanni, 1987b).

Two underlying features are included in this definition—roles and interaction processes repeated in established patterns over time. Both of these features are important aspects of schools confronted by new principals and deserve further elaboration.

Roles. "The concept of role provides the basic mechanism which links individuals and larger social systems without losing track of either the individual or the system" (Smith & Peterson, 1988, p. 73). Role theory provides a concise view of constructs that define the nature of roles in social groups such as schools (Stryker & Statham,1985). According to the precepts of role theory, roles are associated with social positions—such as principal—that constitute forms of identity and fulfill established functions within the group. They designate a commonly recognized set of persons, and each role incumbent is expected to behave in characteristic ways that define the role. While each person filling a role is unique in many ways, people who share a role also share a common identity. Behavior expected of those in a role and adherence to the norms and values associated with a role are induced by the group through shared expectations. Also through these expectations, the group teaches and enforces appropriate behaviors. The experiences described as socialization are common means of role learning (Biddle, 1979; Biddle & Thomas, 1966).

One must take care not to overrationalize the concept of role. People fill many roles at the same time and experience conflicting pressures from different constituencies related to the same role (see the common descriptions of the principalship in textbooks used in educational administration programs). Many conflicting demands develop within roles and between the roles people hold at the same time (principal, son, mother, husband, community leader, church member, political party member). These pressures often are experienced as vague discomfort. When people perceive conflicting or incompatible role expectations from within a group or from different social groups, they experience role stress, which can take the form of conflict, overload, or ambiguity (Bacharach, Bamberger & Conley, 1990, 1991; Bacharach, Bamberger & Mitchell, 1990).

Two outcomes can be identified from the intersection of interaction and role theory: role taking (personal development to fill a role) and role making (role development) (Nicholson, 1984; Nicholson & West, 1988; Turner, 1962). When people largely internalize the existing social definition of a role like the high school principalship, they experience primarily role taking. Through a process of continual testing and reframing people assess their success at fulfilling the role expectations of the group in very conventional ways. This is exactly what Greenfield (1985a, 1985b) observed in the majority of principal successions and professional socialization experiences. Recently Oliver (1992) observed the same outcome.

Role making or role development occurs when a person substantially modifies the tasks, expectations, norms, or beliefs about a social role. In role making people consciously and unconsciously orchestrate their own behavior in order to assert themselves as they enact and alter the role. When role making occurs in schools, the faculty, parents, and others alter their expectations of the principal as a result of the actions of the person filling the role.

This discussion oversimplifies these two outcomes—role taking and role making. For the purposes of discussion it is easier to make them appear discrete and isolated, but they include features of flux and adjustment that make complex a change in the status quo during periods of change like a leader succession. "On the one hand, situations are said to be emergent and unique, while on the other, role learning, roles, and organizations are possible" (Wentworth, 1980, pp. 51–52). Consequently, role taking and role making provide ways of analyzing the process through which new principals enter and affect a school, but they do not provide definitive snapshots of discretely different outcomes.

Leadership research illustrates this complexity. Phillips (1984) found in experimental research that people's expectations about effective leadership outweigh their own observations of effective leaders when they are asked to categorize people as effective or ineffective leaders. The concept or image of an effective leader they subscribe to is more important than their observations of leaders. Others agree: "[T]he category [people] place a leader into is determined by their belief about how effective the leader is as well as by what they actually see the leader do. . . . As long as a characterization of a leader fits the prototype they have established, they will agree with it" (Smith & Peterson, 1988, p.42). These attributions of leaders' effectiveness and characteristics play a part in the combination of personal perceptions, causal inferences, and assignments of responsibility people make when they assess a leader's effects (Lord & Smith, 1983; Ross & Fletcher, 1985).

Writers disagree over the relative freedom people possess to deviate from established norms. Some argue that role structures preclude the possibility that individual leaders will vary within them (Pfeffer, 1981a). They use this argument to explain why school principals are so much alike and have so little direct impact on student performance. Others disagree, while acknowledging the restraining power of firmly established roles: "The creation of roles is an ongoing, indeterminate process, not a quickly reached conclusion" (Smith & Peterson, 1988, p. 74). In addition to their variability, socially constructed roles include a number of facets. Schein (1971b) defined organizational roles as functional, hierarchical, and inclusionary. Functional roles relate to the tasks at hand; hierarchical roles relate to the distribution of rank and responsibility over the actions of others; and inclusionary roles relate to relationships in the social fabric or interpersonal inclusion with the organization. Each particular role has a combination of facets that create the overall role.

Studies of head teachers in England can be used to illustrate these facets of role, which combine to create a sense of isolation in newcomers (Weindling & Earley, 1987, p. 122). Functionally, respondents in one study said, while deputy heads are permitted to "plead ignorance and learn gradually," the head often is "expected to know all the answers immediately." Hierarchically, they are expected to function as mediators between diverse and conflicting interest groups—teachers, parents, pupils, governors, local education authority officers, and the community at large. Their inclusionary role is altered because they "must be prepared to give up the day-to-day camaraderie of the staffroom." This isolation has parallels in the United States. In one study of new principals, the author concluded; "By far the greatest sources of surprise were personal and job-related. Subjects conveyed considerable emotion as they described the unexpected loneliness of the principalship, the unanticipated time press, and the disconcerting feelings of unpreparedness" (Duke et al., 1984, p. 26).

Other views of role facets affecting socialization focus on the scope and demands associated with a role rather than on tasks, hierarchy, and inclusion (Frese, 1982; Mortimer & Simmons, 1978). Nicholson (1984) contended in his theory of work role transition that scope of control and demanding and novel tasks play an important part in the change process. He hypothesized that in roles involving moderate amounts of discretion and novelty and in the absence of other constraints, people are most able to influence the outcomes of their own transitions and shape their own experiences during socialization.

Role clarity is yet another facet of roles operating to affect organizational socialization. Wanous said that new members must be initiated to the tasks of a new job; define their own interpersonal roles with respect to peers, subordinates, and superiors; learn to cope with resistance to change; develop congruence between their own evaluation of their performance and the apparent evaluation of established members of the organization; and learn to work within the given degree of structure and ambiguity (1980, p. 180). Each of these facets appears to some degree in the research reviewed in Chapters 1 and 2 related to leader succession and organizational socialization.

Processes and Roles. A number of specific features of interaction related directly to role constructs deserve reiteration at this point in the discussion of interaction theories. In the case of leaders, role success relies on the outcomes of interactions with others and in large part on the new leader's ability to shape the understanding of others in the group. One can argue that

> The effectiveness of a leader lies in his ability to make activity meaningful for those in his role set—not to change behavior but to give others a sense of understanding what they are doing and especially to articulate it so they can communicate about the meaning of their behavior. . . . If in addition the leader *can put it into words* then the meaning of what the group is doing becomes a *social* fact. . . .This dual capacity. . .to make sense of things *and* to put them into language meaningful to large numbers of people gives the person who has it enormous leverage. (Pondy, 1978, pp. 94–95)

When formal leaders are new to the group, the function of language and sense making become even more important. Leaders must go through a period in which the liabilities of newness apply to them, *and* they must move into a position where they begin to influence the sense making of group members (Allen & van de Vliert, 1984). This relationship is particularly precarious because it relies heavily on social relations between strangers, and trust is more precarious (Stinchcome, 1971). This is a tenuous relationship: "Meaning can only rarely be unilaterally defined. A good deal of managerial success in influencing subordinates as intended is likely to rest upon intimate knowledge of subordinates' goals and their beliefs as to how those goals may be accomplished" (Smith & Peterson, 1988, p. 122).

When superintendent succession and culture are examined in concert, researchers affirm this dynamic, saying, "The stories that count are not created by those who participate in the drama but by those who tell about it, often people other than the executive." Yet, "where executives successfully modify organizational culture, their symbolic work is more successful than that of the keepers of the previous culture" (Firestone, 1989, pp. 3, 4). Experienced mentors often pass on the strong culture to new members. Greenfield (1985b), in fact, links the moral orientation of new principals to that of their principal mentors. Social learning theory explains how this happens: "The performer's behavior conveys information to observers about the characteristics of appropriate responses. Observers must abstract common attributes exemplified in diverse modeled responses and formulate a principle for generating similar patterns of behavior" (Bandura, 1972, p. 37). Role models are important, and so are social learning processes (Bandura, 1978). What people learn about their work roles in organizations is often a direct result of how they learn it.

> Any organizational culture consists broadly of long-standing rules of thumb, a somewhat special language, an ideology that helps edit a member's everyday experience, shared standards of relevance as to the prejudices, models of social etiquette and demeanor, certain customs and rituals suggestive of how members are to relate to colleagues, subordinates, superiors, and outsiders, and a sort of residual category of some rather plain "horse sense" regarding what is appropriate and "smart" behavior within the organization and what is not. All of these cultural models of thinking, feeling, and doing are, of course, fragmented to some degree, giving rise within large organizations to various "subcultures" or "organizational segments." (Van Maanen & Schein, 1979, p. 210)

Examples of the impact of interactions between a new formal leader and an established culture can be found in education research. In one study of "cultural politics" and the managerial succession of superintendents, Firestone (1989, p. 27) found that one superintendent "neither sought nor assumed a role that would facilitate the adoption of the values and interpretations congruent with the formal changes he initiated." This superintendent, who failed to accomplish his goals and left the school district, was never fully integrated, was never accepted as an insider, was never accorded moral legitimacy. He was never socialized into the group to an extent allowing others in the district to give him influence over their values and beliefs.

Environment: Personal and Group Context. In the preceding discussion, the complex interaction of leaders with groups plays a critical part. The nature of existing cultures is viewed as influential in shaping the outcomes of a leader succession. This is not an unconventional view. Martin et al. (1983) describe seven categories of stories that are told and recur in all organizations about how things are done that exert strong influence over organizational outcomes, and three of these categories relate to leadership: "Is the big boss human?"; "Rulebreaking"; and "How will the boss react to mistakes?" The first category of story tells how a superior will act when given opportunity to perform a status-equalizing act. The second category tells how the leader and others in the group interact when confronted with rules or when a senior manager breaks a rule and is then confronted by a junior person. The third category involves the nature of a leader's behavior when subordinates make mistakes. These categories of stories illustrate the critical impact of the personal and group context in shaping leader successions.

Other researchers talk about the ways in which newcomers can learn about the context in which they must function, about the existing culture. Schein (1985, pp. 114–118), for example, listed questions researchers trying to uncover an organizational culture might ask. These questions can easily be adapted to offer advice to new principals:

1. Early in the entry stage, structure active experiences and systematic observation and then deliberately note surprises (Louis, 1980b).
2. By using systematic observation and checking to calibrate surprising experiences, verify that surprising events indeed repeat and are not idiosyncratic. They are part of the school culture.

3. Locate an insider who can (and is willing to) analytically decipher and explain what is going on.
4. Use insiders to reveal surprises and puzzles and to verify hunches. Avoid abstractions and generalizations.
5. Jointly explore possible cultural descriptions with others in the school to find explanations; systematically probe for underlying assumptions and patterns.
6. Formalize explanations that make sense and state operational values that can be derived from observable behavior.
7. Systematically check conclusions with existing documents and records, stories, and other artifacts, in formal conversations, using systematic observations.
8. Push to the level of assumptions. Try to go beyond the articulated values of group members, and try to understand the deeper layer of assumptions behind them.
9. Perpetually recalibrate and adjust your conclusions about the culture as new data continually surface.
10. Formalize the assessment of culture through a written description.

Schein persuasively asserted that a new leader must develop an understanding of an existing cultural environment in order to use it to the advantage of the organization.

Once culture is viewed as a social design that supersedes specific behaviors, it can better be used to understand the context in which leader socialization takes place in a school or other form of organization. Culture can then be viewed as a set of principles organizing the encounters of the new principal with established members of the group.

Outcomes

When organizational socialization begins to take hold and the new principal or other school leader becomes an established group member, many writers conceptualize the result as a new social structure. These new structures may or may not be substantially different from those that preceded the new member's entry, but a number of outcomes have been described. Schein (1971b), for example, offered a useful set of outcome categories for structural responses to socialization:

1. Custodianship. A custodial response often reflects a newcomer's conclusion that the inherited past may have much to recommend it in supporting survival in the organization and functional achievement. The newcomer simply learns the substantive requirements of the job and customary strategies to meet these requirements. A custodial response can occur in both technical and moral socialization in Greenfield's analysis of professional socialization. Its distinguishing feature is its replication.

2. Content Innovation. When content innovation results, the novice has been unwilling for a variety of reasons to limit his or her enactment of the role to the knowledge base transmitted directly through the socialization process. Changes can be made in tactical alternatives as means to certain ends. Substantive changes or improvements in knowledge base or strategic practices can also be made. While traditional norms and ends are accepted, existing strategies or technologies in use are not.

3. Role Innovation. Role innovation is the most radical structural change associated with socialization. During role innovation, the new member may attack and attempt to change the mission associated with the role. In addition to the strategies for accomplishing goals, he or she successfully rejects most of the norms governing conduct and performance of the role, redefining the "ends to which the role functions" (p. 228).

These three structuring outcomes—custodianship, content innovation, and role innovation—do not occur with equal frequency. The most common outcome, even when it is not functional, is custodianship. Much of the organizational socialization literature reviewed in Chapter 1 focuses on ways to enhance the contribution of new members (avoiding custodianship) while retaining the best features of the existing culture or social structure. Furthermore, social systems theories illustrate how difficult changes in structure are and how interactive content and structure can be:

> It is because of the power of past socialization, that is, the tendency for old-system norms to persist so that they may interfere with proper component action in a new system, that students of industrial and other production often recommend a thorough change of personnel in a new system rather than a retraining of the old. (Monane, 1967, p. 19)

When we examine the individual aspects of organizational socialization that affect structure, we bring the discussion full circle. This "paradox of mutual indeterminism" (Skidmore, 1975) may have discouraged the development of organizational socialization frameworks for the study of leader succession. While individuals and the social groups to which they belong depend on each other and affect and shape each other, the relative proportion of influence exerted by one or the other is undetermined.

The related concept of "reciprocal determination" (Bandura, 1978), however, provides a more positive view of inquiry into the mutual effects of formal leaders and groups on each other. Each affects the other, providing guidance related to action in practice and further exploration through research. In management socialization research, for example, newcomers to organizations have been found to use their images of themselves as well as their beliefs about others to evaluate and define their new work situation. They also use these referent points when choosing to act in innovative ways in their new assignments. Those high in self-efficacy tend to define new situations in personal terms, even though their roles are tightly prescribed by the organization. The newcomer thus exerts considerable influence over the definition of the role (Jones, 1986).

Intraorganization power and political analyses, although approaching the study of organizations from a perspective quite different from social learning, affirm the presence of reciprocal determination (Bacharach & Lawler, 1981). Blau (1964, pp. 199–200) summarized the critical importance of the reciprocal relationship as it relates to power, emphasizing the importance of reciprocity in social relations and equilibrium in social structures: "Stable organizing power requires legitimation. To be sure, men [sic] can be made to work and to obey commands through coercion, but the coercive use of power engenders resistance and sometimes active opposition." Using cognitive dissonance theory to explain this effect (Festinger, 1957), Blau goes on to say that, once the group coalesces around support for a new leader,

> shared feelings of loyalty and group norms tend to emerge that make compliance with [the leader's] directives a *social* obligation that is enforced by the subordinates themselves. (p. 207)...The crucial problem for the formal leader, with undeniable power, is to win the loyalty and legitimating approval of subordinates, particularly since his power may tempt him to dominate them instead of winning their respect and willing compliance. (p. 210)

Through this process, legitimation becomes "publicly effective" (Mills, 1959, p. 37). The political exchanges that take place within organizations offer new and insightful views of schools as well. Ball (1987) and, later, Blase (1989) uncovered persuasive evidence that the micropolitical framework reveals much about the organizational outcomes in schools that we may have previously attributed to leaders acting on their own. This power of shared feelings and mutually negotiated realities may explain why Gabarro found that a major determinant of the outcomes of managerial succession is the development of effective working relationships: "The inherent social disruption caused by successions may be one reason why a new manager's ability to develop effective working relationships discriminates so strongly between the failed and successful successions" (Gabarro, 1987, p. 166).

Yet, the difficulty of achieving legitimacy in the group should not be underestimated. Roberts and Wright (1989) argued that this task is one of the most difficult new principals face. Following a one-year study of first-time high school principals, they concluded that

> beginning high school principals reported critical challenges of their first year most frequently in the areas of student management, personal overload, instruction, and most seriously, in the general area of *mobilizing frequently strong, resistant, experienced teachers (or clearly unmotivated teachers) with whom the new principal often lacked credibility* [emphasis added]. (Roberts & Wright, in press, p. 12)

Studies of principals' behavior affirm the influence of the interaction context on outcomes. Martinko and Gardner (1984, 1987) studied high- and moderate-performing elementary and high school principals in an attempt to distinguish differences in their behaviors. Using trained observers, the researchers collected coded observation data on behavior according to the role, ethnic group, and gender of the person with whom it occurred. They applied various coding schemes based on Mintzberg's event categories and Luthan and Lockwood's Leadership Observation System, but could find no distinguishing differences between the high- and moderate-performing principals. Performance for their study was judged according to four criteria: (1) the school's performance on state minimal competence exams, with statistical controls for socioeconomic factors; (2) the school's rank within the district on national achievement test scores; (3) superintendents' ranking of the schools; and (4) superintendents' ranking of the principals. However, the researchers found substantial relationships between various dimensions of school *context* and the behavior of the principals.

The complexity of interactions among people in the context also makes it impossible to definitively judge the essence of and relative usefulness or goodness of particular values within a culture. Schein (1985) suggested strongly that leaders are judged on the basis of criteria drawn from the context, so cultures are good or bad in relation to each value within each context. Evidence is mounting, in fact, that prescriptive models that define a "good culture," such as that offered by Peters and Waterman (1982), are either incomplete or wrong (Hitt & Ireland, 1987). Describing the experience principals often have when attempting to influence school culture, Deal and Peterson (1990, p. 14) pointed out that

> a school's culture has been created well before most principals arrive; it will exist long after most leave. Only a few principals may have the opportunity to start afresh in a brand-new school, but even then the new teachers and students will carry cultural imprints from their previous place—as will the principal.

> Most principals must work with a cultural tapestry that is already woven. They must somehow reinforce thin spots or tears, shape it to cover different or changed surfaces, or even try to reverse the fabric without unraveling the shared meaning. There is a delicate balance between a principal's doing nothing and doing harm. The Chinese call this balance *wei-wu,* the place between inaction and undue force. This balance is at the center of effective symbolic leadership and cultural change.

These authors reinforce the criticality of interactions among individuals (albeit powerful individuals, like principals) and the schools in which they work as outcomes emerge.

Summary

This chapter introduced some concepts from the social and behavioral sciences on which organizational socialization theory is based. These perspectives draw on the study of interaction between groups and individuals and among individuals to understand what happens to people when they join work organizations. The motivation to interact, interaction processes, and the structural outcomes of interaction form the major aspects of these frameworks. Multiple process theories of interaction help explain how utility, behavior, exchange, ritual, and information interpretation shape the outcomes of organizational socialization. In order to explore these aspects further, researchers have delved into situational and core self-concepts, concepts of others and their roles in social groups, and the importance of organizational structures as the setting for all socialization experiences.

These research and theoretical traditions provide plausible explanations for and predictions of observed dynamics and outcomes during organizational socialization. In the next section, the four themes drawn from organizational socialization and discussed in Chapter 1 are applied to specific studies of principal succession to illustrate these effects. Each central theme is used to show how organizational socialization adds important insights to the original research frameworks applied to these succession studies.

II

Principals in Succession:
A Potpourri of Experiences

This section takes a substantially different approach to this inquiry into principal succession. Moving away from the discussion of background material on leader succession and organizational socialization presented in Section I, Section II examines quantitative and qualitative research on principal succession and cases prepared specifically to examine leader succession. The chapters examine challenges that principals have experienced in real schools. They use the frameworks drawn from theory and research presented in Section I to seek understanding and insight into the nature of the leader succession experience in schools for all those involved.

Chapter 4 is a succession case presented from the point of view of a faculty. The researchers who conducted the inquiry concluded that the process resulted in retrenchment and disillusionment on the part of most of the adults who worked in the school. The principal arrived in an atmosphere of promise and anticipation that degenerated into cautious resentment by the end of the year. While some supporters maintained at the end of the first year that the principal was "biding his time," most concluded that nothing of substance was going to change.

Chapter 5 presents a slightly different perspective: a succession case from the viewpoint of the successor and other insider informants that began in an atmosphere of suspicion and resentment and ended in a reasonably productive experience for most of the participants. While a positive assessment prevailed, some involved remained convinced that the original problems with the new principal were irreconcilable. However, the majority of parents, teachers, and staff chose to act on the options for change made available to them by the succession.

Chapter 6 takes a slightly different approach, combining a number of different studies of principal succession and principal professional socialization, relying on qualitative and quantitative data to further explore the utility of organizational socialization as a framework for understanding and improving leader succession experiences and research. This chapter applies many of the insights achieved through the analyses of cases in Chapters 4 and 5 to a broader look at the interactive processes that shape leader succession outcomes.

4

A Faculty's Perspective of a Succession[1]

The Setting

Valley Elementary School[2] was a small school of about four hundred students located in the northern part of a large western school district. The district included a number of suburbs and small cities near a large metropolitan area. Most of Valley School's students were the children of white, suburban, working class families. According to the staff at Valley, families in the area tended to be stable with both parents present in the household. Both parents in the home often worked. The small, well-groomed tract homes adjacent to the school reflected the social and economic characteristics of their occupants.

The Valley Elementary building was typical of elementary schools in the area. Twenty-two years old, it was a single-story building with a low, flat roof. A row of large glass windows shaded with venetian blinds stretched across both the front and rear of the building. A wide lawn, concrete sidewalk, and flagpole dominated the front of the building. Shrubbery, tucked under the windows, covered the front wall. On the eastern end of the building, an asphalt parking lot provided more than ample parking for teachers and guests. An asphalt playground with one basketball standard (in serious disrepair) was located behind the school. Beyond the asphalt, a large lawn, bordered on all sides by the backyards of adjacent homes, provided an expansive play area for students.

The double glass doors of the main entrance led directly into the central module of the school. This central area contained a room that served as a cafeteria and multipurpose room, a gymnasium and auditorium, the office, and the faculty lounge. Two long, uncluttered corridors flanked on both sides by classrooms extended out from this central area. The classrooms in the eastern corridor were reserved for grades three through six, while the western corridor contained classrooms for kindergarten through second grade. Like most elementary schools, the walls of Valley Elementary's halls were covered with students' art work and a variety of handmade posters.

The Participants

Three important groups of people affected the faculty's assessment of their principal's succession: the two principals—predecessor and successor, two school secretaries, and the teachers. Prior to the succession, the Valley Elementary School had twenty classroom teachers, one of whom was a half-time kindergarten teacher. The school also had two special education teachers. In addition, a media coordinator, a psychologist, and a social worker visited Valley on a regular basis. Seventeen women and five men taught at Valley. All the teachers, like most of their students, were Caucasian. Most of the teachers lived in the surrounding neighborhoods.

Valley's faculty was experienced and stable. Their experience in the profession ranged from five to twenty years, while their tenures at Valley ranged from four to sixteen years. Most also were born and raised in the local community or state.

After the succession, there were few changes in the faculty. Two new teachers who had just graduated and were serving in their first teaching assignments replaced two teachers who left for unspecified reasons. Both new teachers, like those they replaced, were Caucasian women.

Mr. Brown, the predecessor principal, worked in the school district for thirty-five years, first as an elementary teacher and then as a principal. He was a principal for nineteen years, twelve of which were spent at Valley—an uncommonly long tenure at one school among the district's principals. Mr. Brown held a master's degree in educational administration from a nearby university. Like most principals, Mr. Brown was white, male, active in community activities (in this case, his church), and raised and educated locally.

The successor principal, Dr. Hamilton, had worked in the district for twenty-three years. He began his career as a junior high school social studies teacher. He quickly transferred to a high school, where he also taught social studies. After teaching on the secondary level for four years, Dr. Hamilton, at the suggestion of a superior, moved to the elementary level to prepare himself for a career in administration. He felt that the move was necessary, because most administrators in the district began their administrative careers as principals of elementary schools. After teaching at the elementary level for two years, Dr. Hamilton received his first appointment as elementary school principal. Over his seventeen-year career, Dr. Hamilton served as the principal of three elementary schools. Valley Elementary School was his fourth administrative assignment.

Dr. Hamilton held three degrees, all earned from the same local university—a bachelor's degree in secondary education, a master's degree in secondary administration, and a doctorate in educational administration. He was born, raised, and educated in the immediate area and pursued his career there.

Viola ("Vi") Fowler had been the secretary at Valley for nineteen years. She preceded Mr. Brown by seven years. A widow, Vi devoted herself to the school. During her time at Valley, she developed very close relationships with several of the teachers and with Mr. Brown, the principal. She was a fixture, someone who had been a part of Valley Elementary School as long as anyone who worked there could remember.

How the Faculty Experienced the Succession

The succession of the principal unfolded for the faculty in four stages. First, upon finding that their principal was retiring, teachers began to think about opening school in the fall with a new principal. They expressed anticipation about possible positive changes and fears that their independence might be violated by a new administrator. One faculty member said that the last thing he wanted was some new principal who wanted to change the world in a year. Second, based upon the fears and expectations with which they approached the arrival of a new principal, the faculty generally found that the successor more than fulfilled their hopes. His surface characteristics matched their expressed hope for a cordial, charismatic leader, and he seemed to leave them alone to teach their classes, a highly valued trait. Third, the initial enchantment gave way to a period of distress for the faculty. In an atmosphere of ambiguity, insecurity, and anger—coming to a head with the transfer of the school secretary—the faculty began to question the successor's commitment to Valley. Fourth, teachers resigned themselves to the existing situation and retreated to their classrooms. Many teachers, assuming that the principal was simply biding his time, continued to expect him to make changes in the school. Teachers approached the end of the school year much as they had approached the previous year, expecting changes but not knowing what form they would take. This time an aura of mistrust rather than hopeful expectation pervaded the atmosphere.

Looking Ahead

Although Mr. Brown had notified the district in March that he would retire at the end of the school year, he decided not to inform the teachers until the last day of school. Vi was the only person on the school's staff in whom he confided. He explained that he did not want people to make an event out of his retirement. According to several teachers, however, rumors were flying about Mr. Brown's impending retirement from early in the school year. It was far from a secret. Finally, Mr. Brown found that a family friend had confirmed his decision to some of the teachers. On April 26, he announced his retirement at a faculty meeting.

The first reaction of the teachers when the rumors of Mr. Brown's retirement were verified was a sense of detachment. This detachment manifested itself in two ways. First, teachers were not involved directly in the succession process. They explained, "Teachers often get called upon to provide input on new curriculum and instructional materials, but not on selecting a principal." They had little reason to feel any involvement in the succession at this stage. The choice of Mr. Brown's successor, according to district administrators, was made entirely at the district level. District officials simply assigned one member of a pool of available administrators to the post at Valley Elementary. That pool included experienced principals designated for reassignment and newly appointed principals awaiting their first assignments.

District officials also revealed that, while they did seek input from leaders among the parents of Valley Elementary School's students about the kind of person they desired as the next principal, they did not request input from teachers. One administrator noted that teachers should not be involved in the selection of principals, because "every teacher has a different opinion." Once the appointment was made, the school district informed Mr. Brown of their choice. Mr. Brown then informed the teachers.

In the days that followed Mr. Brown's announcement, little mention was made of his retirement or the prospects of having a new principal at Valley Elementary. A week and a half after learning that Mr. Brown would be leaving the school, a teacher commented in the faculty lounge that she wished that the district would reveal the name of the new principal. She concluded, "They'll probably announce it during the summer. We'll probably find out about it when we read it in the newspaper." The teachers' emotional distance did not prevent them from throwing a farewell party for Mr. Brown, however. And, although some described him as a "vanilla" principal, they showed genuine affection for him. He was a nice person.

A second reason for the teachers' detachment was grounded in their interpretation of a principal's role in any school. Approximately one-third of the teachers said that a change of principals simply would have little effect on them. One teacher explained: "It doesn't really matter that much." She recounted the following story. She had worked in another school before coming to Valley. In that school, the principal had been killed in a traffic accident. For five months, the teachers and a secretary were left to run the school, and, as this teacher told it, "We did just fine."

The same sentiment seemed to be captured in one line of the poem composed for and read at Mr. Brown's retirement dinner by a teacher: "The principal will retire soon, and another funny principal will take his place." Reinforcing the teachers' detachment from the succession process and from the possible impact of a new principal, the new principal never visited the school during the remainder of the school year.

Fear was the teachers' second response to the succession. Roughly 80 percent of the teachers said they felt some fear or anxiety. They feared two things: the unknown and a loss of independence. About one-third of Valley Elementary's teachers said they feared the unknown. They felt a general resistance to change per se and were not sure how they would get along with the new principal. For example, a third grade teacher said, "It's kind of exciting, but it's scary because you don't know how the new boss will relate to you." Similarly, a sixth grade teacher responded this way to the announcement of Mr. Brown's retirement: "I was real disappointed, because the status quo is safe, especially when we don't know who is coming."

At least half of the teachers specifically feared that a new principal would intrude on their instructional prerogatives or might not be the kind of person they would like to work for. For example, one teacher reflected, "It could be worse. Not a lot to complain about now, because he [Mr. Brown] leaves teachers alone." Several teachers on the faculty also expressed some reservation about female principals in general. They unconditionally hoped that the district would not assign a woman as principal of Valley: "Women principals are picky. I feel they wouldn't let you do your own thing."

Fear was coupled with excitement and anticipation. Teachers communicated a sense of hopeful expectation that this rare change might provide opportunities for the improvement of Valley. All the teachers expressed this sentiment. Their positive expectations focused on the personal and professional characteristics that the faculty hoped the new principal would possess. They looked for three qualities in a principal: (1) a willingness to support teachers, (2) friendliness, and (3) the ability to provide leadership by developing a sense of unity among the faculty. They also all wanted student discipline to receive attention.

Sixty percent of the teachers expressed the hope that the new principal would "support" the faculty. By support, the teachers meant that they wanted a principal who would take an interest in them and reinforce what individual teachers did in their classrooms through schoolwide programs. A fourth grade teacher said it this way: "I would like to have a principal who is more involved in the school and more interested in what teachers are doing." Her expectations reinforced a complaint voiced by one teacher in the spring, that Mr. Brown was not interested in school programs, not involved. A third grade teacher simply said, "I want a principal who is positive, reinforcing." On May 24, just one and a half weeks before the close of school, a teacher commented during a conversation in the faculty lounge that she had heard "good things" about the new principal from a friend who was a school counselor. According to this sixth grade teacher, he was reputed to be "a teacher's principal, supportive."

Over half of the teachers also wanted a principal who had a pleasant interpersonal style. They used words such as *friendly, outgoing,* and *personable* to describe the type of person whom they would like to have as their next principal.

Finally, about one-third of the faculty expressed a desire for a principal who was able to exert leadership by developing a sense of unity in the faculty while moving the teachers together toward a common goal and seeking input from teachers. One teacher hoped that the succession would bring "Someone who'll say, 'Here is a picture of where we can go,' [and ask] 'What do you think?' " Comments from teachers suggested that the sense of unity they sought would revolve largely around an intelligent involvement in instruction and curriculum. For example, one teacher remarked, "I'm hoping for a principal who has a more intellectual approach to curriculum and who shows more intellectual involvement." Another expressed anticipation and fear of intrusion in one breath: "We need someone who can bring the faculty together for a common purpose, but I still want one who will let me do my own thing." He felt this need in part because Mr. Brown was seen as ineffectual, trapped between the parents and the teachers and between the district and the teachers.

In spite of their anxieties, the faculty of Valley School generally looked ahead to the arrival of the new principal with high hopes. While they feared that the new principal might encroach on their instructional autonomy, they also hoped that the successor would be willing to support teachers, be friendly, and be able to develop a sense of unity and involvement in the school.

The Enchantment

Since Dr. Hamilton chose not to visit Valley when his appointment was announced, the teachers' first contact with him occurred with the beginning of the school year. The faculty initially was enchanted with Dr. Hamilton. This feeling lasted for the first three to four months of the school year. Teachers were very much taken with Dr. Hamilton. His reputation as a "teachers' principal" had preceded him, and the faculty's initial impressions confirmed that reputation. Dr. Hamilton was handsome and engaging. He projected the image of a man who could do things for Valley. He exerted his authority, possessed a warm personality, and negotiated successfully with the district on behalf of the faculty. Several events led teachers to reach this conclusion.

First, teachers generally came to believe that Dr. Hamilton would provide the leadership and unity they had hoped for. This belief was rooted in a variety of experiences demonstrating a take-charge personal style, a willingness to make decisions. In the first few faculty meetings of the school year Dr. Hamilton addressed a number of issues the faculty had said were important to them. He pursued the acquisition of duplication equipment for the school and set up schedules for monitoring the playground and hallways during recesses and lunch after seeking the advice of teachers in faculty meetings. Although he sought input, he made the final decision on his own. This behavior matched Dr. Hamilton's description of himself. His style, he said, was to consult teachers but make decisions himself.

Another set of events illustrated this feature. A teacher who had a reputation among other teachers for being a maverick failed to take her assigned post to monitor the hallways during recess. After checking the schedule and the halls, Dr. Hamilton found the missing teacher in the teachers' lounge and asked her if she wasn't scheduled to monitor the halls. After the teacher thanked the principal for reminding her and left the lounge, another teacher remarked, "At least this year it's the principal that reminds you." Teachers approved of his assertive style in enforcing expected behaviors.

Perhaps the most compelling quality the teachers saw in Dr. Hamilton was his friendly manner. All of the teachers said that they were struck initially by Dr. Hamilton's attention to personal relations. A sample of their comments illustrates this assessment: "I've had principals walk past me in the hall and not say 'hello!' Not Dr. Hamilton." "He's one of the few principals who shakes hands. More of a personal contact." "We joke around in the hall. He seems always pleasant." These comments were borne out by the researchers' observations. At the initial faculty meeting in August, he introduced himself and then asked the teachers to introduce themselves. After the last introduction was made, Dr. Hamilton proceeded to recite the names of all the teachers. His charisma and charm contrasted sharply with the bland, but nice, Mr. Brown.

The final trait that endeared Dr. Hamilton to teachers was his ability to get things for them from the school district's central office. They attributed this "can do" ability to him because he acquired a duplicating machine. After asking teachers to submit lists of needed materials or equipment, Hamilton promised that he would try to meet at least some of their requests. As one teacher recalled, "We got a ditto machine. I really felt like he was going to do things."

Despite these positive attributions, the faculty found the few changes made by Dr. Hamilton to be largely insignificant. He changed assembly seating, cafeteria procedures, and the supply requisitioning system. They also expressed some relief that changes were minor. He did not interfere with their teaching, and teachers were glad that achievement test scores and "magazine test" scores would be deemphasized.

Other trivial changes seemed unnecessary to teachers. For example, a change in the policy concerning when and where students would enter and leave the building was seen as unnecessary and disruptive. The change also foreshadowed conflict over Hamilton's practice of seeking input and then proceeding on his own. Hamilton chose to admit students before the bell rang and relaxed restrictions on the doors they could enter. At a faculty meeting in October, where he sought input, teachers voiced concerns about supervising the students before classes began and worried that there was a possibility of disruptive behavior. Teachers also voiced their objections during informal conversations in the faculty room: "If I can walk ten blocks to school, the kids can walk the length of the building." Despite the teachers' reservations, the principal changed the procedures. While the teachers later acknowledged that the change had not affected them to any great degree, they took some pleasure that the principal reversed his decision in February, because students had "abused the privilege."

As time passed, the faculty began to settle into a stable relationship with Dr. Hamilton. His authoritarian style, however, sparked conflict with Vi. Tensions between the school secretary and Dr. Hamilton developed gradually over the ensuing weeks. He wanted changes in office procedures that Vi resisted. In December, Vi was summarily transferred. This event marked a change in teachers' descriptions of the new principal.

The Disenchantment

If anticipation and enchantment had characterized the teachers' assessment of the succession to this point, disenchantment, the seeds of which were partially sown earlier, exploded with Vi's dismissal. Just prior to the Christmas break, Hamilton announced that Vi would be leaving Valley Elementary School for a similar position in another school. Vi had developed strong personal relationships with most of the teachers during her long tenure at Valley. One teacher observed: "Vi is a widow. This school was her family; these people were her friends. She only has two years to go before retiring. She couldn't afford to fight him."

All of the teachers concluded that the secretary had been removed by the new principal. They believed that this was the result of conflict between Dr. Hamilton and the secretary over various office procedures. The following quotations are representative: "There was conflict between Dr. Hamilton and Vi. . . . She had a set way of doing things and he felt that she was a little firm and resistant to change." "When the secretary went, talking to her, she didn't do it exactly the way he wanted it done." "He pushed her out, because he decided from day one that he was in charge and she took too much responsibility."

Teachers' perceptions were corroborated by comments made by the principal both before and after the secretary was transferred. In September, he dodged a question about his goals for the school year; instead, he talked about the secretary. "The secretary has too much control at the front desk. . . . We [he and the office staff] are here to serve the teachers. In the past it's been more like control." Later, in October, Dr. Hamilton commented that he thought that the rule prohibiting students from entering and leaving the school through the main entrance stemmed from the secretary's desire not to be bothered. He referred to his earlier comment about the secretary having too much power. Then, after the decision had been made to transfer the secretary to another school, Dr. Hamilton made the following observation during a conversation in the faculty room: "She had been here for almost twenty years.... You're bound to start thinking of everything as yours, that you know more than everyone else." Dr. Hamilton saw the situation as an authority conflict. He exerted his "leadership," the same quality the teachers initially praised, and rid himself of a rival.

After just three months, the period of enchantment was over. The immediate reaction was anger. As one teacher reflected, "If it came down to the principal or Vi, we'd pick Vi." Another commented: "He really got rude."

The dramatic dismissal of Vi contradicted teachers' personal experiences with Dr. Hamilton. He was still friendly and personable, and teachers continued to praise him for this interpersonal skill. He seemed to get along with people, which made the nature of his response to Vi even more disconcerting.

The anger gave way to insecurity. While they had chosen not to oppose Hamilton's changes, most of the teachers feared that the transfer of the secretary illustrated how he would deal with them if they did oppose his decisions. He had learned their names, was handsome, and was friendly and personable in the halls, yet the teachers realized that they had no idea what he really expected of them—except that they support his decisions. The teachers' expectation that their principal assert his authority conflicted with disapproval over his choice of consequences when resisted. "Everyone is uneasy about where they stand. The action with Vi precipitated this." "He likes to use his authority and show who's boss, and I agree with that. But everyone was sure scared after the Vi thing." "I don't really know what he thinks of me; that's the hardest thing. I don't know if I am approved of." "I wonder what he's watching for. How do we know if he's going to boot you out for not meeting expectations." "I don't feel like I know where I stand. With Mr. Brown [the predecessor] I knew what he expected."

This disenchantment was framed to a great extent by the teachers' general expectations for the succession: change and cordial personal relationships. They expected change, not retribution. While he made no significant changes that affected teachers, Hamilton failed to make known his expectations for teachers' performance. Teachers were uncertain about the changes that would be forthcoming. At the same time, he purged an important member of the group when she resisted his directives. So much for his charming personality.

Hamilton acknowledged that Vi was transferred because she did not readily adopt new office procedures demanded by him. Teachers concluded that he would take this approach in dealing with them if they failed to meet his expectations. They felt vulnerable in a very personal way, even as they continued to praise his cordiality and interpersonal skill. In the absence of known expectations, insecurity spread throughout the faculty. The removal of the school's long-time secretary seemed to focus the teachers' attention on other evidence pointing to his autocratic and arbitrary style.

After the distrust surfaced, teachers began to criticize the principal for other things. They said he lacked commitment to the school and its staff. He seemed to take action on a personal basis, and teachers had difficulty discerning any real plan for the school as a whole. They mentioned his lack of interest in the school, his failure to develop any plan or vision for Valley, his inability to deal with the school as a whole. The mounting criticism centered on three issues: socioeconomic status, the principal's self-serving attitude, and his absence from campus.

Socioeconomic differences between Dr. Hamilton and the faculty became increasingly apparent. Half of the teachers commented that they felt that Hamilton's personal prosperity and home address stood between him and the school. His behavior contributed to this perception. The district in which Valley Elementary School was located was large and included many suburban communities. These communities varied widely in the socioeconomic status of their residents. Wealthy professionals and business people lived in some neighborhoods, while blue-collar workers, some recently laid off, resided in others. Traditionally, the wealthier neighborhoods were located in the southern end of the district, while working class neighborhoods were located in the north. Antagonism between the south and the north often had colored district politics.

Valley Elementary served a working class community in the northern half of the valley, and many of the teachers on Valley's faculty lived near the school. In contrast, Dr. Hamilton lived on the southern side of the valley. His previous school was in the south. Hamilton constantly talked about his neighborhood, his influential neighbors, and his previous assignments. Teachers grew to believe that their new principal did not like being at a north side school: "Maybe, just maybe, it was a letdown to come here from the south side. We're hoping that changes. It's kind of a step down in prestige." " 'Out here,' if I hear him say, 'out here' one more time . . . . " "I don't know how happy he is here . . . . I don't know if we're too far north."

His openly friendly manner did not reduce this perception. Teachers said: "He's more interested in the fact that he lives six houses from the boulevard [a wealthy area] and that he plays tennis. I get the idea that it's a cut to be on this side of town." "His tennis and moving back to the south side [are important to him]. He's very status conscious and money and having the best of everything [mean more to him than Valley]." He did talk about tennis, sometimes emphasizing that his opponents were high-profile members of the community (e.g., the president of a local university). Also, on several occasions he was overheard arranging tennis dates on his office telephone. Further, Dr. Hamilton regularly spoke with various teachers about his boat, his south side home, the new automobile he had just purchased, and his job selling insurance on the side. In one conversation with a teacher he remarked, "My wife didn't like the first [new car] I brought home. I took it back, got another. It cost four thousand dollars more. The music system's worth one thousand dollars!" The teacher responded, "My *car* wouldn't even get four thousand dollars."

About a fourth of the teachers said the principal's attention to social status caused him to favor some teachers in the school over others. As one teacher observed, "He's a snob! He likes some teachers better than others. It sort of depends on what we do in our leisure time, what college we went to, where we live." While this was not a majority sentiment, it underscored the social distance that grew between the principal and large portions of the faculty.

Teachers also believed that Dr. Hamilton expressed a lack of commitment to the school in self-serving behavior, that he placed his own well-being above that of the school as a whole. Half of the teachers noted that he was very concerned with how he looked to the parents and his superiors. As one teacher stated it, "[He wants to] make himself look good. . .to everybody: parents and the community. He wants it to come across that he's doing good. . . . He's concerned about his own image." Faculty and staff said that much of what Hamilton emphasized was designed to place him in a good light with district officials and parents. For example, several teachers and staff members noted that he was a stickler about teacher absenteeism while frequently absent from the school himself. One staff member recalled that he "had teachers with pneumonia but he got upset [over their absences]." Another teacher remarked that when the principal had visited her in the hospital after a serious accident, "He didn't ask about my condition, but said, 'I thought you and I were going to be the ones who weren't going to be absent.'" Dr. Hamilton had attempted to recruit this teacher to his team, his group of leaders and insiders who would set an example. His complete lack of concern over her health appalled her. "He wants us to look good in the eyes of the district. . . . When reports come back [from the district], this upsets him. . . . It's important that he looks good to teachers, district, and parents." Another remarked, "It puts a bad light on him when we have the most absences at our school."

This concern over appearances was manifested in Hamilton's relationship with the school's Parent Teacher Association (PTA). Two teachers passed on a rumor that Dr. Hamilton had problems with the PTA at one of his previous schools. Talk about this rumor replaced previous stories about Hamilton as a "teachers' principal." Another teacher felt that he favored the PTA's side when the PTA and faculty were at odds over an issue. Some teachers believed that the removal of the secretary was precipitated by a complaint from a PTA officer. Others understood that the decision to change the time and locations for student entry to the building in October (over protests from the faculty) was in response to a request from the PTA. The principal did place a call to the PTA president to apprise her of his decision to rescind the change of policy in February and to "check" with her. This conversation occurred before he discussed the issue with the teachers. On another occasion, the principal supported a PTA citizenship award instigated by the PTA over the reservations of his teachers.

The third issue over which teachers criticized the principal and questioned his commitment to the school was his absence from campus. Dr. Hamilton often was away from the school for private as well as school business. One teacher reported that "He usually leaves after recess and comes back before lunch. Then he leaves after lunch and comes back before recess." Another commented, "He's never around when you need him." A staff member said, "He doesn't want you to be gone, but he leaves when he wants to leave—and that's often." The principal often was off campus. In one case, he took a half day off to register his new car. On other occasions, he would leave campus to conduct business at the district office, to do school business, or, frequently, to take a "late lunch." When he left campus for his private late lunches, he would ask the staff to "be sure to tell people that it wasn't early, it was a late lunch. He doesn't want to give them a bad impression." Dr. Hamilton also had a second job as an insurance salesman. He would leave the school immediately at the end of the day to begin his "real work." Teachers said they felt he cared more about his other job than he did about his job as principal.

The faculty of Valley Elementary gradually grew disenchanted with its new principal. This disenchantment came to a head with the transfer of the secretary to a new school but involved much more than a power struggle. Hamilton devalued the school, paid more attention to the opinion of parents than teachers, acted arbitrarily, and fussed over appearances rather than substance.

Teachers also gradually questioned Hamilton's commitment to Valley and its faculty. They felt that he did not want to be at Valley, because the assignment did not reflect real worth nor his social and economic status. Their school and the neighborhoods in which they lived were beneath him. They believed that he bowed to district and PTA influence in order to maintain his own personal image with his superiors and with powerful parent constituencies. They felt that he spent too much time away from campus for his own purposes while criticizing legitimate faculty absences. And they saw his behavior when opposed as arbitrary and overly harsh.

One faculty member summarized the succession this way: "The atmosphere is different. The old principal was not handsome. He was good, kind, decent, deeply concerned about the school at heart. But the teachers were always unhappy. Then there comes this handsome principal. The whole atmosphere changes. The teachers really had high expectations. They lived on hype until the Vi experience. After Christmas, they sort of kept looking over their shoulders to see if they would be next."

An Equilibrium

As the year drew to a close, faculty began to nervously settle into the situation. The faculty swallowed their disappointment and went about their work of teaching children. This phase began in the early spring. Teachers' conclusions about the new principal had four themes: (1) changes did not significantly affect teachers, (2) the principal was biding his time, (3) teachers would isolate themselves in their classrooms and teach, and (4) the principal had a friendly personality.

All of the teachers concluded that changes made at Valley during the year had little or no effect on them. They remarked that the process of requisitioning materials, procedures by which students entered and left the building, and the acquisition of a duplicating machine really did not affect their work. This conclusion stood in contrast to the feeling among some teachers at the beginning of the year that the new duplicating machine marked the first of many positive changes to come.

Several teachers explained that the principal was probably biding his time before making significant alterations or introducing new programs. These teachers either believed that it was simply too soon to expect changes or thought that the principal was sizing up the situation before making changes. Even toward the end of the year, they defended Hamilton's lack of impact on Valley: "We're in a transition. . . . I don't know if he'll float along until he's in a better position." "I don't hear any clear-cut goals coming through. . . . I don't know if he's been bogged down with getting familiar." "Maybe he's just getting a feel for the school and community. . . . Ask me in another year or two."

Teachers dealt with the troubling conflict and feelings of rejection in their school by resorting to an often observed tactic among members of their profession. They isolated themselves in their classrooms. This tactic also served to isolate Hamilton from them. The teachers reported that they focused their attention on teaching students. The emphasis placed by teachers on their classrooms and students also enabled teachers to cope with a situation they found to be either somewhat threatening in its uncertainty or simply negative. By downplaying the atmosphere in the school outside of their classrooms, teachers could deny the impact of the problems that had emerged during the school year. One teacher commented, "I'm still feeling it out. I just stay in my classroom and do what I'm supposed to be doing." Another said, "I close my door and do my best with what I've got. I tend to handle it myself."

During this settling-in phase, despite the insecurity and animosity that had grown out of the secretary's transfer and Hamilton's elite behavior, many of the teachers continued to comment on the principal's personableness. Both the few teachers who were highly critical of the principal and the few teachers who were supportive mentioned this quality, albeit in very different terms. Those highly critical of the principal characterized his style of interaction as "hype" or "phoney" or commented that "he's not a really personable man." Supporters, on the other hand, said he was "positive, genuine, caring,supportive, patient. . . I feel like he's my friend" or a person whose "door is always open if you want to talk with him about things." Between these two extremes, most teachers simply said he was friendly.

By the end of the school year the faculty and staff of Valley Elementary School seemed to have accepted the situation. Regardless of their personal relationship with Hamilton, teachers had largely focused their attention away from a negative school environment and toward their classrooms.

By the end of the school year, assessments were firmly established. The majority of the faculty was noncommittal. Hamilton's supporters were waiting for the next year to see if he would do anything of note at the school. His detractors felt that his image had betrayed them. As one faculty member summarized the experience: "In the beginning we thought we got the prince. We ended up with the frog."

The Teachers' View of Organizational Socialization

The teachers at Valley Elementary had no influence over the appointment of the new principal. They could only wait and see who would be chosen. They were not even given as much input into the process as area parents. Their disengagement in the early stages is not surprising.

After school began, Hamilton's surface characteristics made him seem a likely successor and raised early hopes, because he seemed to match the expectations teachers held for their new principal. As their interactions with him unfolded, teachers and staff came to see these surface characteristics as unimportant. He paid attention to appearances (for superiors and powerful constituencies); he attended to his social contacts far from the school and drew attention to the differences between his friends and the faculty at Valley; he left school frequently for social reasons and on business unrelated to the school. By the end of a year, even his most adamant supporters were trying to explain his lack of integration and impact on the school. He's "biding his time," they said.

Contributions from Organizational Socialization

Organizational socialization concepts applied to the analysis of Hamilton's succession reveal the importance of the general characteristics of the experience, the personal and social contexts, the stages during which the interaction between the new member and the established group unfolds, and the combined effects of these factors. In this district, no deliberate strategy for influencing the effects of organizational socialization was observable from the perspective of the faculty or from interviews with Hamilton. After the appointment was made, informal processes dominated.

Tactics

The characteristics of Hamilton's socialization to the new assignment at Valley Elementary followed patterns commonly identified in the research on principals. It was individual, informal, and random—fixed by social norms but random in its application. The district made no attempt to influence the success of the process. His professional socialization experiences exhibited these characteristics from the time he first decided to pursue an administrative career. Hamilton had left his high school teaching position to acquire experience at the elementary level at the advice of a superior, a mentor who had taken an interest in his career. He began to divest himself of his identity as a teacher to take up the mind-set and skills of an administrator after four years and was rewarded within two years with his first assignment as an elementary school principal. His serial experiences, following stolidly in the footsteps of almost all the top administrators within the district, exposed him to the content of norms, expectations, and values in a carefully accepted sequence of steps reinforced by a social system. The district did not have a program for socializing principals, but convention had created one imbedded in the behavioral norms of the district. Hamilton clearly understood from the beginning of his career that he must follow carefully laid out steps if he wanted to be a principal in this district.

Hamilton's behavior after his appointment suggests that he and his superiors did not interpret his transfer to a new work site as anything but a routine lateral move. He paid no heed to his acceptance by the group. He chose not to visit Valley at all in the spring following his transfer, so the teachers and staff never met him until the beginning of the following school year. It apparently was not important to him or to district administrators that he be introduced earlier. The organization's processes invested the status quo. In content, context, and social features, Hamilton's succession to the principalship of Valley encouraged a custodial response in which he would essentially replicate his previous behavior, suppressing innovation. It may also have encouraged him to feel free to dictate changes in the content/processes by which the school operated, leading in part to his immediate demand that the school secretary conform to his preferred office procedures and adjust practices that she had used for years. Hamilton felt he fit in well in the South side school from which he had come. He had been successful there, and he saw no reason to change his behavior or leadership style for Valley. He spent a great deal of time talking about his wonderful past. With the exception of rumors about his conflict with powerful and assertive members of the PTA, no negative information followed him from his old assignment to his principalship at Valley. If anything, his reputation was a good one—a teachers' principal. The result was that

Hamilton superimposed behavior designed to buy social acceptance from teachers, students, and parents in an affluent neighborhood onto Valley without regard for the needs and beliefs of the faculty. All indications should have been that Dr. Hamilton knew how to manage a school and his past experience did not foreshadow the clashes to come.

Personal and Social Context of Socialization

The personal and social contexts of this succession loom large in the case from the faculty's point of view. Their small tract homes on the north side of the valley contrasted sharply with Hamilton's neighborhood, and he took every opportunity to emphasize the differences.

Social Context. The faculty Hamilton joined was experienced and stable with long experience in teaching and long tenure at Valley. Mr. Brown, the predecessor, also had been a long-established feature (twelve years at Valley prior to his retirement). Vi, the school secretary, had been an influential member of the school organization for longer than the predecessor, nineteen years. This situation set up a social environment with strongly established and widely accepted behavioral and organizational norms reinforced by the surrounding community. Yet the larger district environment and the behavior of Mr. Brown and Dr. Hamilton revealed the belief that teachers had no role in any dynamic related to administration. Brown tried to keep his impending retirement a secret; teachers had no role in the succession; and Hamilton stayed away. After becoming principal, he chose to retain this separation—taking his "late lunches" away from school, presumably with people he valued more than those at Valley.

Hamilton moved into a strong social environment, tight knit and firmly established, under circumstances that his behavior suggests he interpreted as carte blanche to import himself and his preferences unchanged. Teachers acknowledged their powerlessness and prepared for potential problems by discounting the importance of principals in general. At the same time they detached from the potential impact of a new principal, they feared intrusion into their prerogatives and hoped for a charismatic, friendly leader who could create a sense of unity.

Personal Context. Much attention focused on Hamilton's personal traits and their relationships with expectations held by the faculty. Teachers wanted a friendly, outgoing, and personable principal who could unify the faculty around a common purpose while seeking input from teachers and respecting their autonomy. He had these traits and used the self-presentation skills that made him a successful insurance salesman to create a favorable impression on the faculty, memorizing their names, greeting them in the halls. He was a long-time insider in the district, an experienced "teachers' principal," with a warm and friendly personality, who immediately learned teachers' names and was "willing to go to bat for the faculty." These traits in large part dissipated initial uncertainty and apprehension that arose when Brown announced his retirement.

Hamilton's view of himself revolved around his position in the center of authority in the school (illustrated by his complaints about Vi's "control at the front desk" in September interviews) and as a member of the professional upper-middle class. He chose to emphasize these features through stories about himself, his friends, his possessions, and his leisure activities. To Hamilton, Valley was "out here," implying banishment and rejection. He talked about his tennis dates and the social importance of his tennis partners. He bragged about the cost of his new car and the sophistication of its sound system. Teachers noted that their own cars were worth less than the price difference between the car he eventually bought and the one he returned to the dealer because his wife didn't like it. They observed favoritism, apparently based on teachers' addresses and choice of leisure activities.

While his personable nature and the decisive purchase of a ditto machine quickly created cordial relationships with the faculty, personal characteristics that clashed with norms and expectations more central to the social norms of the community surrounding Valley and the teachers themselves soon came to dominate descriptions of him by the majority of faculty members. His assertiveness came to be described as rude and authoritarian; some saw his friendly nature as self-serving, the result of an exaggerated image consciousness and self-absorption. Uncommitted to the school, perhaps even embarrassed to be there, he was a "south side snob." He cared more for the appearance he projected to the PTA and his superiors than he cared for the school, its teachers, and its performance. He chastised a seriously ill teacher in the hospital over her absence, giving the impression that he worried more about how he would look to his superiors if teachers were absent than about her well-being. He sided with the PTA and other parents against the faculty over student use of different entrances to the building and a new citizenship award. He repeatedly ignored teacher input when making decisions.

Teachers saw Hamilton's behavior toward Vi as a reflection on his personality—uncompromising, authoritarian, arbitrary, and insensitive—and translated their own interactions with him according to this new set of personal characteristics. The emotional effect of the purge of the secretary was projected onto their own experience—he could exact swift and uncompromising retribution when crossed, yet the standards and expectations on which he might act remained unclear.

The interaction of Hamilton's charismatic personality and intense feelings of social and professional rejection among many teachers gradually took on mutually exclusive meanings for teachers. His personableness initially satisfied a real need among teachers for a more dynamic school orchestrated by a dynamic principal. He chose not to move beyond these early contacts to integrate himself into Valley any more deeply than the functionary tasks of management required. At any time of the day, he could be heard arranging tennis dates on the telephone. The belief spread that insurance was more important to him than was the school.

Socialization Stages

On the basis of these critical interactions, Fauske and Ogawa (1987) and Ogawa (1991) drew a stage framework to explain this succession. Their stages emphasized interaction between the social context and the new leader more strongly than do traditional succession stage frameworks. Organizational socialization stage frameworks emphasize change in the newcomer *and* the existing social group. Because Hamilton demonstrated so little willingness to change in order to better accommodate the needs of the faculty and staff at Valley, he appears never to have become fully integrated, never to have passed the early stages to full membership and maximum "location" (Wanous, 1976) in the group. Regardless of the labels one attaches to the stages, Hamilton appears to have never passed much beyond the first stage before equilibrium set in.

The first stages of organizational socialization frameworks emphasize the surprise, conflict, and expectations confronted in the reality of a new job content and its personal and social context. This stage is likely to include excitement, the pleasure of discovery, and learning. The social atmosphere, communication patterns, work, and people play important parts. As a powerful new member, Hamilton confronted naturally occurring conflicts with no apparent examination of important aspects of himself in the new setting. He chose to cope with resistance to change from Vi and some teachers by precipitating open conflict and a crisis event around which discontent could focus. He confronted resistance to his interpretations of professional norms (absenteeism, participation in important school-level decisions) and social norms (respect for neighborhood and group values) by forcing acceptance of his point of view through the use of his formal authority. Parents and teachers would disapprove of his frequent lunches away from campus and absences to complete private business. His response was to admonish the new secretary to cover for him. He wasn't absent; he was taking a late lunch. Teachers, however, must not be absent, regardless of the reason.

Initial acceptance for Hamilton based on readily observable personal traits and a story passed on by a teacher that he was a "teachers' principal" kept the encounter/anticipation stage of his organizational socialization cordial. Enchantment gave way to distress when more deeply imbedded behavioral and social norms assaulted by Hamilton began to bring his incongruities into sharp focus. The stories about his previous principalship changed; teachers now told stories about his conflict with the PTA at his previous assignment. He responded to these conflicts by exerting his authority more assertively.

The interactions that might have led from encounter through adjustment and stabilization/integration led instead to a social situation bogged down at anticipation and characterized by ambiguity. At the end of the year, Hamilton's most avid supporters described him as "biding his time." They felt that his friendliness and personal style outweighed the discomfort that resulted over his excessive use of power. Hamilton's supporters also said that they still believed that he would move to affect the changes in the school that their earliest interactions with him suggested might occur and that his personal style seemed to predict.

The changes that actually took place were judged more harshly. Teachers assessed the few changes as largely insignificant. His location in the group remained unsure; teachers said they didn't know what he expected of them, yet they feared retribution should they cross him. In contrast to the predictions of many writers that the first six months of a new leader's tenure in an organization present a critical time frame during which patterns are formed, Hamilton seemed to be forever waiting for some unique, opportune moment.

Outcomes of Socialization

By looking at the outcomes of socialization, we bring the analysis of this case full circle to the characteristics of the process. High role innovation also often results in concert with personal change. Hamilton displayed a custodial response in which his inherited (and imported) past dominated in all but the most superficial ways at Valley. He bought a ditto machine, changed a few entrance/exit patterns, and fought with the secretary over office procedures. Hamilton felt free to change the content of procedures and to emphasize teacher attendance, but he left teachers largely in the dark about his relationship to the central functions of teaching and learning at Valley. Teachers were puzzled. Maybe next year, they said.

An organizational socialization perspective provides an additional insight into this case, focused on the affective outcomes of the succession. Writers in this tradition emphasize the importance of acknowledging the affective states that accompany important changes. Changes in skills, values, and professional identities can result from succession socialization experiences for individuals undergoing the experience. Organizational growth and changes in the existing group can also result.

At the end of a year, the outcome at Valley was not exploration, for there was little role change and no personal change on Hamilton's part. It was not determination, for Hamilton accomplished little change in the way the principal functioned at Valley. He was still an outsider to the school. It was not absorption, for Hamilton did not change, even in ways clearly suggested by the first year's interactions. It can best be characterized as replication—no change. Hamilton made no effort to redefine the goals or ends toward which the faculty and staff might work together. He had little effect on the means—ignoring central functions of instruction and focusing his only "reforms" on office procedures. Hamilton was friendlier than Brown; he shook people's hands; he remembered names easily. But teachers "kept looking over their shoulders to see if they would be next." The prevailing response: (1) teachers judged the few changes instituted to be insignificant; (2) both Hamilton's detractors and his supporters said he was biding his time; (3) teachers returned to the isolation of their classrooms, asserting that the whole process of the year's succession had little or no effect on them.

5

An Outsider Successor's Personal View[1]

The Succession Setting

One of two junior high schools in Lakeview, Eagleton[2] had seven hundred students, grades 7 and 8. The city was fiscally and politically conservative with a slowly growing population of about 45,000. In an attempt to stabilize its revenues and protect the district's budget from state school funding shortfalls, the board of education had sponsored a voted leeway election in each of the two preceding years. Both measures failed, a result that teachers and administrators attributed to a substantial retirement population and opposition by the taxpayers' association. A large university in the city dominated its social, intellectual, and economic life. Two university professors served on the board of education; one was its president. A majority of the university's professors who lived in town had homes within Eagleton's boundaries.

The building was suffering from age. Built with federal supplementary funds in 1932, it had been substantially remodeled only once—classrooms and a gym added in the early 1960s. There were bats in the attic. A series of brightly painted wood panels in brilliant primary school orange, yellow, lavender, and chartreuse—a source of constant student complaint—dominated the main hall and ramps to the second floor.

Dr. Johnson, the superintendent, had come to Lakeview from the superintendency in a wealthy district in the Northeast via a short and restless sojourn as a professor. He preferred, he said, the action of administration. A prevailing sense of rapid change and development permeated the district. Some people complained of innovation overload, others adjusted more easily to changing professional patterns. Districtwide programs of instructional improvement, instructional leadership, and clinical supervision were being implemented. Of the three new principals appointed in 1983, only one was from within the district.

The assistant superintendent, Dr. Gary, was a long-time administrator in the district. He was known for his gregarious, person-centered style and a strong, affectionate personality. Dr. Gary got along well with both the old guard and newcomers alike. In contrast, the superintendent had a reputation as analytical, cool, and task and performance oriented.

Students at Eagleton were mostly white and upper-middle to lower-upper class, although a small number of students from minority groups and some from less affluent backgrounds attended the school, the result of deliberate boundary manipulation by the board of education. Students were prosperous and knew it. They dressed well, in the latest styles. Status and clothes were important; students often checked the labels in others' collars or waistbands. Some students openly flaunted social class differences among students and with the teachers. Many teachers were defensive of parental criticism of the school and parent attempts to control them. Faculty members resented the influence, demands, and pressure parents exerted on the administration and faculty. In the community, Eagleton had the reputation of being "out of control," and school board members, parents, and other principals talked openly about perceived problems with the students there. A few days before school closed in May, the students, by advance arrangement, simultaneously emptied their lockers, filled with papers squirreled away for weeks, onto the floor. They "trashed the halls," a tradition that teachers said was firmly established. Their bravado was impressive.

Mr. Light was principal of Eagleton. He was fifty-eight years old and decided to retire at the end of the 1983 school year after sixteen years as principal of Eagleton and ten years as the assistant principal of a high school in Lakeview. A native of the city, he attended Eagleton as a teenager. He was almost universally described in the community as a kind man. His approach, according to teachers, was fatherly and protective toward students and teachers alike. He emphasized the importance of stability and tradition in the schools, referring to his own long tenure and the even longer tenure of his predecessor. Upon meeting his successor he said, "I don't know how long you'll be here, but Eagleton has had a very solid, consistent past." Then, in an aside to the superintendent, who had just introduced them, "I know how you feel about rotating principals, but. . . ." Like many principals, Mr. Light had chosen his own assistant. Continuing this tradition of mentors appointing their successors and before announcing his retirement he asked a science teacher in the school if he was interested in administration, hinting that he might become the new assistant principal if he wanted. State certification was no problem. That could be taken care of later.

The assistant principal was white and in his early forties. Except for one year, Mr. Cooper also had spent his career in the district, first as an audiologist and then as the assistant principal at Eagleton. He had no classroom teaching experience other than one semester of student teaching—at Eagleton, while working simultaneously as the assistant principal—to get his administrative certificate from the state. The teacher with whom he did his student teaching described the situation as "awkward." A past president of the teachers' union, Mr. Cooper was well known, sociable, and had many friends among district teachers and administrators. In early spring, Mr. Light began hinting he would almost certainly be the next principal. Other insiders with ties to the teachers' union were also candidates for the position. One, a long-time teacher at the other junior high school who assumed no outsiders posed a serious threat, told friends she planned to sue the district for sex discrimination under the Civil Rights Act if she were not appointed.

The teachers at Eagleton ranged in experience from zero to twenty-nine years. They were all white and middle class. The shop teacher had spent his entire career at the school beginning in 1954 and was the only teacher Mr. Light had not hired. Mr. Light also made sure he filled all teaching vacancies before leaving the principalship at the end of June. One of Mr. Light's best friends, a social studies teacher, was a favorite hunting and firewood-cutting companion. Many teachers were loyal to Mr. Cooper, feeling that he deserved to be principal. A highly respected teacher, described by the principal, teachers, and assistant superintendent as perhaps the best teacher in the school, wrote a letter of protest to the superintendent when she heard Mr. Cooper would not be the principal. Two young faculty members were also vocal in their opposition to the new principal. One young man, a math teacher and building representative for the teachers' union with state certification in administration, said to the new principal the following autumn, "Your appointment made me feel like the district was saying there was no hope for me." The union representative the previous year expressed similar dissatisfaction. "There are many good people in the district who are prepared for administration. We really supported Mr. Cooper." Resentment from faculty and staff surrounded the appointment.

The New Principal

In the late winter of 1983 Kate Howard was completing doctoral work in educational administration, preparing to be a school administrator. She had begun graduate school for her own enjoyment and to pursue a master's degree in history. In the process she had taken some administration classes, become entranced, and stayed on for a doctorate. Her most visible talent had always been doing well in school. She supported her academic habit as a research assistant and with the help of graduate fellowships. Thirty-five, white, married, and a mother of four daughters, she differed in many ways from most secondary school principals in Lakeview, the surrounding districts, and the state. At the time of her appointment, she became one of three women principals in secondary schools in the state, joining one high school principal and one junior high school principal. Her work in education had been spent teaching—high school and junior high—in other districts in the state. She had never worked as a principal or assistant principal nor held a line administration position.

Using her fellowship with the state's society of superintendents as an entree, she began talking with several superintendents about a postdoctoral internship in central office administration, where she thought her major interests lay, near the end of her doctoral program. The contact was useful. Several superintendents were helpful and suggested she contact them again.

The Social Dynamic of a Succession

Dr. Johnson was one of the superintendents in the state who encouraged Kate Howard. After several conversations, he invited her to meet with his central office administrators. Not far into the meeting, she realized this get-acquainted talk was bearing a striking resemblance to an interview. Although the tone was relaxed, it was direct. When she said she wanted to be a superintendent, Dr. Gary asked whether she had any particular superintendency in mind. "Do you mean am I gunning for somebody's job?" she replied. He responded with a hearty laugh. "You're all right."

A few weeks later, Dr. Gary called Kate at home. A junior high school principal in the district had decided to take an early retirement. In addition, a reorganization of the central office and another retirement meant a new director of secondary education might be appointed. Would she like to apply for either position?

A second meeting with district administrators came a few days later. This time the director of elementary education joined the central office administrators who had first interviewed her. The conversation ranged from state politics to school improvement, then centered on the relative advantages of various job sequences in an administrative career. Should one take a principal's job—line administration—or a central office role with broader influence but staff position status? The elementary director, superintendent, and assistant superintendent argued and parried, at times almost ignoring Kate Howard. Their talk had the ring of a strategy session. Kate was asked to submit a formal letter of application for both jobs—director of secondary education and junior high school principal. When she pushed the assistant superintendent for advice on which position would be best for her, he was evasive, but the superintendent was more direct. Experience in line administration was an important precursor to district level administration. They would be in touch.

Two weeks followed with no word. Finally Dr. Gary called, asking her to come to an interview for the principalship the next day. The superintendent, assistant superintendent, director of research, and personnel director were all present. After answering questions for nearly two hours on school effectiveness and improvement, discipline, junior high curriculum, personnel action, community relations, and her personal leadership philosophy, she was thanked. They would be in touch. The next day the superintendent called. The board of education was concerned that too many outsiders were being appointed as principals, but they had agreed to support her. She was the new principal of a junior high school in a community in which she had never lived or worked. The board members wanted to meet her the next morning at 7:30.

When she arrived, Dr. Johnson was talking with the president of the board of education. Two members had declined to join them. Those who had come talked quietly but frankly with the superintendent about the others' deliberate absence. She caught only snatches of their conversation but felt herself tighten over what she did hear. The board president came forcefully to the point with his opening comment. "Women don't like to work for women. What are you going to do about that?" "What does your husband think about you accepting this position?" "How many children do you have? How old are they?" "You have all the comforts of life, a husband, a wonderful family. What do you want to do this for?" She explained that her husband was supportive. While the family had talked about the possibility that she would be a principal, she did not ask her children to make her professional decisions. (They were four, seven, nine, and twelve years old.) Firmly but diplomatically changing the subject, the superintendent redirected the questioning. He asked her to comment on administrator effects on schools, effective schools research, instruction, and her dissertation research.

Though women had been elementary principals in the district for four years, no women administrators worked at the secondary level. The district administrators and board of education members did not volunteer this information. They wondered openly whether she could be successful, but they offered little information, a commodity she was to find in short supply.

After the conversation turned from her personal traits, other issues that obviously influenced their decision surfaced in the questions posed by board members. She gathered that the board sought changes in the leadership style at the school. "Your predecessor is not perceived by the community as a strong leader," the board president explained. He prefaced his questions with remarks that revealed definite opinions about the traits that would be important for the principal in this school. She heard herself described as "hard working, high energy, intellectual," with "high standards" for herself and others. If his list of her talents had not been followed by the prediction that people in the school would be "intimidated and upset," she would have felt complimented. Ambivalence filled the room. It dawned on her that board members felt they were taking a calculated risk.

The nature of that risk soon took shape. Implying that, in their search for change, they might create too much disruption, one board member said, "You know, people on this faculty are going to be more afraid of you than you are of them." Fear was an unexpected emotion. Later she learned that only a partial list of fears had surfaced that day. Some district administrators and board members felt she might be "too academic." The superintendent and assistant superintendent called the head of her department at the university and the chairman of her doctoral committee, asking specifically about her human relations skills. When called for references, her most recent principal and a district administrator in a previous district praised her teaching but also were cautious, suggesting that she was too intellectual. Could she work with people or only read books?

The community was discomfited, and board members were concerned about the effect of their decision on teacher morale. A former neighbor of Kate's who lived in the city revealed people's feelings, barely able to disguise her concurrence. "How did *you* get that job? People are pretty upset."

Kate was out of town when the appointment was announced, so a meeting was arranged to introduce her to the faculty. Her predecessor had planned a full agenda for the faculty meeting, so, following an introduction by the superintendent during which she became Dr. Howard, she gave a brief presentation—a summary of professional experiences, description of her personal background, and expression of pleasure and anticipation for the future. She and the superintendent then left.

Uncertainty, exacerbated by the fact that she was an outsider, surfaced again immediately. The union representative also left the faculty meeting, hurrying to catch them in the hall. After describing the frustration and apprehension that faculty members were feeling because so much about her remained unknown, he said, "We don't even know what to call you—Dr., Mrs., Kate. It's not that we question whether you're the boss. We know you're the boss. But there are a lot of worried people who are nervous and upset. . . . People feel a lot better now that they've seen you, but you need to get back here right away. They have a lot of questions." It was late April by this time.

Another faculty meeting was arranged for the next week with more time to talk and answer questions. On the way to the school Dr. Howard stopped and bought four dozen doughnuts; convinced this would be a crucial session, she hoped food would ease the tension. When he saw the boxes of doughnuts, Mr. Cooper smiled and unlocked the soda pop machine. Dr. Howard began by talking about her family, local roots, and teaching experience in junior high schools. This time the faculty was prepared with many questions, some of them only thinly disguising their hostility. The union past-president asked the first question, quoting an eighth grader he had overheard in the hall. " 'I wish we were going to be here next year. We could get away with anything we want with a lady principal.' As a woman, as a lady principal, how do you react to that?" he asked. She replied, "They don't know me very well. But they will." "What do you know about Lakeview?" The question set off a rowdy discussion, reflections on a conservative community, complaints about "difficult" and "elitist" parents. "What have you been told about Eagleton?" Teachers agreed, laughing, that they had a reputation as a difficult faculty, uncooperative, and were anxious to know how they were portrayed to her.

During this second faculty meeting, defensiveness toward parents and discomfort with the new instructional improvement and clinical supervision program surfaced. After the meeting, a small group, including Dr. Howard, talked casually. A teacher, unable to attend because of scheduled parent meetings, came up to chat. "I'm sorry I wasn't here," she said. "I told [the faculty representative] to tell me everything you believe." The faculty representative quipped, "Yeah, she believes in leaving us totally alone, in never coming in our classrooms, and in just letting us do our own thing all the time."

Immediately after the appointment was announced, a group of concerned parents called Dr. Howard at home. They wanted a private meeting in a parent's home, and they wanted no one else from the school to be present. On an afternoon in May in a crowded living room in a fashionable neighborhood overlooking the valley, the agenda was revealed. They were aggrieved about student behavior. Parents perceived blatant violations of behavioral expectations by students—obscenities, drugs, premature dating and sex, rowdiness, devalued academic achievement. Defined as a "problem," their concern about discipline translated into a firmly stated demand that a schoolwide program of assertive discipline be implemented before school opened in the fall. The meeting was cordial, but the parents were adamant. "You're the principal. Make them do it." The dialogue lasted into the late afternoon and was animated at times. The parents complained repeatedly about the "prevailing atmosphere of negativism and lack of discipline" at the school and pressed hard. In a letter to the superintendent a week after the meeting, a group of these parents expressed the belief that "Dr. Howard has the image and professional abilities necessary to succeed," then restated their concerns. The first week in June she made an appointment to talk with the elementary school principal who had implemented the discipline plan the parents wanted.

Following her meeting with parents, Dr. Howard arranged for a series of meetings with the teachers in each department at Eagleton to discuss their priorities and concerns. These meetings yielded a picture of school discipline much like the parents' and cautiousness toward her.

The reasons for their caution became more and more clear. To her surprise, Dr. Howard found she had a reputation. Her education and personal background combined with the belief that the superintendent had chosen her were linked with task orientation and performance-based expectations. The superintendent's perceived abilities, the exceptionally broad search prior to the appointment, and the affirmation of board members who were university professors by profession (while other board members remained openly unsupportive) reinforced her reputation as task oriented, a person deliberately brought in to clean house. In one quiet conversation weeks after the appointment, Mr. Cooper admitted he had expected someone "really into theories," lacking the "kind of commitment and experience necessary to run a junior high school."

While Mr. Cooper wondered about her commitment and experience, some teachers speculated that she had been appointed to clean house. "This faculty has a reputation in the district as being difficult," one reiterated in May. Suffering from an undiagnosed extended illness, one teacher was unable to return to work in the fall. She telephoned her friends repeatedly during the summer and the first few weeks of school, often asking them directly if Dr. Howard could be trusted. Telling a friend that she suspected administrators in the school and district of trying to deprive her of her employee benefits and her job, she sought his help in the protection of her rights. Impending doom was felt by the staff as well as some teachers. Her expression of pleasure and anticipation on meeting the school's two secretaries was greeted acerbically: "Well, we didn't know if we would be here or if you would bring in your own people." A part-time custodian had the same fear. He asked Mr. Light to "put in a good word" for him, and the first time he met Dr. Howard said he hoped she would "let him keep his job."

In addition to resentment and suspicion aimed directly at her, Dr. Howard was the recipient of a general lack of cordiality between the board of education and administration and the teachers that year. While teachers emphasized their willingness to cooperate (one said, "You just tell us what we have to do, and we'll do what you say"), a general level of suspicion toward her motives and the motives of other administrators existed in the school and district. Authority conflict was high, exacerbated by the lack of a teaching contract when school began. With no contract in hand in late September, a district-wide strategy session was planned by the union. The teachers could not decide whether to admit administrators to the session where they would discuss and vote on a proposed contract. Rejecting the suggestion that everyone at the meeting should be a union member (because it would exclude some teachers and include some principals who retained their union membership from years ago), they admitted all professional staff members. While several teachers went out of their way to find Dr. Howard and assure her in private that the pervading resentment was not directed at her, the message was clear: you are an administrator and an outsider.

As time passed and still no contract for teachers could be agreed on, increasing pressure caused by the appointment of outsiders to administrative positions in the district developed. Outsider administrators became a major focus of acrimony in negotiations. In one administrators' meeting, the issue was hotly discussed; principals and district administrators hired from other districts over four years' time said they were surprised at the depth of resentment. Blamed for blocking the careers of "many great teachers who have prepared themselves and are qualified for administration," these appointments were called "unfair" by teachers and many long-time principals. One principal, a young woman who had been with the district for four years, was openly nonplussed at the meeting where these resentments were expressed by principals: "I didn't think I was an outsider. I thought I was part of the team." Increasing confrontation developed through September.

The situation was not completely negative, however. Some teachers expressed a glimmer of hope that the change in principals might nurture new opportunities and points of view, providing many with a chance to catch their breath or recover from a rocky start with the previous administration. "Do us a favor," one teacher said, "and don't believe everything they tell you about us. Get to know us first." The suspicion sparking her remark was justified. Mr. Light had made it a point almost every time he talked with Dr. Howard prior to June to share his perceptions of teachers. One teacher was characterized as making a game of "undermining the assistant principal," another as "someone in this faculty you should listen to." Another comment began: "Now don't get me wrong; she's a bright woman but. . . ." The hope for change expressed first by school board members and then by parents and teachers highlighted the advantages of being an outsider that Dr. Howard might tap. Mr. Cooper also played an important and positive role in the succession, even though his candidacy was a source of early tension. He was not only Dr. Howard's closest associate in the school but also a recent competitor for the job. He was eager to learn, more cautious than she. Under Mr. Light's administration, he said, he had little opportunity to contribute ideas to the school and was relatively invisible to district leaders.

Mr. Cooper was candid about his feelings. A lay leader in a religion in which women never hold authoritative positions, he was, he said, in a completely unfamiliar relationship. His ability to adjust to an unusual and unexpected new authority relationship helped deemphasize her incongruencies and the resentment many felt that he was "passed over." She asked him how he felt about her—an outsider, a woman, a few years younger. His reply: he was hurt when he first learned he would not be the principal. But during three or four long talks in his office after everyone else had left the school,

he shared a gradually changing attitude. (1) Under the circumstances—conflict within the school, old ties and obligations, need for
change, new programs—he felt an outsider had many advantages.
(2) Having a woman principal did not bother him as he thought it
would. (3) He was by nature a loyal and ethical man who would do
his best regardless of who the board chose as principal, and they, he
said, knew it. (4) New experiences brought learning opportunities to
him. (5) An increase in his own visibility as an assistant principal
might improve his chance of a principalship in the near future. Mr.
Cooper's personal integrity, lack of rancor, and flexibility altered the
emotional atmosphere immediately following the succession to a large
degree while providing Dr. Howard with an ally, a badly needed
source of peer support.

At the first meeting with secondary principals Dr. Howard
attended, the status of her peer support network was less clear. A
high school principal asked her to tell them about herself. Blithely
describing training, orientation, and experience, she was interrupted.
"That's not what I mean. Tell us about you. How many children do
you have? Your husband's an attorney?" She complied. Tired of the
reaction to gender, anxious to fit in with her peers, she chose to
interpret these questions in the worst possible light and drove home
disconsolate.

Dr. Howard's worries about the support of her peers turned out
to be exaggerated. The principal of the other junior high called in
July. Within a few hours he was at her door to visit, sustain, and
support. "Please," he later told her he had intoned, "let her be good
at what she does. Let her do a good job so that will give Dr. Johnson
more support for hiring outside the district and looking for other kinds
of people." Anxiety filled his voice. He shared stories about his first
year in the district. "Don't be surprised if some of your faculty hate
you," he said. "I've got three or four that just hate my guts." They
talked a long time about the problems of outsiders and the excitement
of accomplishing goals. Close to her own age, hired recently, with a
similar professional background, his support became an early
strength, a cohort core. Other principals gradually joined in, helping
when they could and offering their acceptance. Over a year later, one
high school principal described her to the dean of the College of
Education at her alma mater as "a real smart little gal."

Additionally, by September colleagues good naturedly goaded
her on her gender, about being an outsider and an out-of-towner (she
continued to commute to Lakeview from her home fifty miles away).
During an early fall meeting, a district policy defining residency for

student tuition requirements was proposed. Because of the proximity of the university, many foreign and out-of-state graduate students brought spouses and children to live in the district. The new policy was designed to help them establish residency and avoid tuition. It stated that "wives and children" of students would be considered residents. Prefacing her comment with, "I'm sorry, I have to do my woman thing," Dr. Howard suggested "spouses" be used in place of "wives" in the policy. "No, you're not sorry," quipped the research director, who was conducting the meeting. They all laughed. "You're right." She joined the laughter. "I'm not."

A net of friendships at the district added to her growing comfort and grew increasingly important to her work. Late in July, Dr. Howard overheard the district maintenance director, complaining about a new elementary school principal. "That little gal," he said, "wants her whole school rekeyed, and she wants me to pay for it." Walking into the room, she joined the conversation, "I want my whole school rekeyed, Rod. When can you have it done?" She stuck out her hand. "Hi, Rod, I'm Kate Howard." "I thought as much," he laughed, shaking her hand vigorously. Later he helped her. A veteran math teacher due to retire that year had kidded at the faculty meeting where she was introduced that they'd like a sink in the faculty lunch room. At Dr. Howard's request, ahead of other work orders in the district, he quietly installed a sink and small water heater (teachers previously had no place to get water or rinse out their dishes after lunch). He didn't charge the school budget. He also made sure the brilliant primary school colors in the main hall at Eagleton were replaced with subdued maroons and neutrals by a district painting crew before school opened. The school counselor asked, "How'd you get that done?" Another good friend turned out to be Dr. Gary. Gradually she worked more closely with him and less often directly with Dr. Johnson.

This net of friendships with cordial, warm, and renowned characters and "people-oriented" veteran administrators provided a comfortable professional environment for Dr. Howard. She also found that, for the first half of the year, people openly compared her with Mr. Light. He interrupted; she was a listener. "You always get the feeling that she is listening to you, whether she agrees with you or not." His kindnesses were described as "patronizing" in contrast with a new "professionalism." The students even joined in. In the lunchroom during the first week of school, she overheard two eighth grade boys joking: "Light didn't know how to dress at all, but this one's okay." Mr. Light took an early beating. But criticism of Mr.

Light and comparison of their very different administrative styles dropped off gradually and almost disappeared by late winter. By then, she was sometimes the criticized as well as the praised administrator.

Before school started, the issue of student control needed to be addressed. The parents were intensely concerned. All the teachers were contacted by mail. Each one was asked to set up an appointment for a private talk about the school with Dr. Howard in August. During the ensuing weeks, she used the ideas shared during these private conversations to outline a schoolwide system of discipline, standardized across classrooms if that was the teachers' preference, more individualized if they preferred. She decided to put the choice to a direct vote of the faculty. The element of choice became more significant than the structure of the plan. One teacher, impressed by her request, called from her summer business in Jackson Hole, Wyoming, to talk with her about the program and offer her ideas and support because she was unable to talk with her in person.

Working with the teachers, union representatives, and the assistant principal, a plan of action for the opening of school was prepared, resisting pressure from parents to mandate a prepackaged program, because the teachers rejected that idea. Concern over discipline allowed people to address a suspicion, unspoken by everyone but the students (and the faculty indirectly), that a woman can't run a tight ship in a secondary school. One teacher quietly expressed his skepticism in late August, saying to the assistant principal, "Don't you really run the school?"

Positive feedback came gradually but more frequently. Change and renewal were spreading through the faculty, confirming the hope some had cautiously expressed in May. The teacher who had written a letter of protest to Dr. Johnson when the appointment was announced told Dr. Howard she had seen an emphasis on the positive coming through to the faculty; they "know where you stand." Good news was reinforcing. Early in August Mr. Cooper said he was "having a good time. For the first time in three years I'm actually looking forward to the start of school." The exchange of perceptions between staff members helped to solidify them. Early in the second week of school, a secretary in the main office overheard a group of teachers talking about the change. They had, she said, "a lot of respect" for Dr. Howard. The faculty representative, the young man who had mourned her appointment as a death knell to his own administrative career ("Your appointment made me feel like there was no place for me in this district"), gradually spent more and more time in her office, talking and joking. By February he felt comfortable enough with her to secretly hang a poster of a naked baby sitting on a potty chair with the caption "Tell them I'm in conference" behind her desk just before her annual evaluation interview by the three head district administrators—the superintendent, assistant superintendent, and personnel director. She didn't see the poster until the personnel director complemented her on it at the end of their two-hour interview. The secretaries began inviting her to their regular lunches in a small back room. They shared stories about family, health, and work.

All staff relationships did not improve as quickly as they had with the secretaries. The amount and kind of attention the custodial staff was accustomed to receiving from the principal clashed with Dr. Howard's intentions. This conflict caught her off guard, surprising her. In her journal she recorded some frustration at the surprise:

> Went on a tour of the building with the head custodian. He wants me to go through everything in the building with him and make all the decisions. There is a lot of old, trashy junk stored in and around the building. The mobile classroom unit is stacked full of trash—old broken desks in a big heap in the middle of the room, equipment, broken pieces of building material, left over ceiling tiles. . . . Behind a fence in the back there is a stack of old pipes, some broken urinals from remodeling in the boys' bathroom years ago, and rolls of fencing. . . . When I told him that the district maintenance director was sending a truck to come and get the old stuff, he acted like that was not what he really wanted to have happen. He said, "Well, some of that stuff we should keep, you know." I said, "What stuff?" "Well, some of those desks can be fixed." I said, "Do you have time to fix them? Can you fix them?" "Well, some of them. And some of them aren't so bad." I told him to go through the desks, pick those that he could easily repair or felt were still good, and keep them. His answer was, "Well, maybe we could go over and go through them together."

The custodian privately complained to Mr. Cooper that "the new principal" was throwing perfectly good things away and neglecting the building. He couldn't figure out what he was going to do "with these female principals."

Mr. Cooper kindly let Dr. Howard know that the custodian was feeling neglected, which gave her the chance to find a middle ground that they could both be comfortable with. She set regular meetings with the custodian and assigned Mr.Cooper to meet with him also. They set new and much higher expectations for keeping the floors polished and other areas cleaned, but the staff was able to make adjustments in other places. The head custodian proudly passed on compliments he began to receive several months after school started. The district supervisor sent other custodians to Eagleton to see how he kept the building, as a good example.

Mistakes, some serious, also helped Dr. Howard develop a better sense of the Lakeview District and Eagleton Junior High. Her lack of experience with the idiosyncrasies of expectations for the principal caused glitches with the teachers as well as the custodians. Planning for the autumn faculty party was one of the ceremonial responsibilities expected of her and a custom of long standing at Eagleton. She was totally unaware of the expectation, having always worked in schools where the faculty representatives and building social committee planned faculty parties. Late in September, the faculty representative asked why plans had not been made for the party. Following complications and conflicts resulting in several changes in the date, he confronted her, irritation in his voice: "When is it? Friday night or Tuesday night? I don't want to take responsibility for it." Dr. Howard replied, "Why not? It's not my party, it's the faculty's party." "I think," he remarked with no attempt to hide the sarcasm in his voice, "that the leader needs to decide when it is and then stick with it."

Another conflict in expectations arose over the office work. Dr. Howard assumed the office was functioning well and that the staff was responsible for making decisions about their work. Late in October the emotional tenor in the office became tense and off balance. Approaching the assistant principal, the financial secretary worried she could not complete her work because Dr. Howard had not examined and approved it as Mr. Light had done. She was afraid that people would not be paid in time. The receptionist, who was also responsible for records and was Dr. Howard's secretary, said she was drowning in the additional work load caused by Dr. Howard's work pace, dictation, and writing. Dr. Howard thought she was granting autonomy. Luckily, Mr. Cooper passed this information on too. The secretaries felt neglected and overworked. A few meetings, new work arrangements with which the secretaries felt comfortable, and the purchase of a typewriter for Dr. Howard to use for rough drafts and notes (cutting down on the amount of transcription needed) alleviated the problems, but a thoughtless mistake was narrowly avoided.

Later in the fall, Dr. Howard committed a more serious error involving territorial imperatives over time and authority. Parent-teacher conferences were traditionally held during regular school hours. Based on her experience in other schools, she assumed that the introduction of evening conferences would be greeted with enthusiasm because of the opportunity for increased participation by parents who found it difficult to leave work to attend conferences (a dilemma with which she identified) and the likelihood that more fathers would attend. She suggested in a faculty meeting that the hours be juggled to include an evening, resulting in time off for teachers the next day, and asked for feedback, questions, objections, and suggestions. The reply was silence, both during and after the meeting. She waited several weeks and then, interpreting silence as agreement, scheduled evening conferences in November. She was wrong. Several days after letters were sent to the parents and only a few days before the conferences, several teachers contacted the president of the district teachers' union. On his recommendation, heated faculty debates were held (with only union teachers present; all others were asked to leave). Following an uncomfortable conversation with the school's union rep, a compromise was struck. Conferences proceeded as scheduled, and a record of parent attendance including the time of day, student name, and parents who attended was kept by teachers to evaluate the response to the evening conferences. Many parents expressed their pleasure and surprise at the new times. Although the evening hours were reduced, the faculty voted to continue to hold evening conferences, and other schools began to adopt the practice.

Professional competence structured a final focus of Dr. Howard's interaction with the teachers at Eagleton. Teachers had never been directly observed in their classrooms before the superintendent began an instructional improvement program in the district. The year before the succession, Mr. Light began to implement the district's teacher supervision program, observing a few teachers but providing little follow-up and no criticism. But the role of principal as instructional leader—operationalized as clinical supervision—was emphasized in the district. Perceived expertise as a teacher and stories about useful feedback helped Dr. Howard when it came time to push this change with the whole faculty. The health teacher exclaimed during one of their conversations, "I can't believe it. A principal who knows something about teaching!" Her visits to classrooms were often the beginning of relationships with individual teachers, particularly those just getting started.

Knowing something about teaching was important to the faculty at Eagleton. Mr. Light felt little association with his past as a teacher; Mr. Cooper had no experience as a teacher, having spent his pre-administrative career as an audiologist and done student teaching only to gain administrative certification. Teachers had never been directly observed in their classrooms before the superintendent began an instructional improvement program in the district.

One additional and very important group helped facilitate Dr. Howard's succession at Eagleton. Students were an important part of her integration into the school. She spent a lot of time in the hall with the kids early in the year. At back-to-school night she heard from parents that their children thought she was "pretty and nice" (great qualities for a leader). But by hustling a group of lingering eighth graders on to class late in September, she sparked a conversation in class. "You know, that new principal's nice, but she can be mean, too." The story passed among the teachers at lunch and came back to her from several different sources.

Other student judgments of Dr. Howard also influenced teachers. While observing in a math class, she helped a few students whose hands had been raised for a long time, because the teacher was busy with others. One student refused her help. He would "wait for [his] teacher." When she protested that she was a teacher, he acquiesced. "You'd make a great TA [teaching assistant]," said one student in the hall later that day. She talked with students a lot, spent time in the halls, mingled with the kids during dances, worked with the counselor to resolve group conflicts some girls were having, broke up fights, joked with boys in the hall. Students began dropping by her office to talk about a problem at school or at home or to just pass the time of day. Toward the end of October an eighth grade boy who had already been in trouble several times told his art teacher that Dr. Howard was "very nice." Many students also felt, however, that the new behavior rules were strict and "not fair."

These positive experiences with students played a major role in Dr. Howard's view of the principalship. Late in December, an eighth grader who was having difficulty getting along with her stepfather had sought her out to talk. For a long time they hashed over alternatives: approaches with her mother, how she could behave, what she could say to her stepfather. Together they decided she would ask her mother for a private drive in the car and a long talk. Early one Monday morning, the student grabbed Dr. Howard in the hall, hugged her fiercely and said, "It worked. It worked. We're going to plan something out together. You were so right. It's just perfect. I'm so happy." Then she hugged her again and ran down the hall with her friends.

By late October, people began appearing in Dr. Howard's office to "explain" their original opposition to her. Justifying her letter of protest to the superintendent, its author volunteered, "I wrote to Dr. Johnson before I knew you. At the time I did not agree with his decision. I want you to know, I've changed my mind." However, even as people voiced their growing support, they made it clear that they continued to oppose the trend toward outside appointments to administrative positions they saw developing in the district. "We like you, but we don't like how you got here."

The board president passed on the community response. He stopped Dr. Howard at the district office one morning late in the autumn. Parents who had openly opposed her appointment had begun to change their minds, he said. Several had approached him in the grocery store to tell him so. "I've heard" became a common intro- ductory phrase in her conversations. A gratifying example, given the rocky start with the custodians, came from another principal: "My custodian says your custodian likes you." Sometimes people heard more about her than she would have liked. Over a month after she said, "Do you give a shit?" in a faculty meeting, she heard about it during another faculty meeting. She had evidently provided a lively conversation topic at lunch one day at the high school.

November brought the appearance of a core of support beginning to solidify in the school, even though the debacle over parent/teacher conferences occurred early in the month. Late one afternoon, a teacher stopped to talk in the parking lot. He had a reputation as the perpetual (and not always loyal) opposition, playing the perpetual devil's advocate. "I can't believe you. I've never encountered an open- minded principal in Lakeview District," he said. "I hope I'm here next year," she cautioned. "I hope you know that the feeling is that if they go after you they'll have to go after a lot of us with you." His open expression of support, although she suspected his motives just a bit, lifted her spirits.

Important ratification also came as the new discipline and positive reward system began to take effect. Although Mr. Cooper handled most daily discipline problems, Dr. Howard usually got involved when he was away or busy or when a serious problem arose. These times of high emotion and conflict were stressful but provided further chances to show that Eagleton was not falling apart under the soft and pliant tutelage of a "lady principal." A vandalism case was solved; a major theft resolved.

The consensus among teachers seemed to be that Dr. Howard was "intense." Her socialization at the university, where sharp verbal interaction is the norm, was sometimes misinterpreted. One teacher remarked to another, "[She's] great to work with when you agree with her, but watch out if you don't." However, this doggedness soon joined other judgments about her as a topic for humor, including the old fears that she would be too academic. The expression—"Get out your dictionaries. Here's a memo from Howard"—became commonplace. They were able to joke about disagreements. During a faculty meeting in November she expressed a strong opinion, then remarked, "I've always been reticent to tell people what I really think." "The hell you are," commented a thirty-year veteran. Between his "hell" and her renowned "shit" and amidst laughter they became a conspiracy of ne'er-do-wells with a "reputation in the district."

In the office during the last hours before the December holidays the faculty and staff were relaxing at their traditional reception. A teacher who had left Eagleton for a counseling position in another school had returned to visit old friends. "I hear from several faculty that they like it better here than they ever have, and you're the only thing that has changed," he said.

When everyone returned to school in January, several teachers greeted Dr. Howard in the office: "So, you decided to come back after all." People seldom mentioned Mr. Light, and, when they did, focused on their personal and usually pleasant memories. Seldom was he excoriated for the way things used to be. It sounded strange to Dr. Howard when anyone referred to her as the "new" principal.

By early spring Dr. Howard felt a renewed impetus to pursue additional perspectives on Eagleton's problems. Although they had successfully implemented a discipline plan, it lacked a coherent positive reward system. With the help of money made available by Dr. Gary, she sent groups of teachers to observe and visit schools in surrounding states to investigate promising programs and alternative ways to organize curriculum and instruction for intermediate students. A few teachers became so excited they demanded a continually increased pace of change and renewal. Responses were never universal, however. Although change became an expected and valued factor, some found the adjustment difficult. Disagreements developed between faculty members and were freely expressed. Two teachers in particular remained critical, unconvinced that Dr. Howard was an appropriate leader for Eagleton. But at the retirement dinner for two teachers and the school's counselor, the counselor's husband sought her out. "I wanted to thank you for this last year," he said. "You've made all the difference for us."

One major test remained—the traditional trashing of the halls the last week of school and an infamous closed campus and student search at every door to control water balloons and shaving cream during the last day. A series of strategy sessions with student leaders, PTA representatives, and teachers resulted in a plan including a locker clean-out early in the week and memory book signing, regular class schedules, no searches, and no closed campus. The trashing did not occur. A district social worker stopped Dr. Howard in a quiet upstairs hall in the middle of the last day. "You really run a tight ship around here, don't you?" he said. The only water balloon came after the final bell: three teachers stuffed it down the back of Dr. Howard's shirt, broke it, and ran out to supervise the final loading of the buses to the enthusiastic cheers of the students.

The last week of school a special education aide dropped by Dr. Howard's office and closed the door. "A lot of us were really unhappy when we found out you were going to be the principal. I was one of them. I worked for a woman principal. . . , and it was not a good experience. But I couldn't let you think that we still feel that way. You helped me realize that it's a personal thing. It's been a pleasant surprise." Another teacher (the author of the previous spring's protest letter to the superintendent) said goodbye for the summer another way. She put her arms around Dr. Howard and gave her a warm hug. "Thank you for showing us a vision of the way things can be instead of focusing on the way they are." Seven years later, long after Howard had left Eagleton for another assignment, an art and history teacher from the school ran into her in the corridor of city hall in the state's capital city. "Aren't you Kate Howard?" she asked. "I thought I recognized you." After exchanging small talk for a few minutes, the teacher remarked, "You were a breath of fresh air at Eagleton."

The Insider's View of Organizational Socialization

Dr. Howard, like Dr. Hamilton at Valley Elementary, replaced a principal who retired. Unlike Hamilton, she was taking over her first assignment as a principal in a district in which she had never worked. Like Hamilton, insight into her experience (cast from her point of view with additions offered by other participants) is provided by an organization socialization analysis.

General Characteristics

In many ways very similar to the first few months of Hamilton's tenure at Valley, Howard's socialization into the district and school was individual, informal, random, and variable. Until she asked, no one even told her where the school was located. Other than regular principals' meetings, she had no contact with either experienced principals taking over in new schools or other new principals. Contact with Mr. Light, Mr. Cooper, parents, and others in the school and district were made as issues came up and usually at her initiative. While she chose to visit the school many times between her appointment and the summer break, she was not required by her superiors to do so.

Because Howard moved from a university setting to school administration and took on responsibilities that contrasted with her previous teaching experience, the principalship at Eagleton represented a divestiture of professional self-concept, moving her farther toward a challenge to her professional identity and sense of self at work that had begun with her preservice professional socialization. It also required that she use many newly acquired skills for the first time in a new situation. Howard had no direct role models; she was the first woman principal at the secondary level in the district and one of only two in the state at the time. She was also an outsider, coming from a city and an organizational environment reputed to advance values and behaviors not necessarily valued by the teachers, administrators, and staff at Eagleton. People openly expressed worries that she was too academic for her new job. In that sense, her socialization experience was disjunctive because she was significantly different from others who had held the role before her.

Many of these organizational socialization factors could have been influenced (or even structured) by school district leaders. The visits to the school, almost immediate interaction with existing members of the group at Eagleton, the community, and the larger organization, and extended interaction and communication with them frequently happened because of casual conversations as Howard learned more about the place.

Personal and Social Context of Socialization

Personal Context. Because this case was undertaken from the principal's point of view, data about Howard's own sense making is available. She recognized changes in her situation/professional self-concept, its interaction with core self-concept over time, and the impact on values, intellectual functioning, and sense of self-direction that her experiences at Eagleton were having. Like the teachers at Valley, the parents, teachers, and school board members associated with Eagleton immediately focused their attention on Howard's personal traits. They used highly visible characteristics to pass early judgment about her potential for success. They praised (or complained about) her "high standards" and academic focus. They gave her tenure a mixed to pessimistic prognosis, depending on whom you talked to. She was inexperienced, overly academic, into theories picked up at the "other university." She was viewed as an outsider during a time when resentment and retrenchment against outsiders was building in the district. Teachers (and her own assistant principal) feared she lacked the "orientation" necessary to run a junior high school. Others worried that she was "cold" and "intimidating" ("They're more afraid of you than you are of them. . . ."), a hired gun mandated to clean house for the superintendent and school board members who were themselves university faculty. At the same time, many doubted any woman could provide the tight ship they felt they needed, and she was a working mother who had usurped a scarce leadership opportunity from a well-liked and well-connected man who had done his duty for district and church.

While Howard had felt compelled to carry her "vision" of an effective junior high school to Eagleton and reproduce it there, the interaction with the school quickly challenged this view. She explicitly stated that the first several months of tenure were spent on issues identified by the parents, teachers, and assistant principal, not by her preconceived notions about the "strong leader" the school board said they wanted in her interview. Descriptions of her personal characteristics evolved, too. While the traits that led to Howard's appointment also worried board members and teachers, the emphasis on her traits shifted from their incongruence and disruptiveness to their utility. Although still an outsider, she possessed the necessary "image" for Eagleton and "needed professional skills." She was intense, yet positive and personable, consultative, sometimes democratic (to the protestations of some veteran faculty members who wanted her to "just tell us what to do, and we'll do it"). Committed to teaching, she knew where she was going, and the teachers knew "where she stood." A strict disciplinarian, she got along well with junior high students. She was decisive enough and enough of a maverick to fit in with a faculty that prided itself on its "difficult" reputation.

Social Context. Howard's experience illustrates markedly the prediction that, in loosely coupled systems like schools, it takes more effort for a successor to establish socially validated authority relationships with the existing group members than it might in, say, a military organization. It also illustrates that strong responses by influential members (Mr. Cooper, a few powerful teachers with long tenure who were respected by their peers) can trigger similar responses from other members. First, in the case of the English department chairperson who protested Howard's appointment and then changed her mind, her status as "perhaps the best teacher in this school" and a supporter of Howard within a few months affected others' developing opinions. Second, the processing of information about Howard across reference groups who were not always allies—the ex-counselor's stories heard around the district, the tales told at back-to-school-night, the favorable feedback from parent-teacher conferences, the praise following an open meeting to explain the new discipline policy, the commendations in response to letters coming from the school, the federal district court judge who returned to the school to volunteer his services for inservice upon meeting the principal—created a new definition and interpretation for Howard's principalship. "You're the only thing that's changed. . . ."

Other aspects of the social context influenced Howard's socialization. Many features of the organizational context were unfavorable. Even at best, by the end of the year, some influential teachers remained unconvinced that Howard was a good principal. Three male faculty members were bitter critics, and she never won them over. They found her leadership and supervisory styles aggressive and her credentials questionable. Another teacher secretly tape-recorded all faculty meetings throughout the year, "just in case" he needed evidence in some future conflict. The board of education member who boycotted the meeting at which she was introduced before her appointment never did introduce himself to her. More favorable features of the context required some digging before they emerged.

First, many people began to see valued similarities in skills and values between Howard and the professionals in the school and district. Her experience affirms that contact breeds respect when the features around which the contact focuses are valuable professional skills and critical personal experiences, beliefs, and orientations. Howard sought out and was given (sometimes through serendipity and extenuating circumstances) a number of opportunities to demonstrate shared professional values, beginning with her approach to the parents' demands for a new discipline system.

Second, communication, centered around core features of teaching and central worries about an orderly learning environment, occurred frequently and with many different people long before the school year began. Howard ran into some difficulties as she misinterpreted silence as assent and continued resistance from opponents. During the first four or five months, all did not go smoothly. Some core values of independence were violated, and the environment (a contract dispute taking place at the same time) played an important part in highlighting problems in communication. A number of major differences in interpretation occurred.

Third, prevailing beliefs about things that make a good principal and make one a leader did not coincide with early beliefs about Howard. Her surface personality characteristics presented an early barrier to her acceptance. People feared she was a "hatchet man"; an egghead ("Get out the dictionary; Howard's written another memo"); an outsider; a woman who can't maintain discipline; a woman who "stole" the promotional opportunity from deserving local men who support their families. These prevailing beliefs remained preeminent for some, even after a year in the principalship.

A fourth aspect of the social environment worked to Howard's advantage. She shared fundamental work and organizational values with many people who held informal and formal positions of influence at Eagleton—respect for the professional teacher, discipline combined with respect for students, high academic values, shared experiences in junior high schools, interest in and support for innovation and change, support for helping interested teachers get involved in shaping new programs and other reforms. Diversity then became possible, because initially visible and incongruent personal characteristics became less and less important as core professional values in the school were reinforced. These events partly grew out of intentional actions on Howard's part. She told stories and shared experiences; she implemented a consultative approach to the development of the new discipline plan that acknowledge parents' concerns and teachers' professional territory. She developed procedures for supervising students that protected teachers from the odious teacher supervision assignments of previous years (at the close of school) and unintentionally emphasized congruent and core values. Other favorable interactions with the social environment came to Howard by chance. She acknowledged that she did not have a deliberate strategy for capitalizing on favorable features of the social context.

The preceding description of social context features oversimplifies the role played by the social context in shaping the Howard succession, however, because interactions reveal more about eventual outcomes than does a catalogue of Howard's actions. She assumed the principalship in a school in which a conservative community had become accustomed to its religious, community, and school leaders being the same people. She was the only woman who was a principal in the secondary schools, even though her supporters worried women would automatically reject her as a leader because she was a woman, and "people [would] be afraid of her." An outsider, standing at the end of a procession of outsiders who were being subjected to escalating hostility, she was appointed by an outsider superintendent and a school board (two of whom boycotted the meeting with her prior to her appointment) dominated by professors.

In this atmosphere of uncertainty, frustration, and apprehension, the faculty was defensive and resentful toward the board, the parents, and Howard. They took the first possible opportunity to point out their "difficult" and "uncooperative" reputation to her. Teachers asked her what "she had been told" about Eagleton. They protested the "critical and effete" attitudes of the patrons/parents. They let Howard know that clinical supervision, a mandated program, unsettled them and outsiders as principals offended them.

In a pattern of parry and thrust, a series of direct conflicts precipitated exchanges between Howard and the faculty, staff, and parents that set up her validation by the group and permission from them to lead at Eagleton. Howard was unaware of the importance of these events at the time they occurred. These events allowed Howard to capitalize on the hopes people shared for a new perspective on the challenges of education and change at Eagleton that existed side by side with strident resentment against her. Howard's first interactions were personal—with Cooper, the assistant principal. Together they spent long, late hours talking about the school. After each of many long meetings with Mr. Light, her predecessor, Howard went to Cooper for information and insight about what she had just heard. Cooper, therefore, had the first and most powerful influence on her interpretation of the school. In turn, he revealed his own disappointment and aspirations, and they planned specific strategies to increase his visibility in the district as a promising administrator.

The second interaction with the social context that shaped Howard's succession was with the teachers. In return for their time, reflection, and insight, she offered the chance to each teacher to criticize and recommend changes in drafts of the new discipline plan demanded by parents. Elected teacher representatives participated directly in the decisions that shaped the ultimate plan features. Howard sidestepped the parents' demands for assertive discipline before school began but gave the parents a new and reassuring system they could count on as well as a community advisory committee that met monthly with her to raise issues and provide input into school programs. During the year, Howard set up repeated opportunities for teacher control over important decisions related to instruction, curriculum, and programs, which many accepted. Even though Howard and some faculty members clashed over her sometimes combative verbal style, which a few labeled confrontational, they openly made it the brunt of jokes, enjoying its effects on adversaries. When the palace revolt over parent-teacher conferences occurred, a parent survey of attendance assessing the experiment mollified the concerns of the majority of teachers. Many teachers passed compliments from parents to other teachers to Howard—especially those from *teachers,* also parents, who had never been able to attend parent conferences in the past because of rigid schedules during which they, too, worked (9:00 A.M. to 3:00 P.M.). In the end, teachers voted to retain the evening conferences in reduced form. Howard lost a few hours from the conferences in the exchange. More importantly, she began to gain the trust of teachers and parents over common concerns about students. She had accumulated important "idiosyncrasy" credits, in Yukl's terms.

The social context at Eagleton provided a developing framework for interpreting events surrounding Howard's succession that deviated from the dominant early interpretations based on her most visible personal characteristics. This framework reinforced the legitimacy she attained as a result of the early conflicts and confrontations over discipline policies and parent-teacher conferences about student achievement and stood in contrast to the overwhelmingly negative view held by the majority of teachers early in her tenure and a minority of teachers at the end of a year. An orderly learning environment and the accomplishments of their children captured parents' attention; these also were core values held by teachers. While parents failed to achieve their immediate goal in April—the implementation of assertive discipline—Howard dignified their concern with actions focused on student discipline, an emphasis she would not have chosen to promote (even after the trashing of the halls she witnessed in May). A year of constant attention to positive relationships between teachers and students at Eagleton culminated in a peaceful and affectionate last day of school that exemplified the concerted efforts of teachers, students, and administrators during the year. Howard was the only person who fell victim to a water balloon—and that at the hands of a teacher.

Interactions, grounded in serious consideration and respect, characterized Howard's relationship with the school's secretaries and custodians as well. Complaints of neglect from her were met, with the unqualified help of Mr. Cooper, with new schedules for regular meetings to assess needs and provide assistance in completing their work. The building was cleaner, and the staff received many compliments as a result. These compliments from outsiders gradually changed their orientation toward "messes." Simple cordiality quieted early fears felt by secretaries that Howard would dump them and "bring in [her] own people." Later, their gentle complaints to Cooper that Howard's work style resulted in an overload for them were met with adjustments in demands and new equipment, along with reinforced requests for independence and performance from them. Everyone worked harder, including Howard.

As Nicholson cautions, affective reactions to succession must not be ignored. Howard was rewarded for her response to staff worries with regular invitations to eat lunch with the staff. The secretaries fed her and fussed over her preference for diet Coke instead of school lunch. They plied her with salads laced with diet dressing, buns without butter.

Many people in the district organization also contributed to the social acceptance Howard gradually experienced from the majority of her coworkers. The district maintenance supervisor provided early credit with their faculty by installing a sink for their lunches and painting the front hall. Other principals provided peer acceptance and legitimacy. Even the most veteran high school principal said she was a "real smart little gal." Board members gave affirmation and support as they passed on tales about the "positive atmosphere" at Eagleton. The assistant superintendent, famous for his people skills throughout the district, turned people's attention toward Howard's affective qualities with his simple, warm support.

Some faculty members remained unsupportive of Howard, emphasizing their anger over male/female and insider/outsider ascension issues and an overly aggressive interpersonal style. Howard heard five years later that three men still spoke angrily about her appointment, asserting that she had usurped the earning power of male breadwinners who had paid their dues in the school and district. Core resistance to her as a principal came from two experienced male teachers who never, to Howard's knowledge, revised their initial negative assessments and opposition to her appointment. The one teacher who made a specific effort to ridicule Howard's husband, a public service attorney ("All my attorney friends say they can't make it in private practice) told friends privately that he never was reconciled to Howard. The social context with its overarching norms supporting teaching and learning held sway over the criticism, resulting in a dominant spirit of support by the end of a year and an open acknowledgment that Howard's impact on the school was apparent.

In the presence of change through interaction with the existing organization, Howard's personal characteristics, the same traits that inspired early suspicion and fear, became the object of warmth, affection, and humor from a critical mass of faculty members by the winter holidays. (They would never dare say "shit" at Eagleton, would they?) Faults became qualities. Deeply imbedded resentments associated with the district and broader issues were untouched by this process, however. Outsider appointments for principals remained a bone of contention. Past experiences with women administrators were bitter memories, often recounted. Teachers who preferred the Light style and era withheld their approval from Howard and made sure she knew it. Her socialization into Eagleton was experienced and interpreted by its participants as a unique, ungeneralizable interaction. They chose to see it as a single event. Past experiences with women administrators remained salient and vivid, unmodified by this single experience. A few who preferred the patriarchal Mr. Light, who had tried to control behavior by telling stories about his grandfather's experiences in the local church, remained unsupportive and critical. Howard's leadership was labeled a "personal thing." They said that they knew where she stood: for an Eagleton exemplified in achievement, dignity, and pride but clearly for a modified power structure that continued to cause discomfort.

Socialization Stages

Unlike Hamilton's happy experience at Valley, Howard's encounter stage brought conflict and disappointment. Parents immediately demanded a hearing in which to present their demands. The "most respected teacher on the faculty" protested her appointment to the superintendent. A valued native son and candidate for promotion (Mr. Cooper) quietly swallowed his pride and mourned in private while his friends took up his torch. Howard's encounter/anticipation/confrontation stage of organizational socialization, as a result of this situation, was turbulent. The advantage this experience gave her emerged as a result of the real therapy it provided—she confronted reality, the expectations, conflicts, and disaffections of organizational members that surrounded her appointment.

Reflecting this concern, Howard recalled thinking on the drive home from her first visit to Eagleton, "I've been set up." At the same time, this experience challenged Howard's conception of her role as a principal and the contribution she might make to a school's performance—measured as student achievement and in terms of teachers' work lives. Light had gleefully presented California Achievement Test scores for the school in years past, claiming them as an achievement of the administration and faculty. But these students' predicted scores belied Light's happy prognosis. Where might they achieve, given their privilege of birth and environment? Right on predicted levels.

The second stage in organizational socialization frameworks, clarity or adjustment and accommodation, aptly characterized stabilizing interactions between Howard and the school and district. Several issues and events controlled Howard's responses: (a) new interpersonal relationships (at first dominated by secretaries and custodians) demanded careful reflection, particularly because she was surprised; (b) events demanding quick agreement on goals and programs among the faculty and staff required assessment; and finally (c) staff complaints received a response acceptable to most of the people involved. Custodians grumbled but received praise from peers for the appearance of buildings. Teachers asserted that Howard's emphasis on learning and respect for people as individuals protected them as well as the students. Howard adjusted to the secretaries' work overload.

This amalgam of events led to a final stage—location—placing Howard within the school, and it happened by December or January. Her place was stabilized. She managed her role. Teachers and staff saw a fit. The words of staff, students, teachers, and parents placed her firmly in the future direction of Eagleton Junior High School, while she never achieved total consensus and praise from all faculty members. By Christmas, eight months after her appointment was announced at a meeting of the school board, Howard was a feature of Eagleton Junior High. No one talked about biding time. Teachers said, "We know where you stand."

Outcomes of Socialization

Several of the tactics experienced by Howard during organizational socialization experience suggest she might be more likely to simply accept many existing procedures, leaving role content alone and taking a custodial stance in search of group and personal security. Where office and other instrumental tasks were concerned, she did just that for a long time. Unlike Hamilton, she did not see control over supplies and paperwork as a central issue in her early months as principal. Other characteristics of this case would predict that she would be more likely to respond with content and role innovation.

Recall from the earlier discussion that the general experience was disjunctive, random, informal, and individual, and that it fell somewhere between investiture and divestiture (as an intermediate step in her professional socialization). These characteristics would be more likely to support role innovation—redefining the mission or goals of the role, rejecting many norms governing conduct and performance, and redefining ends as well as means. They also support the application of new tactics, tasks, and knowledge bases to the challenges of the role and some redefinition of the role of principal. The completely individual nature of the experience increased Howard's early ambiguity. She was not sure how to meet the expectations of the board (for a strong leader), the superintendent (for an instructional leader), angry parents (for a tight ship), and teachers (for professional respect from the principal), let alone the students. Her early interactions—a few interviews with her predecessor, Mr. Light—were so informal as to reduce the likelihood of a completely custodial response. Also, Howard saw Light's efforts to influence her ("I wouldn't make any major changes, if I were you") as a direct effort to manipulate and control her. A number of writers have predicted that this informality is more likely to produce more extreme good and bad outcomes, a factor that may also have contributed to Hamilton's experience.

The outcomes of this socialization were also affective. As the writers whose work is reviewed in Chapter 1 emphasize, changes in values, skills, and behavior all are very important during organizational socialization. These internal changes—both by way of discovering things about herself and acknowledging the validity of feelings expressed by those around her that she would not previously have predicted—may have made it possible for Howard to fit in at Eagleton without sacrificing her individuality. As the faculty reminded her later in the year, they all, including her now, "had a reputation in the district."

All these factors, tactics, the personal and social context, and socialization stages emerging from interactions produced an outcome that the organizational socialization literature describes as exploration—both role and individual development. Nicholson pointed out that high role innovators also report a great deal of personal development and change as a result of a change in work assignments. Exploration is also a more common outcome of socialization than is dogged determination, in which little personal change occurs but significant role innovation takes place. Hamilton appeared to seek content innovation, controlling office procedures, bell schedules, student traffic patterns, and recess assignments, and he had the formal authority to impose these changes. He did so at a price.

The outcomes of Howard's case highlight a need identified by Nicholson (1984) for those involved in major work transitions and those who study them to attend more to the levels at which people do their work creatively and innovatively. Her case also reveals a number of organizational socialization factors that, combined with personal factors, led to both role and personal innovation and social validation, despite the continued opposition of some individuals in the school.

6

The Professional and Organizational Socialization of Principals: Analysis of Additional Research

The preceding two chapters illustrate how the central themes of organizational socialization can be used to expand understanding of the processes through which principals and schools experience succession and profit or fail to profit from the process. These two cases were chosen for their detail and for the views of the principalship they represent—elementary and junior high school, first-time and experienced principals, male/female, principal perspective/teachers' perspective, insider/outsider. In this chapter, recent leader succession and professional socialization studies of principals that include these and additional contextual factors, qualitative and quantitative data, and a number of different research perspectives are analyzed to further demonstrate the application of organizational socialization frameworks to the study and practice of leader succession in schools.

This chapter draws in detail on a study by Cosgrove[1] (1986) and in lesser detail on studies by Crow (1989, 1990b); Lamoreaux (1990); Leithwood, Steinbach, and Begley (in press); Oliver (1992); Parkay, Currie, and Rhodes (1992); Roberts (1989a, 1989b); Roberts and Wright (1992); Weindling and Earley (1987) and Earley, Baker, and Weindling (1990); and Wright (1992).[2] The study by Cosgrove is particularly useful, because she included both first-time and experienced principals and a control group of ongoing principals in her sample and recorded data over time. Most of the other studies also provide longitudinal data. (See also Ackerman, 1991a, 1991b; Beeson & Matthews, 1991; Nytell, 1991; Playko & Daresh, 1989.) They were undertaken as inquiries into the succession or professional socialization of principals and heads in the United States, Great Britain, and Canada. While a number of these studies were concept-ualized by their authors as concerning professional socialization, their samples include principals with previous administrative experience in different roles and at different levels, some in other principalships. Parkay, Currie, and Rhodes (in press), for example, included in their sample of first-time high school principals people who had served as elementary and junior high principals and as assistant principals. Leithwood, Steinbach, and Begley (in press) also chose to include vice principals and principals undergoing inservice training in their study. They placed these principals in the incorporation stage of professional socialization, based on a stage framework developed by Ronkowski and Iannaccone. All these studies were cited briefly in Chapters 1 and 2, which introduced the literature on principal socialization and succession.

The studies discussed in this chapter were chosen for three main reasons. First, they are among the most current available research that focuses on principal succession and socialization. They include qualitative and quantitative data and employ a variety of methods for analysis. They draw on assumptions as varied as those under-girding rational positivism and aesthetic criticism and were analyzed using many techniques, and they looked at socialization and succession from the principals' and the organizations' points of view. The variety of methods and theoretical approaches represented by these studies gives a view of principal succession that supersedes the limitations of perspective. Second, succession studies that include school leaders of varying experience in their samples are scarce, so it was helpful to include studies that chose to define professional socialization in the broadest possible terms, including experienced administrators in their samples, in order to examine the utility of organizational socialization themes for the analysis of principal succession. Finally, the dynamics of organizational socialization exert powerful influence over the successions of first-time principals as well as those of more experienced principals. Those new to administration undergo a more complex set of socializing experience than more experienced principals. Their socialization includes two dimensions: those unique to the profession and those unique to the context in which they begin their administrative careers. These principals should not be overlooked in either research or practice when leader succession is the focus.

The chapter is organized much like the preceding two cases. A description of the studies and their major findings is followed by an analysis of these findings based on the four central themes of organizational socialization.

Studies of Newly Appointed Principals

Ten Principals—Five Successors and Five Continuing

Cosgrove (1986) studied the succession of five elementary school principals in a single district over the course of a year. She began her study by looking for "patterns in the interpretations and perceptions held by members of the educational organization as they experienced a new leader" (p. 4). The study inquired into the antecedents and consequences of leadership, using principal succession as the precipitating event. It looked at teachers' and principals' perceptions and interpretations of the behavior and events connected with the assignment of a new principal. Undertaken primarily from the teachers' perspective, this study provided a basis for assessing the effects of principal succession on elementary schools.

To accomplish her goal, Cosgrove collected data on ten schools— five experiencing succession and five serving as controls. Her research questions sought to probe explanations for the multiple effects of leader succession based on the stage framework provided by Miskel and Cosgrove (1985). Her questions included:

1. What is the reason for the succession?
2. What is the selection procedure for the principalship?
3. What is the reputation of the new principal?
4. What is the school like before the new principal is installed? Culture, expectations, current job satisfaction of teachers.
5. What are the effects of the reasons for the succession and selection procedures?
6. What changes, if any, are attributed to the succession by principals and teachers? Orientation of new principal, culture, effectiveness, job satisfaction.
7. How do schools experiencing succession compare with schools not experiencing succession?
8. What emerging general themes increase knowledge about succession?

To accomplish this goal, Cosgrove studied the five schools experiencing a change in principals in a district (omitting two newly built schools from her study) and five schools (matched demographically with the succession schools) with ongoing principals. Her sample of respondents included forty-eight teachers chosen randomly from faculty in sample schools and twelve principals (the ten principals who were ongoing and successors, and two predecessors). Because her study was conducted in a single district, principal successions during the year in which the study was conducted included transfers. Consequently, two of Cosgrove's successor subjects were predecessors in schools chosen for study. Three principals were both predecessors and successors—located at two different schools included in the study. Two principals in her study were successors only. Both of these were first-time principals who had been assigned to a sample school. The five continuing principals in the study were included as part of a control group.

Data were collected in two forms: (1) individual interviews with five teachers selected at random in the sample schools and with the principals in the same schools and (2) a teacher job satisfaction inventory administered at the time of the succession and one year later. Cosgrove's interviews focused on five areas found to affect leader succession: (1) reasons for the succession; (2) the selection process; (3) the reputation or orientation of the successor; (4) school culture— roles, rules, shared themes or values, principal's role; and (5) school outcomes/effectiveness (positive or negative change or no difference). To avoid the problems associated with spurious causal attributions, Cosgrove chose to conceptualize effects in her study as changes in the prearrival and arrival factors associated with her framework.

Presuccession in Succession Schools. The reasons for the successions were benign in all but one case. Two of the predecessor principals left their positions because they were assigned to newly built schools; there were no deaths, retirements, or resignations. Two of the principals felt their assignments were promotions (larger or newer schools) and three saw them as lateral career moves. Four moves were unforced; one was forced. The subjects saw their information exchange with predecessors as primarily informative. None of Cosgrove's subjects reported that their predecessors tried to alter their decisions, and subsequent information exchange among predecessors and successors generally occurred at the initiation of the successor.

Mentors played little or no role in these successions, not even for the first-time principals. The two new principals did believe that they had mentors, but they expected to receive only limited influence from them in the future.

The expectations of teachers and principals for the succession played a large part in Cosgrove's study. One of the major set of expectations involved expected changes. Principals and teachers differed on their views about changes they could expect from the succession. "Almost all teachers expected their new principal to promote general changes as he took over the school, but this expectation did not cause much discomfort. Comments such as 'It'll work out okay,' 'It won't affect our overall teaching,' 'It'll be hard for us to get used to, but it will be good for us (to change),' and 'It's his right'" dominated. Principals, on the other hand, "felt most things would remain the same" (Cosgrove, 1986, p. 63). "Principals expressed a need to hold back on major changes, while teachers felt these changes were significant."

The perceptions of principals and teachers about district mandates given to principals mirrored those about change. Two-thirds of the teachers thought that a district mandate had been given to the new principal. They believed these mandates related to personnel, curriculum, student achievement, and community relations. They also thought the new principals were given instructions to correct a problem, meet district goals, and so forth. In contrast, the principals identified few mandates. Some were encouraged to improve the condition and appearance of the school building; one was asked to improve relations with the PTA.

Other expectations that existed before the successions took place showed that the principals and teachers shared general norms of participation in decision making by teachers when the decisions involved curriculum and instruction, student behavior, discipline, or staff concerns. At three schools, the teachers expected a lot of teacher input in decision making; at one they expected strong principal decision making; at one, they felt it would be a combination. When decisions involving the whole school were required, those at one school were not sure how involved they might be; at two schools the teachers felt the principal would decide; at two they felt the teachers would decide. Overall, the successors' expectations matched the teachers' fairly well in these areas. Where teacher autonomy was concerned, their expectations matched very closely.

Another important prearrival factor considered by Cosgrove was school culture. She attempted to get a sense of the cultures of the schools in which succession was about to take place by asking teachers and principals to identify key roles played by teachers in the school, social norms or unspoken rules, and shared themes or goals. Teachers in the five schools identified teachers filling the roles of spokespersons, leaders who fill in, and empathizers who listen to personal problems. Few could identify social leaders, problem solvers, peacemakers, complainers, gossips, jokers, troublemakers, or principal's pets. The predecessor principals identified different key roles filled by teachers—social leaders and problem solvers.

The identification of social norms and unspoken rules posed more of a challenge for participants. Principals and teachers had a "great deal of difficulty identifying social norms or unspoken rules" (p. 67). Themes were a bit easier for principals and teachers to describe. All the predecessor principals and most of the teachers could name a specific goal or theme representing a shared value at the school (i.e., school-community unity, self-concepts of students, cooperative work, encouraging excellence), but Cosgrove found little agreement within schools about the themes. "Despite the fact that those who could identify a theme thought that it was generally agreed upon by most of the staff, it was rare that even two people from any of the schools named the same theme or goal" (p. 68). The teachers tended to think the principals were the source of any given theme.

Even though participants could not adequately describe important cultural elements of their schools, they gave extensive credit "to principals in general for the nature of school culture. The principal 'sets the tone' or 'mood for the entire school' and influences the staff through opinions, attitudes, the way support is given, and the level of stress created," they said (p. 68).

> Teachers believe that principal behavior becomes a model for how teachers will treat each other and the types of interaction that will take place. As one teacher said, "How he treats you is the key. There is less gossip and back-biting if the principal is not mean. If he's a tyrant, it will cause you to be guarded and to become like him." (p. 68)

Confusion about the nature of organizational culture seemed to exist among the participants in the study. Some seemed to equate interpersonal relationships with school culture. One teacher said, "It makes a big difference [who he brings in]. They may not team or coordinate and get along. In selection of personnel—he'll pick people like himself" (p. 68). People believed in school culture, but neither principals nor teachers could adequately describe it.

Teachers and predecessor and successor principals expected smooth sailing during the succession. The only possible problems they foresaw were in the area of teacher-principal relationships. Half of the teachers expected no difference in the effectiveness of the school; a third expected the new principal to have a positive influence on outcomes; and the remainder of the teachers thought the effect of the succession would be negative. The principals were far more sanguine about their potential. Two-thirds of the successor principals expected their effect on the new school would be positive. One third of successors thought they would play no causal role in effectiveness.

Teachers at the succession schools generally were satisfied with their work. They scored a mean of 26.7 and a median of 27.7 out of 35 possible on a teacher job satisfaction questionnaire administered at the end of each interview.

Postsuccession Findings—Succession Schools. Successors and teachers perceived no effect of succession factors on the schools. Successors reported no attempts by predecessors to influence the school. The two new principals reported very little input from their mentors. They also felt that "they had incorrectly assumed that new principals were typically given more guidance in the beginning and that being left to their own devices was common practice" (pp. 81–82).

Teachers in all five schools could describe changes in leader focus, leadership style, and decision-making patterns. They generally saw more emphasis on student discipline, new focus on certain curriculum areas, differences in supervision and classroom observation, and changes in the cleanliness of the building. Most seemed comfortable with the changes. In one school where succession had been frequent, the teachers said:

[They] had grown "to expect a lot of change with a new principal. It gets worse at first, then it gets better." They spoke of "retraining principals to our way" and "wasting a lot of time back pedaling while they try things we've already done that don't work." They resigned themselves to the inevitable, saying, "We don't worry," and "We must endure and adapt." (p. 82)

All teachers reported differences between the predecessor's and successor's leadership styles. Two were seen as more relationship oriented; three as more task and goal oriented. The task leaders were seen by the teachers as insensitive to the personal lives of teachers and unsupportive of teachers in parent-teacher interactions. Teachers said they were distant in relationships and dictatorial, emphasizing structure and specific goals, directions, and guidelines. Teachers also felt that the two principals who were relationship oriented could get things done. Little agreement existed between these descriptions and principals' descriptions of their own leadership styles.

A new style of decision making also appeared in each school. "Degree of teacher participation, areas in which input is requested, frequency with which input is used, and decision making participants varied across schools and from the predecessor to the successor in each school" (p. 84). "In the two schools in which much input was both requested and used, teachers were pleased with the decision making style" (p. 84).

Teachers in four of the five schools reported no change in school culture (even though they had little idea what it is). The school in which a change was reported found it positive:

> The faculty had become closer, power was more evenly distributed, males were no longer favored over females, sharing among teachers increased, and grade levels interacted more. Teachers felt they were respected as professionals by the principal. All of these changes were attributed to the new principal, with credit also given to a smaller faculty and enrollment than the previous year. (p. 85)

Respondents saw changes in the teachers filling cultural roles as "the major culture change." In four of the five schools, the new principals brought with them trusted teachers they had known in other settings. "In each case, the faculty perceived this new teacher to have greater influence, access to information, or favor with the principal at the beginning of the year" (p. 86). All teachers—the existing faculty and the new teacher—were aware of this strategy. In three of the schools, the teachers did not mind; in another teachers used the new person as a source of information and influence; in one they had trouble adjusting to the personality of the new teacher. Teachers interpreted changes in interpersonal dynamics and in the individuals filling cultural niches as change in school culture.

All teachers and principals reported that the schools were functioning effectively and the transition had gone smoothly. Teachers at one school said the successor was easier to work with than was the predecessor. At another school, teachers were surprised that none of the problems they had expected had materialized. At another school, the faculty reported that the succession had gone smoothly despite many problems because of "their professionalism and the high quality of the staff" (p. 87). One teacher remarked:

> You expect a lot of change with a new principal. Principals think they are going to offer something no one else can. . . . You have to adapt to their expectations. Some things are easy to adapt to, some are contrary to your own feelings, some you don't care

about. You just have to wait and see. Don't worry, just watch and adapt. (p. 87)

Job satisfaction was not affected by the succession. The teachers scored a mean of 26.7 and a median of 27 out of 35 on the teacher job satisfaction questionnaire.

Presuccession Patterns in Continuing Schools. The patterns of leadership, expectations for change, and culture in the continuing schools chosen as a control group by Cosgrove were much like those in the succession schools. Teachers felt that the principals cared a great deal about district administrators' perceptions of them. Three-fourths of the teachers and all of the principals expected some changes to be made in the school in the coming year. Two of the continuing schools had second-year principals, and teachers in these schools predicted many changes. At one of these schools, teachers felt the potential changes would be positive. At the other, teachers felt threatened by the promised changes. The remaining three schools were perceived by teachers and principals as "very conservative with changes."

Perceptions of leadership style varied widely, and Cosgrove could discern no patterns. Like the succession schools, the teachers and the principals did not agree on task versus relationship orientations of the principal. The teachers in two schools said their principal was totally lacking in leadership. In the school where the principal was in his second year, the teachers expressed anger and resentment at the principal and apologized for "sounding so negative" and "unloading more than you ever wanted to hear" (p. 74).

Like the succession schools, those in the continuing schools could not describe their own school cultures. The roles mentioned by teachers included leaders who fill in, consolers, and squeaky wheels whose complaints are addressed because they are so verbal. The principals added spokespersons.

Teachers could not identify social norms or unspoken rules without great difficulty. When they did, they named fairly shallow things like "Return things to the media center on time. The media lady gets horribly upset about overdue books."

About two-thirds of teachers and four of five principals could name goals or themes that they felt reflected a widely held value. The principal often was the source of the goal or theme, for example, looking for the good in every child—positive self-images. In all five schools, at least three people named the same goal or theme. While the principals thought they had extensive influence on school culture, the teachers disagreed. This was not because teachers did not believe principals could influence culture. "Principals can make an enormous difference. They are the glue to hold things together, but not here" (p. 77). "The principal should, but [our principal] doesn't. If cohesiveness occurs, the team does it. It's not because of him" (p. 77).

Teachers in three schools felt that "major" changes occurred in the year between the first and second interviews. They, too, viewed interpersonal relationships as organizational culture, complaining about increased gossiping, backbiting, transfer requests, cliquish behavior, decreased sharing, and emotional distancing from school problems. In one school where the principal was in his second year, teachers reported that faculty room conversation had become almost exclusively gossip and negative conversation about the principal.

In four of the five control schools, teachers and principals expected no change in the effectiveness of the school in the coming year. In the one where change was expected, expectations were negative, and teachers shared ominous predictions. Only one-fourth of the teachers felt principals had a causal role in the way the school ran.

The job satisfaction of teachers in the control schools was similar to that in the succession schools—a mean of 28.4 and a median of 29 of a total 35 on the teacher job satisfaction questionnaire. At the end of a year, these remained unchanged—a mean of 28 and a median of 28.7.

Postsuccession Data from Continuing Schools. The teachers and principals were accurate in their predictions about what would happen during the intervening year. In the school where major changes were anticipated, they came and were viewed as more negative than positive. Additionally, teachers in three other schools reported differences in areas they interpreted as culture, complaining about more gossiping, backbiting, transfer requests, and cliquish behavior. They felt there was less sharing and that teachers distanced themselves from school problems.

In spite of these complaints, teachers reported no change in the effectiveness of their schools. They said things had gone "smoothly" during the year and teaching had been as expected. They also showed no significant change in teacher job satisfaction (mean of 28; median of 28.7 out of 35).

Differences Between Succession and Continuing Schools. The succession and continuing schools in Cosgrove's study showed little systematic variation along the dimensions identified in her framework. Teachers' descriptions of the principals' leadership styles differed widely. Few differences existed in leadership behavior, decision making, teacher autonomy, or perceptions of mandates from the district.

Some differences emerged. All teachers expected changes in some form to be stimulated by principals—those undergoing succession expected more change and more important changes. Teachers in succession schools "anticipated new leadership; they expected the principal to significantly affect the mood, tone, and interactions in the school." Continuing teachers attributed school culture only minimally to the principal. They saw the culture emanating more from the teachers in the school. In two of the continuing schools, however, teachers felt the mandates given them for change were unreasonable. Principals perceived mandates differently. The continuing principals felt more pressure for planning and more accountable to meet district mandates; successors "felt no external pressure to make changes or accomplish certain goals" (p. 101). Successors believed that external input was intended to help them, not require action.

The majority of differences Cosgrove observed between the two groups of schools related to individual differences among the principals or to teacher preferences rather than to succession per se. Differences in leader orientations, style, and decision making were apparent, but Cosgrove concluded that reactions seemed to depend on "teacher comfort with a particular style of decision making, rather than reactions to change itself" (p. 104).

"Culture changed more in continuing schools than in succession schools" (p. 104). Cosgrove attributed this outcome to the presuccession discontent of four of the five continuing schools with the leadership styles of their principals, while only two of the succession schools were uncomfortable with the new principals' styles. Teachers attributed effects on school culture to principals only when reporting change; they gave them no credit for impact on the culture when it remained the same. Teachers were more likely to report no disruption in the succession schools; and Cosgrove found no significant differences in job satisfaction among the teachers.

General Themes. Cosgrove drew two conclusions from her study that bear directly on the present inquiry into the utility of organizational socialization theory for understanding the interaction of newly appointed principals with schools. First, Cosgrove concluded that succession effects go beyond the first year of a principal's tenure. In one school, the ongoing principal was entering his second year, and the teachers in this school reported the most significant changes of the ten sample schools. Cosgrove noted a tendency on the part of teachers and principals to "wait and see" what would happen as a result of a succession. "Principals and teachers in both succession and continuing schools often reported that the first year of a principal's tenure was a time for assessment and observation to become familiar with staff, students, community, and programs," she said (p. 112).

In spite of these conclusions, the most negative reactions Cosgrove reported occurred at a school during the second year of the continuing principal's tenure. Teachers reported that this principal had passed through his grace period during which changes were to be tolerated and expected. Cosgrove and her subjects acknowledged that it is difficult to balance the appropriate level of change attempted following a succession. While all teachers in the succession schools expected changes to follow the succession, some principals were leery about too much change while others recognized the need to take advantage of teacher expectations for change. "If you make too many changes, teachers get too anxious. Teachers expect some. I did as many as I could the first year. Now I have to sit back and assess for next year" (p. 113). Teachers, too, acknowledged that sometimes a complete lack of influence on the part of the principal looks like a smooth transition. "Things went smoothly this year. It may be because he's not voicing his opinions yet. I don't know about next year. He may relax and open up next year." Cosgrove uses this and other observations by teachers to contend that the cyclical nature of schools affects succession dynamics. "The result of succession is that adjustments to new principals affix their timeliness to the school cycles."

Two telling statements by Cosgrove highlight the importance of timeliness when taking action during leader succession:

(1) The district in this study did not use the succession process as an opportunity to mandate change. Under what conditions do districts promote change through succession? (p. 129)

(2) Future research could focus on school culture and its effects on succession. More in-depth study is needed to determine the nature, process, degree, and relevance of the influence of teachers on the succession process. With a clearer understanding of school culture, a successor principal could direct shared expectations, values, and attitudes held by the faculty towards

a smooth transition into the principalship so that the majority of their collective energy could be aimed at common goals and improving school effectiveness. (p. 130)

This last statement is tied to Cosgrove's second conclusion: Teachers influence the effects of principal succession. The social system of the school affects leader succession.

This study supports the notion that the effects of principal succession can be influenced by teachers' attitudes, reactions, and culture.... Regardless of adverse reactions to change or to the new principal, anxiety created by unknowns, increased need for adjustment, or different leadership and decision making styles, teachers' scores on the job satisfaction questionnaire did not change significantly from one year to the next in any single school or group of schools.... [The school] allows them to receive the same rewards and satisfaction from their work irrespective of the principal. (pp. 116, 118) (See also Podsakoff, 1982)

Other data support this conclusion about the effects of the group: Respondents in this study banded together in the face of adversity. Sometimes staff cohesiveness provided mutual support, other times it was aimed at "retaliation or plans to prevent the principal from taking action...." (p. 118).

In the face of unknowns and potentially unwanted changes, teachers deny the possibility that disruptiveness and instability might occur and instead rely on their personal autonomy and collective power to successfully resist unwanted changes, adapt to reasonable or welcome changes, *and fundamentally to remain the same* [emphasis added]. (p. 120)

Based on these observations, Cosgrove drew a number of specific conclusions (pp. 126–127):

1. Successor principals should recognize that there are a variety of responses to succession. Their early assessments should focus both on how this school uniquely anticipates a change in administrative incumbents and what each teacher expects.
2. Succession is a process initiated by the assignment of a new principal to a school, not a single event.

3. Principals should forge ahead with needed changes. Teachers expect principals to initiate change and are prepared to adapt and adjust to it, often looking forward to change with anticipation. While principal succession and the accompanying changes can create apprehensions and doubt, negativism can be overcome.
4. Principals need to recognize the limits of their influence on schools and to take heart in small changes.
5. District-level decision makers should evaluate the frequency with which they reassign principals. Succession disrupts the normal flow of activity within the school.

An Educational Criticism of a Principal's Succession

The succession experiences of new principals have also been studied using qualitative, descriptive, or comparative case study techniques. One such study, reported by Lamoreaux (1990), provided a look at the work of a new principal from an aesthetic perspective using the vehicle of educational criticism to convey the succession experience. Lamoreaux believed, with Duke (1987), that this "aesthetics-based" view of leaders yields important information about new leaders missing from role, control, influence, or behavior-based approaches.

Highly descriptive and unique views of succession reveal the depth and texture of succession missing from some research perspectives. Those who undertake this form of research point out that some things about succession remain in an ineffable realm, difficult to approach using more rationalistic methods but resonating with the experiences of every newly appointed principal. "There is something different around a school when a new principal takes command. Teachers notice it; students notice it; parents notice it. This difference, especially when it's something special, is often called leadership" (Lamoreaux, 1990, p. 3). The distinct contribution of an aesthetic-based educational criticism of leader succession is the way in which it renders "situations, events, or objects in such a way as to provide others with an understanding of what makes them significant" (p. 4), providing interpretations that are reliable *within* the individual case.

Leigh Miller, a new principal assigned to Chesterfield High School, was the subject of Lamoreaux's inquiry. Leigh had been an administrator prior to her assignment at Chesterfield and had considerable experience with school discipline. On the day of her interview at the district office, she also visited Chesterfield. She found the setting, its students, and its problems familiar, personally identifying with the challenges educators face in a large, comprehensive high school. At the same time, she saw many advantages of an administrative experience at Chesterfield. The school was located in a small community and provided a very different setting than her previous assignment as an assistant principal in a large, metropolitan area.

Leigh immediately felt at home at Chesterfield during her interview visit. At one point, she almost intervened to hurry some rowdy, tardy students to class. The teachers with whom she was talking at the time were upset, "nearly in hysterics," that she took over so assertively, even if automatically. She apologized, saying, "I've done discipline at Metro for so long that I wanted to see what was going on with those kids; I just wanted to get them wherever they belonged" (p. 6).

Leigh is meticulous—in appearance and in personal habits. Lamoreaux's description provides repeated evidence of this: "Her shortly cropped, more-salt-than-pepper, silver hair is always impeccably groomed; her clothes are not only fashionable and elegant, but noticeably expensive; her jewelry is 24 karat. She dresses in shades of black, gray, and white, most often with an accent in red." One day she wore a "crisp, fashionable, black and white checked, jersey dress and short red coat" (p. 1). An important part of her day-long interview experience for the principalship at Chesterfield was a "$400 gray hounds tooth checked suit" (p. 6). When Leigh noticed a spot on her skirt during lunch, she went to a cleaner's during a break in her interview schedule. She had the skirt dry-cleaned on the spot while she stood in her slip in the back room, to the amusement of the attendant. Other personal habits reinforced this image of the meticulous woman. The ashtray of her car was "overflowing with white Virginia Slims, each smoked almost meticulously to three-quarters of the way to the filter" (p. 1).

Leigh approved of the casual dress and accepting attitude of the students at Chesterfield, however. These attitudes differed from those of the students at the school in which she worked as the assistant principal. She found the students at her previous assignment more judgmental and elite, more unaccepting of others who deviated from their narrow conception of acceptable dress styles and behavior.

Leigh was a twice-divorced career educator. She came to administration after moving through a number of traditional teaching assignments, including librarian. She interpreted several of her important career experiences in terms of her sex, seeing them centered in her differences as a woman. Leigh said she missed out on an assistant principal's position in a neighboring district because her principal wanted to keep her on his staff. He chose to give a favorable recommendation for her major competitor for the position, a male counselor at the same school, because he did not care whether the man remained at the school or not. He wanted Leigh to stay. She felt she was eventually appointed an assistant principal (one of three women serving in this position in her district) because her principal "was in her debt" over this incident (p. 10).

Gender played an important role in Leigh's leadership experiences. She believed that the actions of women administrators are more carefully scrutinized than those of men, and decisions that are on their face sex neutral (improving the appearance of the school) often are attributed to being female, "just like a woman." In a confrontation with a student whose request she had denied, the student blurted, "If they'd hired a man to be principal, they wouldn't have someone so incompetent" (p. 12). Leigh believed that this dynamic would not contaminate the tenure of a male school administrator; no one says "That's just like a man" when criticizing the choices made by male administrators.

The career path Leigh followed prior to her appointment at Chesterfield was similar to that of other women administrators (Shakeshaft, 1989). She moved first from teaching to a semisupervisory role as a media specialist/librarian and as a coordinator of a schoolwide drug and alcohol intervention program. She then was appointed an assistant principal. Like many others, she did not see administration as a career goal until late in her teaching career (after numerous moves from place to place in support of two husbands' careers). She was young—forty-two—an exception to the rule for many women administrators.

Other features of Leigh's experience highlighted apparent sex differences (Shakeshaft, 1989). She joked about herself rather than others; she used the language of support and cooperation in her communication with parents. She apologized to the faculty for decisions that were later criticized:

> Leigh apologized for opening her mouth long enough to exchange feet in setting up an Open House this early in the year without first consulting with the staff. . . . Leigh asked for a faculty advisory committee to work with her and help her avoid future pitfalls/goofs due to her being so new to the job and district. (p. 14)

In a conversation with a male faculty member in response to the inquiry "How's it going?" Leigh recounted the events of the day in a tone of confidence while acknowledging the challenges she was facing. In response to the same inquiry from two female friends—a secretary and teacher with whom she had worked previously—she began to cry. She recounted the pressures of getting organized and completing reports. She was frustrated because she had always been very organized and now was overwhelmed. She felt pressured, watched, with no time to herself. Leigh's self-evaluation of her first nine weeks as principal of Chesterfield High School were self-critical: C for organization; C for curriculum; B+ or A− for staff relations; B− in staff evaluations; C+ in establishing rapport with students.

Lamoreaux's view of Leigh's first nine weeks diverged from this mediocre assessment. He saw her impact on the school in a very different light. Drawing on the literature on effective principals, Lamoreaux argued that a clear communication of vision, an impact on the way in which people living and working in the school view themselves, was a better measure of impact. Leigh's messages about her vision for the school, he contended, were consistent from her very first meeting with the faculty shortly after her appointment. Her view was communicated to students and faculty. Leigh valued people. She saw high school as a critical time—a period in which students formed central and long-lasting views of themselves and their potential in the world in which they lived.

Lamoreaux believed that Leigh communicated this vision of high school to students and teachers in the first nine weeks of her tenure as principal of Chesterfield High School. He described her behavior in ways that illustrate how much she wanted to know the students and staff well, wanted the students to see this as "the best years of their life." Lamoreaux saw Leigh's vision as healthy and productive, one of "caring, of sharing, and of relationships," and he observed that vision manifest at Chesterfield within nine weeks of Leigh's succession.

This conviction that Leigh affected Chesterfield in a mere two and one-half months is illustrated by Lamoreaux through the words of the students at Chesterfield High School. The students formed quick impressions of their new principal on the basis of her appearance and carriage. Within nine weeks, they altered these perceptions. They told Leigh, "When you first came to Chesterfield, we thought you were just like Nancy Reagan. We called you the Nancy Reagan of Chesterfield High. Now we probably like you better than most of the others in the school" (p. 19).

Tying Professional Socialization to School Outcomes in Canada

Leithwood, Steinbach, and Begley (in press) studied the nature and contribution of professional socialization experiences to principals' instructional leadership. The study was an attempt to explore how instructional leadership develops in principals by examining "how a variety of 'socialization' experiences influenced the development of instructional leadership among several groups of Canadian educators" (p. 3). They applied a four-part framework of socialization to their research: (1) relationships (with peers, superordinates, and subordinates); (2) experiences with formal policies and practices (especially those related to selection and promotion, performance appraisal, and professional development); (3) formal training; and (4) outcomes of socialization (image of role, skills and knowledge, norms and values). They looked at these aspects across three stages that parallel professional and organizational socialization stages—initiation, transition, and incorporation. When assessing their own performance during the initiation stage, they contended, people attend primarily to how others judge them. During transition, a person moves toward an internal set of criteria for judging performance. At incorporation, principals draw comparisons with their own past performance, focusing on their level of achievement and the quality of development or change toward a professional ideal they have achieved.

From their review of literature, Leithwood, Steinbach, and Begley hypothesized that some socialization experiences would promote qualities associated with instructional leadership in three ways. They would contribute to a professional self-image as an instructional leader (role orientation). They would foster increased and refined knowledge and skills needed to be successful as an instructional leader—technical socialization in Greenfield's (1985b) terms. And they would contribute to consensus among administrators on central organizational norms and values operating at the school and district levels (moral socialization in Greenfield's terms). These effects would be seen across the three stages of initiation, transition, and incorporation.

The research was a survey study employing statistical and text analysis techniques. Fifty preservice graduate students and thirty-eight principals and vice principals with from one to twenty years of experience responded to a thirty-two item questionnaire. The researchers analyzed responses for patterns that would support the hypothesis that particular characteristics of the socialization experience would predict instructional leadership self-concept, behavior, and values in principals. Socialization patterns examined included such things as having a mentor; the extent of encouragement they received to pursue an administrative role; exposure to helpful role models; hiring and promotion practices; administrator evaluation practices; opportunities to interact with peers about classroom, schoolwide, and district issues; and opportunities for leadership roles.

The analysis suggested that respondents believed their socialization experiences were helpful, that few differences existed between the experiences of men and women, and that incumbent principals and vice principals had opportunities to participate in socialization activities that promoted instructional leadership more frequently than those earlier in their careers. The researchers concluded: "Those forms of socialization valued most appear to be embedded in the context of school life, available both regularly and often and focused directly on the role of administration and leadership" (p. 20). As socialization experiences related to instructional leadership increased, more respondents described their images of the role of principal in terms consistent with instructional leadership.

Some surprising results emerged from the study as well. The researchers hypothesized that respondents who reported experiencing socialization patterns thought to help promote instructional leadership and described their professional role image in terms consistent with instructional leadership would see tasks related to instruction as the most important tasks associated with the principalship. They believed that these experiences would shape the principals' professional self-concepts as instructional leaders. Results did not support this conclusion. Instead, 74 percent of important tasks named by those respondents who had experienced the two socialization patterns considered most helpful in developing instructional leadership were unrelated to instructional leadership. Instructional leadership tasks included such things as curriculum and instructional leadership; effective administrative problem solving; leadership as a role model, motivator, or facilitator; and acquisition of new knowledge. Instead, the principals considered their most important tasks to be interpersonal (communication and positive climate personal relations), managerial (budget and discipline), and legal (policies and collective bargaining).

Twelve New High School Principals

Wright (in press), Roberts (1989a, 1989b), Parkay, Currie, and Rhodes (1992), and Parkay and Hall (1992) analyzed case studies of twelve first-time high school principals. They report the patterns of school culture, supervisory priorities, and career development of these new principals in a series of papers, chapters, and articles. These scholars, part of a body of inquiry known as the Beginning Principals Study (BPS), contribute multiple views of the leader succession and socialization experiences of high school principals. Six male and six female principals from five states in the Midwest, East, West, and Southeast were selected on the basis of their location (rural, suburban, urban), school size, and sex of administrator. The eventual sample represented a range of demographic variables.

Data included visits to the site (at least three, two-day observations) and bimonthly interviews, either in person or by telephone) conducted over the course of the principals' first year. Follow-up interviews were conducted twice a year for two subsequent years. The researchers used interviews of teachers, district personnel, and community members to verify data, as well as documents collected from the twelve study sites. Questions in the regular interviews were open ended and nondirective: "(1) What critical events are occurring? (2) How are you spending your time? (3) To whom did you turn for support and whom did you support? (4) What decisions have you made? (5) What joys, successes, and frustrations are you experiencing?" (Wright, 1992). Data analysis included two phases. The first phase applied the principles of grounded theory research in search of patterns common to and unique to individual principals. The second phase used a multiple case study design that allows comparison of major themes across cases, duplicating the replication rationale of quantitative research.

Principals' supervisory priorities and developing professional identity formed the core of Wright's (1992) inquiry. This choice of focus primarily sprang from Blumberg's (1989) contention that the kind of supervisory tasks principals emphasize when they first enter a school have an impact on their developing professional identities as people who will lead instructional improvement efforts. To accomplish his analysis, Wright defined supervision broadly as those tasks undertaken within the context of the school that contribute to instructional improvement and teacher professional growth (Sergiovanni, 1987a). He developed an integrated classification system to identify tasks (administrative and directly supervisory) that related to the improvement of instruction and teacher growth. These included goal setting; planning; organizing the work; staffing; directing the continuous accomplishment of tasks; coordinating the work toward a recognized purpose; reporting progress and keeping superordinates and subordinates informed about task achievement; budgeting; communicating; managing conflict; influencing culture—"initiating changes in or altering the belief systems, goal orientations, and ways of relating to colleagues and students" (Roberts & Wright, 1989, p. 6); giving direct assistance; making formal evaluations; developing curricula; building teams (working together on mutual issues related to instruction); performing action research; and solving student problems (related to academics).

Wright found that principals ranked communication, team building, influence on school culture, and goal setting as among their most important first-year tasks. Among these groups of tasks, influence on school culture remained the concept least clearly defined. Wright (in press) classified "changing or partially altering how faculty did their work" and rethinking "why they did their work in certain ways and how they related to each other as peers in getting things done" as cultural tasks.

Two less important groups of tasks were also identified by the principals. The tasks ranked as secondary in importance were direct assistance to teachers, curriculum development and directing, organizing and staffing, and student problem solving. The least important tasks were coordinating and formal evaluation planning, budgeting, managing conflict, and action research. Few of the principals actually described themselves as instructional leaders.

Wright concluded that first-time principals' induction/socialization period included the first two years of service and that principals need improved skills supervising "within the context of the school as a complex organization." He recommended that further study focus on ways in which the developing professional identities of principals can be conceptualized and described. Further, he suggested that researchers and practitioners need to attend to the "uncontrollable or previously undetectable factors (organizational arrangements, social structures, personal orientations, etc.)" with which new principals must interact. When she analyzed the same twelve case studies in search of a relationship between new principals and the school culture, Roberts (1989a, 1989b) concluded that first-time principals have difficulty establishing a cultural orientation.

The researchers undertook this particular focus of data analysis because of widespread expectations that principals exercise cultural leadership. Roberts pointed out that

learning about the school's value system and gaining acceptance for one's efforts to change or build a school's culture are doubly difficult. Indeed, principals are expected to do more than supervise; they are to inspire and to ensure that appropriate values are embodied in the actions of all school staff members. (Roberts, 1989a, p. 2)

The focus of Roberts's study was the impact of new principals on the culture of the school. She asked about cultural linkages recognized, exhibited, and manipulated by beginning principals; about the coupling patterns related to student performance; and about the leadership values espoused and displayed by new principals. As previously noted in the discussion of social information processing in Chapter 3, Roberts's subjects had a great deal of trouble using communication or influencing interpretations.

Stories circulating among faculty members were not principal-initiated, positive, culture-building tales but rather complaints in which the new principal was often the target. Making changes without sufficient communication, being critical of all instead of a guilty few, being negative about faculty in an article, constantly pointing out errors, and even being inappropriately silent. . . . Most who faced these difficulties reacted defensively. . . . In only a couple of cases were new principals able to handle such complaints from faculty in a sensitive, constructive manner which resulted in a positive outcome. (1989a, pp. 16–17)

Roberts went on to report that shared values and trust were almost nonexistent for one-fourth of the principals.

Although these new principals identified influence on school culture as among their most important tasks, Roberts found that her twelve subjects had some difficulty with the concept of school culture and behaved counterproductively. Their efforts to build cultural linkages to improve instruction internally were weak, often nonexistent. They concentrated on establishing tightly coupled linkages among system components in the school, demonstrating a high need for control. Finally, they provided limited cultural leadership linked to their own values.

Roberts and Wright (1989) also applied survey techniques to reveal areas in which new principals experience their greatest difficulties related to change management. They concluded that new principals focused early change activities on management activities, morale, and climate, but that their long-range planning was weak and unfocused, and their influence over "vision" and culture, especially related to instruction, was weak.

Beginning high school principals reported critical challenges of their first year most frequently in the areas of student management, personal overload, instruction, and, most seriously, in the general area of mobilizing frequently strong, resistant, experienced teachers (or clearly unmotivated teachers) with whom the new principal often lacked credibility. (1989, p. 12)

Parkay, Currie, and Rhodes (1992) concluded that a stage framework could also be developed from the experiences of these twelve high school principals. They classified these stages as survival, control, stability, educational leadership, and professional actualization. At the survival stage, surprise functions as the most powerful element. The researchers quoted Van Maanen (1977a, p. 15) that this " 'breaking-in' phenomenon (i.e. occurring when individuals first join an organization) represents a prototypical crisis period. . . ." Principals described this period as "traumatic, chaos."

The control stage represented a focus on "setting priorities and seeking ways to manage the overwhelming flow of new demands" (p. 16), what Van Maanen (1977a, pp. 23–30) has called "normalizing the setting." Principals in this stage fear losing control, being ineffective. They tend to rely on their formal sources of power, vested in their role as principals.

During stability, the third stage identified by Parkay, Currie, and Rhodes, management tasks become effective and efficient routines. Events that previously were sources of frustration become routinized. Less intent on promoting change, the principal acknowledges the importance of doing a good job.

Educational leadership, the fourth stage these researchers observed, was represented by a strong vision of the school. While the first three stages were defensive in nature, this stage was a step toward "long-term success for change strategies" (Parkay, Currie & Rhodes, 1992, p. 58). Harmony is not necessarily the result. Because principals in this stage take concrete steps to promote career growth and advancement for teachers and for themselves and press hard for effective outcomes, conflict with established ways of doing things at the school can result.

The fifth stage represented in this research was professional actualization. Principals in this stage of interaction with a school do not attempt to impose their own vision on an unwilling faculty. This stage is analogous to transformational leadership (Burns, 1978) in that "faculty members believe that they have been truly empowered and work collegially and harmoniously to improve the school" (Parkay, Currie & Rhodes, 1992, p. 58). Principals bring out the best in the "incipient vision the faculty has for the school" (p. 18).

An additional theme in this stage framework deserves note. Parkay and his colleagues observed principals moving from positional power to personal power (Etzioni, 1975) and from coercive behaviors to those that facilitate learning and growth for themselves and others (Parkay, Currie & Rhodes, 1992). Only a few of the principals they observed moved along this stage framework to the fifth stage within three years of their appointment to their first high school principalship. They also noted that principals made "little movement beyond the level of development that had begun to emerge after the first year" (1992, p. 61). For these twelve principals, the first year was "the handwriting on the wall" (pp. 61–62) projecting a principal's eventual effectiveness.

The proportion of principals reported by Parkay, Currie, and Rhodes (1992) who developed to the top stages in three years is not overwhelmingly encouraging. They found that five of the principals had reached stage four, educational leadership, and two had developed to stage five, professional actualization. One principal at this stage, Mindy, told the researchers: "In terms of leadership, I've gone from directing to trying to guide and develop other people" (in press, p. 31). Another stage five principal, Hank, previously had held a position as a junior high school principal. "From the beginning, Hank's actions clearly reflected a strong commitment to Stage 4 and Stage 5 concerns" (1992, p. 69).

> Although Hank had his share of emergencies and crises during his first year..., he responded to each with a high degree of skill and insight. Throughout the year, he set high expecta-tions... and he empowered others—students as well as teachers. According to his criteria for excellence (and those of his teachers and superiors at the district office), Hank had a very successful first year—so successful, that after his second year in the principalship he was made assistant superintendent for instruction. (pp. 69–70)

This was not, however, Hank's "second year in the principalship." It was his second year as a high school principal.

Parkay, Currie, and Rhodes concluded that their analysis supports the description by Hall et al. (1984) of effective principals who display an "initiator" change style. These principals "promote clearly articulated policies and goals for their schools that are based on a compelling vision of what their schools might become. . . .[They] convey high expectations to faculty and students, and they continually evaluate their actions according to what is best for the school" (Parkay, Currie & Rhodes, 1992, p. 71). These principals "tend to receive much of their confirmation from within" (in press, p. 34). They respond to an inner locus of control while realizing that "they can't do everything, that they must learn to empower others in meaningful ways" (p. 71).

The researchers concluded that more systematic methods that provide support for the effective patterns they identified need to be developed. They recommended the Peer-Assisted Leadership (PAL) program advocated by Barnett (1985). They also advocated the development of increased sensitivity to the dynamics of educational change and "greater respect for the goals, dreams, and abilities of their faculties" (p. 71) on the part of new principals. Other recommendations: "Beginning principals (and, perhaps more importantly, their supervisors) should be encouraged to develop analytical skills that will enable them to understand how the informal socialization processes which new principals experience mitigate against their developing into Stage 4 or 5 leaders" (p. 72). Parkay and his colleagues believed that this would help mitigate against the prediction offered by Greenfield:

> The dominant role orientation among administrators focuses on activities aimed at maintaining organizational stability, and while instructional leadership and educational improvement continue to be the preferred orientation espoused by school administrators, few actually pursue those ends or engage in activities associated with such a conception of the role. (Greenfield, 1985b, p. 110)

These scholars also believed that a knowledge of the "shape" of the career will help new administrators feel less inadequate and, "knowing that their experiences are common and lead eventually to higher stages of development" (p. 72), will spark a confident growth toward more effective interaction with the school, toward more effective leadership.

New Secondary Heads in Great Britain

In a footnote to their study, Parkay and colleagues acknowledged their indebtedness to Dick Weindling for visiting their research sites and for sharing his research techniques, study results, and survey instruments. It is fitting, therefore, to conclude this description of varied socialization/succession studies with the research undertaken by Weindling and his colleagues. This research group conducted the largest study undertaken to date of new principals or heads. Their goal has been to document critical components of leader succession among secondary heads in Great Britain, responding to a claim made in a Department of Education and Science Green Paper referred to in Chapter 1: "The character and quality of the head teacher are by far the main influence in determining what a school sets out to do and the extent to which it achieves those aims" (Weindling & Earley, 1987, p. 1). Not an investigation of succession *effects* per se, these studies were undertaken to (1) document the demands made on heads in their first year of headship, (2) describe the range of strategies employed to cope with these demands, and (3) identify requisite skills and knowledge needed to carry out the new role and provide guidelines for in-service agencies concerned with senior management training in secondary schools (1987, p. 6). The transition to headship formed the focus of study, not succession effects.

This study combined survey and case study methods. It resulted in cross-sectional and longitudinal data. Subjects were placed in three groups—newly appointed secondary heads; secondary heads with three to eight years of experience; and local education authorities (LEAs). All newly appointed heads in England and Wales in 1982–83 were included in the population. Sampling techniques reduced the one hundred new secondary heads hired in September of 1982 (through the use of a stratified random sample) to a research sample representative of the schools throughout England and Wales. Forty-seven schools in thirty-two local education authorities were eventually selected for the longitudinal study. Of the forty-seven initial schools examined, one-third were selected for two or more visits by researchers—sixteen schools in all. Over three hundred teachers were interviewed in the sixteen schools.

The sample schools were chosen to represent a range of factors—geographical location, age range of pupils, internal promotions versus external promotions, income levels of neighborhoods. In a first round of interviews, the researchers talked with the new head, members of the senior management team, the chairperson of governors, and the senior local education authority (LEA) officer. A survey of all heads selected during the 1982 school year provided a check on data from the cases investigated in depth. A second visit and round of interviews emphasized comparisons between the style of the new head and the general reactions or expectations of the staff. The third visit in the summer of 1984 lasted four days. During this visit, researchers interviewed at least four department leaders and a variety of teachers—from heads of year to scale one or two (beginning) teachers. These interviews focused on the kinds of change introduced by the new head, the change process, styles of the new head, consultation and participation in decision making, and general staff reactions to the new head. The last (third and final) set of interviews raised issues over time—change, perceptions, professional isolation, peer relationships, positive aspects of the role.

Weindling and Earley (1987) estimated that 7 percent of heads turn over in Great Britain every year. A total of 249 heads entered their first headship in 1982–83, the first year of the study. While the majority of these new heads said they had not aspired to leadership at the beginning of their teaching careers, they recounted a number of experiences leading to headship. They were assigned a leadership task that they completed successfully; they felt the time was right to move on; they received encouragement from their own heads; they felt the need for a fresh challenge.

The researchers found a number of differences between their subjects and earlier pools of school administrators. For example, the new heads held significantly more certificates and advanced diplomas and higher degrees that did the older heads they were replacing. Only 25 percent of heads in the interview/case study sample were promoted within their schools, and only 10 percent of heads in the survey sample were promoted from within. Sex differences also were clear. While 25 percent of men served as acting head before their appointment as head, 40 percent of women were assigned an acting or assistant role before their official appointment as leaders of British schools.

Heads in Great Britain also agreed about their greatest challenges. Women had to surmount a perception that they might not "maintain discipline," that they constituted a "greater risk than appointing a man" (1987, p. 30). All heads had to obtain information about the school and establish relationships with the staff, especially with senior teachers.

Interactions with teachers revolved around a number of factors. Teachers wanted to ask questions that would reveal whether the new head was concerned enough about the school. They judged concern in part by the number of visits a new head made to the school, sometimes at considerable personal expense. Teachers judged whether the new head was "in charge."

Successors told a tale that centered on learning and on influence. They said that the time they spent with outgoing heads was rarely well spent; that they wanted more data about the impressions of faculty; that "the experience of becoming a head" was the single part of their new job they were least prepared for (1987, p. 37). Heads felt that the power to appoint a new assistant head of their choosing would be an advantage, but only 51 percent had been able to appoint at least one new deputy during their first two years.

The data from this study revealed a vital link between trust and delegation. New heads were uncertain what the strengths and weaknesses of the senior staff might be, and they hesitated to risk accountability for decisions entrusted to others—exhibiting a high need for control. The most successful heads, however, used deputies and teams of teachers to accomplish their most important goals. The way in which Weindling and Earley reported their study lends itself to a stage framework focused on the prearrival and entry stages.

Selection and Prearrival. When the new heads arrived, faculties sometimes asked, "Can they walk on water?" Weindling and Earley responded by pointing out that "Heads taking up appointment in a school are likely to face an organizational structure and social system which has been temporarily suspended on their arrival and can therefore take advantage of this 'to manoeuvre and reshape the structural patterns of the social system'" (p. 66). At the same time they "enter a situation where many relationships have to be established anew, and to a considerable extent participants' reputations have, once more, to be made" (p. 66). Because of reported poor relationships between the predecessor and the faculty, some heads spent considerable energy "to gain an understanding of both their predecessor's style and the quality of the relationships enjoyed with staff" (1987, p. 66).

At all sixteen research sites where in-depth data were collected, faculty described the tone dominating the appointment of a new head as "an atmosphere of expectancy." Many staff members "were excited and optimistic, looking to the head for a fresh start and knowing that the new head would want to introduce changes" (1987, p. 67). Even those with "a hard act to follow" found they were "given a sincere welcome." Others were seen as the school's "new champion or saviour." One new head said, "I think the staff here had unrealistic

expectations of me and wanted someone who could 'walk on water.'"
The vast majority of teachers interviewed in all sixteen schools
expected changes to take place and recognized the need for change;
what was more problematic,...was the speed and timing of the
change process" (1987, pp. 67–68).

The notion of a "honeymoon period" appeared in all the case
studies undertaken by Weindling and Earley (1987). Disagreement
raged, however, over the length of this period of grace. Some
contended it lasted only a few days; others as long as eighteen months.
One deputy promoted to head raised an intriguing question. He
contended that he had no honeymoon period, that his administration
was a continuum of the previous administration. Others said they
observed their support growing noticeably over time.

Teachers and new heads also identified specific tensions that
developed either during the selection process or as a result of events
that occurred during selection. First, internal candidates seldom were
appointed and often were treated differently from external candidates.
Internal candidates who "clearly had no chance at a position" (p. 71)
were "short-listed" and then given private interviews to explain to
them personally why they might not be right for the job. As a result,
the new head felt some effect from staff perceptions that internal
candidates had been "hard done by" or "having a bad deal" (p. 70).
"[T]he perceived 'poor' treatment of internal candidates had a
deleterious effect not only on the individuals concerned, but also on
the staff as a whole" (p. 71). Second, selection procedures—
applications, interviews—were viewed as inconsistent, including
varying levels of formality that resulted in accusations of favoritism.
Third, existing faculty complained about the appointment of "whiz-
kids" or that a new head wanted "to bring in her own people" (p.
71). Weindling and Earley note that many faculty clearly believed
in the importance of the headship as a reward for long service but
appointments violated these expectations with increasing frequency.

Arrival/Entry. Once the new heads arrived, the researchers
identified interaction dynamics between faculties and new heads that
produced common themes across sites. First, in thirteen of the sixteen
case study schools, faculty complained that the new head consulted
and communicated with them far too infrequently. Second, in five
schools, teachers suggested that the successor favored students or
parents, providing insufficient support for teachers. "Some heads were
seen as giving preference to parents and were seen as having gone
too far in wooing them" (p. 74). Third, experienced successors erred

when they tried to make a point with new faculties by referring to how well practices had worked at their "old school," with the accompanying implied criticism of the new. Weindling and Earley (1987) noted that "heads should be more aware that what worked at the 'old' schools need not necessarily work in the different context of the 'new'" (p. 74).

Contrary to the general conclusion drawn by Gordon and Rosen (1981), Weindling and Earley found that a popular predecessor was not a disadvantage for their subjects. The only serious problems they identified revolved around conflicts between the successors' and predecessors' communication and consultation styles. Successors said they found that it was important to learn as much as possible about the style of the previous head and set up deliberate transitions and changes over time.

The most important focus of early activities identified by Weindling and Earley's subjects was their relationship with the teachers at the new assignment. The new heads named eight top staff-related difficulties that arose in their first two years:

1. Problems arising out of merit award points given by the previous head that did not reflect current assignments.
2. Persuading teachers to accept new ideas.
3. Dealing with a weak member of the senior management team at the school.
4. Challenges associated with the dismissal or reassignment of an incompetent teacher.
5. Poor staff morale.
6. Promoting staff development.
7. Reduction in faculty resulting from falling enrollment.
8. Restrictions on teacher recruitment imposed by the local education authority (district).

While staff morale was named as one of the top eight problems, in some study schools teachers said that staff morale had risen "largely as a consequence of a change in leaders" (Weindling & Earley, 1987, p. 85).

Change developed as a major theme of succession. Almost all of the new heads said that "it had been made clear at their interviews or soon after . . . that various changes were seen as necessary" (p. 92). After the first year, only 10 percent of the first-time heads and 9 percent of the more experienced heads said no major changes had been introduced in their schools. Almost all these changes were made by the new head. They often related to communication and interaction patterns, school image and community relations, building improvements, liaisons with feeder schools, and student discipline. The changes named were not frequently of long-range importance nor did they affect the overall structure of the school. Teachers expected new heads to introduce change. The only exception came with an insider, a former deputy whom teachers expected to continue existing practices. While the few insiders in the sample felt they had little trouble finding out about daily routines and persuading teachers to accept new ideas, they also implemented fewer changes. Even more change is now occurring. The Education Reform Act of 1988 imposed a number of changes, undermining some of the traditional power and autonomy that head teachers have had in the past. Among these changes will be a national curriculum and national testing.

No particular pattern characterized teachers' assessment of the quality of changes initiated by new heads. While the vast majority of teachers interviewed said they felt changes were needed, assessments of the changes once initiated were varied. Reactions were favorable in six schools, negative in four schools, and mixed in the remaining six schools (p. 106). Further, teachers emphasized the need for successors to openly acknowledge the good things that were going on in the school upon their arrival.

The pacing and timing of change also was an important issue for the new heads. While many said they had planned to wait out the first year, they found they could not delay. Heads strongly defended the need to start planning and laying the groundwork for change almost immediately upon their succession. Two important features of timing and pacing emerged from the responses of successors. First, they sought early cosmetic changes in noncontroversial areas because they "recognized the importance of being seen by staff as someone who could get things done" (p. 103). Second, they observed that length of tenure of their predecessors affected teachers' expectations for change. Expectations for change were particularly high when the predecessor had held his or her position for a long time.

Weindling and Earley provide an insightful description of the widely divergent assessments of faculties at two of the study sites that illustrate some developing interaction patterns. Similar changes were implemented at the two schools—curriculum, shared management with teachers, student grouping patterns, organizational changes. At school A, the teachers accepted and worked with the changes, were involved in the planning, and helped set up starting dates for the changes that would gradually occur over time. The new head felt "it was best to introduce only superficial change initially," but worked from the beginning to prepare "the ground for more fundamental change." He "sowed the seeds," (p. 110) focusing on senior staff members first, uniting them around proposals, and then worked with the middle-level teachers and with any interested parties. His rationale was to prevent any surprises when decisions to adopt innovations were made. At school B, the teachers described the new head as a man who said he wanted democracy and consultation but operated differently in practice: "He sees himself as a great democrat and then behaves in a very autocratic way" (p. 112). Although the teachers and the deputy head were evenly divided over the desirability of the changes initiated, they were united in their condemnation of methods. "He just came in and swept things away" (p. 112). The new head responded, "I found that so many things had to be started at this school that I couldn't be democratic. I had to provide the institution with a philosophy and the institution needed a wallop. I had to hit them when they were down" (p. 112). Weindling and Earley summarized the assessment of the new head at school B this way:

> At the beginning, the majority of staff seemed optimistic but during the first two years the head appeared to have alienated almost all the staff, whose views ranged from extreme anger to general unhappiness. . . . They felt the new head had a blueprint for the school and he had ignored their views and imposed his own, saying that it *would* work because it did at his last school. (p. 113)

In a follow-up study conducted five years later, Earley, Baker, and Weindling (1990) found their larger sample of subjects even more adamant about the need to move quickly, but with consultation, to establish a pattern for change than were the heads in the sixteen schools where in-depth data were collected. Their advice to others carried a number of themes (1990, pp. 24–25).

1.   Seek to build confidence in what you do.
2.   "Don't sit around too long."
3.   Decide on your objectives and put a plan together.
4.   "Timing is important. You have got to be an opportunist. . . seize the opportunity when you see an interest."
5.   Support people who will make changes.
6.   Be flexible but clear about principles on which you stand.

7. Make sure that people who will be affected by changes have a say.

8. Spend a lot of time listening and establishing a sense of direction and long term vision.

Another major theme of the Weindling and Earley (1987) study was professional support and isolation. A majority of heads expressed feelings of isolation that differed from their experiences as deputy heads. While there were no differences among the subjects by size of school or for men and women, heads were less likely to feel isolated if they described themselves as well prepared for their new role. They pointed out that, while deputies are permitted to "plead ignorance and learn gradually," heads are "expected to know all the answers immediately." They also must be "prepared to give up the day-to-day camaraderie of the staffroom" (p. 122). Heads who were caught between interest groups—teachers, parents, students, district/LEA offices, the community—felt the most isolated, particularly during labor disputes.

New heads drew much of their support from deputy heads and from their peers. Deputies' support depended in large part on whether they were seen as subordinates or as fellow managers, in which case they provided trust and consultation. Successors also felt they needed feedback and interaction with an objective outsider, a person who could be open and honest about the school. In districts where considerable competition between schools existed, new heads felt more isolated. One head said, "I don't really trust the other heads in the borough, too many things seem to get back" (p. 127). Support staff in the school, "most notably, secretarial and administrative assistance within the school itself," provided a "very important form of support" (p. 150).

Little support during succession was provided by the central governance administration. While new heads usually were invited to the school for an introduction day, it was just that, an introductory visit. The local education authorities had two major explanations for this situation: (1) more involvement was not viable or appropriate; and (2) the informal approach to taking over was more important, and successors should arrange regular and informal interaction on their own. What little orientation did exist centered around LEA (district) policies and procedures with little content related to the problems and issues facing those experiencing succession.

Conclusions. Weindling and Earley concluded their study with a number of concrete recommendations. First, they recommended that improvements in preparation should include a concentration on in-service work with aspiring deputy heads. Second, "new heads should fully recognize the importance of their relationships with the senior management team" of the school (p. 186). With involvement in planning and implementation of change and collegial relationships, new secondary heads avoid many unnecessary problems. Third, successors should concentrate on establishing good working relationships with teachers. This includes gathering information about the predecessor, careful planning of their first formal staff meeting, improved communication and consultation, carefully setting up rewards and appointments to talk with teachers, and keeping references to their previous administrative assignments to a minimum. Fourth, successors need to learn more about the management of change, including careful strategies for each stage, managing the pace of change, support for innovations, involvement throughout the planning process (not just implementation), and evaluation. The authors believe that successors should "capitalize on their 'honeymoon period' by establishing the groundwork for major changes and achieving a short-term objective" (p. 189). Finally, central administration should provide more support for newly appointed heads and planned programs of induction, including more official time for visits and interactions at the new school.

The Organizational Socialization of New Principals

The preceding studies represent a broad look at the "taking charge" experiences of many principals. Some of these new leaders had previous experience as principals or assistant principals; some were tackling the role for the first time. They all shared one thing in common—interaction with an established social system as a formally appointed new leader. In this section of the chapter, the four general themes of organizational socialization are applied to an analysis of the experiences of leader succession described in these studies.

Tactics

Like Hamilton and Howard, the many principals and heads included in these studies went through an initial period of socialization characterized by individual experiences with many people. The quality of these experiences often depended on the quality of their relationships with established members of the organization or with formal and informal mentors. Even those who reported having mentors, however, found that they exercised little influence, finding instead that "being left to their own devices was common practice" (Cosgrove, 1986, p. 82). When mentors received no preparation and support for their activities with these new members, the quality of their experiences were extremely idiosyncratic. They also tended to promote a custodial response in the successors, because they affirmed and inculcated in new members the values, beliefs, and behaviors of established veterans. Weindling and his colleagues argued that this oversight unnecessarily jeopardizes the quality of early experiences for newly appointed school leaders, leaving it primarily to chance and ignoring the relative importance (depending on the needs of each school) of innovative leadership reinforcing valuable and successful practice or providing needed innovations in content and leadership role.

Socialization also was primarily informal, with few established procedures aimed at enhancing the quality of the resultant inter-actions and integration. The nature, number, and character of principals' experiences were random and their order was variable. Principals' superiors seemed unaware or unconcerned with the critical process of succession.

These studies reveal far less conformity of organizational socialization features experienced by principals along two important dimensions: (1) the relative investiture or divestiture of work and personal values and identities they entail and (2) the presence of role models who possess significantly similar personal characteristics. These two features played a major role in the custodial responses or content and role innovation and change that result from the interaction of the new principal with the existing social system of the school.

Investiture/Divestiture. Depending on the amount and intensity of previous experience, the features of principals' successions ranged along a continuum from partial divestiture to almost complete investiture. None described a succession that deeply assailed their identities as educators. None entered the principalship devoid of preservice experience, and none felt completely divested of their professional identities. The principals in all of these studies (even those focused on professional socialization) were experienced with issues of administration at some level. For good or ill, this feature of socialization to school administration should enhance the likelihood of a custodial response, and the findings of all the studies reviewed in this chapter bear out this prediction. For example, Cosgrove's sample was remarkably homogenous—all male, most with previous experience as elementary school principals.

Lamoreaux's educational criticism of Leigh Miller illustrates why the investiture/divestiture feature is less likely to be a dichotomy than a continuum for principals, and how many school principals move along this continuum. Leigh was an assistant principal and sought the principalship assertively for some time before receiving her appointment at Chesterfield. She felt very much at home at Chesterfield from her first interview visit, so much so that she almost took charge of a school discipline incident when still only a visitor.

Evidence of divestiture differed among studies. Leithwood and his colleagues found evidence of some divestiture in the socialization of principals and assistant principals—changes in self-images as instructional leaders developing as a result of socialization experiences. They also found that these experiences were far more common for those already holding formal administrative positions than they were for preservice students in their sample, that the experience was not really professional socialization but was most salient and effective when imbedded in a school during the actual leadership experience. While Cosgrove's subjects exhibited many individual differences, the question of principal professional image played almost no role, an understandable outcome given the lack of diversity.

All these studies reveal how thin is understanding of the development of professional identities contributing to principals' success. Wright and Roberts both pointed to the lack of sufficient knowledge about this important aspect of principal succession. Wright emphasized the paucity of data and organizational practice targeting the effects of organizational arrangements, social structures, and personal orientations that contribute to professional self-image. Roberts emphasized the dysfunctional impact of this lack on principals' ability to develop a rudimentary understanding of the organizational culture into which they are thrust as leaders.

Role Models (Serial or Disjunctive). These successions tended to be serial. Role models were common for all the men who were white. A number of the subjects, particularly assistant principals and first-time principals, identified mentors to whom they could turn, yet none identified them as a strong presence in their leadership work. In Cosgrove's study, new principals were surprised at how little influence their mentors—informal or assigned—had on their regular work. Weindling and Earley detected little difference between the men and women in their sample, with the exception that women tended to be older and to have experienced demotions during their career paths, often because of circumstances in their private lives.

The importance of helpful role models formed a major focus for Leithwood and colleagues. They tied the presence of "helpful" role models and interactions with peers on issues important to instructional leadership (classroom, schoolwide, and district). Perhaps because none of these studies included significant inquiry into the dysfunctional effects of assigned mentors with whom working relationships are not good, they tended to call for more emphasis on formal mentor relationships, at least for all first-time principals or for principals undergoing a significant role transition (from junior high principal to high school principal).

Although principalships have been around for a long time, the organizational socialization literature emphasizes that, when current role incumbents are significantly different in important personal characteristics from those previously filling the role, the experience takes on the dynamics of a disjunctive socialization. These studies bear out this prediction. The lack of role models for women preceding them in similar roles contributed to the ambiguity and anxiety these principals reported. In a number of the studies (Parkay, Currie & Rhodes, 1992; Leithwood, Steinbach & Begley, in press; Lamoreaux, 1990), women experienced higher levels of performance anxiety as they faced the new school. Leigh revealed the level of her anxiety to her female friends in an emotional exchange but kept it to herself when talking with a male teacher. She was even different from most women in her role—younger, attractive, twice divorced. Leigh's self-evaluation after her first nine weeks as principal was mediocre at best—a view Lamoreaux did not share. These differences functioned separately from one characteristic Weindling and his colleagues emphasized. They found no significant differences among subjects on the feelings of isolation as a result of school size or sex. They did find that principals who described themselves as well prepared for their new role felt less isolated, but they did not elaborate what constituted being well prepared.

Personal and Social Context

These studies provide considerable evidence that the personal context plays an important role in succession, a result that should surprise no one. Principals paid particular attention to interpersonal relationships—between the new principal and teachers. But these studies to varying degrees provide strong evidence of the influence of interaction between the personal and social contexts than they provide for any given set of personal features that promote success, belying the importance of traits per se. The research methods providing longitudinal, qualitative, and in-depth data also provided rich detail about the nature of personal context factors shaping the succession process.

Personal Context. Cosgrove's subjects revealed a mind set that emphasized the importance of newcomers—principals and the teachers they "bring in"—conforming to the expectations and behavioral norms of the existing groups. This orientation suggests that the teachers in her sample see the school's part in socializing newcomers as a critical factor in their future satisfaction with events. Despite this focus in their interviews, no significant differences in teacher satisfaction were found in any of her subject schools a year following succession. Regardless of their assessment of the experience, they saw their work lives in much the same light as before. They saw no change in the effectiveness of their schools. This outcome draws attention to the possibility that sufficient time must pass and interaction occur before even powerful organizational members can effect a discernible impact on an organizational culture. When combined with Rowan and Denk's (1984) finding that some effect on student achievement is apparent two years after a succession and evidence from the studies reviewed in this chapter that the window of opportunity must not be lost, these findings support calls for persistence in concert with patience. Cosgrove's subjects identified the important principal characteristics influencing their interactions with the new principal as centered around leader orientations, style, and decision-making preferences. She attributed these reactions to "teacher comfort with a particular style" rather than to a reaction to change.

The emphasis in Leigh's case on personal characteristics was more apparent. Her dress, personal habits, sex, experience, private life, and meticulous habits caught everyone's attention. Leigh, too, attributed many dynamics of the succession to personal traits— pointing out that she felt that women administrators were subject to more scrutiny that were men, emphasizing that people never say "that's just like a man" in reference to a male principal's decisions.

Some potentially salutary personal traits received attention in these studies. Leithwood and colleagues focused on professional self-image as an instructional leader. They hypothesized that role orientation would eventually lead to behavioral change and enhanced instructional leadership.

Social Context. The interaction of these personal traits identified by a number of writers with the social context in the new work assignment provided a far more revealing picture of the succession process than did attention to traits alone. For example, Leithwood and others built the rationale for their study on evidence from the literature that principals' development of a professional self-image as an instructional leader would contribute to the application of refined knowledge and skills needed to be successful as an instructional leader and to the development of norms and values in the organizations in which they worked that contributed to instructional performance. They found that principals implicitly valued socialization experiences aimed at instructional leadership embedded in the context of the school. To their disappointment, they also found that principals who reported having experiences that should have fostered instructional leadership did not focus on tasks related to instruction in their daily work. The social context and focus of tasks remained unchanged.

The social context as a general concept received considerable attention from the British heads. All said they needed a lot of information about the school, established relationships among staff members, and the social role of senior teachers. Women had to overcome perceptions that they would not maintain discipline. The impressions of the faculty and their own potential for influence received a great deal of attention from successful heads. Teachers' view of this process was often couched in social terms—a judgment whether or not the new head was "in charge." Other general features of the context revealed outcomes that conflict with some other research. While Gordon and Rosen (1981), for example, predicted that a popular predecessor would make succession more difficult and play an important part, Weindling and his colleagues found that heads reported a "sincere welcome" regardless of the favorable light in which successors were held. They also said that time spent with predecessors was generally unproductive (Cosgrove found this factor to be "benign"). These school leaders describe the most difficult part of their succession in social terms, saying that the experience of becoming the head was the part of their job they were least prepared for—the process itself.

The culture of the school was another social context factor to which many of these studies turned for insight into the succession process. Cosgrove made it a major focus of her study, yet she found that neither the principals nor the teachers were able to identify core cultural features of their schools. They had "a great deal of difficulty" identifying any norms or unspoken rules deeply imbedded as assumptions and beliefs. This, despite the fact that those who did identify a "theme" for their schools believed these themes were shared by others. This situation was unaffected by succession. When teachers did talk about culture, they attributed it to the teachers, not to the principal, yet they seemed to place importance on the notion of school culture and the principal's responsibility to affect it.

These results suggest a lack of understanding of the deep-seated nature of organizational culture. Many of Cosgrove's subjects seemed to confuse culture with interpersonal relationships—talking about getting along with the new people. Wright and Roberts's findings support this conclusion. While principals said their most important first-year goals included influence on school culture, research revealed not only no effects but no understanding or focus on aspects of the school critical to understanding culture. Roberts went so far as to assert that there was little evidence their twelve subjects recognized, used, or manipulated cultural linkages. She saw little evidence that values espoused by new principals received significant attention in the schools. Instead, new principals showed evidence that they had difficulty with the concept of culture and behaved in counterproductive ways—concentrating on control and the establishment of tight, principal initiated linkages throughout the social system of the school.

These writers also highlight a common error committed by new leaders—falling back on old times and places and favoring other pressure groups over teachers. Any too-apparent preference for other referent groups—district supervisors, parents, community members, or the faculties of other schools—offended teachers in the new setting. One serious error teachers identified was the reference to how well things worked in their old schools. As with Hamilton, who alienated faculty members with constant references to past successes and practices, Weindling and Earley found that teachers interpreted these examples as implied criticism. And parents and students should not be favored over teachers, who came to feel that they received insufficient support.

One final aspect of the social environment that received attention from the majority of these studies—faculty expectations for change—also became entwined with socialization stages. These writers emphasized the anticipation, the high expectations for change that accompany changes in school leadership. Some found that the longer the tenure of the predecessor, the greater the expectation for change (Weindling & Earley, 1987), but these studies make it clear that teachers expect changes from new principals and that the manner in which these changes occur and the timing and pacing of change are important factors in any succession. Cosgrove found that teachers emphasized their belief in mandates for change more than did principals—expecting, almost demanding, that this disruptive process have some effect on their work. The issue of "honeymoon" periods and missed opportunities also emerged from these studies. These issues of timing and pacing may be a very important aspect of the stages of organizational socialization for new leaders.

Socialization Stages

Like the case studies of Hamilton and Howard, these studies reveal ways in which the stages of the organizational socialization of new school leaders can affect outcomes. Encounter or entry was dominated by anticipation of change and confrontation with problems, conflicts, and opportunities. The need for careful data gathering and school analysis by new principals constantly reappeared. The balance of adjustment, accommodation, and clarity had a number of effects ranging from status quo custodial replication of the previous situation to major exploration and development for both principals and faculties. Parkay and colleagues asserted that the challenges and discouragement that some principals seem to feel as they move through (or fail to progress through) important stages of integration and influence may in part result from their lack of knowledge of the "shape" of this process. Better understanding of its dynamics and universality may help new school leaders feel less inadequate and lead to a high level of development for a greater number.

Encounter. As I pointed out in the preceding section, the expectation of change dominates prearrival and early encounter experiences in schools. All the studies reviewed for this book that looked at the situation in schools preceding succession reveal expectations for change of some kind. But a major controversy surrounds the timeliness of change efforts and the depth and scope of change.

Cosgrove concluded that the nature of the school year might dictate that principals look on their second year as a part of the succession time frame and moderate change initiatives with that in mind, but her own data reveal a serious risk in that decision. While she associated differences in perceptions about district mandates among principals and teachers in continuing and succession schools as evidence of second-year effects, they also could be associated with a "window of opportunity" that, when passed, results in new resentment toward perceived and resented mandates for change. Teachers expect change from new principals. In her conclusions, Cosgrove moved toward this interpretation, recommending that principals forge ahead with needed changes because teachers are prepared to adapt and look forward to change with anticipation.

Other studies reveal similar dynamics during the early period of succession. Weindling and Earley's extensive sample and the follow-up study by Earley, Baker, and Weindling argued that this "wait and see" attitude often precluded the introduction of new ideas in the future. Their subjects adamantly insisted that it was critical to move quickly. The most successful began immediately with some surface changes that provided highly visible commitment and ability to get things done (much like Hamilton's copy machine and Howard's faculty room sink) but were basically surface changes and caused no disruption. At the same time, they recommended that newly appointed leaders begin immediately to study the school and plan for more significant changes related to the content of the work at the school, bring people along, and base their actions on a knowledge of the aspirations and dreams of the teachers. By developing a long-range strategy, these heads contended, one can maneuver to reshape the structural patterns of the social system over time.

The length of the "window of opportunity" is less certain. Weindling and Earley's subjects said eighteen months; Cosgrove suggested two years; Lamoreaux argued that evidence of effects can be visible as early as nine weeks; Parkay and colleagues set no time limit but found only two of twelve principals at their highest stage after three years. But general agreement exists that "wait and see" is not good advice; that teachers must be involved; that principals often show a remarkable lack of respect for the norms, beliefs, and skills and knowledge of their faculties and pay the price for it.

Parkay and colleagues found that a few principals fail to move beyond the first two stages of organizational socialization in which they rely too heavily on formal sources of power and fear losing control. These principals were not successful. They can be in danger of remaining in a state of damage control, "chaos," and conflict.

Adjustment and Accommodation. The above discussion has intruded somewhat into this second stage. The studies reveal that, having once seized the opportunity during the early period in which change is expected, successful principals move past cosmetic changes into further diagnosis and understanding of the particular school in which they are working to develop plans for development, acquire a clear and accurate understanding of faculty perceptions and the nature of the culture and social system into which they have moved, and begin to accommodate and adjust (not just demand accommodation and adjustment from others as a result of their formal authority). Careful diagnostic work and planning and respectful interactions yield some early signs that principals are beginning to have an impact. Lamoreaux detected signs of this stage within nine weeks of the beginning of the school year.

During accommodation, which Parkay and colleagues called stability, a level of effectiveness and routinization develop. They argued that principals become less intent on promoting change and begin to move toward the development of a strong vision for the school.

Stabilization. Whether one looks at final stages as the start of a new cycle (as Nicholson argued) or as a career stage (as did Parkay and colleagues), interaction patterns between the formal leader and the social system appear consistently to characterize final stages. This stage was clearly visible in only longitudinal studies that extended over months. Not necessarily dominated by harmony or absolute consensus, it represents a move toward what Parkay, Currie, and Rhodes called "long-term success for change strategies" and movement toward a kind of professional self-actualization represented by collegial work toward school improvement. While they found only two principals at this stage at the end of a three-year study, they also contended that the first year revealed whether or not these principals would develop this integration and success—the "writing on the wall" (p. 22).

Others are less effusive about the final stage than Parkay and colleagues, but this group of writers agree that some principals stop far short of achieving healthy and productive levels of group integration. They also describe patterns that echo outcomes predicted by organizational socialization research—replication, absorption, determination, and exploration.

Outcomes of Socialization

Greenfield's studies suggested some years ago that the custodial response is the most frequent when principals take over in new schools. If the first year establishes the norm and if custodial responses resulting in a replication of the existing order are as frequent as these studies seem to suggest, then he may have been right. However, these studies provide important insight into ways in which other outcomes can emerge from the succession process. A too-frequent pattern of successions may exacerbate this outcome. Cosgrove, for example, found in one school where succession had been frequent that replication was the dominant and repeated result (teachers talked about "retraining principals to our way").

Cosgrove; Parkay, Currie, and Rhodes; Lamoreaux; Leithwood, Steinbach, and Begley; and Weindling and his colleagues all observed a respectable level of content innovation in schools as a result of leader succession as well. There were new approaches to decision making, new respect for and awareness of the skills and knowledge important for improved instruction and the exercise of instructional leadership, new ways of interacting with students during conflicts over discipline (a caring vision). These effects occurred at varying depths. Leithwood's group found that the knowledge and orientation for instructional leadership developed but that principals continued to view their most important tasks to be interpersonal, managerial, and legal.

Some principals attempted a determined remaking of the group while they remained unchanged, but this goal was not successfully achieved in any of the reported studies. Personal change seemed a pervasive partner of organizational change. This outcome parallels Wanous's (1980) assertion that the most successful newly appointed managers report personal and role change in concert (exploration). Healthy growth, it appears, is contagious.

A new principal's deep-seated reevaluation of goals and values accompanied by significant personal development was the most praised outcome of the interaction of new leaders with existing groups in schools. Parkay, Currie, and Rhodes compared it with transformational leadership a la Burns (1978). On a more instrumental level, the Canadian researchers seemed to have been aiming for this outcome as they looked for instructional leadership behaviors within schools accompanied by the requisite values and knowledge in principals as a result of socialization activities. This outcome—labeled exploration by Nicholson (1984)—received praise from scholars and appeared most frequently in the advice offered by subjects in follow-up studies.

Conclusions

The writers whose work is considered in this chapter either explicitly or implicitly offered a number of conclusions as a result of their inquiries that relate directly to the dynamics of *interaction* that have been called organizational socialization. A number of these conclusions can be summarized:

1. The process of taking charge in an existing professional organization like a school is complex. Principals and aspiring principals by their own and researchers' accounts are ill-prepared for this experience and their superiors rarely provide assistance with it.
2. The specific tactics districts or LEAs might choose to adopt will have different outcomes for promoting the replication of superb programs, the development of individual principals, the introduction of promising innovations, or the redefinition of mission and goals in schools. These factors are not, however, causal predictors, and each case must be handled with skill as an individual mix of organizational, personal, and environmental dynamics.
3. Organizational culture—its complex nature, deeply imbedded characteristics, resilience, unconscious influence, and interaction with formal leaders—may not yet be well understood as it relates to principal succession. Schein's admonition that one person should probably not try to change a culture but understand and use it may deserve more attention. At the same time, successors should concentrate on gathering information about the new social system they have joined and establishing good working relationships with teachers. Teachers influence principal succession and are the major source of group support validating the leader.
4. Newly appointed principals need to understand more about the management of change, its pacing and timing. At the same time that they remain sensitive to the pressures of change overload, they should proceed with needed changes, recognizing the limits of their influence on schools and taking satisfaction in their accomplishments.

In addition to these general conclusions, the writers on whose work I have relied so heavily for this discussion created a picture of the interaction of principals and schools as an ongoing process along a complex set of continuums. Changes in professional self-image do not guarantee changes in actions. Progress toward understanding and managing the taking-charge process does not guarantee that all successions will result in a healthy balance between personal, role, and organizational development. In short, succession remains a unique, complex, and exciting experience.

III

Leader Succession and Socialization:
The Future in Research and Practice

This last section of the book takes the lessons learned from the preceding sections and applies them to research and development in educational administration. The section is divided simply.

Chapter 7 explores the implications of hypotheses that can be generated when organizational socialization theory is applied to leader succession research, particularly in schools where long-established traditions about schools in general exist side by side with individual school cultures. In this chapter, I recommend future directions for research based on an expanded, interactive framework applied to inquiry on leader succession in established organizations.

Chapter 8 moves away from this focus on theory and research. In it, I take the research propositions presented and discussed in Chapter 7 and assess their implications for the practice of educational administration. In Chapter 8, I raise implications that spring from the "persistent problem" occurring whenever individuals interact with established social groups during leader succession. The chapter addresses ways in which those who appoint and assist principals can improve the overall quality of succession processes in their schools and school districts. It also confronts ways in which principals can improve the likelihood that their successions will be rewarding for them professionally and personally while being productive experiences for the schools they are asked to lead.

7

Implications for Research on Leader Succession in Schools

In the past few decades, inquiry on leader succession has been isolated from the interaction perspectives provided by professional socialization and organizational socialization research and theory. The unique strengths of each of these approaches applied to discreet views of school organizations warranted this isolation during early stages of knowledge development because of those strengths and the need for control in research designs focusing on small numbers of variables. Traditional succession frameworks facilitated the identification of variables affecting succession processes and outcomes (such as race, sex, insider/outsider status, selection agent, and so on). Professional socialization and induction research revealed the processes through which new professionals develop their skills and come to adopt the values, beliefs, and assumptions characterizing the profession. These frameworks promoted increased control over extraneous sources of influence on outcomes.

With its traditional focus on the leader, search for effects, and lists of related variables, principal succession research is in danger of faltering. While it provides correlations between variables (e.g., qualities of selection agent/superior are attributed to the successor; outsiders institute higher levels of change; ethnic minorities function outside the common circle of mentors; women experience higher performance anxiety), the number of factors is so large that meaningful relationships evade description. Ogawa (in press) recently asserted that the conventional approach to succession research in schools may have outlived its usefulness, because it has failed to generate useful new hypotheses and empirical research for almost a decade. Only increased interest in the influences of organizational culture on principals and assertions that leadership is a measure of attributed rather than real effects offered new insights (Pfeffer, 1981b;

Schein, 1985). A long list of variables and processes resulted from this research but little recent progress in understanding their interaction in real school settings occurred. Future progress depends on the use of more interactive frameworks that provide guidance for research and promote its application to practice.

In addition to the need for research designs that include the successor and the organization in the same studies, the wide variation among successions and methodological debates lead to a disagreement over the utility of further exploration into the positive, negative, or neutral effects of succession per se. In actuarial studies based on large existing data sets, scholars partialed out variance attributable to past organizational performance, industry (or public sector), and environmental factors, then looked for variance attributable to changes in leadership. Research using this method (following on the work of Lieberson and O'Connor, 1972) has come under attack. (See the discussion of general leadership effects in Chapter 2.) First, the magnitude of effect (as measured by attributable variance) is small, and the authors of these studies have reached widely varying conclusions about its importance. Second, critics contend that the findings are an artifact of the method. They provide little insight into the variables of interest in leader succession. The search for general leadership effects retains such power over the imagination, however, that scholars continue to explore the actuarial approach and the methods of analysis seeking variance in performance resulting from changes in leadership. Recent reanalysis of some of these studies and further exploration by Thomas (1988) provides support for continued methodological development and "definite support for the individualist view of leadership" (p. 388).

Abandoning succession frameworks, perhaps for these reasons, researchers in educational administration turned to professional socialization theory to better understand principals' experiences taking charge in schools. They used these theories to frame research and provide explanations for the induction experience and for principals' observed impacts during the taking-charge phase (Duke et al., 1984; Greenfield, 1985b; Oliver, forthcoming; Parkay & Hall, in press; Pellicer et al., 1988). But these approaches are limited by the theory; they focus on first-time principals (or other professionals). When scholars fail to control for experience in research samples, the validity of results is threatened. The use of new principals to study principal socialization or leader succession is most useful for understanding the socialization of new principals (effects on the individual— assistant principals or principals in their first-time administrative assignments). When school effects and the interactions between the school and new leader become the focus of inquiry, they falter.

Carefully designed professional socialization studies reveal much of worth about induction into the principalship and other leadership roles in education, but they also leave the vast majority of leader successions in schools out of the picture. Because few new principals are completely free of administrative experience at other levels (e.g., elementary, middle school or junior high, and high school) or in intermediate positions (e.g., assistant principal), these successions require somewhat different conceptualizations and framing (Parkay & Currie, in press). While principals and other managers will probably experience between six and eight leader successions in their careers, only one of these will be a first-time experience. The strengths of the socialization frameworks researchers have garnered for professional socialization research need to be more broadly distributed in the scholarly agenda on school leadership.

By extending research and theory in leader succession to embrace both professional and organizational frameworks, scholars can help rectify these problems. Organizational socialization theory, too, has limitations grounded in its perspective, primarily emerging from its emphasis on the group's impact on newcomers. These limitations present an almost reverse image of those in traditional leader succession frameworks. The emphasis on the group can lead one to discount the creative input of each new leader, while isolated focus on the new leader presents a view of succession almost divorced from context. However, when the two traditions—succession and socialization—are viewed as complementary and their major strengths combined, a more accurate picture of the complex processes of leader succession in schools emerges. The power of the group and the creativity of the individual can be tapped by such a synthesis.

Socialization and leader succession research literatures both rely on some version of the four main themes to which I have repeatedly referred throughout this book. These themes are organizational tactics, stages, personal and social context, and outcomes. Each of the research traditions on which this discussion draws brings different insights to these themes, contributing parts of the whole.

Table 7.1 illustrates the contributions of socialization and succession approaches to the study of newly assigned school leaders. Leader succession research to date contributes to inquiry along a number of dimensions, providing insight into important variables. By seeking correlations and predictive validity among variables such

TABLE 7.1

A Research Synthesis

Organizational Socialization	*Leader Succession*
1. Tactics: Discussion of tactics provides more opportunity for organization to influence leader and organizational growth — exploration.	1. Tactics: No discussion of tactics after the selection of leader.
2. Stages: entry, accommodation and adjustment/stabilization. Emphasizes interaction of new member and organization. Provides insight into the group impact on the leader and the social validation of leader legitimacy.	2. Stages: pre-arrival, entry, accommodation, stabilization. Details about presuccession factors and organizational history assist successor in planning tactics. Insight into taking charge processes and exercise of influence.
3. Context	3. Context
Personal: congruence and growth.	Personal: established traits.
Social: facilitates cultural analysis and process of influence, including how influence is exerted and why—shared reality. Shows how varying selectivity affects level of socialization needed. Helps leaders assess impact on them, emphasizing adjustment.	Social: assessment and diagnosis and emphasis on shared expectations and timely changes, emphasizing what should be influenced. Identifies selection problems. Helps the leader understand need for change, emphasizing taking charge.
Conceptualizes context as dynamic, process of interaction affecting personal and organizational growth.	Conceptualizes context as static, a set of features for the leader to change.
4. Outcomes: Custodial—no change in leader of organization or some personal development in leader. Organizational change—innovation in content of leader's role or content/role innovation and personal development in leader.	4. Outcomes: Variance in organizational performance, no effect, or symbolic effect.

as processes that precipitate succession, the selection of a new principal, and the impact of superiors on perceptions, expectations, and successor influence, it structures inquiry into relationships among personal traits of successors, organizational characteristics, and outcomes. Consequently, succession research examines the impacts of prearrival factors, organizational history, superordinate influence, and selection process on expectations and events in schools.

Succession writers also introduced the notion of sense making to research on principal succession (Hart, 1987; Fauske & Ogawa, 1987; Ogawa, 1991) and raised the all-important possibility that the whole process is attributional (Pfeffer, 1981b). This approach called attention to the power and creativity of the individual principal to shape interpretations and outcomes and to the importance of people's beliefs about succession in schools. It reminded researchers that improved school performance is the fundamental reason for this inquiry and highlighted the window of opportunity for change accompanying each principal succession.

A number of issues that arose from this research tradition remain tantalizingly unresolved. The characteristics and ambient boundaries of a possible window of opportunity, for example, require further investigation, along with the nature of social processes included in sense making and other dynamic processes. The majority of this research suffers from a static organizational and individual view of succession, neglecting in-depth analysis of the emergent, dynamic processes that shape the interaction among elements.

Organizational socialization presents an interactive view of individuals and groups during succession and can encompass the research issues and variables of interest in induction/professional socialization research when structured appropriately (if the socialization to professional norms, beliefs, and values is added to studies including first-time role incumbents). It provides descriptions of organizational tactics whose effects on school and principal outcomes deserve further investigation—an aspect of succession almost completely neglected by succession researchers, as Weindling and his colleagues (1987, 1991) pointed out. Organizational socialization research expands understanding of leader succession by providing theoretical models for interaction processes that shape outcomes. These theories include propositions that can be used to formulate testable hypotheses about *how* and *why* certain individual and group effects emerge, changes in schools develop, and sense making creates a shared reality. This approach thus supplies theoretical explanations for the social dynamics of succession that include the full complement of important participants, processes, and context variables.

As part of this expanded view, organizational socialization draws attention to impacts on the successor as well as the school, offering explanations and predictions for personal and organizational growth. These theoretical linkages can be used to construct research projects that examine the effects of organizational socialization on human resource development. They also reveal dynamic linkages among participants, at different organizational levels, and across stages in a view of the continuing cycle of transition and outcomes becoming inputs that characterizes principal succession. This cycle of outputs becoming inputs is fundamental to understanding social system interpretations of succession. It builds on the critical first succession during which a new school leader is inducted and socialized and allows for a continuing professional development view of succession events from the individual perspective. It also allows for the unique mix of variables in each setting to be better conceptualized and understood.

Finally, organizational socialization offers the advantages of professional socialization research frameworks while protecting the trustworthiness of the results from the threats of sample contamination. Since few school administrators are truly novices to the profession of school administration (as law school graduates, for example, are certain to be novices to the practice of law), research on the professional socialization of principals can be protected from a lack of control over level of experience in research samples.[1] At the same time, the uniqueness of first-time successions, during which the magnitude of impacts on professional self-concept and future professional values is great, can be preserved in the overall research agenda.

Issues in the Organizational Socialization of Principals

The potential of organizational socialization theory to enrich leader succession research in schools opens up three issues for future research. First, the findings of stage framework research in schools support a call for organizational analysis including the organization and new leader in the same research design. These studies also support the prediction that careful organizational analysis by the successor can play a critical part in promoting productive interactions and, subsequently, outcomes. Second, researchers presently are best at identifying social validation as an outcome rather than as a process. The specific interactions that lead to social validation, what some researchers prefer to call transformational leadership (Bass, 1981; Burns, 1978; Parkay, Currie & Rhodes, 1992) or value-added leadership (Sergiovanni, 1991), require detailed and careful explication in school settings. Schools possess powerful and explicit social histories, norms, and expectations that affect leader legitimacy. Third, the interaction of processes and situations that results in effective outcomes for schools and the people who work there during principal succession requires careful analysis.

Organizational Analysis

Socialization frameworks present an interactive view of the individual/group relationships. At the same time, the impact of the group is a clear focus of this perspective. Researchers engaged in succession inquiry framed as organizational socialization will need to conduct in-depth organizational analyses of schools in order to reveal and analyze significant interaction variables and processes. Some of the debate over the methods of analysis used in large actuarial studies may spring from frustration over the inappropriate decoupling of variables from context, given the nature of the social phenomenon under study.

The use of organizational socialization to frame principal succession research highlights the role of the new leader in organizational analysis as well. The dialogue between individual and group that socialization represents can be more or less conscious, and it is possible that principals who conduct a practitioner's version of total participant observation inquiry while filling a powerful role in a school may provide important insight into the socialization process. Principals clearly have limited time to devote to inquiry (Willower and colleagues studies—Kmetz & Willower, 1982; Martin & Willower, 1981). One can say that principals must analyze and understand a school, but complex practical and ethical issues accompany participant observation inquiry by practicing school administrators. That this research might be conducted by people who will use it to take action in the school only complicates the situation.

While the research methods and data analytical techniques for socialization inquiry conducted by researchers are well established and involve simultaneous examination of the setting and the new member, analyses conducted by leader/participants benefits from no firmly established tradition of inquiry. Not only does participant observation research pose challenges, but principals seeking improved organizational understanding must conduct this inquiry, attempt an analysis that includes *themselves* as one component, and take action based on the outcome. Little is known about rigorous and trustworthy processes for gathering data and completing analysis by a new member who also possesses formal authority in the school and can take actions affecting others.

Some guidance can be found in recent literature that sees action, rather than research, as the primary goal of inquiry (Argyris, Putnam & Smith, 1985). Schein (1985) argued persuasively and provided guidelines for in-depth cultural analysis by an outside researcher in organizations. He affirmed the need for new leaders to understand linkages between culture and leadership and provided useful questions for structuring this inquiry. Other social science researchers also provided cogent arguments for the inclusion of the insider, native view in any cultural analysis (Gregory, 1983). But the role of the new leader as researcher requires much more careful examination.

A number of questions for scholars arise in consideration of this issue. How might multiple case study designs facilitate the development of models that include multiple variables, participants, and levels of interaction and expand understanding of the interaction process between the new leader and the school context in a leader succession experience? What is the appropriate role of a successor as subject and inquirer in leader succession research? What methodologies found to be productive in research lend themselves to adjustment and application by new school leaders seeking a guide to action? Hart (1986) asserted that some systematic data gathering and analysis techniques common to qualitative methods can be modified for use by principals. Action research (Argyris, Putnam & Smith, 1985) suggests methods that hold promise. How do these compare with such concepts as "reflection-in-action" and "reflection-on-action" proposed by Schon (1983, 1987) as models for effective professional practice? How might principals be better prepared to take on this challenge? What forms of organizational socialization and support do principals require to develop the habit and expectation of reflection and analysis (Dewey, 1933)?

Social Validation of Principals—the Road to Leadership

Organizational socialization theory and research provide researchers with important frameworks for analyzing the process and magnitude of social acceptance and validation from group members achieved by new leaders during succession. As an outcome, social validation makes a lot of sense. It can be identified when it occurs, and it amplifies a new leader's ability to affect the actions taken by members of the organization. Interviews and surveys of participants delineate the scope and impact of the group's support for a principal and the actions attributed to that validation. Without much expanded knowledge about the types of interaction and forms of social process that yield this outcome, little progress will be made toward penetrating the black box of cause and effect relationships in which leader succession research has languished.

The need to understand types of interaction and forms of social process also raises the issue of power and influence among participants during succession. Leadership is, after all, the desired outcome—leadership validation that springs from and results in social power. The studies reviewed for this book do not capitalize on research and theory on power in organizations—neither from a positivist, micropolitical perspective nor in the voice of social criticism. Because social analysis, inquiry, and reflection such as that required for the interaction studies called for in this chapter are "essentially a political act" (Kemmis, 1985), more diverse views of power in school organizations deserve attention.

Questions for researchers emerge from inquiry focused on the social validation of leaders (Blau, 1964; Dornbusch & Scott, 1975). What tactics undertaken by a new leader's superiors facilitate social validation processes? What specific information actions by principals predict social validation by teachers, the community, and the new principal's superiors, and under which conditions? What actions assist the development of influential relationships with the group? How do the ethnicity, sex, social class of origin, and race of the new leader affect validation processes and outcomes, and what tactics used by superiors and new leaders help socially incongruent new leaders become successful, contributing, and integrated members of a school organization? How are these group level relationships predicted by or emergent from exchange relationships with individuals? How does this inquiry push knowledge beyond the exchange theories of leadership and the purchase of idiosyncrasy credits referred to in previous chapters (Yukl, 1989)? How does information processing contribute to this outcome? What are the critical features of social information processing in professional or semiprofessional work systems such as schools? How does the first-time succession (and the resultant induction and professional socialization effect) shape future succession experiences, and what factors are most critical for superiors to consider in setting up these experiences? How does the social psychological view of succession offered by organizational socialization compare with political models such as micropolitics as an explanatory or research framework (Bacharach & Lawler, 1981; Blau, 1964; Ball, 1987)?

Principal and School Growth and Performance

A third and final issue arising from an organizational socialization analysis of school leader succession relates to effects—personal and organizational. The focus on effects that succession research maintained through so much ambiguity and so many contradictory findings should not be abandoned because early, highly controlled models failed to produce stable results. Professional socialization research on school principals has begun the refocusing of inquiry by asking questions about personal and school effects of the induction process. Organizational socialization research predicts a number of group and individual outcomes that can stabilize these results and that deserve elaboration. Additionally, researchers should attend to the processes that participants and their superiors manipulate that yield desired outcomes—with outcome measures explicitly described in advance.

Personal and organizational growth are valued outcomes of succession. This value raises questions about the utility of succession as a deliberate strategy for improving school performance and promoting the professional development of principals. What are the relationships between succession variables and personal growth by the successor? What are the relationships among succession factors, content innovation in the enactment of the principal's role in a particular school, and major role innovation that challenges the fundamental assumptions of the principal's role in schools? How might knowledge about these relationships be used to inform action aimed toward promoting the recommendations of so many school reform and restructuring reports and teacher work redesign (Bacharach, Bamberger & Mitchell, 1990; Hart, 1990b)? What is the relationship between principal and school growth and the window of opportunity for change presented by group expectations that accompany succession? What ambient boundaries confine the window of opportunity for change, and what relationships do these boundaries have with the school year and conventional school schedules? How do these expectations and outcomes differ from those in other kinds of organizations? What are the benefits and costs of transferring principals to new schools on a set schedule with no clear goals? What group and individual benefits accrue from the succession of principals and other school leaders from underrepresented groups, such as women and members of racial and ethnic minorities?

Implications for Research Methodologies

These three substantive issues have methodological implications for principal succession research. While the question of positive, negative, or no effects of succession per se appears to have been answered with "it depends," the methods best used to identify the specific variables and process on which these effects depend deserve examination.

First, longitudinal, in-depth case studies including multiple data types and sources, participant perspectives, and socialization factors need to be completed. These cases can be used to develop cross-case analyses and pattern development. Only longitudinal research that includes participants, processes, and outcomes can trace the interaction dynamics among individuals and within groups that characterize principal succession. Some of these data must be in the words of participants, because so much depends on their expectations and interpretations—their sense making—and on researchers' ability to trace the growth of an emergent shared reality and identify its distinguishing features.

Researchers also require multiple forms of longitudinal data from many sources to trace the processes and the critical variables involved in the social validation of the new leader. Some of these data should be specifically designed to assess the outcomes of succession— levels and salutary forms of change; organizational development using well-established measures of work design and healthy organizations; outcome and performance (teacher and student); principal development measures; impacts of race, sex, and ethnicity; and goal-outcome congruence. (Did the succession and the deliberate tactics chosen predict outcomes desired by the superintendents, other superiors, the district, the community?) The earliest succession studies began this inquiry; researchers should pursue its development.

Second, studies need to move beyond the focus on principals and outcomes isolated from interactions in schools. Methods that fragmented levels of analysis, isolated variables, and dissected relationships provided insight about discrete variables that may affect succession at early stages of this research tradition but failed to reveal how principals and schools interact in real settings under real performance and outcome pressures from superintendents, school boards, and communities. Like the child psychology researchers who now know how three-year-olds react to stress in artificial environments under contrived stressor conditions, it is time to move on and come to understand how these responses emerge for normal people in real environments (Kagan, 1978). We know that outsiders make more changes; many respond to this information with "so what?" For a decade, succession research in schools has languished, perhaps because it is time for researchers to develop more complex, interactive models of leader succession as a social process. Hypothesis testing related to personal traits and projected outcomes appears to be of little utility in this research, because it so simplifies the social environment that it renders findings trivial at best. By imbedding all succession inquiry in the social environment that creates its legitimacy and interprets each variable, researchers will be better able to develop predictive models based on multiple correlations.

Finally, the neglect of social criticism in the succession literature is glaring. Racial and ethnic differences and the "sexuality of organizations" (Hearn, Sheppard, Tancred-Sheriff & Burrell, 1989) affect groups' assessments of people, shaping their judgments of whether a person is appropriate for or fit for leadership. This reality became apparent in the earliest small group studies of leadership conducted by the military, in which researchers found that people are less likely to attribute expertise to minorities and women and less willing to give them credit for positive outcomes. These studies revealed that sex and race are significant independent variables that shape outcomes; they fail to reveal the interactions among individuals and between the leader and organization or group that produce these effects. Many scholars offer useful methods and paradigms for opening the study of organizational socialization and leader succession to more critical perspectives (Cooper & Burrell, 1988; Burrell, 1988; Giroux, 1991). These approaches deserve further attention and application.

Research Propositions

Research and theory drawn from a synthesis of leader succession, professional socialization, and organizational socialization research can be used to structure propositions about relationships among variables during principal succession. While these propositions should not be viewed as hypotheses, the development of testable hypotheses on the basis of these propositions is possible. The propositions that follow are grouped according to the three research issues emerging from organizational socialization inquiry during principal succession discussed above.

Organizational Analysis

Administrative work is dominated by demands for action and effects (Mintzberg, 1973). Theorists and researchers can productively pursue frameworks that promote organizational analysis focused on interaction. New principals and other school leaders, too, might benefit from systematic analyses that replicate professional reflection models (Dewey, 1933; Hart, Sorensen & Naylor, 1992; Schon, 1983, 1987). Administrators face an environment rife with pressures for assertive action, power, and demonstrations of "leadership." This poses a challenge for successors who are basically naive about the critical social features of the new environment in which they must function or who (if insiders) must overcome strong preconceptions about themselves held by others as well as past relationships and social "debts." The need for interaction analysis thus exists for researchers and successors, grounded firmly in recognition of the social constraints the role places on the analyst who is simultaneously an actor.

1. Principals skilled in cultural analysis will be able to describe the performance/outcome needs of the school and the finest professional aspirations of professional teachers and others who work there in ways that accurately represent the descriptions of the established members of the group. They will be able to analyze the social context in which they must pursue these goals and promote these outcomes.

2. Principals who understand the interaction processes of succession (know about the two-way effects of interaction and ways to analyze and diagnose the social setting) will have a greater and earlier impact on the school following a succession than those who are not prepared with this knowledge and skills. They will be less likely to resort to formal authority, dictates, and control and more likely to move quickly through the stages of integration, influence, and actualization described by researchers.

3. Succession/socialization stages are normative, not functional. They do not predict functional outcomes *desired* by superiors, organizational leaders, successors, or school members. Adjustment and equilibrium do not guarantee a successful succession from the point of view of the organization. Outcomes may suppress desired innovation and individual creativity and signal the end of the window of opportunity brought on by the succession event. The relationships among stages, organizational inertia, and personal and school growth remain unclear and need exploration.

Social Validation of Principals—the Path to Leadership

A social interaction view of succession emphasizes the power of the group to control actions by individuals while acknowledging that any new member also affects a group. A teacher may oppose a new principal's initiatives, but if the group supports and affirms his vision for the school, it will enforce compliance and support. A new principal (or teacher leader) need not resort to formal authority, because the group will bestow legitimacy and support to the new effort. Depending on the norms of the group, an overreliance on formal authority may be dysfunctional. The power of the group to promote major changes in schools in the face of individuals' opposition is illustrated in research reports of school reform and teacher work redesign (Bacharach, Bamberger & Mitchell, 1990; Hart, 1990a).

Social validation and legitimacy emerge from social interaction processes, however, and schools are organizations with strong distinguishing social, professional, and school-level norms, beliefs, and assumptions that shape these processes. Knowledge about the means through which validation outcomes emerge is sparse.

1. Successor influence is amplified when group pressure supports the goals and orientations of the new leader and functions separately from the loyalty and cooperation of individuals. Actions that promote the development of this group affirmation in schools need further description and analysis.
2. Group pressure supportive of the new leader's goals develops as a series of events along a continuum, beginning with the individual and moving toward group-level relationships—a continuum requiring description, elaboration, and categorization, particularly in professional/semiprofessional organizations such as schools.
3. A quick mastery of technical skills and knowledge valued and needed by the school (and organizational support toward that end) speeds up new leaders' validation. By achieving this validation based on valued skills and knowledge, principals and other school leaders are freed to attend to more subtle and difficult aspects of school performance imbedded in social interpretations, speeding up the adjustment and stabilization stages of leader succession.
4. Contact, communication, and congruent traits among new principals and schools predict positive outcomes during succession only if they are *interpreted* as legitimate in the context by the participants. The processes through which these interpretations emerge can be predicted using social information processing, symbolic interactionism, micropolitics, the presentation of self, ethnomethodology, or other theoretical frameworks. The utility of various theoretical perspectives for predicting outcomes in schools remains unknown.

5. Leader successors with personal traits that appear to conflict with
    established norms and traditions in the social system (ethnic and
    racial minorities and women) can enhance the process of social
    validation and acceptance by the group (and consequently their
    ability to function as leaders, influencing the behavior of others).
    Yet the processes through which they can accomplish this goal
    remain poorly understood. The utility of competing information,
    cognition, or social processes remains unknown. "Socially
    incongruent" principals who use information exchange and
    interpretation (social information processing) to emphasize
    functional and valued similarities such as technical and moral
    skills and basic approaches to education and deemphasize surface
    incongruities will be more successful and will have a greater
    impact on schools than those who do not. Principals' superiors
    can positively affect the success rate of newly appointed women
    and people of color by using tactics specifically designed to assist
    them during the taking-charge stage of leadership.

Growth and Performance

Superintendents and school boards appoint principals and
anticipate positive outcomes from these appointments. Positive effects
for the school are the major goal. A long-range quality strategy also
includes the development of the district's human resources, however.
Principal growth consequently is also an admirable goal of succession,
as schools in the district will rely in the future on the leadership of
talented, skilled, and knowledgeable principals. These personal and
school-level growth outcomes interact, but circumstances shape the
relative balance of personal and school growth that can result.

1. School organizations can enhance the adjustment of new
    principals (and others in authority who undergo transitions, such
    as teacher mentors and lead teachers) by employing socialization
    processes that minimize negative surprises about the nature of
    the work and the work group and facilitate sense making. This
    can be achieved by teaching participant observation skills and
    organizational analysis, providing peers with whom to discuss
    emerging frameworks, and rewarding the habit and expectation
    that organizational analysis will occur.
2. The most productive balance between organizational and
    personal change during succession depends on the characteristics
    of the successor and the needs of the school organization. School
    district leaders can explicitly structure tactics, training, and

organizational support to maximize benefit in each succession. These outcomes can be predicted and traced through well-designed research.

3. If superiors do not deliberately plan socialization tactics, socialization of principal successors will occur nevertheless; outcomes can be predicted based on content, process, and context. Variables of importance include the collective/individual, formal/informal, sequential/variable, fixed/variable, serial/disjunctive, and investiture/divestiture characteristics of the socialization experience. During principal socialization, the outcomes of various combinations of these tactics remain substantially untested, because school district leaders have neglected to employ deliberate tactics during principal socialization occurring with succession.

4. Those interested in role innovation and school restructuring can predict potent effects from a lack of role models and from requirements inherent in reform that teachers and principals abandon their established professional self-concepts. Tactics and support structures described above should predict outcomes of teacher work/leadership reform, just as it will predict outcomes of principal succession. The relationships of role stress and professional and personal concept with significant work role transitions require careful study in schools (Bacharach, Bamberger & Conley, 1991).

5. Mentors (and predecessors) have functional and dysfunctional effects during succession. Contact with the immediate predecessor suppresses innovation. Contact with mentors who exemplify and model desired innovation leads to enhanced levels of change and organizational development. Contact with mentors who exemplify traditional practice predicts replication of current practice.

6. Custodial responses are promoted by principal succession processes now employed by school districts. By altering and studying these processes, school districts should be able to test this proposition.

Summary

Implications for succession research are numerous when one expands inquiry to include a synthesis of professional and organizational socialization with leader succession theory. They include issues of substance and methodology that deserve the attention of researchers.

Issues of substance suggest a reframing of inquiry to include expanded use of longitudinal, comparative case study frameworks that include all participants' perspectives and focus on interactions between the organization and the new leader; the implications of data gathering and analysis by a powerful, new organizational member; the need for the *group* validation of the legitimacy of a new principal in order for the school to act on her goals and toward outcomes to which she aspires; and the personal and organizational growth potential provided by succession events.

Methodological implications that organizational socialization raises relate primarily to the need for longitudinal data from many sources, in many forms, from many points of view. Methodologies also should be expanded so that the successor/leader is not studied in isolation from the organization. Although expensive and time consuming, longitudinal case studies including quantitative and qualitative data hold the greatest promise (Yin, 1985). Leader succession is a complex process. It emerges from interactions. It occurs over time. It depends upon the interpretations of groups of people and upon their willingness to act on those interpretations. Additionally, the research on leader succession would benefit from the application of critical methods and paradigms to the research. This point of view is currently absent from the literature.

These research issues and the methodological implications also affect practice. In the concluding chapter that follows, the implications of an interaction perspective combining succession and socialization frameworks are discussed.

8

Improving Leader Succession in Schools

I had already made the right beginning—I had already figured out where the big fish would be and why.... Then an odd thing happened. I saw him. A black back rose and sank in the foam. In fact, I imagined I saw spines on his dorsal fin until I said to myself, "God, he couldn't be so big you could see his fins." I even added, "You wouldn't even have seen the fish in all that foam if you hadn't first thought he would be there." But I couldn't shake the conviction that I had seen the black back of a big fish, because... I know that often I would not see a thing unless I thought of it first.

—Norman Maclean, *A river runs through it*

During leader succession, when the relationships and patterns that shape a principal's impact on the school are formed, the organization and the new principal exert influence on each other. A successor who possesses knowledge about social influencing processes and skill in applying that knowledge can have a substantial impact on the outcomes of her own succession experience. District leaders can use the same body of knowledge to plan succession processes and design support activities for principals that make the results they desire more likely to occur. They can use knowledge about the interaction between a new member and the organization to modify principal evaluation processes and refocus principals' attention.

This final chapter examines some of the practical implications of a synthesis of leader succession and organizational socialization frameworks to improve the outcomes of principal succession—personal and organizational. These implications follow from the research: (a) on organizational tactics that shape interactions among a new leader, his superiors, and the community; (b) on the outcome predicted by individual and organizational variables; (c) on the process of socialization across time; (d) on the stages of socialization; and (e) on the social and personal context of the school.

The homage leadership receives in our culture and in literature leads many principals to conclude that they stand alone at the center of the ideas, planning, culture, and action that drive schools' performance. Experience and research belie this simple conclusion. While the principal is an important member of the school organization, her opportunity to exert influence in a school depends in large part on her ability to understand and use the personal and social context. As her knowledge about the social processes in which she is embroiled and her ability to use that knowledge to interpret and shape events increase, a successor will be more likely to see and respond to the important factors that affect the outcomes of the succession. She will be in a position to notice and take action on the critical factors central to the performance of the school that she can influence effectively. It is important that principals and their superiors become aware of and experienced in diagnosing and working with the powerful social forces of the school, district, and community.

Three fundamental beliefs about the relationship of new principals with schools emerge from an organizational socialization/ leader succession synthesis. First, principal succession is best understood as a group experience in which the school and new principal influence each other. When attention turns too exclusively toward the new principal, information, action, and the potential impact of the principal are limited. This holds true whether this is a first appointment and the new principal will experience professional and organizational socialization simultaneously or whether the new principal is a veteran taking on a new assignment. The opposite extreme holds dangers as well. When the school's power to shape the principal is overemphasized, the creative input of the new principal suffers.

Second, the complexity of the leader succession process does not make the experience undecipherable. While it is important not to underestimate the complexity of the social realities with which a new principal must deal, it also is important not to underestimate the ability of people to develop skill and experience understanding and working within socially complex situations. There is a danger that the many significant factors that principals and researchers find affecting successions will cause some to conclude that no one can really understand the phenomenon. Cases, actuarial statistics, and correlational studies fail to support this conclusion: the interaction context is too complicated to understand. Rather, they affirm that a principal who chooses not to hone his knowledge and skill in analyzing and understanding the social dynamics of organizational socialization during succession does so at his own risk. Individuals and organizations can develop strategies to deal with the process (Andrews, 1971).

Finally, by acknowledging the impact schools have on new principals (personally and professionally), one does not relinquish the belief that principals affect work, relationships, and outcomes in schools. A better understanding of the nature and power of the group does not negate the potential for creative contributions by the individual. In our culture, a deep desire exists to maintain the belief that strong, assertive, and dynamic leaders are proactive, not reactive, that they shape the culture and outcomes of the school. This desire reflects the popularity of cultural and symbolic leadership in the literature on schools (Deal & Peterson, 1990). It emerges in the search for new metaphors for leadership (Bredeson, 1985; Beck & Murphy, in press), new images (preferably heroic) that will explain the difference between an inspirational principal and the dull administrator who does little more than reconcile the budget, change the bells, plan the yearly schedule, and supervise the lunch periods.

This desire for heroic leaders also makes it difficult to focus attention on the social, interactive nature of leadership in schools. Some fear that an emphasis on interaction denigrates the importance of leaders. One person, commenting on the succession experience of Dr. Howard (presented in Chapter 5), complained that Kate Howard perpetuated stereotypical beliefs about women as passive leaders. By emphasizing the part played by moral legitimacy and social validation in her own interpretation of her succession, this critic argued, Dr. Howard behaved in a stereotypically female way. No woman wants to be accused of failure as an active leader; neither does any man.

In spite of the accusation that leaders must be assertive and quickly find and pursue solutions to problems, models or metaphors for leadership that emphasize complexity and responsiveness are far from rare. In a recent essay on leadership, for example, Bennis (1990) said that "sooner or later, each of us has to accept the fact that complexity is here to stay. . . . " In another essay over a decade ago, Weick (1978) emphasized the importance of the docile leader. The type of leadership most called for in our complex social institutions, he pointed out, is not aggressive and intrusive, not the heroic leadership of politics, war, and mythology, but complex, varied, and responsive, and it draws on cognitive processes (Weick, 1979). He offered the carpenter's tool used to replicate two-dimensional patterns in physical objects, the contour gage, as a metaphor for docile leadership. This tool is a series of moveable spines suspended side by side in a metal frame. The spines move independently of each other, so that, when pressed against an object, they create a negative and positive image on opposite sides of the frame. These images allow an outline to be traced. For example, a piece of floor tile can be cut to fit exactly against a door frame modeled by the contour gage.

Weick used the contour gage as a metaphor for leadership. He argued that leaders must be able to register the elements of the organization in their own knowledge, skills, and features. As they make themselves more complex (increasing the number of their "spines"), they can register and respond to more complex organizations in appropriate ways. While decisive and immediate action that is not reflective may be called for, Weick cautioned that these occasions are rare.

In the abstract, decoupled from fears about male and female stereotypes or cultural and ethnic imperatives, Weick's ideas about the "spines of leadership"—responsive and tailored to the needs of each school—sound reasonable and creative. In practice, each principal fears being labeled "not a leader" and feels the pressure to act a part that may actually be inappropriate in a professional work setting. Images and beliefs denigrating the interactive, responsive nature of leadership continue to plague those who want to improve their own leader succession experiences and those who appoint and supervise school leaders. An interaction view of principal succession does not belittle or ignore the importance of the individual principal in each school. Rather, it adds insight and power gathered from an expanded understanding of the social realities in which leaders work and the effects of organizational socialization on new members of a group— even powerful new members. Heroic expectations aside (Peters & Waterman, 1982), the experiences of principals and of managers in all kinds of organizations affirm that succession is a social process, however salient a personal experience.

Other writers offer images of leadership that require less heroic points of view and use more interactive and conceptual approaches, as well (Bolman & Deal, 1992; Greenfield, 1991). Smith and Peterson (1988) promoted a view of leadership as event management. They asserted that the leadership needed in modern organizations is best characterized as the management of complex events. Because organizational work is a series of events each of which has importance for a number of different organizational issues and activities, administrators must become proficient in analyzing and managing the interactions, dynamics, and implications of events directed toward multiple purposes simultaneously. They asserted that social analysis may be the only avenue for a truly cross-cultural understanding of leadership. For example, a faculty meeting may be a single event important for a number of reasons. It can be an opportunity for structuring collaborative decision-making norms in the school. A group of teachers might simultaneously use the event to block or promote a curriculum reform, drawing on coalitions formed before the meeting to set up a confrontation. In the same meeting, the principal could demonstrate and model new instructional techniques. Each of these aspects of the school and its work is important; each may be a part of a single event; each demands response and complexity from the principal.

A succession is one major event and a series of smaller events. A principal undergoing succession profitably analyzes and manages this series of events to secure the validation and support she needs. Because event management requires the analysis and understanding of the culture, a nested series of contexts grounds the experience.

As I pointed out in Chapter 7, the major contributions of the traditional leader succession literature focus attention on the successor. Practice is enhanced by features similar to those that inform research. While primarily a static view of the new principal, the school, and the district, traditional literatures emphasized several important aspects of succession. Disillusionment with the progress being made by traditional succession perspectives turned people's attention toward issues of cultural change and social interpretation. The following are traditional succession contributions to practice:

1. Insight into the impacts of superordinates, prearrival organizational factors, and selection processes on the expectations of people in the school and district. These insights can be used by successors and their superiors to plan tactics and experiences likely to yield desired outcomes.
2. Individual creativity and effort on the part of the principal, providing support for successors' continued efforts to affect schools and information about ways this can happen.
3. A view of the window of opportunity for change during succession stages that encourages principals to pay attention to the pace and scope of innovation following succession. Action plans that use this window of opportunity to affect desired changes can be developed.

4. The individual influence of a new principal on school performance and aspects of the school likely to provide inroads into these areas of influence.
5. The notion of sense making, turning attention away from the more static explanations for succession effects and toward more symbolic and emerging explanations. Principals can thus ask how they make sense of their succession and what interpretations others in the school, district, and community are drawing from events.

Succession frameworks failed to reveal how and why some successions affect schools while the majority seem to result in a minor disturbance followed by the replication of the presuccession status quo. Consequently, scholars turned to the few studies that applied social analysis to succession and sought explanations for participants' beliefs and explanations. While culture and symbol provide ammunition with which to debunk a succession effect, others used cultural analysis, belief, and meaning to explore the dynamic, emergent processes of leader succession. An organizational socialization perspective makes major contributions to this search, exploring how and why some successions make a positive difference in schools. The major contributions of the organizational socialization perspective are the following:

1. It provides an understanding of organizational tactics that principals' superiors can use to influence the outcomes of succession beyond the selection stage.
2. It expands understanding of the interaction processes that result in succession effects—how and why outcomes occur, changes in the organization develop, and sense making shapes a new shared reality on which people in the school then act. New principals can act to affect this process.
3. It is a dynamic, cyclical view (rather than a static view emphasizing lists of features and conditions) that acknowledges the impact of the social group on each new member, the power of social validation of principal legitimacy to affect the behavior of participants, and the processes through which social validation occurs. It gives principals insight into specific ways they can influence their own validation and leadership.
4. It provides an expanded and complex look at personal and organizational growth during leader succession rather than focusing exclusively on school performance. This view enhances

the professional development of principals as well as outcomes in schools. It consequently combines with professional socialization knowledge to provide guidance in designing experiences for first-time and experienced principals during succession.

5. It reveals the dynamics and processes through which linkages among participants and the school and district are formed across stages of organizational socialization/succession, creating the new context that sets the stage for the next transition. This view of processes allows for deliberate organizational tactics to affect succession and action plans by each successor principal are more likely to affect outcomes.

A synthesis of leader succession and socialization perspectives offers some pivotal considerations for the practice of educational administration to which principals and policy makers should pay attention. These considerations can be used to design action plans to improve the likelihood that desired results will emerge from the exciting and complex process of leader succession in schools:

1. Succession occurs in stages that eventually lead to a situation of stability (or preparation for new cycles of change). Quiet, however, does not necessarily signal a productive final stage. Comfort or resignation may signal inertia. Principals and their superiors should not assume that no news is good news and accommodation means a succession has been successful. It may be a replication of the status quo for the school and the principal.

2. A successor requires the validation of his leadership by the teachers and other members of the school in order to act in their behalf and influence their goals and actions. Principals should establish exchanges with individuals but also attend to processes that lead to social validation by the school as a whole. The group then will enforce compliance by other members.

3. New principals should promote the validation of their authority by demonstrating that they possess and know how to use valued social, technical, and moral skills for the benefit of the school as a whole.

4. Districts can design and utilize a variety of deliberately structured processes to shape the organizational socialization of principals toward desired outcomes.

5. Current practice in educational administration virtually assures a custodial response from newly assigned principals. Districts should continually reevaluate current practice and match the

experiences new principals will have to desired outcomes as much as possible.

6. Socialization will occur with or without deliberate planning because of the nature of social groups. Principals can become knowledgeable about and be able to exploit their organizational socialization experience. They should take responsibility for diagnosing and influencing these interactions and shaping the use of information and the sense-making process toward a new shared reality that productively promotes goal accomplishment and organizational development.

7. Succession provides an opportunity to implement reform in schools, because everyone expects change. Principals can make changes, even if they are minor, that keep these expectations alive while they plan appropriate interventions for the future. They thus extend the window of opportunity that the expectation of change presents.

8. The need for a principal to respect an existing culture and work within it and the need for change and innovation will conflict during succession. Principals should be aware of and plan to deal with this conflict. They should also balance the tension between stability in the social group and their individual creativity.

9. Principals can help shape information processing and action during succession. Because belief and interpretations play a vital part in determining the actions people take, shaping these beliefs and interpretations of "objective" events is an important task of the successor. Recognizing that interpreting the facts is as important as getting the facts, principals can take action to learn about critical presuccession events, selection criteria and processes, and expectations that influenced interpretations.

10. Knowledge about organizational socialization can help women and people from diverse social and ethnic backgrounds to be successful upon taking leadership positions in schools by enhancing their moral legitimacy as leaders. Principals in these groups can deemphasize unimportant social incongruities and play to professional strengths and values shared with the school. Superiors should provide direct, individual, and collective assistance with this process.

These contributions result from organization processes and deserve attention from principals, their superiors, and policy makers in school districts. Each can be used to facilitate change, development, and growth in principals and schools as a result of leader succession.

Socialization Stages

Socialization stages during organizational socialization relate directly to practice. Anticipation almost universally accompanies leader succession. It facilitates exploration and development for everyone in a school. Yet often, the outcome is a replication of the status quo after the initial disruption, what scholars call a custodial response. This last stage highlights the misconception that tranquility is always a good thing. While equilibrium emerges and fear and apprehension subside (Ogawa, 1991), the existing order may be protected. Often teachers retreat to their classrooms as a form of damage control. Unless overt conflict occurs, the principal and her superiors can misinterpret this response as progress. If little or no disruption seems prominent in initial interactions, it could mean that the new principal is much like the rest of the school, so much like her predecessor that no difference can be expected. Repeated examples of this outcome appear in the literature—principals begin to seem interchangeable.

Accommodation takes on a flavor of finality, while it signals a truce of sorts. If progress stops here, a major opportunity will be lost. The failure to take advantage of teachers' expectations for change in the early stages of succession appears repeatedly in case studies of principal succession. This failure leads to a rapid return to comfort (with relief or disappointment) or reconciliation with the status quo. Principals then lose the chance to make changes as they become integrated into the school. New principals who "wait and see" too long may lose the opportunity to make important changes, allowing the succession to reach its final stages when expectations for change have diminished. Even small, highly visible changes can keep the climate for change more favorable, maintaining interest in the opportunities that succession provides for everyone in the school and community to reexamine their professional practices and goals.

When succession ends with accommodation and adjustment accompanied by no change, teachers may withdraw. In spite of the excitement that accompanies the succession of a new principal, discomfort, conflict, and disappointment can drive teachers to the all too convenient privacy of their own classrooms. The nature of teachers' work and conventions of privacy make isolation and insulation from the principal popular coping mechanisms for teachers, an easy way to accommodate and adjust while protecting themselves. This withdrawal can look tranquil to uncritical observers, yet it may signal an undesirable outcome—protectionism. Teachers time and time again explain a poor experience with principal succession by insisting that they are fundamentally unaffected: "Principals come and principals go." Or they may simply withdraw to avoid conflict.

Knowledge that organizational socialization and succession occur in stages also highlights the need to balance overload with inaction. While innovation overload and resentment come as a result of a too-aggressive and sweeping attack on existing school practice by a new principal, the reverse outcome occurs far more frequently. Many newly appointed principals take the advice given them to "wait and see," leading teachers to excuse their lack of impact by saying they are "biding their time." But carefully conducted investigations into successions that yield the most promising outcomes belie the wisdom of this advice. Organizational inertia threatens to undermine the potential of a new principal to lead and innovate in a school even as disruptive change undertaken in complete disregard for the school threatens innovation and social stability.

Groups Empower Principals through Social Validation

This staged view of the organizational socialization of principals emphasizes that the principal must eventually move toward a position of leadership granted to him by those with whom he works. This leadership effect emanates from the school as a whole, not from individuals.

Leaders do their work through others, especially in professional workplaces like schools. Formal authority provides some basis from which to affect others' actions, but excellent work springs from each person's commitment to act. Years of experience in schools and hundreds, perhaps thousands, of studies affirm that formal authority alone is an insufficient base from which to accomplish goals and exert influence over desired outcomes. Loyalty, exchanges and obligations, and personal professional commitment from some teachers provide impetus for action by individuals, but concerted effort requires social affirmation, validation, and reinforcement of leader legitimacy. Validation lends the power of the group to the principal's goals and initiatives, enforcing expectations and stimulating action by others in the school and community. Validation emerges gradually and cumulatively from the group as a result of the observation that valued outcomes are being achieved. It is difficult to observe and difficult to identify. If a new principal hopes to affect this process, she should give careful attention to the complex array of people, conditions, and events in the school and cultivate the skills of cultural and organizational analysis.

Having said that validation is a complex process and difficult to identify as it occurs, it remains worthy of attention by and accessible to principals undergoing succession. The benefits are worth the cost in time and attention. When teachers, students, and parents coalesce around common beliefs and goals, they act to support each other. More instrumentally, they enforce compliance within the group, applying sanctions against those who deviate from validated expectations. If students, teachers, parents, and staff find the goals, values, and beliefs of a new principal compelling and support the changes these views bring with them, the principal's influence can be amplified far beyond the boundaries of his individual authority. Without diminishing the value of individual relationships, new principals should work to move beyond the personal level in their efforts to exercise influence over the work of the school. Attention to detail and dynamics that support this goal, as well as a great deal of patience, support the new principal who is moving through the validation process.

Group affirmation emerges gradually from repeated interactions among all those who work in and with the school. Trust and respect grow as principals seek out and arrange interactions that yield outcomes valued by the group. Principals may bring a fine reputation with them; they may have prestigious degrees or possess special expertise. But the validation of their right to act for the group, to speak for the group, to lead the group toward new goals and new ways of pursuing them emerges from social affirmation, from what Dornbusch and Scott (1975) call the moral legitimacy of authority.

By emphasizing the importance of groups, I do not argue that individuals are unimportant. But, while personal relationships may form the foundation of social bonds between the new principal and the school during the early stages of succession, a principal and some individuals in the school may like and respect each other long before group affirmation emerges. Dr. Hamilton (see Chapter 4), for example, was very well liked as an individual, and teachers praised his personality one on one even as they came to distrust his actions and dismiss his impact on the school as a whole. While teachers praised his personable style, they complained that he had no discernible plan for the school and never moved beyond the individual level in his interactions with people. Even when he wanted to pressure influential teachers for support, he approached them on a personal, "how can you do this to me . . . ?" basis (his pressure on the hospitalized teacher who "agreed not to be absent," for example).

An overreliance on personal loyalty can actually work against a new principal. If others see unacceptable privilege and influence on the part of a few teachers, the group may respond with sanctions against favored teachers and resistance to the principal.

While the path to social validation may be poorly articulated and its achievement hard to identify, actions that promote the desired outcome can be described. First, successors should spend time and effort learning about the unique plans, beliefs, and expectations of each teacher and other important people associated with the new school. They should find out which people are respected spokespersons for the group and which can be counted on as friendly critics of the status quo to provide them with an "outlier's" look at events. Friendly (or neutral) critics can be immensely valuable, because they can provide a successor with important details different from her previous experiences or expectations.

Second, the successor can use this information to develop an understanding of patterns, cultural values, and beliefs that characterize the school as a whole and represent a shared reality. He can check his perceptions as his experience within the school builds, by talking with superior, peers, and people in the school. Successors benefit from time spent in cultural or social analysis. They can work toward understanding the norms, beliefs, and assumptions that are essential components of the new group's sense of professional and social worth and the essence of good practice and decent behavior in the school that must not be violated. Schein's (1985) cultural analysis questions (see Chapter 1) provide a useful guide for this kind of inquiry. The core assumptions that make up the existing school culture will not be readily visible, but they will provide important clues to the ways in which a new principal can use the existing organizational culture to move toward the accomplishment of valued existing or new goals.

Third, a newly appointed principal or other school leader should not assume that patterns and actions that worked in her previous assignment will work in a new assignment. Nor can she assume that stories about previous successes will be well received in the new setting. Tales about the way she did things before (used as illustrations of how poorly things are now being done or, more benignly, to argue for a change) can cause a great deal of difficulty and inspire resentment and resistance. One should learn through experience (past experience is a critical component of professional knowledge); but the way in which this knowledge is used plays a critical part during succession. An effective new principal uses her experience to inform her choices, demonstrate the utility of her recommendations, and shape her options, not to remind new colleagues of past triumphs and present failings.

School Leaders Should Demonstrate
Valued Knowledge and Skills

One way in which a successor influences this process and establishes himself in a school (working toward the goal of social validation) is to seek opportunities to demonstrate that he possesses valued technical, social, and moral skills that can help the group accomplish its goals. Experience speaks louder than words, free of the negative effects that emerge from storytelling as an object lesson. Chances to demonstrate expertise can be deliberately set up. A school leader can also take advantage of serendipity, seizing additional opportunities to demonstrate skill as they arise. Successors determined to enhance the outcomes of their successions will constantly be on the lookout for these chances to demonstrate that they have critical skills, experiences, and contacts from which the entire school can benefit.

Schools present a number of regular opportunities for successors to make their talents and skills visible to the faculty and community. Once a successor has progressed in his cultural and social analysis of the school, he can use the values and needs he has identified to match his own best features with aspects of the school warranting attention. Immediate and long-range intervention planning can then follow. For example, if the school is suffering from poor relationships with parents and misunderstandings between the school and community, a successor might seize the chance to show her skills at public relations and communication with parents and the community, "marketing" the good things people are doing. In the process, she might discover situations in the community (having improved communication in both directions) that provide potential for school development and goal accomplishment.

The press of administrative work makes it easy to neglect this need to demonstrate expertise. Especially during succession, when new situations require nonroutine responses, a principal can be very busy. This busyness can interfere with a new principal's ability to notice opportunities for demonstrating valued skills and knowledge. Often, these opportunities slip by because a successor is not specifically looking for them. A regular faculty meeting may present the chance to use an innovative teaching technique in which the successor is particularly skilled, but a conventional agenda with a presentation and discussion format takes less time to prepare. Yet instructional skills are valued by many faculties, and chances to demonstrate instructional skill may be rare. Unless a principal sets up regular teaching times in classrooms so that teachers can see him teach, he may have little opportunity to strut his stuff.

Other opportunities can slip by as well. A poorly organized assembly; a halting or inaccurate presentation to students, parents, or faculty; or a poorly written memo can go far in undermining perceptions of a principal's academic skill and ability to represent the group. Social and political skills are also valued by many faculties. Successors perceived as influential with their superiors and skilled at acquiring valuable resources for the school are viewed more favorably than those who are seen as lacking in influence. Principals who have mastered the social skills needed for intraschool or district politics and contact with the public can structure situations in which these skills are demonstrated while teachers and others are present.

While the foregoing progresses may seem self-aggrandizing, they need not be. The discussion is not meant to make succession sound like pure self-presentation, the construction of a fictional, heroic leader who reflects only the status quo expectations held by those in the school. Teachers often see that kind of empty, symbolic behavior as manipulative and false, as public relations constructed to control and subvert. The simple point is that, like the fisher in this chapter's opening quotation, a principal sees opportunities when she expects to see them as a result of her knowledge, experience, and analysis. A school leader who has mastered the technical skills of instruction, supervision, curriculum design, and subject area knowledge and finds ways to demonstrate to the faculty that she has these skills will be freer to exert influence over these important aspects of school performance. Skill and knowledge are important facets of legitimacy in new leaders. These skills need to be real, and they must be apparent to observers if they are to exert influence on perceptions and expectations. The successor's responsibility is to find ways to highlight her best characteristics that match those needed and valued by the setting. The more skilled and knowledgeable the principal, the more prepared she will be to adjust to a new school and move through the stages of leader succession and organizational socialization that will bring her to a position of influence in the school.

The Socialization of Principals Can Be
Deliberately Influenced by Superiors

While the organizational socialization of principals is an emergent process, it is not unresponsive to deliberate intervention. School district officials can act to deliberately improve the outcome of each succession and the professional socialization of principals new to the profession. Planned interventions can shape the growth and development of the principal and the salutary outcomes of succession for the school as a whole. Deliberately structured experiences can also target different outcomes depending on the social and personal context of the school and the goals of district leaders. These processes should minimize negative surprises by providing critical positive and negative information about the challenges to be faced by the principal in her new assignment and by providing accurate information about the social and cultural features of the new school.

Recall that tactics of organizational socialization are described along a number of dimensions. Although the characteristics of socialization these dimensions represent provide no guarantees that any individual succession will have a given outcome (because each person experiences the processes individually and responds on the basis of his own experience), they do make certain desired outcomes more likely.

First, to increase commitment, provide preparation for major change across schools, or decrease ambiguity, collective socialization experiences can be designed by district leaders. The school year and the subsequent cycle of administrative appointments in school districts makes this process relatively easy in education. Principals can be grouped in a number of ways, depending on the district's size and goals (i.e., all successor principals with new assignments; all first-time principals; all successor elementary principals; all high school principals).[1] Were district leaders interested in using successor principals and the opportunities for change that succession opens to forge new paths for all the schools in a district, collective experiences that develop, reinforce, and nurture innovations and new behaviors would be most appropriate. These activities are aimed toward divesting old professional identities, expectations, and values and replacing them with the values, skills, and assumptions necessary to support new ways of doing things. Valued instructional leadership behavior, participative decision making, or other desired leadership orientations, styles, and behaviors benefit from this kind of support. Collective experiences can build esprit in the group, a sense of unity of purpose, and commitment to the district and desired innovations. Such activities can also be adapted to fill other needs for change in school districts. Bredeson (1991) argued that successfully restructured schools require that many principals let go of "outlived professional identities" while remaining in the same school. In a sense, they experience the divestiture and change pressure of a major transition while remaining in the same assignment.

By contrast and depending on their goals, district leaders can rely on completely individual experiences. In the extreme, these experiences are left to chance. A principal can be shaped by mentors or the training that each successor completes on his own. District leaders can select mentors for their qualities, experiences, and orientation, depending on desired outcomes, or they might simply assign administrators with long experience in a role or in the district to assure the preservation of existing attitudes and practices. If, for example, all principals new to a district or to a particular role (i.e., high school principal) are assigned a mentor, and all mentors are conventional old-timers in the district, the effect will be to further invest established professional identities and assure the perpetuation of conventional practice—a custodial outcome. If a newly assigned principal possesses highly valued innovation skills and new knowledge that her superiors want her to use to change a principal-school relationship and its outcomes, individual socialization that limits her contact with certain mentors or predecessors is advisable. While this technique leaves people feeling more ambiguous about the expectations others hold and about the best choices they might make, it also leaves them freer to challenge the underlying rationales and assumptions on which their role is based. It leads to more variety and change.

A second dimension along which structured socialization experiences differ is in their formality or informality. Informal arrangements often occur spontaneously, like the mentor relationships that develop naturally between established members of a group and those new to the group or organization. Informal mentor relationships also develop among principals new to a school and veteran teachers, secretaries, and parents. These, too, shape organizational socialization experiences.

Districts increasingly formalize the assignment of mentors to all newcomers. Sometimes little thought is given to the pairings. These mentor relationships are vulnerable to the quality of interaction within each pair of administrators, and the relationship significantly affects the performance of the successor principal. As

I asserted earlier, more deliberate planning, training, and pairing make mentor relationships powerful tools with which to change and reinforce desired leadership behavior in principals. Other ways of formalizing the socialization experience include separating newcomers from established members in a highly structured and tradition-bound series of experiences. (The military is everyone's favorite example of this form of socialization.)

Each time a principal takes on a new assignment, the district can reinforce district goals and influence the outcome by formalizing reorientation/socialization experiences. For example, the district can encourage principals to engage in more systematic school analysis by establishing regular meetings of all principals in new or first-time assignments to talk about ways in which they gather information and to share their emerging perceptions and interpretations. At these meetings, principals can share the methods for assessing school process they have found helpful (Porter, 1991), gather ideas from the group about issues in the schools needing immediate attention, and share ways to demonstrate their skills to the faculty. They can challenge each other's interpretations and test alternative views. Experienced successors will function as models and mentors of sorts for first-time successors.

Formalized socialization activity appears to result more often in two extremes, favoring either custodial outcomes or highly innovative outcomes. These outcomes depend on several factors: the principals, people in charge of the formal experience, and the structure of activities. Weindling and Earley (1987) recommended that all districts consider more formalized organizational socialization experiences for successor principals, not just those new to a district. They suggested that these formal experiences set the stage for many of the interventions by principals' superiors and actions by successor principals recommended in this chapter. For example, more time for visits to the new school before a principal takes charge provides the chance to observe, question, diagnose, and prepare tentative interpretations to be confirmed (or disconfirmed) during subsequent contacts. Interaction between outgoing and new principals provides data to the newcomer (but can shape his thinking), and formal interactions with other school leaders affect emerging interpretations of this information.

The recommendations made by Weindling and Earley include aspects of a third group of organizational socialization characteristics—whether experiences are sequential or random. If no formal plan is in place, principals will undergo organizational socialization in a random fashion, and the form and substance of socialization will be idiosyncratic for each principal. If districts plan activities, however, they also can deliberately capitalize on the effects of sequential tactics. For example, all principals newly assigned to schools might be required to undergo the same set of orientation experiences and in the same order. This choice would increase uniformity, with or without the effects of a collective experience. This tactic improves the likelihood that major changes will take hold and have long-lasting impacts by providing a social system support for change. Or principals might be asked to participate in a number of activities such as training, site visits, and meetings with faculty and community, but they may be left free to do so on their own.

The time frame in which events occur—a fourth tactic of organizational socialization—may also be set (within six months of appointment, for example) or variable. The more tightly controlled this dimension, the more likely the district will be to shape and predict the outcomes of the experience and the less likely they will be to benefit from the individual creativity and unpredictable positive contributions of the new principals. The trade-off for the organization is that negative consequences are also more tightly controlled. If loyalty and commitment are among the district's goals, sequential and fixed socialization processes present tried and true means to this end.

A fifth and final organizational socialization tactic—the presence or absence of role models—seldom varies for principals under current practice. School successions usually occur in the presence of role models and, if the available research is accurate, districts seldom structure experiences to either separate successors from conventional role models or control the quality of the models principals encounter.

Principals often have access to and contact with their predecessors. Some recommend more contact than currently is common, because it reduces anxiety and ambiguity. Women and members of minority groups need strong role models and mentors (Shakeshaft, 1985). Yet, when major innovation is desired, minimal contact with predecessors may be the best course of action. While it leaves newcomers more ambiguous about the social features and interaction dynamics of the new school, it leaves them freer and, perhaps, more likely to innovate. When the second alternative is preferred, women and minority group members need extra support and reinforcement to carry them through the resulting ambiguity and uncertainty.

All five of these organizational socialization tactics can be used to divest successors of their core professional values and identities or invest current identity, norms, and practice, to emphasize and reinforce valued leadership styles and norms in the district. Divestiture can be combined with training and support that replace the old professional orientation with a new set of professional values more desirable to the school or district. Instructional leadership, for example, and the actions and priorities that promote it can be reinforced within the social context in which it must be exercised, guarding against outcomes such as that reported by Leithwood, Steinbach & Begley (in press). Transferred principals might be asked to alter decision-making norms, for example, implement curriculum reform, or design and pursue any number of restructuring goals that have implications for the design of teachers' work and students' instruction (Firestone & Bader, 1991). Succession presents an ideal time for this kind of organizational intervention in schools.

The ways in which districts choose to structure successors' organizational socialization depends on the outcomes desired. If all is well and no changes are desired, a high-quality principal who will maintain existing practices and relationships in their current productive form (custodial response) might be desirable. A more common situation occurs when the general role of the principal seems to serve the school well, but innovation and organizational change make alterations in the content of the principal's role desirable. This content can include such things as instructional supervision techniques, curriculum reform, or school/community interaction patterns. In these cases, collective experiences that are formal and take place in the absence of substantial influence from predecessors are appropriate.

A less common but increasingly demanded outcome of a principal succession is substantial change in the content of the principal's role—supervision, curriculum, instruction, decision making—and in the norms and authority relationships governing the core definition of the functions of the principal in the school (Sorensen, 1991). When real parental choice becomes a policy of the district, for example, a principal becomes a market analyst and salesperson—designing and selling a school to a particular target population in order to attract parents (Kerchner, 1990). When site-based management (grounded in substantive new structures of shared decision making) is expected, the principal must reconstruct authority, expertise, and control. She must shape not only her own but also parents', teachers', and the community's beliefs about her responsibilities and relationships with others in the school and about standards and measures of her performance. These outcomes require a genuine effort on the part of the principal to redefine the outcomes of a successful succession as well as the means that will be used to achieve them. When this role innovation is desired, new principals require strong personal support from the district level. They need to work outside the influence of their predecessors, buffered from the way things were done in the past. Finally, they may need to divest themselves of a role concept of "principal" developed over years of experience as educators, and they will need support investing a new role concept into their own core beliefs about themselves as principals, educators, and leaders. The principals leading restructuring programs that substantively reconfigure instruction, curriculum, and authority structures fall in this category, particularly if they are taking on a major role innovation as a pilot program while other principals with whom they work continue to function as usual (Hart & Murphy, in press).

After carefully designing socialization experiences that instantiate desired behaviors, provide assistance with organizational analysis and careful reflection on practice to help principals increase their social influence, and reinforce behaviors through the use of carefully chosen and trained mentors and models, districts can use principal evaluation to reinforce these skills and professional orientations. Superintendents supervise and districts pay principals, so evaluation provides a powerful tool for promoting valued skills related to productive socialization experiences (Duke, 1987). Organizational socialization frameworks also provide categories and methods that can reshape evaluation criteria. Among the important categories emerging from this framework is healthy working relationships. In Chapter 1, I noted: "The inherent social disruption caused by successions may be one reason why a new manager's ability to develop effective working relationships discriminates so strongly between the failed and successful successions" (Gabarro, 1987, p. 166).

A number of criteria appear in principal evaluation schemes (Duke & Stiggins, 1985). These often emphasize processes—student management, communication skills. They also highlight congruence and conformity—loyalty, personal appearance. Among the most common criteria used to evaluate principals, superior (superintendent) and patron satisfaction are the most frequent precipitating cause of support or dismissal. Other evaluation criteria commonly applied include key leader behaviors (as defined by experts) that focus on important goals and the competencies necessary to achieve them (Hoyle, 1985) and student achievement (Duke & Imber, 1985; Glasman & Heck, 1987; Glasman, 1984). The use of student outcome assessments for principal evaluation remains vulnerable to the inherent challenge in determining what constitutes student achievement and how it will be measured. In addition, some principals may "overattend to variables that are not as important in facilitating strong educational outcomes." These models that provide them with guidance and the development of a conceptual framework that "recognizes the importance of the school's social context in determining student achievement" should improve the outcomes of principal evaluation (Heck, Larsen & Marcoulides, 1990, p. 122).

Other problems plague these traditional approaches to principal evaluation. These highlight the central functions an organizational interaction perspective serves. First, a principal's work is often decoupled from the teaching and learning experience. Principals exert little direct control over the teaching and learning process, even as they function as the "focal point" of organizational process and governance (Kmetz & Willower, 1982; Martin & Willower, 1981). They lack the absolute power or even direct influence that allows causal linkages (even inferred causal linkages) to be drawn with confidence. Thus, indirect interaction skills become more important. Second, others besides the principal may function as the instructional leader in effective schools (Duke, 1987; Edmonds, 1982). To attribute the subsequent gains in student achievement to principals would be impossible. This, too, returns attention to the group.

In contrast, the interaction between principal and school social unit is within the influence of the principal, amenable to examination, and known to affect the actions and outcomes of organizations. Superintendents or other supervisors can examine principals' use of the organizational analysis techniques that can enhance their success as school leaders and provide opportunities to promote the instructional practices and goals valued by the school district. First, principals can be asked to provide descriptions or other evidence that they have examined and understand the unique professional goals and aspirations of the school's faculty that can be marshalled as resources for facilitating and improving student outcomes. Second, principals can identify key spokespersons for the faculty, opinion leaders, outliers, and respected opponents to demonstrate their ability to conduct and use organizational analysis. They can use this information for planning sessions with other principals as they move to implement important school improvement strategies. Third, principals can prepare in written or oral form a cultural analysis of the school, a description of shared realities, beliefs, and values along with diversions from this group assessment. These analyses can be used to identify differences, seek organizational ways of doing things that can be used as avenues for achieving goals, and diagnose points of conflict between the principal and the school that require attention. Principals should be able to tell their superiors what norms, beliefs, assumptions, and ways of knowing and doing shape work and sense making in the school. They can then identify areas with high potential and areas in which they face opposition or social system obstructions. Fourth, principals should be held accountable for knowledge about teachers' professional values. They can provide evidence of means through which they seek opportunities to demonstrate their own knowledge and skills that are valued by faculties. Another way in which evaluation can be used to enhance and enforce principal effects on the social organization of schools involves resources. Successors who demonstrate ways in which they have garnered valued resources needed for teachers to do their work will improve and speed their own acceptance and social validation. Superiors can ask for evidence that principals are working to secure school resources (staff development, information, training, reallocation of funds, and so on) that teachers value and use in their instructional work. In short, by evaluating organizational and cultural analysis and healthy social interactions between principals and others who work in schools, superiors redefine the processes and outcomes they value and refocus principals' attention on the knowledge and skills provided in the organizational socialization processes they design and use.

This discussion of the tactics and outcomes of planned organizational socialization experiences and principal evaluation strategies that reinforce them is not exhaustive or prescriptive, because each succession presents a unique set of circumstances that makes different outcomes desirable. Until a new principal and a school are matched, one cannot predict whether personal development on the part of the principal, role change, or both would be the most productive effects. The desired balance between individual principal development and organizational change also depends on the needs of the school and district. This balance and the personal characteristics of each new principal should be the critical factors shaping decisions about the structure of socialization processes districts wish to employ.

The need to tailor experiences also makes it impossible to provide prescriptive advice about the best structure for principal succession/socialization a district might adopt on an ongoing basis. Each appointment requires some attention (Kimberly & Quinn, 1984).

Unlike the programs in large organizations (like IBM or the military) that process large numbers of people who fill very similar roles, each principal must work in a unique setting with a different constellation of problems and people than those faced by other principals. "When the phenomenon at hand eludes the ordinary categories of knowledge-in-practice, presenting itself as unique or unstable, the practitioner may surface and criticize his initial understanding of the phenomenon, construct a new description of it, and test the new description by an on-the-spot experiment" (Schon, 1983, pp. 62–63).

To improve the likelihood and quality of this process, district leaders should attend to specific structures of the socialization process as they make their decisions about programs to improve principal succession outcomes: (a) whether experiences will be collective or individual—will principals have experiences alone or with a cohort group; (b) whether formal or informal tactics will be employed; (c) whether the same sequence of experiences will be required of all new or newly reassigned principals or whether they will vary, depending on circumstances; (d) whether the time frame within which socialization processes must be completed will be fixed for everyone or variable; and (e) whether newly assigned principals should spend substantial portions of their time interacting with role models and mentors and how mentors should be selected, matched with principals, and trained.

A number of outcomes appear most likely, depending on which combination of these structures districts choose. First, replication—with little change in the principal or the school—can be a desired outcome, although it is hard to conceive of a school that is functioning so well and a successor so proficient that no change or growth in either is desirable. Second, the development of future leaders within excellent existing schools also might be a desired goal. Were this the case, personal development on the part of the successor would be a major goal. Third, a succession may occur when a school and the principal's role are in need of development. In this case, the new principal might be an organizational star, someone who has a track record of making a positive difference in schools. Changes in the school itself or in the way the principal role functions in the school would be the most desirable outcome of such a succession. Finally, and more commonly, districts may hope for both personal growth on the part of the principal and innovation and development in the role of the principal resulting in positive changes in the school. When this is desired, both role and personal development are hoped-for outcomes. Scholars call this outcome exploration; it moves both the individual and the school into new territory. Within the constraints of available resources, time, and energy, districts can design plans for principals (newly reassigned or appointed for the first time) that are flexible enough to meet the demands of each situation while avoiding the problems that arise from a more laissez-faire approach (Kelleher, 1982).

Four common outcomes, then, are possible goals—replication, personal development, role and school development, or *both* personal and role/school development. Situations where replication may be called for have already been discussed. The other three desired outcomes require elaboration.

Personal development—growth in the principal's skill and knowledge—can always be beneficial as a personnel or human resource development strategy. Personal development can also occur along a number of fronts. A principal can improve his individual coping responses and the bonds of affiliation and professional commitment associated with his work. New values, skills, and knowledge can emerge from his responses to the situation. And a principal can learn and perfect new skills as he responds to the demands of leadership in a new setting. This learning process might reinforce the culture of the school or result in significant transformation for the school.

Too often, the technical side of personal development is emphasized while affective/emotional growth is deemphasized. Friendship and strong feelings of commitment and affiliation promote the integration and eventual contribution of a new principal to a school. Since growth opportunities are so important for people to be able to do creative and innovative work, the personal development of school leaders that succession provides deserves attention along with its potential for improving school performance.

Yet schools do not hire principals so that adults can achieve self-actualization and professional growth. Principals serve students in schools. Consequently, role and school development are also desired outcomes of succession. In Chapter 1, I reported the findings of research showing that innovation and change in the school and principal role will most likely be accompanied by personal change and growth in the principal. Principals who explore new vistas professionally will be more creative and innovative at the same time. Succession stimulates this process. This is a noteworthy finding, for it supports the assertion made at the beginning of this chapter that principals can make a difference in complex school settings, and they can do this while they grow and develop personally and professionally. They will actually be more likely to contribute to the school *if* they grow.

With the knowledge in mind that positive outcomes of succession can come in the form of personal and professional development for the principal and role and organizational development for the school, district leaders can examine the experiences and programs they provide and the probable effect they might have on principals and schools. If assigned mentors will be used, each person should be carefully chosen for the impact she will have. Mentors should not be left to their own devices. They need guidance about the means most likely to yield desired outcomes, consultation about the person to whom they are assigned, and training. All the possible tactics discussed above should be considered and choices made from a wide array of possibilities. Finally, no organizational socialization plan for newly appointed principals should ignore the potential for surprise, innovation, and creativity emerging from the talent and inspiration within each new principal. Organizations can benefit from the creative and innovative work people do best at the school level. While the rhetoric about principal leadership tends to favor heroic enterprise and dramatic cultural interventions, exploration—concurrent role and personal development—is a more likely outcome of a healthy leader succession process than are either dramatic role or personal change. Effects will be two-way; principals who innovate and affect change in schools will do so as they change and grow personally and professionally. Both kinds of development are worthy goals as management policy.

Before leaving this discussion of the personal and school development that can result from principal succession, a word of caution is warranted about the importance of individual and social context. In the midst of enthusiasm for the change and development that succession can bring with it, district leaders should recall that an established record of inquiry also demonstrates that succession is a disruptive experience for a school. If it were not disruptive to some extent, it would not carry with it the potential for change. Patterns of too-frequent succession—one principal following quickly and regularly on the heels of another—lead to many dysfunctional outcomes. Retrenchment, resistance, and teacher professional isolation are among the negative effects observed by researchers. The history and people in a school provide an important social context for each succession. Sometimes a district has no choice—a principal resigns or retires—but some districts have automatic transfer policies. The length of time a principal has served, not the context, stimulate the change. The experiences of many principals described in preceding chapters call the wisdom of this kind of automatic transfer policy into question. While it requires little effort, it may yield sporadic (if any) benefit.

Current Practice Promotes a Custodial Response

What we now do promotes the status quo. By uncritically assigning experienced principals to socialize new principals with little forethought or training, we turn the future without question over to the past. We recreate what we already have. By appointing principals whose experience is just like their predecessors, district administrators give them little or no substantive guidance about change or innovation they may hope will occur and no models for change; superintendents move principals from school to school for no apparent reason other than an established cycle of principal transfers. These practices guarantee that principals will feel obligated to function as custodians of current practice, values, and culture. They also guarantee deeply felt angst when superiors or policy makers demand substantial change after setting up a succession that reinforces the status quo and continued difficulties for socially incongruent new school leaders (women and minority group members).

A certain cynicism and a decided fatalism can result from a perusal of the studies of principal socialization that dominate the field. Repeatedly, the process of replication emerges from current practice. In the face of calls for dramatic leadership, writers point out that principals are so much alike, experience so many powerful social-ization processes, and are subject to so many constraints that no difference can or should be expected from them. The organizational socialization literature helps explain why principals become custodians of conventional practice; it also provides insight into changes in current practice holding potential for breaking this cycle. Instead of lamenting the resilience and inertia of current practice, educational leaders can use powerful strategies to assault undesirable conventions.

Socialization Occurs With or Without Planning

Whether or not school districts plan socialization activities like those just discussed, successors will be socialized by their interactions within the school. Duke (1987) asserted that informal socialization processes are much more common and exert much more influence over principals than formal socialization experiences. Only a tiny proportion of principals receive any formal orientation to their new jobs (Duke et al., 1984). Consequently, the "formal and informal mechanisms by which new principals are socialized convey an impression of variability and arbitrariness" (Duke, 1987, p. 272). If districts wish to have any impact on the outcomes of this socialization, they should intervene to shape some of the experiences that are a part of the process each time a new principal takes charge. Much of the organizational socialization experience will occur outside the control or influence of a principal's superiors and will depend on the social and personal context of the school. In the event a principal finds himself succeeding to a new leadership role in the absence of district support, it will help him to be aware of the informal and naturally emerging forces shaping the outcomes of his succession.

First, a new principal can attend to the amount of change from her past role that the succession brings (status, role requirements, work environment), the contrast and carryover of people and ideas, and the surprises (positive and negative) that she encounters in the new school. When consciously noted and analyzed, each of these factors will affect her immediate judgments, and her responses will shape much of what follows. She will face the task of fitting in while retaining her own best talents and working to contribute to goal achievement in a new social world. This action can be particularly salutary for minorities and women. It can provide options that promote their own professional goals, preserve their finest personal aspirations, and protect them from pressure they feel to abandon their own unique heritage (Hodgkinson, 1983).

Second, the new principal can design his own support structure—help from others in interpreting his experience and adjusting appropriately. If he has not been assigned a mentor and feels the need for peers with whom to discuss and interpret experiences, he can seek out and nurture these relationships. If the job includes responsibilities or structures that are unfamiliar to him or require new skills, he can work to develop the knowledge and skills that will help him grow and develop personally in the new role. He can watch for powerful social dynamics and seek to better understand how he fits in. He might work to modify existing work or social patterns to capitalize on his abilities and best talents. Finally, he can assess his most promising sources of support and develop an understanding of the methods and criteria on which he will be evaluated. If ambiguity and conflict are high, he can seek ways to capitalize on ambiguity to promote change and manage conflict rather than succumb to either.

Finally, a new principal can seek a growing understanding of her professional growth and development cycle and place the succession within this cycle and within the social context (Ashford, 1989). As she negotiates her new relationship with superiors and the faculty, she can look to the future as well as the past for clues about where she can best seek to explore and develop. In the process, she should be able to better understand how she might make a contribution to the accomplishment of valued goals by those who work in the school. This process requires that she work carefully to understand the new context as thoroughly as possible from the point of view of established members, not just from her own point of view. Principals should take responsibility for integration as well as impact.

Anxiety about performance and potential for making a contribution are major sources of stress during succession (and this anxiety seems to be higher among women than men). By working toward a positive relationship with superiors and faculty, performance anxiety can be lessened. As he comes to reconcile his evaluation of his performance with the groups' evaluation, a new principal will come to better understand how he fits into the school. The legitimacy of his relationship with the faculty can gradually be shaped through this process. By consciously observing himself in the new context, he can learn how his behaviors match the expectations of the group and work to shape their expectations to include his best talents and greatest potential for making a substantive contribution.

Over time, a successor can look forward to developing a strong commitment to the school. Her values and professional self-image will change along with her growing skills and knowledge. She will benefit from new relationships with teachers and other principals. Knowledge about this process and the ability to reflect on its meaning for her and for the school will help a successor develop strategies for taking charge and maximize the positive potential of this all-important professional transition (Bennis & Nanus, 1985).

People Expect Change During Succession

While I believe it is easy to overemphasize the importance of change in any discussion of school leadership, one critical characteristic of organizational socialization that appears repeatedly in research, theory, and practice deserves further elaboration in this final chapter. This feature is the strong expectation that change will occur with principal succession. People begin to speculate about change as soon as they hear that a succession is impending and continue to watch for some change in their work throughout early interactions among teachers, students, parents, superiors, and the new principal.

In the section of this and other chapters on tactics, the importance of change was emphasized. The expectation that change will occur deserves special emphasis, because there has been so much contradictory advice about the amount and kind of change a new principal should undertake. The preceding discussion of role, personal, and school development introduced the possibility that principal succession might provide an ideal opportunity to introduce major changes.

The importance of the succession period for change continually reappears in reports of research and practice. Teachers anticipate change, watch closely for hints of changes to come during early interactions with the new principal, and express surprise, disappointment, relief, disenchantment, or resignation when no substantive changes emerge. Teachers who have experienced a number of principal successions sometimes become cynical about these expectations, arguing that they quickly socialize new principals, controlling their actions and protecting the school from them.

These results of inquiry into principal succession suggest two things. First, powerful and persuasive evidence emerges to show that organizational socialization affects principals. Teachers who are experienced with principal succession describe in detail ways in which they change principals, influence and alter their behavior, and guard against changes made by the principals who rotate through their schools. Second, some change, even if it initially leaves fundamental assumptions and work arrangements untouched, sets the stage for later changes that might emerge as a result of the succession over a longer time span. Principals can take action that extends thinking about change beyond the first year of a tenure, just as Cosgrove (1986) suggested researchers extend their inquiry beyond the first year.

This second conclusion forms the core of the recommendations related to change that emerge from the literature. None of the research offers easy answers about how much change should be attempted and when, but the preponderance of evidence suggests a number of guidelines to which principals can attend. First, principals should not rush in to initiate change without regard for the specific needs and norms of the school and on the basis of insufficient understanding of the school.

Second, the expectation for change should be met, even if only in small ways early in the succession. These actions preserve the expectation for change and protect against the conclusion that no early change means no change ever. The nature of the school year leads some to assume that a principal should spend the first year observing and planning and should not make any real changes until the second year. It leads others to conclude that the first year forms the ambient boundaries of the window of opportunity provided by succession. Researchers who carry their studies into the second or third year following a succession describe substantial resentment from teachers in schools where change was introduced late in the game (Cosgrove, 1986). Teachers felt that some bargain or tacit agreement forged through inaction had been broken. They expressed considerable frustration against principals who were not integrated into the school (Parkay, Currie & Rhodes, 1992).

Third, a careful social and cultural analysis of the school should protect principals from inadvertent violations against social system taboos or sacred totems. It will help them understand how people feel about established procedures, methods and norms of instruction, student relationships, community relations, office procedures, and other critical aspects of the school. While interaction and validation purchase credits from the group for unique or somewhat idiosyncratic behavior (see Chapter 2), principals become new members and seek to exercise leadership in established social groups and should not violate the core assumptions that support the value and worth of the group. Even when new schools are built and staffed, the principal takes charge in the school in an environment that fosters the replication of many firmly established practices (Blanch, 1989). Change congruent with the finest professional values of the teachers who work in the school and the central norms and values of the school community will go far toward accomplishing school goals. Once these changes begin to yield valued outcomes for the members of the school community, principals can move on toward more extensive innovation and change.

These three recommendations—to gather sufficient knowledge, to make some change quickly, and to balance the pace and scope of change to respect the fundamental nature of the existing school culture—may appear contradictory. They need not be so. Rather they are meant to call successors' attention to the importance of constant balance and sensitivity to emerging responses to their leadership within the school. Succession remains a balancing act between stability and change.

The Need for Stability and the Need for Creativity Will Conflict

This tension between the need to respect and adjust to a new school and the need for creativity and innovation from a new principal will never disappear. It is a ubiquitous factor in the career cycle of principals. It also is, as they say, life.

In Chapter 3, the central conflict between the power of the group to shape and create each new member through socialization and the creativity of the individual as the source of much that is valuable and interesting in social life was discussed. This central tension between the group and the individual should be continually in the forefront of observation, analysis, and action by principals during succession. As a principal's ability to balance these two aspects of leadership increases, her ability will increase to make action decisions that show respect for the people with whom she works while enabling her to move the group forward toward the discovery and accomplishment of important goals. Succession places the group and individual aspects of leadership in schools immediately at the surface, because the principal must come to know the school and be accepted while working creatively and innovatively to have some schoolwide influence. While it may be frustrating to principals that this knowledge provides no decision rules nor explicit guidance about how to act in what situations, those who achieve this balance will have developed their own decision rules to guide them.

School Leaders Can Affect the Processing of Information that Shapes Interpretations and Actions During Succession

The fundamental assumptions and beliefs arising from an interactionist perspective on principal succession provide insight into ways in which principals can affect the outcomes of succession. This approach builds on the advantages gained when a successor learns to balance the group's needs for stability with the potential of individual creativity. In Chapter 3, I introduced theories exploring the means through which people come to share a view of the real world based on their interpretations of their experiences. These theories can be used to develop a description of the way in which events (all of which people experience as individuals) can come to have a common meaning for the members of a group. The core event of interest here is principal succession. Social information processing helps us understand how the interaction between a new principal and others eventually shapes a common view of reality.

In the attempt to control important events in schools, participants seek to objectify experiences, to get to the core of the matter, to find out what really happened. Much energy is expended railing against "unfair" expectations and conclusions or "inaccurate" perceptions, but people act on the basis of these expectations and perceptions. While responsible school leaders continually act rather than rely solely on impression management, they enhance their succession by attending to the interpretations people attach to their actions, working to shape perceptions and beliefs in desired directions. While it may seem noble to "damn the torpedoes" and forge ahead, information processing, like organizational socialization in general, will occur, and a perceptive successor will pay attention to factors that influence the process.

Information processing is the means through which people take information, assess its accuracy and reliability, assign a meaning to what is learned, and pass on the information along with their interpretation. A teacher may ask others, following the new principal's first appearance at a faculty meeting, "So, what do you think?" As they discuss the event all have just experienced, they may find that they initially have very different perceptions about what happened, what was said, and what it meant. The opinions of teachers who are well respected by others on the faculty may carry more weight, causing others to reevaluate their interpretations. If the experience is processed to conclusion, a shared version of the faculty meeting will emerge from the group's discussion of events.

A principal who is aware of this process can pay particular attention to the relevance and salience of information emphasized in interactions with the faculty—in groups and as individuals. He can seek feedback from influential teachers and community members about the nature of the shared version of events that is taking hold, take action to provide additional information about himself, and structure interactions that affirm a positive interpretation of his potential. He can pay particular attention to the meaning others attach to his actions and less attention to his own intentions. As Likert (1967) so perceptively pointed out decades ago, an administrator is supportive only if his subordinates feel that he is supportive. His intentions are of little import. In this way, a new principal can avoid the pitfalls that befell Dr. Hamilton (see Chapter 4) when he interpreted a power struggle between himself and the secretary as a simple issue of authority, a conflict confined to the working relationship between two people. Meanwhile, teachers were interpreting the secretary's involuntary transfer as a portent of things to come, a new pattern of responses facing anyone who crossed the principal.

Information processing, in a series of feedback communication loops among the people in the school, creates interpretations of the interactions that influence the succession process. An understanding of this process can help a new principal share important information about her technical, social, and moral skills valued by the group while working to influence the interpretations people assign to her characteristics and skills. In order for the group to see her as a leader who will benefit the school as a whole, the successor's skills need to be interpreted in a positive light. Social information processing also shapes validation, through which people come to view the new principal as their spokesperson and representative and vest authority in her to act in their behalf.

Socially Incongruent Leaders Can Succeed and Contribute

The meaning that people attach to a succession as they interpret events and come to share beliefs about the experience thus can have a profound impact on their willingness to move into uncomfortable territory with a new principal. For principals who obviously do not fit prevailing images of a leader or who lack the conventional traits that the group identifies with good principals, this process is even more critical. They need to work constantly toward a deeper understanding of the social nature of the school while building respect for their own qualities and aligning them with central norms and beliefs, shaping an altered shared view of the school, and working toward making a creative contribution. Many schools and school districts desire to increase the diversity of their principals. African-Americans, Latinos, Asians, and women of all races are woefully underrepresented in the ranks of American school leaders. Policy makers seek to improve diversity among educational leaders in order to enhance the pool of ideas and creativity available to the school, expand on the norms and traditions of the existing social system that can restrict the flow of new ideas, and give access to leadership positions to those from previously underrepresented groups. At the same time, these principals face challenges over and above the conventional problems that come when a new principal is assigned to a school. They must deemphasize personal traits that may appear to conflict with established norms and traditions about "leaders" or "principals." These challenges include isolation, preconceived beliefs that are unfavorable, a lack of face validity as leaders, and inexperience working in similar social settings.

Isolation presents one of the major obstacles faced by people who surmount institutional and social barriers and succeed to leadership positions in schools. People tend to increase their contact and interaction with those with whom they feel comfortable (people who are similar to them or similar to others who fill the same role) and limit their contact with people who are unfamiliar and with whom they feel uncomfortable. This tendency makes the challenge of achieving integration and validation as leaders during succession even more problematic for women and minority group members than it is for other newly appointed principals. The first response of faculty who feel uncomfortable may be to isolate the new principal, thus limiting her ability to demonstrate the valued technical, social, and moral skills that will help allay fears and increase comfort. A second problem can arise if the principal herself unintentionally intensifies perceptions of incongruence by drawing attention to her differences. While these differences are often superficial, they also are often highly visible. Socially incongruent principals particularly need to achieve social validation and acceptance by the group in order to function as leaders and they begin with a power as well as a social disadvantage. They often lack models and mentors and powerful social networks on which they can rely. On the basis of their visible characteristics, they may lack validity in the eyes of many whom they are assigned to lead. They can improve the likelihood that they will achieve validation by using information exchange and interpretation (social information processing) to emphasize ways in which they provide a valuable resource and demonstrate critical knowledge and skills that can help the group achieve its goals. They can also seek deliberately to deemphasize surface traits that may seem incongruous.

The organizational socialization process for new principals from diverse backgrounds also may be more disruptive for them. For example, taking charge in a school district where few or no principals share their sex, race, or ethnic background leaves principals without role models, experiencing role ambiguity and uncertainty that other newly assigned principals may not be experiencing. Some researchers argue that women and minorities experience a much different succession process than do white males in American schools, and these differences deserve attention from those who appoint principals and have a stake in their succession. They may also feel pressure to abandon aspects of their own culture and development that they value and that could prove a valuable source of creativity and a resource for achievement (Burrell, 1988).

But incongruity can also be an advantage, and district leaders and policy makers with influence over future principal appointments should attend to these advantages. Because they bring diverse experiences, new points of view, and untapped creativity, women and minority group members constitute a largely untapped resource. If the social challenges they face can be overcome through the application of organizational socialization and interaction perspectives on leader succession, a new resource for development in our schools can be made available. The disjunctive experience of succession under these circumstances can also result in an environment free from many of the assumptions and beliefs that limit the vision of more conventional principals.

Conclusion

Change and complexity dominate the work of school leaders and shape the dynamics and outcomes of succession. Throughout this book, I have returned repeatedly to the notion that leader succession is a frequent organizational event of tremendous importance to those who work in schools. It is disruptive, and its outcomes can be dysfunctional if the new principal fails to become an integrated and respected member of the social system whose leadership has received the affirmation of the school as a whole. In contrast, when a successor achieves this goal, her ability to have a positive impact on the school and its performance is substantially enhanced.

Whatever our idealized view of leaders and despite calls for principals who shape the fundamental culture, structure, and goals of schools, research and practice support a more complex, interactive view of principal succession. Although they fill a legitimate and powerful authority position in the school structure, successors still are new members of a group and are subject to the social forces that shape people who join established social groups. Organizational socialization provides a useful theoretical perspective for understanding the interaction between principals and schools during succession. This is especially true when combined with the traditional strength of principal-centered approaches like leader succession.

Specifically, it provides a framework from which researchers and practitioners can understand the succession process and manage its outcomes. Principals, their superiors, and school policy makers can use an organizational socialization perspective on principal succession to enhance the practice of school administration and the professional development of principals.

School district leaders can assess their current practice and design flexible processes that support principals undergoing succession and lead to outcomes that advance district policies and goals. They can reexamine their use of mentors and match the design of their mentor programs to the outcomes appropriate to each school, provide systematic support and time for the visits, diagnosis, and planning activities by principals that facilitate their transition to a new school, and consciously work to improve the outcomes of a succession *beyond* the careful search for and appointment of the best principal for a school. This includes training and support specifically designed to assist principals who are taking charge in a new assignment, recognizing that they face challenges common to major transitions, acknowledging that a unique mix between the principal and the school will give rise to the outcomes of the succession, and preparing principals for the impact the school will have on them as well as the impact they hope to have on the school. Districts can also capitalize on the expectation for change that succession brings to implement new programs and work toward the improvement of schools. They can seize the opportunity that this major role transition presents to shape and expand the professional orientation, knowledge, and skills, both moral and technical, of the principals who lead their schools.

School leaders undergoing succession can also improve their experience substantially by increasing their knowledge about the process they will undergo and their skill in influencing the social dynamics that will occur. They can systematically engage in social analysis, seeking a deep understanding of the fundamental values and beliefs shaping the attitudes and actions of those in the school. New principals can use this knowledge, which they periodically check for accuracy and usefulness, to assess the areas in which they have the greatest potential for making a positive contribution and plan their activities to improve the likelihood that this will happen. They can seek out and design opportunities to demonstrate their skill, knowledge, and commitment to the school, plan changes that preserve the window of opportunity accompanying succession, and nurture their own exploration and growth. They can work to affect the interpretations that events and information take on in the school as people talk about and process the succession experience.

The best possible outcome of a succession—personal and professional growth for the new leader and growth and development for the school—results when succession is understood and managed as a group process. The chances that this outcome will occur will be improved as principals and other school leaders and their superiors become better versed in the organizational dynamics that shape each succession event. While the forces shaping succession outcomes are complex, the improved results for the successor and for the school are well worth increased effort aimed at improving the outcomes of leader succession. By focusing on the principal and underemphasizing the organization, traditional leader succession literature fails to adequately address the complex environment in which succession occurs. By adding insights and actions based on an interactive, organizational perspective, school leaders and their superiors acquire a healthy command of the complexities of schools and impact on the outcomes of this frequent and significant organizational event. Organizational socialization factors affecting these desired outcomes will otherwise remain invisible: successors and their superiors will not see them because they do not think of them first.

Notes

Chapter 3

1. This chapter provides no more than an introduction to the extensive literature in many disciplines on which scholars of organizational socialization draw. It can, however, be used as a guide by those interested in further exploration.

2. See, for example, the succession case in Chapter 5, where the view of the Eagleton faculty as wave-makers and "difficult" (and proud of it) that teachers presented to the new principal was actually resented by the faculty.

Chapter 4

1. For a description of the research methods used in the preparation of this case, Ogawa (1991). This is the story of one faculty's experience with the succession of its principal, told over time and, for the most part, using the words of the teachers collected in a series of interviews. The succession record began just prior to the predecessor's announcement of his retirement at the end of the school year. It covers the teachers' responses to the announcement that the school would have a new principal. Data gathering continued in the fall with the opening of school and the faculty's introduction to the successor and ended with the close of the school year. The case is used with the permission of the authors. For research reports of the case, see Fauske and Ogawa (1987) and Ogawa (1991).

2. To facilitate the story and protect participants, places and people are given fictional names.

Chapter 5

1. For a description of the research methods used in the preparation of this case, see Hart (1988). Collected from the point of view of the successor, this case presents one view of leader succession. While a single case seen from a single point of view has obvious limitations, it provides an important part of the overall picture of interaction and beliefs characterizing a dynamic view of leadership in schools (Gregory, 1983). The importance of one

participant's view is amplified by the official expectations of managers in organizations—that they will shape the attitudes and behaviors of others (Smircich, 1983).

2. As in Chapter 4, to facilitate the story and protect participants, places and people are given fictional names.

Chapter 6

1. The extensive material drawn from Cosgrove is used with the permission of the author.

2. Parkay and Hall (1992) was in press at the time this book was in production. Quotation pages for Parkay and Currie, Roberts and Wright, Wright refer to the chapters in manuscript form. The reader is encouraged to refer to the published versions.

Chapter 7

1. A recent informal survey of students in the graduate administrative certification program at the University of Utah, for example, revealed that almost half the students already had some administrative experience and many were filling administrative positions during their anticipatory socialization and education at the university.

Chapter 8

1. Evidence suggests that the induction experiences of beginning principals certainly warrant special attention (Daresh, 1986; Playko & Daresh, 1989).

References

Ackerman, R. H. (1991a). *Becoming a principal*. Paper presented at the annual meeting of the American Educational Research Association, Chicago.

Ackerman, R. H. (1991b). *Portraits of practicum life: Toward an understanding of field experience for aspiring principals*. Paper presented at the annual meeting of the American Educational Research Association, Chicago.

Adams, J., Hyes, J., & Hopson, B. (1976). *Transition: Understanding and managing personal change*. London: Martin Robinson & Company.

Alderfer, C. P. (1971). Effect of individual, group, and intergroup relations on attitudes toward a management development program. *Journal of Applied Psychology, 55,* 302–311.

Alderfer, C. P., & Cooper, C. L. (Eds.). (1980). *Advances in experiential social processes. Vol. 2.* New York: Wiley.

Allen, M. P. (1981). Power and privilege in the large corporation: Corporate control and managerial compensation. *American Journal of Sociology, 86,* 1112–1123.

Allen, M. P., & Panian, S. K. (1982). Power, performance, and succession in the large corporation. *Administrative Science Quarterly, 27,* 538–547.

Allen, M. P., Panian, S. K., & Lotz, R. E. (1979). Managerial succession and organizational performance: A recalcitrant problem revisited. *Administrative Science Quarterly, 24,* 167–180.

Allen, V. L., & van de Vliert, E. (1984). *Role transitions: Explorations and explanations*. New York: Plenum Press.

Alvey, H. B. (1983). The problems of new principals. (Doctoral dissertation, University of Montana, 1983). *Dissertation Abstracts International, 44,* 1979–A.

Andrews, D. R. (1971). *The concept of corporate strategy* (rev. ed.). Homewood, IL: Richard D. Irwin.

Argyris, C. (1954). *Organization of a bank*. New Haven: Yale Labor and Management Center.

_____. (1979). Reflecting on laboratory education from a theory of action perspective. *Journal of Applied Behavioral Science, 15*(3), 296–310.

_____. (1982). *Reasoning, learning, and action.* San Francisco: Jossey-Bass.

Argyris, C., & Schon, D. (1974). *Theory in practice: Increasing professional effectiveness.* San Francisco: Jossey-Bass.

Argyris, C., Putnam, R., & Smith, D. M. (1985). *Action science.* San Francisco: Jossey-Bass.

Ashford, S. J. (1988). Individual strategies for coping with stress during organizational transitions. *Journal of Applied Behavioral Science, 24,* 19–36.

_____. (1989). Self-assessment in organizations: A literature review and integrative model. In L. L. Cummings & B. Staw (Eds.), *Research in organizational behavior,* Vol. 2, (pp. 133–174). Greenwich, CT: JAI Press.

Bacharach, S. B., Bamberger, P., & Conley, S. (1990). Work process, role conflict, and role overload. *Journal of Work and Occupations, 17*(2), 199–228.

_____. (1991). The work/home conflict among nurses and engineers: Mediating the impact of role stress on burnout and satisfaction at work. *Journal of Organizational Behavior, 12,* 39–53.

Bacharach, S. B., Bamberger, P., & Mitchell, S. M. (1990). Work design, role conflict, and role ambiguity: The case of elementary and secondary schools. *Educational Evaluation and Policy Analysis, 12,* 415–433.

Bacharach, S. B., & Lawler, E. J. (1981). *Power and politics in organizations.* San Francisco: Jossey-Bass.

Bales, R. F., & Slater, P. (1955). Role differentiation in small social groups. In T. Parsons, R. F. Bales, & E. A. Shilo (Eds.), *Family, socialization, and interaction process* (pp. 259–306). Glencoe, IL: Free Press.

Ball, S. (1987). *The micro-politics of the school: Toward a theory of school organization.* London: Methuen.

Baltzell, D. C., & Dentler, R. A. (1983). *Selecting American school principals: A sourcebook for educators.* Washington, DC: U.S. Department of Education, National Institute of Education.

Bandura, A. (1971). Analysis of modeling processes. In A. Bandura (Ed.), *Psychological modeling* (pp. 1–67). Chicago: Aldine-Atherton.

_____. (1972). Modeling theory: Some traditions, trends, and disputes. In R. D. Drake (Ed.), *Recent trends in social learning theory* (pp. 35–61). New York: Academic Press.

_____. (1978). The self-system in reciprocal determination. *American Psychologist, 33,* 344–358.

Barnabe, C., & Burns, M. L. (unpublished paper). A test of the utility of the job characteristics model for diagnosis of motivation in education.

Barnett, B. (1985). Peer-assisted leadership: A stimulus for professional growth. *Urban Review, 17,* 47–64.

Barr, R., & Dreeben, R. (1983). *How schools work.* Chicago: University of Chicago Press.

Barrows, H. S. (1988). *The tutorial process.* Springfield, IL: The Southern Illinois University School of Medicine.

Bass, B. M. (1981). *Handbook of leadership: A survey of theory and research.* New York: Free Press.

_____. (1985). *Leadership and performance beyond expectations.* New York: Free Press.

Beatty, R. P., & Zajac, E. J. (1987). CEO change and firm performance in large corporations: Succession effects and manager effects. *Strategic Management Journal, 8,* 305–318.

Beck, L., & Murphy, J. (in press). *Understanding the principalship: A metaphorical analysis from 1920 to 1990.* New York: Teachers College Press.

Becker, H. S. (1963). *Outsiders: Studies in the sociology of deviance.* New York: Free Press.

Becker, H. S., Geer B., Hughes, E. C., & Strauss, A. L. (1961). *Boys in white: Student culture in medical school.* Chicago: University of Chicago Press.

Beeson, G. W., & Matthews, R. J. (1991). *Emerging power and leadership: The developing role of new principals in Australia.* Paper presented at the annual meeting of the American Educational Research Association, Chicago.

Bennis, W. (1989). *On becoming a leader.* Reading, MA: Addison-Wesley.

_____. (1990). *Why leaders can't lead: The unconscious conspiracy continues.* San Francisco: Jossey-Bass.

Bennis, W. G., & Nanus, B. (1985). *Leaders: Strategies for taking charge.* New York: Harper & Row.

Berlew, D. E., & Hall, D. T. (1966–67). The socialization of managers: Effects of expectations on performance. *Administrative Science Quarterly, 11,* 207–223.

Biddle, B. (1979). *Role theory: Expectations, identities, and behaviors.* New York: Plenum Press.

Biddle, B., & Thomas, E. J. (1966). *Role theory: Concepts and research.* New York: Wiley.

Bidwell, C. E., & Kasarda, J. D. (1980). Conceptualizing and measuring the effects of school and schooling. *American Journal of Education, 88,* 401–430.

Birnbaum, R. (1971). Presidential succession: An interinstitutional analysis. *Educational Record, 52,* 133–145.

Black, J. S. (1988, Summer). Work role transitions: A study of American expatriate managers in Japan. *Journal of International Business Studies,* pp. 277–294.

Blake, R. R., & Mouton, J. S. (1964). *The managerial grid.* Houston: Gulf.

Blanch, M. C. (1989). *Culture as a control mechanism in schools.* Unpublished dissertation, Department of Educational Administration, The University of Utah.

Blase, J. J. (1985). The socialization of teachers: An ethnographic study of factors contributing to the rationalization of the teacher's instructional perspective. *Urban Education, 20,* 235–256.

———. (1989). The micropolitics of the school: The everyday political orientation of teachers toward open school principals. *Educational Administration Quarterly, 25,* 377–407.

Blau, G. (1988). An investigation of the apprenticeship organizational socialization strategy. *Journal of Vocational Behavior, 32,* 176–195.

Blau, P. M. (1964). *Exchange and power in social life.* New York: John Wiley.

———. (1977). *Inequality and heterogeneity: A primitive theory of social structure.* New York: Basic Books.

Blau, P. M., & Scott, W. R. (1962). *Formal organizations.* San Francisco: Chandler.

Blumberg, A. (1989). *School administration as a craft.* Boston: Allyn and Bacon.

Blumer, H. (1962). Society as social interaction. In A. N. Rose (Ed.), *Human behavior and social processes: An interactionist approach* (pp. 179–192). Boston: Houghton Mifflin.

———. (1969). *Symbolic interactionism: Perspective and method.* Englewood Cliffs, NJ: Prentice-Hall.

Boldt, E. D. (1978). Leadership succession among the Hutterites: Ascription or achievement? *Canadian Review of Sociology and Anthropology, 15,* 395–396.

Bolman, L., & Deal, T. E. (1992). Leading and managing: Effects on context, culture, and gender. *Educational Administration Quarterly, 28*(3), 314–330.

Bossert, S. T. (1988). School effects. In N. J. Boyan (Ed.), *Handbook of research on educational administration* (pp. 341–354). New York: Longman.

Bossert, S. T., Dwyer, D. C., Rowan, B., & Lee, G. V. (1982). The instructional management role of the principal. *Educational Administration Quarterly, 18*, 34–64.

Bosworth, S., & Kreps, G. A. (1986). Structure as process: Organization and role. *American Sociological Review, 51*, 699–716.

Boud, D., Keogh, R., & Walker, D. (1985). *Reflection: Turning experience into learning.* New York: Nichols Publishing.

Bowers, D. G., & Seashore, S. E. (1966). Predicting organizational effectiveness with a four-factor theory of leadership. *Administrative Science Quarterly, 11*, 238–264.

Brady, G. F., & Helmich, D. L. (1985). *Executive succession: Toward excellence in corporate leadership.* Englewood Cliffs, NJ: Prentice-Hall.

Brady, G. F., Helmich, D. L., & Moore, J. N. (1983). The comparative advantage of variation among diversified and non-diversified firms. *Proceedings of the Eastern Academy of Management,* Annual Meeting, Pittsburgh.

Bredeson, P. V. (1985). An analysis of the metaphorical perspectives of school principals. *Educational Administration Quarterly, 21*(1), 29–50.

Bredeson, P. V. (1991). *Letting go of outlived professional identities: A study of role transition for principals in restructured schools.* Paper presented at the annual meeting of the American Educational Research Association, Chicago.

Brett, J. M. (1980). The effect of job transfer on employees and their families. In C. L. Cooper & R. Payne (Eds.), *Current concerns in occupational stress* (pp. 99–136). Chichester, England: Wiley.

Brief, A. P., & Downey, H. K. (1983). Cognitive and organizational structure: A conceptual analysis of implicit organizing theories. *Human Relations, 36*, 1065–1090.

Brookover, W. B., Beady, C., Flood, P., Schweitzer, J., & Wisenbaker, J. (1979). *School social systems and student achievement: Schools can make a difference.* New York: Holt, Rinehart, & Winston.

Brousseau, K. R. (1983). Toward a dynamic model of job-person relationships: Findings, research questions, and implications for work system design. *Academy of Management Review, 8*, 33–45.

Brown, M. C. (1982). Administrative succession and organizational performance: The succession effect. *Administrative Science Quarterly, 27,* 1–16.

Buchanan, B. (1974). Building organizational commitment: The socialization of managers in work organizations. *Administrative Science Quarterly, 19,* 533–546.

Buchanan, F. (forthcoming). *The making of a modern school system.*

Bucher, R., & Stelling, J. G. (1977). *Becoming professional.* Beverly Hills, CA: Sage.

Bullough, R. V., Jr. (1990). Supervision, mentoring, and self-discovery: A case study of a first-year teacher. *Journal of Curriculum and Supervision, 5,* 338–360.

———. (in press). Exploring personal teaching metaphors in preservice teacher education. *Journal of Teacher Education.*

Bullough, R. V., Jr., Knowles, J. G., & Crow, N. A. (1989). Teacher self-concept and student culture in the first year of teaching. *Teachers College Record, 91,* 209–233.

Burns, J. M. (1978). *Leadership.* New York: Harper & Row.

Burrell, G. (1988). Modernism, postmodernism, and organizational analysis 2: The contribution of Michael Foucault. *Organizational Studies, 9*(2), 221–235.

Campbell, J. P. (1977). On the nature of organizational effectiveness. In P. S. Goodman & J. M. Pennings (Eds.), *New perspectives on organizational effectiveness* (pp. 13–55). San Francisco: Jossey-Bass.

Campbell, J. P., Dunnette, M. D., Lawler, E. E., III, & Weick, K. E., Jr. (1970). *Managerial behavior, performance, and effectiveness.* New York: McGraw-Hill.

Campbell, R., Fleming, T., Bennion, J., & Newell, J. T. (1987). *A history of thought and practice in educational administration.* New York: Teachers College Press.

Carlson, R. O. (1961). Succession and performance among school superintendents. *Administrative Science Quarterly, 6,* 210–227.

———. (1962). *Executive succession and organizational change.* Chicago: University of Chicago, Midwestern Administration Center.

———. (1972). *School superintendents: Careers and performance.* Columbus, OH: Charles E. Merrill.

Carnegie Forum on Education and the Economy. (1986). *A nation prepared: Teachers for the 21st century.* Hyattsville, MD: Author.

Carroll, G. R. (1984). The dynamics of publisher succession in newspaper organizations. *Administrative Science Quarterly, 29,* 93–113.

Cartwright, D. & Zander, A. (1968). *Group dynamics: Research and theory, 3rd ed.* New York: Harper & Row.

Carver, C. S., & Scheier, M. F. (1981). *Attention and self-regulation: A control-theory approach to human behavior.* New York: Springer.

Chaganti, R., & Sambharya, R. (1987). Strategic orientation and characteristics of upper management. *Strategic Management Journal, 8,* 393–401.

Child, J., & Kieser, A. (1981). Development of organizations over time. In P. C. Nystrom & W. H. Starback (Eds.), *Handbook of organizational design,* Vol. 1 (pp. 28–64). London: Oxford.

Cicourel, A. V., Jennings, S. H. M., Leiter, K. C. W., Mackay, R., Mehan, H., & Roth, D. R. (1974). *Language use and school performance.* New York: Academic Press.

Collins, R. (1985). *Three sociological traditions.* New York: Oxford University Press.

──────. (1987). Interaction ritual chains, power, and property. In J. Alexander, R. Munch, N. J. Smelser, and B. Giessen (Eds.), *The micro-macro link* (pp. 193–206). Berkeley, CA: University of California Press.

Comer, J. P. (1980). *School power.* New York: Free Press.

Cooper, R., & Burrell, G. (1988). Modernism, postmodernism, and organizational analysis: An introduction. *Organizational Studies, 9*(1), 91–112.

Corbett, H. D., Firestone, W. A., & Rossman, G. B. (1987). Resistance to planned change and the sacred in school cultures. *Educational Administration Quarterly, 23,* 36–59.

Corcoran, T. B. (1985). Effective secondary schools. In *Reaching for excellence: An effective schools sourcebook* (pp. 71–98). Washington, DC: National Institute of Education.

Cosgrove, D. (1986). *The effects of principal succession on elementary schools.* Unpublished doctoral dissertation, Department of Educational Administration, The University of Utah, Salt Lake City, Utah.

Costa, P. T., & McCrae, R. R. (1980). Still stable after all these years: Personality as a key to some issues in adulthood and old age. In P. B. Baltes & O. G. Brim (Eds.), *Life-span development and behavior,* Vol. 3. New York: Academic Press.

Cowherd, D. M. (1986). On executive succession: A conversation with Lester B. Korn. *Human Resource Management Journal, 25,* 335–347.

Crouch, A., & Yetton, P. W. (1988). The management team: An equilibrium model of manager and subordinate performance. In J. G. Hunt, B. R. Baliga, H. P. Dachler, & C. A. Schriesheim (Eds.), *Emerging leadership vistas* (pp. 107–127). Boston: Lexington.

Crow, G. M. (1989). The perceived opportunity structure of educational administration. *Journal of Research and Development in Education, 22,* 70–78.

_____. (1990a). Career incentives of elementary school principals. *Journal of Educational Administration, 28,* 38–52.

_____. (1990b). *Conceptions of the principalship: A career history perspective.* Paper presented at the annual meeting of the American Educational Research Association, Boston.

Curcio, J. L., & Greene, E. (1989). *Crises of integrity of the first-time high school principal.* Paper presented at the annual meeting of the American Educational Research Association, San Francisco.

Dachler, H. P. (1984). On refocussing leadership from a social systems perspective of management. In J. G. Hunt, D. M. Hosking, C. A. Schriesheim, & R. Steward (Eds.), *Leaders and managers: International perspectives on managerial behavior and leadership* (pp. 100–108). Oxford: Pergamon.

Dalton, D. R., & Kesner, I. F. (1983). Inside/outside succession and organization size: The pragmatics of executive succession. *Academy of Management Journal, 26,* 736–742.

_____. (1985). Organizational performance as an antecedent of inside/outside chief executive succession: An empirical assessment. *Academy of Management Journal, 28,* 749–762.

Dansereau, F., Graen, G., & Haga, W. (1975). A vertical dyad linkage approach to leadership in formal organizations. *Organization Behavior and Human Performance, 13,* 46–78.

Daresh, J. C. (1986). Support for beginning principals: First hurdles are highest. *Theory into Practice, 23* 169–173.

Daresh, J. C., & Playko, M. A. (1989). *The administrative entry year: A resource guide.* Westerville, OH: Ohio LEAD Center.

Darling-Hammond, L., Wise, A. E., & Pease, S. R. (1983). Teacher evaluation in the organizational context: A review of literature. *Review of Educational Research, 53,* 283–328.

Daum, J. (1975). Internal promotion—a psychological asset or debit. *Organizational Behavior and Human Performance, 13*, 404–473.

Dawis, R. V., & Lofquist, L. H. (1984). *A psychological theory of work adjustment.* Minneapolis: University of Minnesota Press.

Day, D. V., & Lord, R. G. (1988). Executive leadership and organizational performance: Suggestions for a new theory and methodology. *Journal of Management, 14*, 453–464.

Deal, T. E., & Peterson, K. D. (1990). *The principal's role in shaping school culture.* Washington, DC: U.S. Department of Education, Office of Educational Research and Improvement.

Dewey, J. (1933). *How we think.* Chicago: Henry Regnery Company.

Dienesch, R., & Liden, R. (1986). Leader-member exchange model of leadership: A critique and further development. *Academy of Management Review, 11*, 618–634.

Dornbusch, S. M., & Scott, W. R. (1975). *Evaluation and the exercise of authority.* San Francisco: Jossey-Bass.

DuBose, E. (1986). *A study of the task specific assistance and information needs of incoming elementary school principals in South Carolina.* Unpublished doctoral dissertation, University of South Carolina.

Duke, D. L. (1986). The aesthetics of leadership. *Educational Administration Quarterly, 22*, 7–27.

_____. (1987). *School leadership and instructional improvement.* New York: Random House.

Duke, D. L., & Imber, M. (1985). Should principals be required to be effective? *School Organization, 5*(2), 125–146.

Duke, D. L., Isaacson, N. S., Sagor, R., & Schmuck, P. A. (1984). *Transition to leadership: An investigation of the first year of the principalship.* Portland, OR: Lewis and Clark College, Transition to Leadership Project. [Shortened version in School Organization]

Duke, D. L., & Stiggins, R. J. (1985). Evaluating the performance of principals. *Educational Administration Quarterly, 21*, 71–98.

Durkheim, E. (1915). *Elementary forms of religious life, a study in religious sociology.* Translated from the French by Joseph Ward Swain. New York: Macmillan.

Earley, P., Baker, L., & Weindling, D. (1990). *Keeping the raft afloat: Secondary headship five years on.* London, England: National Foundation for Educational Research in England and Wales. (ISBN 0 7005 0975 5).

Edmonds, R. (1979). Some schools work and more can. *Social Policy, 9,* 32–36.

_____. (1982). Programs of school improvement: An overview. *Educational Leadership, 40*(3), 4–11.

Edwards, A. L., & Klackars, A. J. (1981). Significant others and self-evaluation: Relationships between perceived and actual evaluations. *Personality and Social Psychology Bulletin, 7,* 244–251.

Eitzen, D. S., & Yetman, N. R. (1972). Managerial change. *Administrative Science Quarterly, 17,* 110–116.

Emerson, R. M. (1962). Power-dependence relations. *American Sociological Review, 27,* 31–41.

Epstein, S. (1973). The self-concept revisited or a theory of a theory. *American Psychology, 28,* 404–416.

Erikson, E. H. (1950). *Childhood and society.* New York: Norton.

Etzioni, A. (1964). *Modern organizations.* Englewood Cliffs, NJ: Prentice-Hall.

_____. (1975). *A comparative analysis of complex organizations: On power, involvement, and their correlates.* New York: Free Press.

Fauske, J. R., & Ogawa, R. T. (1987). Detachment, fear, and expectation: A faculty's response to the impending succession of its principal. *Educational Administration Quarterly, 23,* 23–44.

Feldman, D. C. (1976). A contingency theory of socialization. *Administrative Science Quarterly, 21,* 433–452.

Feldman, D. C., & Brett, J. M. (1983). Coping with new jobs: A comparative study of new hires and job changers. *Academy of Management Journal, 26,* 258–272

Festinger, L. (1957). *A theory of cognitive dissonance.* Evanston: Row, Peterson.

Fiedler, F. E. (1957). A theory of leadership effectiveness. New York: McGraw-Hill.

Fiedler, F. E., & Garcia, J. E. (1987). *New approaches to effective leadership: Cognitive resources and organizational performance.* New York: Wiley.

Firestone, W. A. (1989, November). *Cultural politics and executive succession in a modernizing school district.* Paper prepared under a grant by the U.S. Department of Education (Grant no. OERI-G00860011) to the Center for Policy Research in Education (CPRE). NJ: Rutgers University.

Firestone, W. A. (1990). Succession and bureaucracy: Gouldner revisited. *Educational Administration Quarterly, 26*(4), 345–375.

Firestone, W. A., & Bader, B. D. (1991). Professionalism or bureaucracy? Redesigning teaching. *Educational Evaluation and Policy Analysis, 13*(1), 67–86.

————. (in press). *The redesign of teaching: Professionalism or bureaucracy?* New York: SUNY Press.

Fleishman, E. A. (1953). The measurement of leadership attitudes in industry. *Journal of Applied Psychology, 37,* 153–158.

————. (1957). A leader behavior description for industry. In R. M. Stogdill & A. E. Coons (Eds.), *Leadership behavior: Its description and measurement.* Columbus: Ohio State University, Bureau of Business Research.

Fredrickson, J. W., Hambrick, D. C., & Baumrin, S. (1988). A model of CEO dismissal. *Academy of Management Review, 13,* 255–270.

French, J. R. P., Jr., & Raven, B. H. (1959). The bases of social power. In D. Cartwright (Ed.), *Studies in social power* (pp. 150–167). Ann Arbor, MI: Institute for Social Research, University of Michigan.

Frese, M. (1982). Occupational socialization and psychological development: An underemphasized research perspective in industrial psychology. *Journal of Occupational Psychology, 55,* 209–224.

————. (1984). Transitions in jobs, occupational socialization and strain. In V. L. Allen & E. Van de Vliert (Eds.), *Role transitions: Explorations and explanations.* London: Plenum.

Friedman, S. D. (1985). *Leadership succession systems and corporate performance.* New York: Center for Career Research and Human Management, Graduate School of Business, Columbia University.

————. (1986). Succession systems in large corporations: Characteristics and correlates of performance. *Human Resource Management, 25,* 191–213.

Fromm, E. (1941). *Escape from freedom.* NY: Rinehart.

Frost, P. J., Moore, L. F., Lundberg, C. C., & Marin, J. (Eds.). (1985). *Organizational culture.* Beverly Hills, CA: Sage.

Fulk, J., & Cummings, T. G. (1984). Refocusing leadership: A modest proposal. In J. C. Hunt, D. M. Hosking, C. A. Schriesheim, & R. Stewart (Eds.), *Leaders and managers: International perspectives on managerial behavior and leadership* (pp. 63–81). Oxford: Pergamon.

Gabarro, J. J. (1979, Winter). Socialization at the top—how CEOs and subordinates evolve interpersonal contracts. *Organizational Dynamics*, pp. 3–23.

_____. (1987). *The dynamics of taking charge*. Boston: Harvard Business School Press.

Gabarro, J. J., & Kotter, J. P. (1980, January-February). Managing your boss. *Harvard Business Review*, pp. 92–101.

Gamson, W. A., & Scotch, N. A. (1964). Scapegoating in baseball. *American Journal of Sociology, 69*, 21–31.

Ganz, H. G., & Hoy, W. K. (1977). Patterns of succession of elementary principals and organizational change. *Planning and Changing, 8*, 185–196.

Garfinkel, H. (1967). *Studies in ethnomethodology*. Englewood Cliffs, NJ: Prentice-Hall.

Garland, H., & Price, K. H. (1977). Attitudes toward women in management and attribution for their success and failure in managerial positions. *Journal of Applied Psychology, 62*, 29–33.

Gecas, V. (1981). Contexts of socialization. In M. Rosenberg & R. Turner (Eds.), *Social psychology: Sociological perspectives*. New York: Basic Books.

_____. (1982). The self-concept. *Annual Review of Sociology, 8*, 1–33.

Gephart, R. (1978). Status degradation and organization succession. *Administrative Science Quarterly, 23*, 23–44.

Getzels, J. W., & Guba, E. G. (1957). Social behavior and the administrative process. *School Review, 65*, 423–441.

Giddens, A. (1984). *The constitution of society: Outline of the theory of structuration*. Cambridge: Polity Press.

Ginsberg, R., & Barnett, B. (1990). The folklore of principal evaluation. *Journal of Personnel Evaluation in Education, 3*(3), 205–230.

Giroux, H. (Ed.). (1991). *Postmodernism, feminism, and cultural politics: Redrawing educational boundaries*. Albany, NY: SUNY Press.

Glasman, N. S. (1984). Student achievement and the school principal. *Educational Evaluation and Policy Analysis, 6*(3), 283–296.

_____. (1986). *Evaluation-based leadership: School administration in contemporary perspective*. Albany, NY: SUNY Press.

Glasman, N. S., & Heck, R. H. (1987). Administrator engagement in evaluation for decision making: The case of teacher assignment to classrooms. *Administrator's Notebook, 32*(5), 1–4.

Glasman, N. S., & Nevo, D. (1988). *Evaluation in decision making: The case of school administration*. Boston: Kluwer Academic Publishers.

Goffman, E. (1959). *The presentation of self in everyday life*. New York: Doubleday.

_____. (1967). *Interaction ritual: Essays on face-to-face behavior*. Garden City, NY: Anchor Books.

_____. (1974). *Frame analysis*. New York: Harper & Row.

Goldman, M., & Fraas, L. (1965). The effects of leadership selection on group performance. *Sociometry, 28*, 82–88.

Goodman, S. J. (1982). *How to manage a turnaround*. New York: Free Press.

Goody, J. (1966). *Succession to high office*. London: Cambridge University Press.

Gordon, G. E., & Becker, S. (1964). Organizational size and managerial succession: A reexamination. *American Journal of Sociology, 70*, 227–254.

Gordon, G. E., & Rosen, N. (1981). Critical factors in leadership succession. *Organizational Behavior and Human Performance, 27*, 227–254.

Gouldner, A. (1952). The problem of succession in bureaucracy. In R. Merton (Ed.), *Reader in bureaucracy* (pp. 339–351). Glencoe, IL: Free Press.

_____. (1954). *Patterns of industrial democracy*. Glencoe, IL: Free Press.

Green, G., & Novak, M. A. (1982). The effects of leader exchange and job design on productivity and satisfaction: Testing a dual attachment model. *Organizational Behavior and Human Performance, 30*, 109–134.

Greenblatt, M. (1983). Management succession: Some major parameters. *Administration in Mental Health, 11*, 3–10.

Greenfield, T. B. (1975). Theory about organizations: A new perspective and its implications for schools. In M. Hughes (Ed.), *Administering education: International challenge* (pp. 77–79). London: Athlone.

Greenfield, W. D., Jr. (1977a). Administrative candidacy: A process of new-role learning—Part I. *Journal of Educational Administration, 15*(1), 30–48.

_____. (1977b). Administrative candidacy: A process of new-role learning—Part II. *Journal of Educational Administration, 15*(2), 179–193.

_____. (1985a). *Being and becoming a principal: Responses to work contexts and socialization processes*. Paper presented at the annual meeting of the American Educational Research Association, Chicago.

_____. (1985b). The moral socialization of school administrators: Informal role learning outcomes. *Educational Administration Quarterly, 21,* 99–119.

_____. (1991). Toward a theory of *school* leadership. Paper presented at the annual meeting of the American Educational Research Association, Chicago.

Gregory, K. L. (1983). Native-view paradigms: Multiple cultures and culture conflicts in organizations. *Administrative Science Quarterly, 28,* 359–376.

Griffin, R. W. (1983). Objective and social sources of information in task redesign: A field experiment. *Administrative Science Quarterly, 28,* 184–200.

Griffiths, D. E. (Ed.). (1991). Nontraditional theory and research [Special issue]. *Educational Administration Quarterly, 27*(3).

Gronn, P. C. (1982). Neo-Taylorism in educational administration. *Educational Administration Quarterly, 18,* 17–35.

Gross, E., & Etzioni, A. (1985). *Organizations and society.* Englewood Cliffs, NJ: Prentice-Hall.

Grusky, O. (1960). Administrative succession in formal organizations. *Social Forces, 39,* 105–115.

_____. (1961). Corporate size, bureaucratization, and managerial succession. *American Journal of Sociology, 67,* 261–269.

_____. (1963). Managerial succession and organizational effectiveness. *American Journal of Sociology, 69,* 21–31, 72–76.

_____. (1964). Reply to scapegoating in baseball. *American Journal of Sociology, 70,* 72–76.

_____. (1969). Succession with an ally. *Administrative Science Quarterly, 14,* 155–170.

Guest, R. H. (1962). Managerial succession in complex organizations. *American Journal of Sociology, 68,* 47–54.

Gupta, A. K. (1986). Matching managers to strategies: Point and counterpoint. *Human Resource Management, 25,* 215–234.

Guy, M. E. (1985). *Professionals in organizaitons: Debunking a myth.* New York: Praeger.

Habermas, J. (1984, published originally in 1981). *The theory of communicative action.* Translated from the German by Thomas McCarthy. Boston: Beacon Press.

Hall, D. T. (1986). Dilemmas in linking succession planning to individual executive learning. *Human Resource Management, 25,* 235–265.

_____. (1987). Careers and socialization. *Journal of Management, 13,* 301–321.

Hall, G., & Hord, S. (1987). *Change in schools: Facilitating the process.* New York: SUNY Press.

Hall, G. E., Rutherford, W. L., Hord, S. M., & Huling-Austin, L. L. (1984). Effects of three principal styles on school improvement. *Educational Leadership, 41,* 22–29.

Hallinger, P., & Murphy, J. (1987). The social context of effective schools. *American Journal of Education, 94*(5), 328–355.

Halpin, A. W., & Winer, B. J. (1957). A factorial study of the leader behavior descriptions. In R. M. Stogdill & A. E. Coons (Eds.), *Leader behavior: Its descriptions and measurement.* Columbus: Ohio State University, Bureau of Business Research.

Hamblin, R. (1958). Leadership and crises. *Sociometry, 21,* 322–335.

Hambrick, D. C., & Finkelstein, S. (1987). Managerial discretion: A bridge between polar views of organizational outcomes. In B. M. Staw & L. L. Cummings (Eds.), *Research in organizational behavior,* Vol. 9, (pp. 369–400). Greenwich, CT: JAI Press.

Hambrick, D. C., & Mason, P. A. (1984). Upper echelons: The organization as a reflection of its top managers. *Academy of Management Review, 9,* 193–206.

Hannan, M. T., & Freeman, J. H. (1984). Structural inertia and organizational change. *American Sociological Review, 49,* 149–164.

Hart, A. W. (1986). The reflective principal. In E. Ducharme & D.S. Fleming (Eds.), *The rural and small school principalship* (pp. 133–138). Chelmsford, MA: Northeast Regional Exchange, Inc., National Institute of Education.

_____. (1987). Leadership succession: Reflections of a new principal. *Journal of Research and Development in Education, 20*(4), 1–11.

_____. (1988). Attribution as effect: An outsider principal's succession. *Journal of Educational Administration, 26*(3), 331–352.

_____. (1990a). Impacts of the school social unit on teacher authority during work redesign. *American Educational Research Journal, 27* (3), 503–532.

_____. (1990b). Work redesign: A review of literature for education reform. In S. B. Bacharach, (Ed.), *Advances in research and theories of school management,* Vol. 1 (pp. 31–69). Greenwich, CT: JAI Press.

Hart, A. W., & Murphy, M. J. (1990). New teachers react to redesigned teacher work. *American Journal of Education, 98*, 224–250.

_____. (in press). Preparing principals to lead in restructured schools. In P. Thurston, & N. Prestine, (Eds.), *Advances in educational administration*, Vol. 2. Greenwich, CT: JAI Press.

Hart, A. W., & Ogawa, R. T. (1987). The influence of superintendents on the academic achievement of school districts. *Journal of Educational Administration, 25*(1), 72–84.

Hart, A. W., Sorensen, N. B. & Naylor, K. (1992). Learning to lead: Reflective practice in preservice preparation. In F. Wendel (Ed.), *Leadership in the profession* (pp. 5–22). University Park, PA: University Council for Educational Administration.

Hartup, W. W., & Coates, B. (1972). Imitation: Arguments for a developmental approach. In R. D. Drake (Ed.), *Recent trends in social learning theory*, (pp. 63–75). New York: Academic Press.

Hearn, J., Sheppard, D. L., Tancred-Sheriff, P., & Burrell, G. (Eds.). (1989). *The sexuality of organization*. Beverly Hills, CA: Sage.

Heck, R. H., Larsen, T. J., & Marcoulides, G. A. (1990). Instructional leadership and school achievement: Validation of a causal model. *Educational Administration Quarterly, 26*(2), 94–125.

Helmich, D. L. (1974). Organizational growth and succession patterns. *Academy of Management Journal, 17*, 771–775

_____. (1975). Corporate succession: An examination. *Academy of Management Journal, 18*, 429–441.

_____. (1977). Executive succession in the corporate organization: A current integration. *American Management Review, 2*, 252–266.

_____. (1978). Leader flows and organizational process. *Academy of Management Journal, 21*, 463–478.

Helmich, D. L., & Brown, W. B. (1972). Successor type and organizational change in the corporate enterprise. *Administrative Science Quarterly, 17*, 371–381.

Hemphill, J. K. (1964). Personal variables and administrative styles. In D. E. Griffiths (Ed.), *Behavioral science and educational administration*, Part II, (pp. 178–198). Chicago: University of Chicago Press.

Hemphill, J. K., & Coons, A. E. (1950). *Leader behavior description*. Columbus: Personnel Research Board, Ohio State University.

Heritage, J. (1984). *Garfinkel and ethnomethodology*. Cambridge, England: Polity Press.

Hitt, M. A., & Ireland, R. D. (1987). Peters and Waterman revisited: The unended quest for excellence. *Academy of Management Executive, 1*, 91–98.

Hodgkinson, C. (1983). *The philosophy of leadership.* New York: St. Martin's.

Hollander, E. P. (1958). Conformity, status, and idiosyncrasy credit. *Psychological Review, 65*, 117–127.

_____. (1960). Competence and conformity in the acceptance of influence. *Journal of Abnormal and Social Psychology, 61*, 361–365.

_____. (1978). *Leadership dynamics: A practical guide to effective relationships.* New York: Free Press.

_____. (1979). Leadership and social exchange processes. In K. J. Gergen, M. S. Greenberg, & R. H. Willis (Eds.), *Social exchange: Advances in theory and research* (pp. 103–118). New York: Winston-Wiley.

Hollander, E. P., Fallon, B. J. & Edward, M. T. (1977). Some aspects of influence and acceptability for appointed and elected group leaders. *Journal of Psychology, 95*, 289–296.

Hollander, E. P., & Julian, J. W. (1978). A further look at leader legitimacy, influence, and innovation. In L. Berkowitz (Ed.), *Group processes* (pp. 153–165). New York: Academic Press.

Holmes Group. (1986). *Tomorrow's teachers.* East Lansing, MI: Author.

Homans, G. C. (1961). *Social behavior: Its elementary forms.* New York: Harcourt, Brace & World.

Hopson, B., & Adams, J. (1976). Towards an understanding of transition: Defining some boundaries of transition dynamics. In J. Adams, J. Hyes, & B. Hopson (Eds.), *Transition* (pp. 3–25). London: Martin Robertson.

Hosking, D. M., & Morley, I. (1988). The skills of leadership. In J. G. Hunt, B. R. Baliga, H. P. Dachler, & C. A. Schriesheim (Eds.), *Emerging leadership vistas* (pp. 80–106). Boston: Lexington.

House, R. J. (1988). Power and personality in complex organizations. In B. M. Staw (Ed.), *Research in organizational behavior*, Vol. 10 (pp. 305–357). Greenwich, CT: JAI Press.

Hoy, W. K., & Miskel, C. G. (1991). *Educational administration: Theory, research, and practice*, 4th ed. New York: McGraw-Hill.

Hoy, W. K., & Rees, R. (1977). The bureaucratic socialization of student teachers. *Journal of Teacher Education, 28*, 23–26.

Hoy, W. K., & Woolfolk, A. E. (1990). Socialization of student teachers. *American Educational Research Journal, 27,* 279–300.

Hoyle, J. R. (1985). Programs in educational administration and the AASA preparation guidelines. *Educational Administration Quarterly, 21*(1), 71–93.

Hunt, D., & Michael, C. (1983). Mentorship: A career training and development tool. *Academy of Management Review, 8,* 475–485.

Immegart, G. L. (1988). Leadership and leader behavior. In N. J. Boyan (Ed.), *Handbook of research on educational administration* (pp. 259–278), New York: Longman.

James, D. R., & Soref, M. (1981). Profit constraints on managerial autonomy: Managerial theory and the unmaking of the corporation president. *American Sociological Review, 46,* 1–18.

James, W. (1979). *The works of William James: The will to believe, and other essays in popular philosophy.* F. H. Burkhardt, F. Bowers & I. K. Skupskelis (Eds.). Cambridge, MA: Harvard University Press.

_____. (1984, first published in 1890). *The principles of psychology.* Cambridge, MA: Harvard University Press.

Jencks, C. L., Smith, M., Acland, H., Bane, M. J., Cohen, D. K., Gintis, H., Heyns, B. L., & Michaelson, S. (1972). *Inequality: A reassessment of the effects of family and schooling in America.* New York: Basic Books.

Jentz, B., with Cheever, D. S. Jr. (Eds.) (1982). *Entry: The hiring, start-up, and supervision of administrators.* New York: McGraw-Hill.

Jones, G. R. (1983). Psychological orientation and the process of organizational socialization: An interactionist perspective. *Academy of Management Journal, 26,* 464–474.

_____. (1986). Socialization tactics, self-efficacy, and newcomers' adjustments to organizations. *Academy of Management Journal, 29,* 262–279.

Kagan, J. (1978). *The growth of the Child: Reflections on human development.* New York: Norton.

Kanter, R. (1977). *Men and women of the corporation.* New York: Basic Books.

Katz, D., & Kahn, R. L. (1978). *The social psychology of organizations,* 2nd ed. New York: Wiley.

Kelleher, P. (1982). A bad beginning as principal. In B. Jentz (Ed.), *Entry* (pp. 75–86). New York, McGraw-Hill.

Kemmis, S. (1985). Action research and the politics of reflection. In D. Boud, R. Keogh, & D. Walker (Eds.), *Reflection: Turning experience into learning* (pp. 139–163). New York: Nichols Publishing Company.

Kerchner, C. T. (1990). Educational administration: Choice as a reflection of today's *social* values. In S. B. Bacharach (Ed.), *Education reform: Making sense of it all* (pp. 270–281.) Needham Heights, MA: Allyn and Bacon.

Kimberly, J. R., & Quinn, R. E. (1984). *Managing organizational transitions.* Homewood, IL: Irwin.

Kmetz, J. T., & Willower, D. J. (1982). Elementary school principals' work behavior. *Educational Administration Quarterly, 18,* 62–78.

Knight, P. A., & Weiss, H. M. (1980). Effects of selection agent and leader origin on leader influence and group member perceptions. *Organizational Behavior and Human Performance, 26,* 7–21.

Koch, J. L. (1978). Managerial succession in a factory and changes in supervisory leadership patterns: A field study. *Human Relations, 31,* 49–58.

Kohn, M. L., & Schooler, C. (1983). *Work and personality.* Norwood, NJ: Ablex.

Kotter, J. P. (1979). *Power in management.* New York: ANACOM.

_____. (1982). *The general managers.* New York: Free Press.

_____. (1985). *Power and influence.* New York: Free Press.

Kriesburg, L. (1962). Careers, organizational size, and succession. *American Journal of Sociology, 68,* 355–359.

Kunz, D., & Hoy, W. L. (1976). Leader behavior of principals and the professional zone of acceptance of teachers. *Educational Administration Quarterly, 12,* 49–64.

Lamoreaux, D. (1990). *New shoes: An educational criticism of a new principal's first quarter.* Paper presented at the annual meeting of the American Educational Research Association, Boston.

Leithwood, K. A., Begley, P., & Cousins, B. (in press). *Developing expert leadership for future schools.* New York: Falmer Press.

Leithwood, K. A., Steinbach, R., & Begley, P. (1992). The nature and contribution of socialization experiences to becoming a principal in Canada. In F. W. Parkay & G. E. Hall (Eds.), *Becoming a principal: The challenges of beginning leadership.* Boston: Allyn and Bacon.

Liden, R. C., & Graen, G. (1980). Generalizability of the vertical dyad linkage model of leadership. *Academy of Management Journal, 25,* 451–465.

Lieberman, S. (1956). The effects of changes in roles on the attitudes of role occupants. *Human Relations, 9,* 385–402.

Lieberson, S., & O'Connor, J. F. (1972). Leadership and organization performance: A study of large corporations. *American Sociological Review, 37*, 117–130.

Likert, R. (1967). *The human organization: Its management and value.* New York: McGraw-Hill.

Lipham, J. A. (1964). Leadership and administration. In D. Griffiths (Ed.), *Behavioral science and educational administration, Sixty-Third Yearbook of the National Society for the Study of Education* (pp. 119–141). Chicago: University of Chicago Press.

Little, J. W. (1982) Norms of collegiality and experimentation: Workplace conditions of school success. *American Educational Research Journal, 19*(3), 325–340.

———. (1990). The mentor phenomenon and the social organization of teaching. In C. Casden (Ed.), *Review of research in education,* Vol. 16 (pp. 297–352). Washington, DC: American Educational Research Association.

Lord, R. G., & Smith, J. E. (1983). Theoretical, information processing, and situational factors affecting attribution theory models of organizational behavior. *Academy of Management Review, 8*, 50–60.

Lortie, D. C. (1968). Shared ordeal and induction to work. In H. Becker, B. Geer, D. Reisman, & R. Weiss (Eds.), *Institutions and the person* (pp. 252–264). Chicago: Aldine.

———. (1975). *Schoolteacher: A sociological study.* Chicago: University of Chicago Press.

Louis, M. R. (1980a). Career transitions: Varieties and commonalities. *Academy of Management Review, 5*(3), 329–340.

———. (1980b). Surprise and sense making: What newcomers experience in entering unfamiliar organizational settings. *Administrative Science Quarterly, 25*(2), 226–251.

Louis, M. R., Posner, B. Z., & Powell, G. N. (1983). The availability and helpfulness of socialization practices. *Personnel Psychology, 36*, 857–866.

Lundberg, C. C. (1986). The dynamic organizational contexts of executive succession: Considerations and challenges. *Human Resource Management, 25*, 286–303.

Maclean, N. (1976). *A river runs through it and other stories.* Chicago: University of Chicago Press.

MacPherson, R. J. (1984). On being and becoming an educational administrator: Some methodological issues. *Educational Administration Quarterly, 20*(4), 58–75.

Manning, P. K. (1977). Talking and becoming: A view of organizational socialization. In R. L. Blankenship (Ed.), *Colleagues in organizations* (pp. 181–201). New York: Wiley.

Manz, C. C., Adsit, D., Campbell, S., & Mathison-Hance, M. (1988). Managerial thought patterns and performance: A study of perceptual patterns of performance hindrances for higher and lower performing managers. *Human Relations, 41*, 447–465.

March, J. G. (1976). The technology of foolishness. In J. G. March & J. P. Olsen (Eds.), *Ambiguity and choice in organizations* (pp. 69–81). Bergen, Norway: Universitetsforlaget.

Markus, H., & Zajonc, R. B. (1985). The cognitive perspective in social psychology. In G. Lindzey & E. Aronson (Eds.), *Handbook of social psychology. Vol. 1: Theory and method* (pp. 137–230). New York: Random House.

Marrion, B. (1983). A rationalistic study of the experiences of first-year elementary school principals. (Doctoral dissertation, University of Colorado at Boulder, 1983). *Dissertation Abstracts International, 44*, 939–A.

Martin, J., Feldman, M. S., Hatch, M. J., & Sitkin, S. B. (1983). The uniqueness paradox in organizational stories. *Administrative Science Quarterly, 28*, 438–453.

Martin, W. J., & Willower, D. J. (1981). The managerial behavior of high school principals. *Educational Administration Quarterly, 17*, 69–90.

Martinko, M. J., & Gardner, W. L. (1984). The observation of high-performing educational managers: Methodological issues and managerial implications. In J. G. Hunt, D. M. Hosking, C. A. Schriescheim, & R. Stewart (Eds.), *Leaders and managers* (pp. 142–162). New York: Pergamon.

_____. (1987). The leader/member attribution process. *Academy of Management Review, 12*, 235–249.

Mayhew, L. (1984). In defense of modernity: Talcott Parsons and the utilitarian tradition. *American Journal of Sociology, 89*, 1273–1305.

McCleary, L. E., & Ogawa, R. (1989). The assessment center process for selecting school leaders. *School Organization, 9*(1), 103–113.

McEachern, A. (1975). *Managerial control and performance.* Lexington, MA; Heath.

McGivern, C. (1978). The dynamics of management succession. *Management Decision* (U.K.), *16*, 32–42.

McNeil, E. B. (1969). *Human socialization.* Belmont, CA: Brooks/Cole.

Mead, G. H. (1934, 1962). *Mind, self, and society: From the standpoint of a social behaviorist.* Edited and with introduction by C. W. Morris. Chicago: University of Chicago Press.

Merton, R. K. (1949). *Social theory and social structure.* New York: Free Press.

Merton, R. K., Reader, G. G., & Kendall, P. L. (1957). *The student physician.* Cambridge, MA: Harvard University Press.

Meyer, P. S. (1979, July 18). The ITT coup: Why Harold Geneen got the board to strip power from Hamilton. *Wall Street Journal,* pp. 1, 27.

Miklos, E. (1988). Administrator selection, career patterns, succession, and socialization. In N. J. Boyan (Ed.), *Handbook of research on educational administration* (pp. 53–76). New York: Longman.

Milkovich, G. T., Anderson, J. C., & Greenhalgh, L. (1976). Organizational careers: Environmental, organizational, and individual determinants. In L. Dyer (Ed.), *Careers in organizations: Individual planning and organizational development* (pp. 17–30). Ithaca, NY: Cornell University.

Mills, C. W. (1959). *The sociological imagination.* New York: Oxford University Press.

Mintzberg, H. (1973). *The nature of managerial work.* New York: Harper & Row.

Miskel, C., & Cosgrove, D. (1985). Leader succession in school settings. *Review of Educational Research, 55,* 87–105.

Miskel, C. G., & Owens, M. (1983) *Principal succession and changes in school coupling and effectiveness.* Paper presented at the annual meeting of the American Educational Research Association, Montreal.

Mitroff, I. I. (1983). *Stakeholders of the organizational mind: Toward a new view of organizational policy.* San Francisco: Jossey-Bass.

Mizruchi, M. S. (1983). Who controls whom? An examination of the relationship between management and boards of directors in large American corporations. *Academy of Management Review, 8,* 426–435.

Monane, J. H. (1967). *A sociology of human systems.* New York: Appleton, Century, Crofts.

Moreland, R. L., & Levine, J. M. (1983). Socialization in small groups: Temporal changes in individual-group relations. *Advances in Experimental Social Psychology, 15,* 137–192.

Morgenthau, H. J. (1972). *Politics among nations: The struggle for power and peace.* (5th ed.). New York: Knopf.

Mortimer, J. T., & Lorence, J. (1979). Work experience and occupational value socialization: A longitudinal study. *American Journal of Sociology, 84*, 1361–1385.

Mortimer, J. T., & Simmons, R. C. (1978). Adult socialization. *American Review of Sociology, 84,* 1361–1385.

Murphy, J. (Ed.). (1990). *The educational reform movement of the 1980s: Perspectives and cases.* Berkeley, CA: McCutchan.

Myers, I. B. (1975). *Manual: The Myers-Briggs type indicator.* Palo Alto, CA: Consulting Psychologists Press. (Originally published 1962)

National Commission on Excellence in Educational Administration. (1987). *Leaders for America's schools.* Tempe, AZ: University Council for Educational Administration.

National Policy Board for Educational Administration. (1989). *Improving the preparation of school administrators: An agenda for reform.* Charlottesville, VA: Author.

Nicholson, N. (1984). A theory of work role transitions. *Administrative Science Quarterly, 29,* 172–191.

———. (1986). Turning points, traps, and tunnels: The significance of work role transitions in the lives of individuals and organizations. In H. W. Schroiff & G. Debus (Eds.), *The psychology of work and organization: Current trends and issues* (pp. 257–265). Amsterdam: North-Holland.

———. (1987). The transition cycle: A conceptual framework for the analysis of change and human resources management. In K. M. Rowland & G. R. Ferris (Eds.), *Research in personnel and human resources management,* Vol. 5 (pp. 167–222). Greenwich, CT: JAI Press.

Nicholson, N., & West, M. A. (1987). *Managerial job change.* Cambridge: Cambridge University Press.

———. (1988). *Managerial job change: Men and women in transition.* Cambridge: Cambridge University Press.

———. (1989). Transitions, work histories, and careers. In M. B. Arthus, D. T. Hall, & B. S. Lawrence (Eds.), *Handbook of career theory* (pp. 181–201). New York: Cambridge University Press.

Nota, B. (1988, August). The socialization process at high-commitment organizations. *Personnel,* 20–23.

Nytell, U. (1991). The school principal in Sweden: A boss or a leader? Paper presented at the annual meeting of the American Educational Research Association, Chicago.

O'Connor, J. T., & Barrett, D. A. (1981). Educating management engineers and alleviating the crisis in health care: Any connections? *Engineering Education, 71*(8), 795–97.

Ogawa, R. T. (1991). Enchantment, disenchantment, and accommodation: How a faculty made sense of the succession of its principal. *Educational Administration Quarterly, 27,* 30–60.

_____. (forthcoming). Leadership succession. In S. B. Bacharach & B. Mundell (Eds.), *Organizational behavior in schools.* Boston: Allyn and Bacon.

Ogawa, R. T., & Hart, A. W. (1985). The effect of principals on the instructional performance of schools. *Journal of Educational Administration, 23*(1), 59–72.

Ogawa, R. T., & Smith, J. (1985). *How a faculty made sense of the succession of its principal.* Paper presented at the annual meeting of the American Educational Research Association, Chicago.

Olesen, V. L., & Whittaker, E. W. (1977). Characteristics of professional socialization. In R. L. Blankenship (Ed.), *Colleagues in organization* (pp. 157–165). New York: Wiley.

Oliver, J. (1992). *The professional socialization of principals.* Unpublished dissertation, Department of Educational Administration, University of Utah.

Ortiz, F. I., & Marshall, C. (1988). Women in educational administration. In N. J. Boyan (Ed.), *Handbook of research on educational administration* (pp. 123–142). New York: Longman.

Oskarsson, H., & Klein, R. H. (1982). Leadership change and organizational regression. *International Journal of Group Psychotherapy, 32,* 145–162.

Parkay, F. W., & Currie, G. (1989). *Sources of support for first-time high school principals during selection and entry.* Paper presented at the annual meeting of the American Educational Research Association, San Francisco.

_____. (1992). Sources of support for beginning principals. In F. W. Parkay, & G. E. Hall (Eds.), *Becoming a principal: The challenges of beginning leadership.* Boston: Allyn and Bacon.

Parkay, F. W., Currie, G., & Rhodes, J. W. (1992). Professional socialization: A longitudinal study of twelve high school principals. *Educational Administration Quarterly, 28*(1), 43–75.

Parkay, F. W., & Hall, G. E. (Eds.). (1992). *Becoming a principal: The challenges of beginning leadership.* Boston: Allyn and Bacon.

Parkay, F. W., Rhodes, J., Currie, G., & Rao, M. (1989). *First time high school principals: Their characteristics and professional concerns.* Paper presented at the annual meeting of the American Educational Research Association, San Francisco.

Parsons, T. (1937). *The structure of social action.* New York: McGraw-Hill.

_____. (1978). *Action theory and the human condition.* New York: Free Press.

Pellicer, L. O., Anderson, L. W., Keefe, J. W., Kelley, E. A., & McCleary, L. E. (1988a) *High school leaders and their schools, Vol. I: A national profile.* Reston, VA: National Association of Secondary School Principals.

_____. (1988b). *High school leaders and their schools, Volume II: Profiles of effectiveness.* Reston, VA: National Association of Secondary School Principals.

Peters, T. J., & Waterman, R. H., Jr. (1982). *In search of excellence.* New York: Harper & Row.

Peterson, M. F. (1985). Experienced acceptability: Measuring perceptions of dysfunctional leadership. *Group and Organization Studies, 10*, 447–477.

Pettigrew, A. (1979). On studying organizational cultures. *Administrative Science Quarterly, 24*, 570–581.

Pfeffer, J. (1978). The micropolitics of organizations. In M. W. Meyer (Ed.), *Environments and organizations* (pp. 29–50). San Francisco: Jossey-Bass.

_____. (1981a). Management as symbolic action: The creation and maintenance of organizational paradigms. In L. L. Cummings & B. Staw (Eds.), *Research in organizational behavior* Vol. III (pp. 1–52). Greenwich, CT: JAI Press.

_____. (1981b). *Power in organizations.* Marshfield, MA: Pitman.

Pfeffer, J., & Davis-Blake, A. (1986). Administrative succession and organizational performance; How administrator experience mediates the succession effect. *Academy of Management Journal, 29*, 72–83.

Pfeffer, J., & Lawler, J. (1980). Effects of job alternatives, extrinsic rewards, and behavioral commitment on attitude toward the organization: A field test of the insufficient justification paradigm. *Administrative Science Quarterly, 25*, 38–56.

Phillips, J. S. (1984). The accuracy of leadership ratings: A cognitive categorization analysis. *Organizational Behavior and Human Performance, 33*, 125–138.

Pinder, C. C., & Schroeder, K. G. (1987). Time to proficiency following transfers. *Academy of Management Journal, 30*, 336–353.

Pitner, N., & Ogawa, R. T. (1981). Organizational leadership: The case of the school superintendent. *Educational Administration Quarterly, 17,* 45–66.

Playko, M. A., & Daresh, J. C. (1989). *Beginning principals: Entry year programs and principal development.* Paper presented at the annual meeting of the University Council for Educational Administration, Phoenix, AZ.

Podsakoff, P. M. (1982). Determinants of a supervisor's use of rewards and punishments: A literature review and suggestions for further research. *Organizational Behavior and Human Performance, 29,* 58–83.

Podsakoff, P. M., Todor, W. D., & Skov, R. (1982). Effects of leader contingent and noncontingent reward and punishment behaviors on subordinate performance and satisfaction. *Academy of Management Journal, 25,* 810–821.

Pondy, L. R. (1978). Leadership is a language game. In M. W. McCall, Jr., & M. M. Lombardo (Eds), *Leadership: Where else can we go?* (pp. 88–99). Durham, NC: Duke University Press.

Pondy, L. R., Frost, P. J., Morgan, G., & Dandridge, T. C. (Eds.). (1983). *Organizational symbolism.* Greenwich, CT: JAI Press.

Porter, A. C. (1991). Creating a system of school process indicators. *Educational Evaluation and Policy Analysis, 13*(1), 13–30.

Porter, L. W., Lawler, E. E., III, & Hackman, J. R. (1975). *Behavior in organizations.* New York: McGraw-Hill.

Pounder, D. G. (1988). The male/female salary differential for school administrators: Implications for career patterns and placement of women. *Educational Administration Quarterly, 24,* 5–20.

———. (1989). The gender gap in salaries of educational administration professors. *Educational Administration Quarterly, 25,* 181–201.

Purkey, S. C., & Smith, M. S. (1983). Effective schools: A review. *Elementary School Journal, 83,* 427–453.

Redlich, F. C. (1977). Problems of succession. Paper presented at the annual meeting of the American Psychiatric Association, Toronto.

Reinganum, J. R. (1985). The effect of executive succession on stockholder wealth. *Administrative Science Quarterly, 30,* 46–60.

Rice, R.W., Bender, L.R., & Vitters, A.G. (1980). Leader sex, follower attitudes toward women, and leadership effectiveness: A laboratory experiment. *Organizational Behavior and Human Performance, 25,* 46–78.

Richards, E. W. (1984). Undergraduate preparation and early career outcomes: A study of recent college graduates. *Journal of Vocational Behavior, 24,* 279–304.

Roberts, J. (1989a). *Cultural orientations of first-time high school principals during selection and entry.* Paper presented at the annual meeting of the American Educational Research Association, San Francisco.

_____. (1989b). *Principal preparation: The school culture component.* Paper presented at the annual meeting of the University Council for Educational Administration, Phoenix, AZ.

_____. (1992). Building the school culture. In F. W. Parkay & G. E. Hall (Eds.), *Becoming a principal: The challenges of beginning leadership.* Boston: Allyn and Bacon.

Roberts, J., & Wright, L. V. (1989). *A study of the change efforts among first-time high school principals.* Paper presented at the annual meeting of the American Educational Research Association, San Francisco.

_____. (1992). Initiating change. In F. W. Parkay & G. E. Hall (Eds.), *Becoming a principal: The challenges of beginning leadership.* Boston: Allyn and Bacon.

Rosenberg, M. (1979). *Conceiving the self.* New York: Basic Books.

Rosenthal, T. L., & Zimmerman, B. J. (1978). *Social learning and cognition.* New York: Academic Press.

Ross, M., & Fletcher, G. J. O. (1985). Attribution and social perception. In G. Lindzey & E. Aronson (Eds.), *Handbook of social psychology, Vol. 2: Special fields and applications* (pp. 73–122). New York: Random House.

Rowan, B., Bossert, S. T., & Dwyer, D. C. (1983). Research on effective schools: A cautionary note. *Educational Researcher, 12,* 24–31.

Rowan, B., & Denk, C. E. (1984). Management succession, school socio-economic context, and basic skills attainment. *American Educational Research Journal, 21,* 517–537.

Salaman, G. (1977). An historical discontinuity: From charisma to routinization. *Human Relations, 30,* 373–388.

Salancik, G. R., & Meindl, J. R. (1984). Corporate attributions as strategic illusions of management control. *Administrative Science Quarterly, 29,* 238–254.

Salancik, G. R., & Pfeffer, J. (1977). An examination of need-satisfaction models of job attitudes. *Administrative Science Quarterly, 22,* 427–456.

_____. (1978). A social information processing approach to job attitudes and task design. *Administrative Science Quarterly, 23,* 224–253.

_____. (1980). Effects of ownership and performance on executive tenure in U.S. corporations. *Academy of Management Journal, 23*, 653–664.

Samuelson, B. A., Galbraith, C. S., & McGuire, J. W. (1985). Organizational performance and top-management turnover. *Organization Studies, 6*, 275–291.

Schein, E. H. (1971a). The individual, the organization, and the career: A conceptual scheme. *Journal of Applied Behavioral Science, 7*, 401–426.

_____. (1971b). Occupational socialization in the professions: The case of the role innovator. *Journal of Psychiatric Research, 8*, 521–530.

_____. (1978). *Career dynamics: Matching individual and organizational needs*. Reading, MA: Addison-Wesley.

_____. (1984). Culture as an environmental context for careers. *Journal of Occupational Behavior, 5*, 71–81.

_____. (1985). *Organizational culture and leadership*. San Francisco: Jossey-Bass.

_____. (1986). A critical look at current career development theory and research. In D. T. Hall and Associates (Eds.), *Career development in organizations* (pp. 310–331). San Francisco: Jossey-Bass.

Schein, E. H., & Bennis, W. G. (1965). *Personal and organizational change through methods*. New York: Wiley.

Schon, D. A. (1983). *The reflective practitioner: How professionals think in action*. San Francisco: Jossey-Bass.

_____. (1987). *Educating the reflective practitioner*. San Francisco: Jossey-Bass.

Schriesheim, C. A., & Kerr, S. (1979). Theories and measures of leadership: A critical appraisal of current and future directions. In J. G. Hunt & L. L. Larson (Eds.), *Leadership: The cutting edge* (pp. 9–45). Carbondale, IL: Southern Illinois University Press.

Schutz, A. (1967). *The phenomenology of the social world*. Evanston, IL: Northwestern University Press. (Original work published 1932.)

Schwartz, D. B., & Menon, K. (1985). Executive succession in failing firms. *Academy of Management Journal, 26*, 680–686.

Scott, W. R. (1982). Managing professional work: Three models of control for health organizations. *Health Services Research, 17*, 213–240.

_____. (1987). *Organizations: Rational, natural, and open systems*, 2nd ed. Englewood Cliffs, NJ: Prentice-Hall.

Selznick, P. (1957). *Leadership in administration.* New York: Harper & Row.

Sergiovanni, T. J. (1987a). *The principalship: A reflective practice perspective.* Boston: Allyn and Bacon.

Sergiovanni, T. J. (1987b). The theoretical basis for cultural leadership. In L. T. Shieve & M. B. Schoenheit (Eds.), *Leadership: Examining the elusive* (pp. 115–129). Alexandria, VA: Association for Supervision and Curriculum Development.

_____. (1991). *The principalship: A reflective practice perspective,* 2nd ed. Boston: Allyn and Bacon.

Sergiovanni, T. J., & Corbally, J. E. (Eds.). (1984). *Leadership and organization culture.* Urbana: University of Illinois Press.

Shakeshaft, C. (1985). Strategies for overcoming the barriers to women in educational administration. In S. S. Klein (Ed.), *Handbook for achieving sex equity through education* (pp. 124–144). Baltimore: Johns Hopkins University Press.

_____. (1989). *Women in educational administration,* 2nd ed. Newbury Park, CA: Sage.

Shedd, J. B., & Bacharach, S. B. (1991). *Tangled hierarchies: Teachers as professionals and the management of schools.* San Francisco: Jossey-Bass.

Sherman, J., Smith, D., Howard, L., & Mansfield, E. R. (1986). The impact of emergent network structure on organizational socialization. *Journal of Applied Behavior Science, 22,* 53–63.

Shrauger, J. S., & Schoeneman, T. J. (1979). Symbolic interactionist view of self-concept: Through the looking glass darkly. *Psychological Bulletin, 86,* 549–573.

Skidmore, W. L. (1975). *Sociology's models of man.* New York: Gordon and Breach.

Smircich, L. (1983). Concepts of culture and organizational analysis. *Administrative Science Quarterly, 28,* 339–358.

Smircich, L., & Morgan, G. (1983). Leadership: The management of meaning. *Journal of Applied Behavioral Science, 18,* 257–273.

Smith, J. E., Carson, K. P., & Alexander, R. A., (1984). Leadership: It can make a difference. *Academy of Management Journal, 27,* 765–776.

Smith, K. K., & Simmons, V. M. (1983). A Rumpelstiltskin organization: Metaphors on metaphors in field research. *Administrative Science Quarterly, 28,* 377–392.

Smith, M., & White, M. C. (1987). Strategy, CEO specialization and succession. *Administrative Science Quarterly, 32,* 263–280.

Smith, P. B., & Peterson, M. F. (1988). *Leadership, organizations and culture: An event management model.* London: Sage.

Smylie, M. A. (1988). The enhancement function of staff development: Organizational psychological antecedents to individual teacher change. *American Educational Research Journal, 25,* 1–30.

Smylie, M. A., & Denny, J. W. (1990). Teacher leadership: Tensions and ambiguities in organizational perspective. *Educational Administration Quarterly, 26,* 235–259.

Smylie, M. A., & Smart, J. C. (1990). Teacher support for career enhancement initiatives: Program characteristics and effects on work. *Educational Evaluation and Policy Analysis, 12,* 139–156.

Sonnenfeld, J. (1986, summer). Heroes in collision: Chief executive retirement and the parade of future leaders. *Human Resource Management,* pp. 303–333.

Sorensen, N. B. (1991). *Participative decision making in public schools: The effects of structural and process properties on the decision equilibrium in four decision content domains.* Unpublished dissertation, The Department of Educational Administration, University of Utah.

Starbuck, W. H., Hedboerg, B. L. T., & Greve, A. (1977). Responding to crises. In C. F. Smart & W. T. Stanbury (Eds.), *Studies on crisis management* (pp. 111–137). Toronto: Institute for Research on Public Policy.

Stinchcome, (1971). Social structure and organizations. In M. W. Meyer (Ed.), *Structures, symbols, and systems* (pp. 260–290). Boston: Little, Brown.

Stogdill, R. M. (1974). *Handbook of leadership: A survey of the literature.* New York: Free Press.

_____. (1980). Traits of leadership: A follow-up to 1970. In B. M. Bass (Ed.), *Stogdill's Handbook of leadership* (pp. 73–97). New York: Free Press.

Stryker, S. (1980). *Symbolic interactionism: A social structural version.* Menlo Park, CA: Benjamin/Cummings.

Stryker, S., & Statham, A. (1985). Symbolic interaction and role theory. In G. Linzey & E. Aronson (Eds.), *Handbook of social psychology, Vol. 1* (3rd ed.) (pp. 311–378). New York: Random House.

Swann, W. B. (1983). Self-verification: Bringing social reality into harmony with the self. In J. Suls & A. Greenwald (Eds.), *Psychological perspectives on the self,* Vol. 2 (pp. 33–66). Hillsdale, NJ: Erlbaum.

Terborg, J. R. (1977). Women in management: A research review. *Journal of Applied Psychology, 62,* 647–664.

Thomas, A. B. (1988). Does leadership make a difference to organizational performance? *Administrative Science Quarterly, 33,* 388–400.

Thomas, J., & Griffin, R. (1983). The social information processing mode of task design: A review of literature. *Academy of Management Review, 8,* 672–682.

Turner, J. (1988). *A theory of social interaction.* Stanford, CA: Stanford University Press.

Turner, R. H. (1962). Role-taking process versus conformity. In A. M. Rose (Ed.), *Human behavior and social processes: An interactionist approach* (pp. 20–40). Boston: Houghton Mifflin.

_____. (1968). The self-conception in social interaction. In C. Gordon & K. Gergen (Eds.), *The self in social interaction.* New York: Wiley.

_____. (1978). The role of the person. *American Journal of Sociology, 84,* 1–23.

Turner, R. H., & Colomy, P. (1988). Role differentiation: Orienting princples. In *Advances in group processes.* Greenwich, CT: JAI Press.

Tyack, D., & Hansot, E. (1982). *Managers of virtue: Public school leadership in America, 1820–1980.* New York: Basic Books.

Valverde, L. A. (1980). Promotion socialization: The informal process in large urban districts and its adverse effects on non-whites and women. *Journal of Educational Equity and Leadership, 1,* 36–46.

Van Maanen, J. (1976). Breaking in: Socialization to work. In R. Dubin (Ed.), *Handbook of work, organization, and society* (pp. 67–130). Chicago: Rand McNally College Publishing.

_____. (1977a). Experiencing organization: Notes on the meaning of careers and socialization. In J. Van Maanen (Ed.), *Organizational careers: Some new perspectives* (pp. 15–45). New York: Wiley.

_____. (1977b). *Organizational careers: Some new perspectives.* New York: Wiley.

_____. (1978). People processing. *Organizational Dynamics, 7,* 18–36.

_____. (1980). Career games. In C. B. Derr (Ed.), *Work, family, and the career.* New York: Praeger.

Van Maanen, J., & Barley, S. R. (1984). Occupational communities: Culture and control in organizations. In B. M. Staw & L. L. Cummings (Eds.), *Research in organizational behavior,* Vol. 6 (pp. 287–365). Greenwich, CT: JAI Press.

Van Maanen, J., & Schein, E. H. (1979). Toward a theory of organization socialization. In B. M. Staw (Ed.), *Research in organizational behavior*, Vol. 1 (pp. 209–264). Greenwich, CT: JAI Press.

Vroom, V. (1976). Leadership. In M. D. Dunnette (Ed.), *Handbook of industrial and organizational psychology* (pp. 1527–1551). Chicago: Rand McNally.

Vroom, V., & Deci, E. L. (1971). The stability of post-decision dissonance: A follow-up study of the job attitudes of business school graduates. *Organizational Behavior and Human Performance, 6,* 36–49.

Wagner, W. G., Pfeffer, J., & O'Reilly, C. A. (1984). Organizational demography and turnover in top-management groups. *Administrative Science Quarterly , 29,* 74–92

Wanous, J. P. (1976). Organizational entry: From naive expectations to realistic beliefs. *Journal of Applied Psychology, 61,* 22–29.

———. (1977). Organization entry: Newcomers moving from outside to inside. *Psychological Bulletin, 84,* 601–618.

———. (1980). *Organizational entry: Recruitment, selection, and socialization of newcomers.* Reading, MA: Addison-Wesley.

Watts, W. D., Short, A. P., & Well, C. B. (1987). Fitting the professional to the job: Idealism and realism. *Journal of Student Financial Aid, 17,* 22–30.

Webster, M., Jr., & Sobieszek, B. (1974). *Sources of self-evaluation: A formal theory of significant others and social influence.* New York: Wiley.

Weick, K. E. (1976). Educational organizations as loosely coupled systems. *Administrative Science Quarterly, 21,* 1–19.

———. (1977). Enactment processes in organizations. In B. Staw & G. Salancik (Eds.), *New directions in organizational behavior.* Chicago: St. Clair.

———. (1978). The spines of leaders. In M. W. McCall, Jr., & M. M. Lombardo (Eds.), *Leadership: Where else can we go?* (pp. 37–61). Durham, NC: Duke University Press.

———. (1979). Cognitive processes in organizations. In B. Staw (Ed.), *Research in organizational behavior,* Vol. 1 (pp. 41–74). Greenwich, CT: JAI Press.

Weindling, D. (1991). Evolving leadership styles: A longitudinal study of headteachers in England and Wales. Paper presented at the annual meeting of the American Educational Research Association, Chicago, IL.

Weindling, D., & Earley, P. (1987). *Secondary headship: The first years.* Philadelphia, PA: NFER-Nelson.

Weiner, N., & Mahoney, T. A. (1981). A model of corporate performance as a function of environmental, organizational, and leadership influences. *Academy of Management Journal, 24,* 453–470.

Weiss, H. W. (1978). Social learning of work values in organizations. *Journal of Applied Psychology, 63,* 711–718.

Wentworth, W. M. (1980). *Context and understanding: An inquiry into socialization theory.* New York: Elsevier.

West, M. A., Farr, J. L., & King, N. (1986). Innovation at work: Definitional and theoretical issues. Paper presented at the annual convention of the American Psychological Association, Washington, DC.

White, J. K. (1978). Individual differences and the job quality-worker response relationship: Review, integration, and comments. *Academy of Management Journal, 21,* 36–43.

Woolfolk, A. E., & Hoy, W. K. (1990). Prospective teachers' sense of efficacy and beliefs about control. *Journal of Educational Psychology,* 82, 81–91.

Worrell, D. L., & Davidson, W. N., III. (1987). The effect of CEO succession on stockholder wealth in large firms following the death of the predecessor. *Journal of Management, 13,* 509–515.

Wright, L. V. (1992). A study of supervisory priorities of first-time high school principals. In F. W. Parkay & G. E. Hall (Eds.), *Becoming a principal: The challenges of beginning leadership.* Boston: Allyn and Bacon.

Yin, R. K. (1985). *Case study research: Design and methods.* Beverly Hills, CA: Sage.

Young, F. E., & Norris, J. A. (1988). Leadership change and action planning: A case study. *Public Administration Review, 48,* 564–570

Yukl, G. A. (1989). *Leadership in organizations,* 2d ed. Englewood Cliffs, NJ: Prentice-Hall.

Yukl, G. A., & Nemeroff, W. (1979). Identification and measurement of specific categories of leadership behavior: A progress report. In J. G. Hunt & L. L. Larson (Eds.), *Crosscurrents in leadership* (pp. 164–200). Carbondale, IL: Southern Illinois University Press.

Index

Accomodation, *see* socialization or succession stages

Ackerman, R. H., 197

Acland, H., 54

Action, distinction with interaction, 91-92

Adams, J., 29

Adjustment, *see* socialization or succession stages

Adsit, D., 44

Alderfer, C. P., 60, 125

Alexander, R. A., 55

Allen, M. P., 48, 74, 79

Allen, V. L., 130

Alvey, H. B., 20, 115

Anderson, J. C., 84

Anderson, L. W., 50, 248

Andrews, D. R., 267

Anticipation, *see* socialization or succession stages

Argyris, C., 59, 60, 76, 254

Ashford, S. J., 109, 124, 292

Bacharach, S. B., 122, 123, 127, 134, 226, 255, 260, 262

Bader, B. D., 33, 283

Baker, L., 78, 197, 228

Ball, S., 135, 255

Baltzell, D. C., 7, 50

Bamberger, P., 122, 123, 127, 226, 260, 262

Bandura, A., 90, 102, 115, 130, 134

Bane, M. J., 54

Barley, S. R., 104

Barnett, B., 221

Barrett, D. A., 67

Barrows, H. S., 117

Bass, B. M., 62, 64, 113, 252

Baumrin, S., 83

Beady, C., 7

Beatty, R. P., 47

Beck, L., 267

Becker, H. S., 38, 71

Becker, S., 81

Beeson, G. W., 197

Begley, P., 7, 10, 11, 19, 123, 197, 198, 214, 233, 283

Belief and meaning during succession, 86-87

Bender, L. R., 69

Bennion, J., 81

Bennis, W., 63, 125, 267

Berlew, D. E., 15

Biddle, B., 126

Birnbaum, R., 71

Black, J. S., 60

Blake, R. R., 65

Blanch, M. C., 68, 97, 294

Blase, J. J., 12, 135

Blau, G., 24,

Blau, P. M., 9, 12, 13, 35, 57, 94, 97, 98, 99, 100, 101, 102, 108, 111, 134, 255

Blumberg, A., 216

Blumer, H., 94, 95, 108, 115, 116, 121, 122

Boldt, E. D., 73

Bolman, L., 268

Bossert, S. T., 7, 54, 62

Bosworth, S., 97

Bowers, D. G., 65

Brady, G. F., 6, 85

Bredeson, P. V., 267, 280

Brief, A. P., 84

Brookover, W. B., 7
Brousseau, K. R., 29, 33
Brown, M. C., 45, 68, 82
Brown, W. B., 70, 71
Buchanan, B., 101
Buchanan, F., 73
Bucher, R., 11
Bullough, R. V., Jr., 12
Burns, J. M., 62, 101, 220, 240, 252
Burrell, G., 258, 298

Campbell, J. P., 64
Campbell, R., 81
Campbell, S., 44
Carlson, R. O., 6, 66, 70, 73
Carnegie Forum on Education and the Economy, 62
Carroll, G. R., 45, 79
Carson, K. P., 55
Cartwright, D., 65
Carver, C. S., 124
Change. *See* succession as an impetus for change
Cheever, D. S., Jr., 58
Child, J., 76
Clarity. *See* socialization or succession stages
Climate, affecting succession, 56
Coates, B., 14, 115
Cognition, 107
Cohen, D. K., 54
Collins, R., 96, 118
Comer, J. P., 76
Communication, effects on socialization, 33-35
Confrontation. *See* socialization or succession stages
Conley, S., 122, 127, 262
Contact, negative and positive effects, 34-36
Context, of socialization, 15-17. *See also* organizational socialization source of leader power 13-14

Contingency, 66-69, 78-87. *See also* leader contingency
Continuing principals, compared with successors, 199-210
Conversation. *See* ethnomethods
Coons, A. E., 65
Cooper, C. L., 125
Cooper, R., 258
Corbett, H. D., 57
Corcoran, T. B., 7, 76
Cosgrove, D., 9, 28, 36, 58, 72, 87, 197, 199, 231, 293
Costa, P. T., 120
Cousins, B., 7, 10
Creativity, 16-17, 20-24, 40
   individual, 15
   leader, 15
   need for, 294-295
Criticism, educational, 210-214
Crouch, A., 32
Crow, G. M., 56, 197
Culture, organizational
   leaders, 66-68
   ethnomethodology, 104-105
   leader influence on, 215-222
   organizational, understanding, 131-132
   principal effects on, 218-219
   role, 130-131
   as social context, 68-69, 131-132
   structures of interaction, 92-94, 125-126, 241
Cummings, T. G., 30
Curcio, J. L., 68
Currie, G., 11, 68, 197, 198, 219, 220, 221, 233, 249, 252, 294
Custodial, 290. *See also* outcomes of socialization

Dachler, H. P., 17
Dalton, D. R., 82
Dandridge, T. C., 33
Dansereau, F., 23
Daresh, J. C., 23, 68, 197, 304

Darling-Hammond, L., 76
Daum, J., 71
Davidson, W. N. III., 82, 83
Davis-Blake, A., 45, 69
Dawis, R. V., 29
Day, D. V., 54
Deal, T. E., 97, 136, 267, 268
Denk, C. E., 49, 54, 55, 234
Denny, J. W., 27
Dentler, R. A., 7, 50
Detachment, of teachers, 146-147
Development, leader. See
  socialization or succession stages
Dewey, J., 254, 259
Dienesch, R., 23
Divestiture, 26-27, 231-232. See
  also organizational socialization
  tactice
Dornbusch, S. M., 35, 57, 255, 275
Downey, H. K., 84
Dramaturgy, 115-118
DuBose, E., 20
Duke, D. L., 7, 11, 12, 14, 17, 18,
  24, 26, 30, 39, 50, 57, 62, 85,
  128, 210, 248, 284, 285, 290, 291
Dunnette, M. D., 64
Durkheim, E., 95
Dwyer, D. C., 7, 54, 62

Earley, P., 7, 11, 16, 24, 62, 63,
  69, 71, 72, 73, 77, 78, 84, 85,
  110, 113, 114, 128, 197, 222, 223,
  224, 225, 226, 228, 229, 236, 251,
  281
Edmonds, R., 7, 285
Edward, M. T., 86
Edwards, A. L., 106
Effective
  relationships in succession, 8
  principal-school, 8
  school, 7
Eitzen, D. S., 48
Emerson, R. M., 41
Encounter. See socialization or
  succession stages

Entry. See succession or
  socialization stages
Environment, role context, 131-132
Epstein, S., 120
Erikson, E. H., 33
Ethnomethods, 103-106
  context, 105-106
  conversation, 105
  stories, 106
Etzioni, A., 40, 63, 220
Evaluation of principals, 284-286
Exchange, 98-103
Expectations
  effects on exchange, 99-100
  group or social, 19
  organizational levels, effects, 100
  principal, 19

Fallon, B. J., 86
Family. See leader traits
Farr, J. L., 38
Fauske, J. R., 56, 162, 251, 303
Favors. See exchange
Fear, of teachers about principal
  succession, 147-148
Feldman, D. C., 29, 30
Feldman, M. S., 131
Festinger, L., 100, 134
Fiedler, F. E., 65, 66
Finkelstein, S., 77
Firestone, W. A., 9, 33, 57, 66, 79,
  102, 119, 130, 131, 283
Fleishman, E. A., 65
Fleming, T., 81
Fletcher, G. J. O., 128
Flood, P., 7
Folk practices. See ethnomethods
Fraas, L., 75
Fredrickson, J. W., 83
Freeman, J. H., 49, 84
French, J. R. P., Jr., 40
Frese, M., 20, 41, 128
Friedman, S. D., 58, 79, 80, 81, 83
Fromm, E., 27
Frost, P. J., 33
Fulk, J., 30

Gabarro, J. J., 5, 49, 59, 60, 61, 71, 73, 75, 76, 77, 78, 96, 102, 110, 112, 135, 284
Galbraith, C. S., 49, 71
Gamson, W. A., 47, 56, 83, 86
Ganz, H. G., 71
Garcia, J. E., 65
Gardner, W. L., 135
Garfinkel, H., 94, 103
Garland, H., 69
Gecas, V., 33, 121
Geer, B., 38
Gender moderating succession. *See* sex, social incongruence
Gephart, R., 15, 48, 55, 84, 86
Getzels, J. W., 65
Giddens, A., 108, 109, 110, 121, 123
Gintis, H., 54
Giroux, H., 258
Glasman, N. S., 284
Goffman, E., 94, 96, 116, 118
Goldman, M., 75
Goody, J., 6
Gordon, G. E., 57, 79, 81, 85, 87, 96, 226, 235
Gouldner, A., 6, 15, 40, 46
Graen, G., 23, 75
Green, G., 67
Greenblatt, M., 60
Greene, E., 68
Greenfield, T. B., 87
Greenfield, W. D., Jr., 11, 14, 17, 19, 24, 39, 50, 57, 109, 127, 214, 221, 248, 268
Greenhalgh, L., 84
Gregory, K. L., 57, 87, 254, 303
Greve, A., 15
Griffin, R., 38
Griffin, R. W., 67
Gronn, P. C., 103
Gross, E., 40
Grusky, O., 6, 47, 71, 81, 82, 83, 84, 87
Guba, E. G., 65

Guest, R. H., 15, 45
Gupta, A. K., 81
Guy, M. E., 11

Habermas, J., 104
Hackman, J. R., 8
Haga, W., 23
Hall, D. T., 15, 33, 80, 84
Hall, G. E., 61, 68, 215, 221, 248, 304
Halpin, A. W., 65
Hamblin, R., 86
Hambrick, D. C., 49, 77, 83
Hannan, M. T., 49, 84
Hansot, E., 50, 51
Hart, A. W., 7, 15, 17, 25, 27, 33, 35, 53, 56, 57, 82, 84, 85, 86, 87, 119, 251, 256, 259, 260, 284, 303
Hartup, W. W., 14, 115
Hatch, M. J., 131
Head teacher, succession of, 222-230
Hearn, J., 258
Heck, R. H., 284, 285
Hedboerg, B. L. T., 15
Helmich, D. L., 6, 70, 71, 73, 83, 84, 85
Hemphill, J. K., 65
Heritage, J., 103
Heyns, B. L., 54
Hitt, M. A., 136
Hodgkinson, C., 291
Hollander, E. P., 69, 75, 76, 86, 101
Holmes Group, 62
Homans, G. C., 94
Honeymoon. *See* succession stages
Hopson, B., 29
Hord, S., 68
Hord, S. M., 221
Hosking, D. M., 114
House, R. J., 82
Howard, L., 37
Hoy, W. K., 13, 63, 64, 65, 66, 71, 76

Hoyle, J. R., 284
Hughes, E. C., 38
Huling-Austin, L. L., 221
Human systems theory, 35
Hunt, D., 23

Imber, M., 284
Immegart, G. L., 63, 66
Improvement
    school, 287–290
    of succession outcomes, 277–290
Induction. *See* professional
    socialization
Influence, two-way, 9–10
Insider-outsider. *See* leader traits
Instructional leadership, affected
    by succession, 214–215, 216
Interaction,
    beliefs about, 266–267
    culture, structuring interaction,
        92–93, 241
    dynamics 35, 168–184
    as ethnomethods, 103
    leader-group, 14–15
    models, 92–97
    motivation to interact, 94–97
    multiple process theories, 97–119
    principal-school, 7–8
    processes, 95–96
    rituals, 118–119
    as social information processing,
        113–115, 295–297
    structures of, 125–132
    structuring processes, 96–97
    with teachers, 223–224
    as unit of analysis, 91–97
    validation resulting from, 275
Investiture, 26–27, 231–232. *See also*
    organizational socialization tactics
Ireland, R. D., 136
Isaacson, N. S., 11, 14, 17, 18, 24,
    30, 39, 50, 57, 85, 128, 248, 291

James, D. R., 79, 82, 83
James, W., 90

Jencks, C. L., 54
Jentz, B., 58
Jones, G. R., 21, 23, 37, 91, 105,
    134
Julian, J. W., 75, 76, 86

Kagan, J., 257
Kahn, R. L., 65
Kanter, R., 50
Katz, D., 65
Keefe, J. W., 50, 248
Kelleher, P., 288
Kelley, E. A., 50, 248
Kemmis, S., 255
Kendall, P. L., 10, 57, 123
Kerchner, C. T., 283
Kerr, S., 74
Kesner, I. F., 82
Kieser, A., 76
Kimberly, J. R., 286
King, N., 38
Klackars, A. J., 106
Klein, R. H., 15, 46, 75, 82
Kmetz, J. T., 103, 253, 285
Knight, P. A., 86
Knowledge, of successor, 277–278
Koch, J. L., 45
Kohn, M. L., 29, 33
Kotter, J. P., 44, 112
Kreps, G. A., 97
Kriesburg, L., 81, 82
Kunz, D., 76

Lamoreaux, D., 56, 197, 210, 233
Larsen, T. J., 285
Lawler, E. E. III, 8, 64
Lawler, E. J., 134, 255
Lawler, J., 112
Leader. *See* leader socialization
    and succession
    behavior, 65–66
        affecting succession, 74–78
        contingency, 66–69, 78–87

exchange theories, 100–103
situation, 64–65
  affecting succession, 78–87
teachers, 25
traits, 63–64
  affecting succession, 69–74
  kinship or family, 73–74
  insider-outsider, 70–73, 212–213
  situation, 64–65
  sex, 69–70, 212
Leadership. *See also* leader traits,
situation, behavior, contingency
endorsed, 12–14. *See also*
interaction, legimacy, validation
  as event management, 268–269
  heroic, 267
  improvement through succession, 266–272
  organizational socialization contributions, 270–271
  passive, 268
  succession, contributions to, 269–270
  succession and socialization, synthesis of, 172–272
Learning
  principal, 15
  social, 15–16
Lee, G. V., 7, 62
Legitimation
  leader, 9, 12–14
  processes, 135–136
  See also validation
Leithwood, K. A., 7, 10, 11, 19, 123, 197, 198, 214, 233, 283
Levine, J. M., 29
Liden, R. C., 23, 75
Lieberson, S., 49, 52, 53, 75, 248
Lipham, J. A., 65, 101
Little, J. W., 13, 23, 25
Location. *See* socialization or succession stages
Lofquist, L. H., 29
Lord, R. G., 54, 127
Lorence, J., 29

Lortie, D. C., 13, 38
Lotz, R. E., 48, 74
Louis, M. R., 14, 19, 29, 32, 33, 93, 131

MacPherson, R. J., 11, 17, 20, 57
Mahoney, T. A., 53
Manning, P. K., 33
Mansfield, E. R., 37
Manz, C. C., 44
Marcoulides, G. A., 285
Markus, H., 111
Marrion, B., 20
Marshall, C., 25
Martin, J., 131
Martin, W. J., 103, 253, 285
Martinko, M. J., 135
Mason, P. A., 49
Mathison-Hance, M., 44
Matthews, R. J., 197
McCleary, L. E., 50, 64, 248
McCrae, R. R., 120
McEachern, A., 79, 83
McGivern, C., 85
McGuire, J. W., 49, 71
McNeil, E. B., 8, 89
Mead, G. H., 94, 95, 106, 121, 122, 123, 124
Menon, K., 82
Mentors
  role in socialization, 23–24, 280–281
  as role models, 282
Merton, R. K., 10, 57, 89, 123
Meyer, P. S., 83
Michael, C., 23
Michaelson, S., 54
Miklos, E., 5, 10, 11, 17, 55
Milkovich, G. T., 84
Mills, C. W., 135
Minority leaders. *See* leader traits and social incongruence
Mintzberg, H., 75, 258
Miskel, C., 9, 28, 36, 58, 87, 199
Miskel, C. G., 48, 63, 64, 65, 66

Mitchell, S. M., 123, 127, 226, 260
Mitroff, I. I., 39
Mizruchi, M. S., 74
Monane, J. H., 3, 34, 35, 90, 113, 133
Moreland, R. L., 29
Morgan, G., 33, 111
Morgenthau, H. J., 62
Morley, I., 114
Mortimer, J. T., 128, 229
Motivation
    to interact, 94–97
    processes, 94–96
Mouton, J. S., 65
Murphy, J., 7, 267
Murphy, M. J., 27, 119, 284

Nanus, B., 292
National Commission on
    Excellence in Educational
    Administration, 50
National Policy Board for
    Educational Administration, 7
Naylor, K., 7, 17, 259
Nemeroff, W., 74
Newell, J. T., 81
Nicholson, N., 15, 27, 29, 32, 37, 38, 61, 127, 129, 195, 240
Nota, B., 25
Novak, M. A., 67
Nytell, U., 197

O'Connor, J. F., 49, 52, 53, 248
O'Connor, J. T., 67
O'Reilly, C. A., 79
Ogawa, R. T., 3, 10, 15, 43, 50, 53, 56, 64, 84, 87, 162, 251, 273, 303
Olesen, V. L., 123
Oliver, J., 197, 248
Ontological security, 111–112
Organization
    analysis by principals, 253–254, 259, 276–277, 281
    implicit theories of, 84

Organizational socialization. *See*
    Socialization, organizational
Ortiz, F. I., 25
Oskarsson, H., 15, 46, 75, 82
Others, concepts of, 124–125
Outsider. *See* leader traits
Owens, M., 48

Panian, S. K., 48, 74, 79
Parkay, F. W., 11, 61, 68, 197, 198, 215, 219, 220, 221, 233, 248, 249, 252, 294, 304
Parsons, T., 96, 97
Pease, S. R., 76
Peer support, 84–85. *See also*
    succession
Pellicer, L. O., 50, 248
Peters, T. J., 136, 268
Peterson, K. D., 97, 136, 267
Peterson, M. F., 9, 17, 32, 74, 79, 90, 97, 111, 113, 114, 123, 126, 127, 128, 130, 268
Pettigrew, A., 97
Pfeffer, J., 6, 8, 16, 45, 49, 51, 53, 56, 60, 66, 67, 69, 74, 79, 83, 99, 112, 128, 247, 251
Phillips, J. S., 64, 127
Pinder, C. C., 60
Pitner, N., 50
Playko, M. A., 23, 68, 197, 304
Podsakoff, P. M., 113
Pondy, L. R., 33, 107, 129
Porter, A. C., 281
Porter, L. W., 8
Posner, B. Z., 14
Pounder, D. G., 35
Powell, G. N., 14
Predecessor, as a succession factor, 85
Presentation of self. *See*
    Dramaturgy
Price, K. H., 69
Professional socialization. *See*
    Socialization, professional
Purkey, S. C., 7, 76
Putnam, R., 76, 254

Quinn, R. E., 286

Rao, M., 11, 68
Raven, B. H., 40
Reader, G. G., 10, 57, 123
Reciprocal determination, 134
Redlich, F. C., 58
Rees, R., 13
Reinganum, J. R., 71
Research
    implications for, 249–258
    methodoligies, 256–258
    propositions, 258–259
Rhodes, J., 11, 68
Rhodes, J. W., 197, 198, 219, 220,
    221, 233, 252, 294
Rice, R. W., 69
Richards, E. W., 32
Rituals. *See* interaction rituals
Roberts, J., 10, 11, 68, 115, 135,
    197, 215, 217, 218, 219
Role
    ambiguity, 25–26
    clarity, 129
    conflict, 128
    innovation, 37–38, 133
    management. *See* socialization
      or succession stages
    models, 25, 232–233, 282. *See also*
      organizational socialization
      tactics and mentors overload
    processes, 129–131
    role-taking, role-making,
      127–128
    socialization outcomes, 37–40,
      132–133, 283–284
    stress, 25–26
    structures, 126–129
    theory, 126–129
Role theory. *See* Role, theory
Rosen, N., 57, 79, 85, 87, 96, 226,
    235
Rosenberg, M., 116
Rosenthal, T. L., 106, 107
Ross, M., 128

Rossman, G. B., 57
Rowan, B., 7, 49, 54, 55, 62, 234
Rutherford, W. L., 221

Sagor, R., 11, 14, 17, 18, 24, 30,
    39, 50, 57, 85, 128, 248, 291
Salaman, G., 15, 46
Salancik, G. R., 53, 74, 79, 83, 99
Samuelson, B. A., 49, 71
Scarcity, affecting exchange, 99
Scheier, M. F., 124
Schein, E. H., 11, 12, 14, 16, 17,
    21, 23, 24, 26, 33, 36, 67, 68, 93,
    97, 104, 106, 108, 109, 110, 115,
    116, 122, 124, 125, 126, 128, 130,
    131, 132, 135, 248, 254, 276
Schmuck, P. A., 11, 14, 17, 18, 24,
    30, 39, 50, 57, 85, 128, 248, 291
Schoeneman, T. J., 120
Schon, D. A., 59, 117, 254, 259,
    287
Schooler, C., 29, 33
Schreisheim, C. A., 74
Schroeder, K. G., 60
Schutz, A., 96, 124
Schwartz, D. B., 82
Schweitzer, J., 7
Scotch, N. A., 47, 56, 83, 86
Scott, W. R., 14, 35, 57, 82, 101,
    255, 275
Seashore, S. E., 65
Self-concept, 119–130
    core or stable, 108, 120–121
    of others, 124–125
    professional, during succession,
      216–218
    situational, 26–27, 121–124
    stable, 120–121
Selznick, P., 101
Sense making, 56, 111–115
Sergiovanni, T. J., 102, 216, 253
Sex, 212, 223, 297–299. *See also*
    leader traits
Shakeshaft, C., 212
Shared reality, 109–111

Sheppard, D. L., 258
Sherman, J., 37
Short, A. P., 30
Shrauger, J. S., 120
Simmons, R. C., 128
Simmons, V. M., 105
Sitkin, S. B., 131
Size, organizational affecting
    succession, 81–82
Skidmore, W. L., 134
Skov, R., 113
Smircich, L., 33, 67, 68, 111, 304
Smith, D., 37
Smith, D. M., 76, 254
Smith, J., 56, 87
Smith, J. E., 55, 127
Smith, K. K., 105
Smith, M., 54, 65
Smith, M. S., 7, 76
Smith, P. B., 9, 17, 32, 74, 79, 90,
    97, 111, 114, 123, 126, 127, 128,
    130, 268
Smylie, M. A., 27
Sobieszek, B., 121
Social incongruence of leaders,
    297–299
Social information processing
    exchange, during, 108. See also
        exchange
    by leaders, 295–297
    message exchange, 108–109
    as sense making, 111–115
    symbolic interactionism, 107
Social system, affecting succession,
    209, 215
Socialization
    adult, 10–11, 38–39, 123
    definition, 10
    formal, informal, 18, 23–24
    instructional leadership, as a
        stimulus for, 19–20
    of minority group members,
        25–26
    moral, 19
    organizational, 11–14

characteristics, personal,
    184–185
context, 32–36, 131–132
    personal, 32–33, 185–186, 234
    social, 33–35, 186–192,
        235–236
research implications, 252–254
role, 126–131
tactics, 21–28, 230–233, 241,
    279–282
    content, 25, 158–160, 283–284
    context, 22–25, 160–162,
        233–237
    sociality, 25–28
    stages, 28–32, 162–163,
        192–193, 221, 237–239
    outcomes, 27–28, 36–40,
        132–136, 163–164, 193–195,
        239–240, 282–284, 287–290.
        See also organizational
        socialization, outcomes of
    absorption, 37
    custodial response. See
        replication
    deliberately structured, 283–284
    determination, 37
    exploration, 37
    knowledge and skills, 277–279
    personal and organizational,
        36–40
    replication, 37, 39
    oversocialization, suppressing
        creativity, 17–18, 294–295
    power, 15
    principal, 10–11, 17–21
    professional, 20–21
        features, 17
        induction, 217–218, 249
        isolation, 229
        personal outcomes, 36–40
        of principals, 17–21
    role, 14–15
    situation. See leader situation
    stages, 28–32, 192–193, 219–221,
        224–226, 273–274
    technical, 19

Sonnenfeld, J., 81
Soref, M., 79, 82, 83
Sorensen, N. B., 7, 17, 259, 283
Stabilization. *See* socialization or
    succession stage
Stage. *See* succession stage or
    socialization stage
Starbuck, W. H., 15
Statham, A., 126
Steinbach, R., 7, 11, 19, 123, 197,
    198, 214, 233, 283
Stelling, J. G., 11
Stiggins, R. J., 284
Stinchcome, 130
Stogdill, R. M., 43, 63, 65
Strauss, A. L., 38
Stryker, S., 116, 126
Succession
    behavior. *See* leader behavior
    boundaries. *See* succession tenure
    change, 76–78, 208–210, 221,
        226–229, 279–280, 283–284,
        292–294
    contingency. *See* leader
        contingency
    constraints of on effects, 49–52
    effects of on succession, 55–57
    culture, 202–206, 207, 208, 217,
        218–219, 241
    definitions, 6
    effects, 43–44, 45–51
        negative, 46–47
        no effect, 47–49
        positive, 45–46
    forced or unforced, 82
    frequency, 5, 210
    implicit theories, 84
    isolation of the principal, 229
    leader, 62–63
    outcomes, 15, 60, 214–215
        organizational, as a reason for
            succession, 83, 256, 261–262
    peer support, 84–85
    perspectives, in social science, 6
    predecessor, 85

principal, 5–8, 215–221
problems, 226
situation. *See* leader situation
stages, 44, 57–62
    actualization, professional,
        219–220
    anticipation, and excitement,
        148
    arrival, 60, 225–229. *See also*
        entry
    control, 219
    disenchantment, 151–156
    enchantment, 149–151
    entry, 57–58. *See also* arrival
    equilibrium, 156–158
    frameworks, 199–200, 219–221
    leadership, educational, 219
    prearrival, presuccession,
        200–203, 205–206, 224–225
    post-succession, 203–205,
        206–207
    time frame, 208–209
    stability, 219
    survival, 219
    unity, desire for, 148–149
systems, 79–81
tenure, of the leader, 44
    as a boundary of leadership,
        52–55
traits. *See* leader traits
variables, factors affecting, 44
Superiors, improving succession,
    279–290
Supervision, shaping succession,
    216–217
Swann, W. B., 120, 123
Symbol
    dimension in succession, 85–87
Symbolic interactionism, 106–119
    cognition, 107
    information processing, 107
    roots, 106
    self-concept, 122–123

Taking charge, 16–17, 61–62, 241
Tancred-Sheriff, P., 258

Teacher leaders. *See* leader, teachers
Terborg, J. R., 69
Thomas, A. B., 49, 52, 54, 55, 62, 84, 248
Thomas, E. J., 126
Thomas, J., 38
Todor, W. D., 113
Traits. *See* leader traits
Turner, J., 56, 91, 92, 94, 95, 103, 110, 111, 117, 118, 123
Turner, R. H., 113, 120, 127
Tyack, D., 50, 51

Validation, social, 12–14, 254–256, 259–261, 274–277
Values
    culture, 136
    exchange relationships, 99–100
Valverde, L. A., 25, 35, 50
van de Vliert, E., 130
Van Maanen, J., 12, 14, 16, 18, 21, 23, 24, 26, 36, 104, 106, 109, 122, 130, 219
Vision. *See* organizational culture, succession culture, values
Vitters, A. G., 69
Vroom, V., 66

Wagner, W. G., 79
Wanous, J. P., 30, 37, 59, 60, 129, 162, 240
Waterman, R. H., Jr., 136, 268
Watts, W. D., 30

Webster, M., Jr., 121
Weick, K. E., 35, 38, 64, 267
Weindling, D., 7, 11, 16, 24, 62, 63, 69, 71, 72, 73, 77, 78, 84, 85, 110, 113, 114, 128, 197, 222, 223, 224, 225, 226, 228, 229, 236, 251, 281
Weiner, N., 53
Weiss, H. M., 29, 86
Well, C. B., 30
Wentworth, W. M., 13, 22, 32, 44, 97, 120, 121, 127
West, M. A., 27, 29, 32, 38, 61, 127
White, J. K., 15
White, M. C., 65
Whittaker, E. W., 123
Willower, D. J., 103, 253, 285
Winer, B. J., 65
Wise, A. E., 76
Wisenbaker, J., 7
Woolfolk, A. E., 13
Worrell, D. L., 82, 83
Wright, L. V., 11, 68, 135, 197, 215, 216, 217, 218, 219

Yetman, N. R., 48
Yetton, P. W., 32
Yin, R. K., 263
Yukl, G. A., 63, 66, 74, 94, 255

Zajac, E. J., 47
Zajonc, R. B., 111
Zander, A., 65
Zimmerman, B. J., 106, 107